MORE ADVANCE PRAISE FOR
OPPOSE ANY FOE

"Mark Moyar has written an important history of US Special Operations Forces that eloquently records their recent rise in prominence. In this well-referenced and highly readable book, Moyar highlights the chronic challenges that Special Operations Forces have faced in working for conventional commanders and describes the limits of the military instrument in its current configuration in achieving US foreign-policy objectives. He shows the need for fresh thinking on how America conducts its own irregular warfare activities and a better understanding by policymakers and their senior military advisors on what is possible through military force."

— Charles T. Cleveland, Lieutenant General (ret.), commander of the United States Army Special Operations Command, 2012–2015

"Historian Mark Moyar weaves together nuggets of history from Special Operations past to create an in-depth account of America's elite forces. But *Oppose Any Foe*'s best part comes at the end. Moyar offers advice to future Special Operations Forces. Recommended reading for the current administration and future SOF leaders."

— Kevin Maurer, coauthor of *No Easy Day: The Firsthand Account of the Mission that Killed Osama Bin Laden*

"It is exceptional to find a writer who has the diligence and depth of the careful scholar, with the skill to tell a rattling good tale—but Mark Moyar is that author. This is a masterly account of the rise of American Special Forces, a compelling account not just of the derring-do, but the Washington politics and organizational rivalries that went into forging the tip of the American armed forces' spear."

— Eliot A. Cohen, Robert E. Osgood Professor of Strategic Studies, Johns Hopkins SAIS, and author of *The Big Stick*

"Simply put, *Oppose Any Foe* is now the single best account available of US Special Operations Forces from their creation in World War Two to today's brushfire wars. An accomplished military historian, author Mark Moyar writes with the precision of a scholar and the vibrancy of a journalist. Moyar's sweeping history will superbly serve government and military professionals, and the nation's citizens, in fully understanding the extraordinary character and capabilities—and limitations—of this elite grouping of American warfighters."

— Dr. Kalev I. Sepp, former deputy assistant secretary of defense for Special Operations and Counterterrorism

"Mark Moyar's first-rate book is the best popular history of the Special Operations Forces to date and will remain an indispensable source of information, with memorable personalities and dramatic battle scenes, for the foreseeable future."

— Thomas Henriksen, senior fellow, Hoover Institution, and author of *Eyes, Ears, and Daggers*

OPPOSE ANY FOE

OPPOSE ANY FOE

The RISE of
AMERICA'S SPECIAL OPERATIONS FORCES

MARK MOYAR

BASIC BOOKS

New York

Published by Basic Books, an imprint of Perseus Books, LLC, a subsidiary of Hachette Book Group, Inc.

Books published by Basic Books are available at special discounts for bulk purchases in the United States by corporations, institutions, and other organizations. For more information, please contact the Special Markets Department at Perseus Books, 2300 Chestnut Street, Suite 200, Philadelphia, PA 19103, or call (800) 810-4145, ext. 5000, or e-mail special.markets@perseusbooks.com.

Designed by Amy Quinn

Library of Congress Cataloging-in-Publication Data

Names: Moyar, Mark, 1971– author.
Title: Oppose any foe : the rise of America's Special Operations Forces / Mark Moyar.
Other titles: Rise of America's special operations forces
Description: First edition. | New York : Basic Books, [2017] | Includes bibliographical references and index.
Identifiers: LCCN 2016047871 (print) | LCCN 2016048644 (ebook) | ISBN 9780465053933 (hardcover) | ISBN 9780465093014 (ebook)
Subjects: LCSH: Special forces (Military science)—United States—History. | United States. Army. Special Forces—History. | Special operations (Military science)—United States—History.
Classification: LCC UA34.S64 M69 2017 (print) | LCC UA34.S64 (ebook) | DDC 356/.160973—dc23
LC record available at https://lccn.loc.gov/2016047871

10 9 8 7 6 5 4 3 2 1

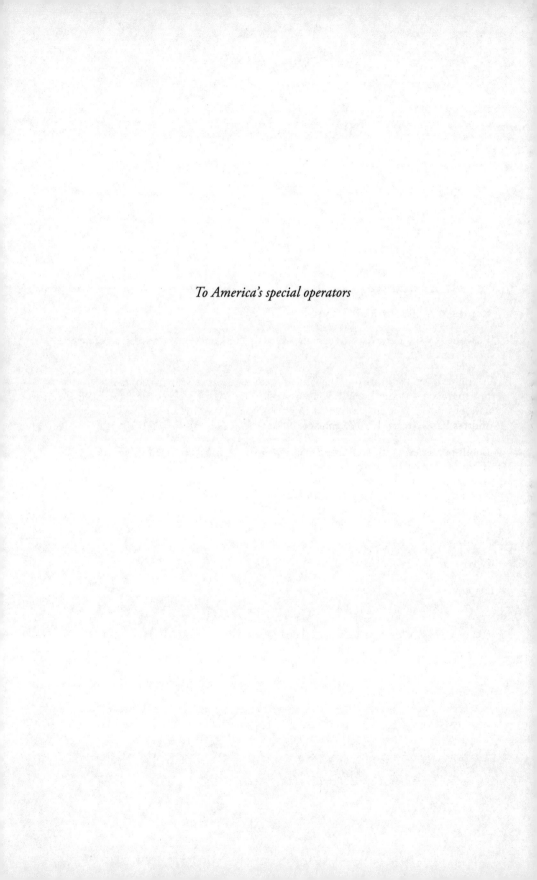

To America's special operators

CONTENTS

PROLOGUE

The airplanes entered Somali air space several miles above the earth's surface, at an altitude where one would expect to find an intercontinental passenger jet traveling from Paris to Singapore. Had a Somali high-adventure company been offering nighttime skydiving excursions, their planes would have been flying at something less than half as high. These aircraft had nonetheless shown up for parachuting, of a sort known in the military as High Altitude, High Opening, or HAHO for short. Designed to prevent hostile ground forces from hearing the parachutes popping open, HAHO jumps require parachutists to spread their canopies after a free fall of only a few seconds, leaving them floating at such high altitudes that they need oxygen tanks to keep breathing on the way down.

Twenty-four US Navy SEALs, each of them specially trained in the technique, had been assigned to parachute from these fearsome heights onto Somali territory. They checked over their gear one last time, then leaped from the aircraft, one at a time, into a frigid and moonless night. Once the chutes jerked the SEALs out of free fall, the men extended their arms and legs like flying squirrels, so as to guide their canopies during the long glide.

Monitoring their locations with global positioning system devices, the parachutists steered toward predesignated landing zones near the town of Adado, the capital of a Somali district with several hundred thousand people. American planners had chosen a landing zone several miles out-side of town, a clearing where reconnaissance flights on previous nights had spotted no Somalis at this hour. During the descent, the SEALs real-ized that the intended drop zone was enshrouded in fog, so they initiated a midair discussion over their helmet microphones, at the end of which the team commander decided to shift to an alternate location.

The burly SEALs, bearing sixty-pound armored vests and a panoply of other gear, thudded down in an area of scrub brush and acacia trees, all twenty-four of them landing safely. With night goggles strapped to their foreheads, they caught sight of one another by the infrared beacon that each man wore on his uniform. The SEALs were not carrying grenades or heavy machine guns but instead brandished precision weapons that would minimize harm to innocent persons, including Heckler & Koch MP-5 and MP-7 machine pistols, highly lethal at short distances, and Heckler & Koch 416 assault rifles, lethal at longer ranges owing to their larger shell and higher muzzle velocity. Each SEAL also possessed a long fighting knife, which could kill an unsuspecting guard without a sound.

The SEALs had been sent to rescue two captives, thirty-two-year-old Jessica Buchanan of the United States and sixty-year-old Poul Hagen Thisted of Denmark. The pair had been abducted three months earlier while working on a demining project for the Danish Refugee Council. On October 25, 2011, they had been driving by car through southern Soma-lia when their vehicle was cut off by a large Toyota Land Cruiser, out of which swarmed pirates who banged the butts of their AK-47s on the car's windows and windshield. Hauling Buchanan and Thisted from the vehi-cle, the thugs drove them to a desert hideout. A pirate spokesman issued a demand of $45 million in ransom for the two of them.

The pirates had moved the prisoners almost daily to keep foreign gov-ernments and rival kidnappers off their scent. Separated from one another, Buchanan and Thisted received one small can of tuna and one piece of bread per day. After three months of this bleak existence, Buchanan con-tracted a urinary tract infection. She notified the captors that the infection was going to kill her if left untreated, a piece of information that they conveyed to an American hostage negotiator in an effort to strengthen their bargaining position. When Washington learned that her life was in jeopardy and that US intelligence had drawn a bead on her location, President Barack Obama decided to send in the SEALs.

According to the intelligence reports, at least nine Somali men were guarding the prisoners, and they were likely to be well armed. The guards might also have dogs, which would begin barking well before the SEALs reached their preferred attack positions. As soon as the guards caught wind of American intruders, moreover, they could alert other pirates or clan members in the area, who could drive to the site with heavy machine guns. The guards might even choose to kill the hostages out of spite or desperation. Then there was the possibility that the SEALs might inadvertently kill the hostages, as had occurred fifteen months earlier when a SEAL team tried to rescue Scottish aid worker Linda Norgrove from the Afghan Taliban.

Fortunately for the SEALs, the men guarding Buchanan and Thisted had not been trained in the finer arts of hostage handling. They did not have dogs, perhaps because of the generally low esteem in which Somalis held the creatures. More egregiously, all nine of the Somali guards had fallen asleep earlier in the night. At least one of them was supposed to be awake at all times, but the men had trouble keeping their eyes open during night hours because by day they chewed khat, a stimulant whose afternoon high was followed by a big downer in the evening. When the SEALs reached the target, they were astonished to find that the only person walking around was a gaunt Caucasian woman who appeared to resemble the person they had seen in a "proof-of-life" video of Buchanan provided by the kidnappers one month before.

Earlier that evening, Buchanan had gone to sleep on a mat that was surrounded on all sides by the sleeping mats of six guards, each of whom lay within twelve inches of her. She and the guards had developed a routine whereby she would say "toilet" when she needed to go to the bathroom in the middle of the night, and then a guard would give his consent for her to make for the bushes. On this night, however, none of the guards had responded when she awoke in the dark and uttered the word. Walking toward the bushes, she flashed her pen light in order to show any awakening guards that she was not trying to escape. Once she had taken care of business, she returned to her mat and lay back down.

Moments later, Buchanan began to hear noises. They were faint, but she thought she could make out the breaking of twigs and the scratching of insects or small animals. Five minutes after her trip to the bushes, she heard one of the guards next to her jump to his feet and cock his rifle. The man called the name of his boss once, panic in his voice. Silence. He called the name again, and then other guards sprang up, weapons at the ready.

Bursts of gunfire shattered the serenity of the night. Buchanan listened as the Somalis screamed orders at one another. Lacking night-vision equipment, the guards were firing blindly in the general direction of the incoming fire. They were knocked to the earth in quick succession, as if a giant bowling ball had rolled into the camp. Buchanan heard shrieks of mortal agony from several men who had been snoozing next to her seconds earlier.

Remaining flat on the ground, Buchanan bundled herself in a blanket, hoping that the bullets would not find her there. She guessed that another Somali group was trying to kidnap her and her fellow hostage. They might be from al-Shabaab, the Al Qaeda affiliate in Somalia, whose fanatical fighters would surely kill the hostages if they gained possession of them.

Buchanan had not been listening to gunfire for long when she felt someone tugging at her blanket. She clung to it with mad desperation, as if it could protect her from falling into another captor's clutches. "Jessica!" said a male voice. To her bewilderment, the man had an American accent. She relaxed her grip on the blanket and saw the outlines of several men in black masks. "Jessica! This is the American military. We've come to take you home."

A big man picked Buchanan up in a fireman carry position and ran from the camp with the speed and grace of an athlete burdened by nothing more than a T-shirt and shorts. She was puzzled by the fact that neither he nor any of the other Americans seemed to need a flashlight to find their way. At a small clearing, the man set her down, then went back to the site of the shooting to retrieve her sandals and medicine bag. More figures arrived in the dark, one of whom she made out as Thisted.

The gunfire had not lasted long. The SEALs had killed all of the guards without a single injury to themselves or the hostages, and evacuated the camp before any enemy reinforcements could arrive. Once the twenty-four SEALs had assembled at the clearing, they jogged for a few minutes with their precious cargo to a landing site where they had scheduled a rendezvous with the extraction helicopters.

Through the darkness and the whirling sand, Buchanan could discern three helicopters, one of which she boarded at the signal of a SEAL. Once the aircraft lifted off she was able to see the faces of her rescuers for the first time. Many were younger than she, and they impressed her with their courteousness. One SEAL gave her a folded American flag. "I just started to cry," Buchanan remembered afterward. "At that point in time I have never in my life been so proud and so very happy to be an American."

Eight thousand miles away, Barack Obama was preparing to deliver his 2012 State of the Union Address. He entered the House chamber a few hours after the SEALs had parachuted into Somalia, whereupon he prefaced his address by looking over at Defense Secretary Leon Panetta and saying, "Leon, good job tonight. Good job tonight."

The president did not utter any further words about the raid in his remarks to the Congress, leaving millions of Americans wondering what the Defense Department had been up to that night. His address did, however, make mention of another recent SEAL operation, the killing of Osama bin Laden on May 2, 2011.

"One of my proudest possessions is the flag that the SEAL team took with them on the mission to get bin Laden," the president remarked. "On it are each of their names. Some may be Democrats. Some may be Republicans. But that doesn't matter." The SEALs had shown how Americans worked together regardless of political party, the president averred. "Each time I look at that flag, I'm reminded that our destiny is stitched together like those 50 stars and those 13 stripes," he said. "No one built this country on their own. This nation is great because we built it together. This nation is great because we worked as a team."

Obama's address also included a reference to his new defense strategy, which involved downsizing the nation's conventional forces on the premise that smaller special operations forces were a more effective and less expensive substitute. "Working with our military leaders," he said, "I've proposed a new defense strategy that ensures we maintain the finest military in the world, while saving nearly half a trillion dollars in our budget."

Obama did not explain the rationale for the new strategy in the speech, but the announcement of Buchanan's rescue hours later gave the White House an opportunity to cite special operations successes as justification. On the next day, January 26, the *Washington Post* relayed statements from unnamed US officials that "the raid, by members of the Navy SEAL Team 6 unit that killed Osama bin Laden in May, demonstrated President Obama's focus on the narrow, targeted use of force after a decade of large-scale military deployments." The Associated Press reported later on the same day that "the Navy SEAL operation that freed two Western hostages in Somalia is representative of the Obama administration's pledge to build a smaller, more agile military force that can carry out surgical counterterrorist strikes to cripple an enemy. That's a strategy much preferred to the land invasions of Iraq and Afghanistan that have cost so much American blood and treasure over the past decade."

THE FIRST MONTH of 2012 was, indeed, a highly auspicious time to wave the banner of special operations forces in support of a new national security strategy. Through the Bin Laden raid and other recent victories, special operators had amassed unprecedented prestige both within Washington and in the country more generally. Special operations forces seemed not only more exciting, but also more efficient and decisive than the large conventional military forces that had been employed in the wars of Iraq and Afghanistan. Hollywood was releasing movie after movie extolling the virtues of the special units, including a film called *Act of Valor* that starred active-duty SEALs. On the Internet, dating sites were hit by epidemics of men pretending to be special operators in order to win the hearts of unsuspecting women.

Although President Obama relied mainly on subordinates to sell his new strategy to the public, he did cite the special operators while explaining the strategy during an interview with journalist Mark Bowden, who was writing a book on the Bin Laden operation. "Special Forces are well designed to deal with very specific targets in difficult terrain and oftentimes can prevent us from making the bigger strategic mistakes of sending forces in, with big footprints and so forth," he explained. "So when you're talking about dealing with terrorist networks in failed states, or states that don't have capacity, you can see that as actually being less intrusive, less dangerous, less problematic for the country involved."

What Obama had called "Special Forces" were in actuality the special operations forces (SOF)—the official term for all the units dedicated to the conduct of special operations. Special operations forces include not only the US Army's Special Forces, but also the Army Rangers, Navy SEALs, Air Force Night Stalkers, and Special Operations Marines, among others. Mixing up Special Forces with special operations forces was a common enough mistake, and one that might have been unworthy of mention had the president merely been dispensing praise to an obscure federal bureaucracy, on the order of the Japan-U.S. Friendship Commission or the American Battle Monuments Commission. But SOF had become the centerpiece of Obama's national security strategy, and hence the misstep encouraged doubts about the amount of thought that had gone into the strategic redesign. Later events were to confirm that administration strategists had not given adequate consideration to the strengths and limitations of special operations forces before hoisting them to the apex of the world's most powerful military.

It was not the first time that presidential ambitions for special operations forces had outstripped presidential familiarity with those forces. Indeed, no president, Republican or Democrat, has ever demonstrated a commanding grasp of special operations forces and their capabilities, although John F. Kennedy at times came close. Presidential unfamiliarity acquired a new significance under Obama, however, because US special operations forces were larger and more prominent than ever before, and because their ascent in Obama's first term contributed to a terrific crash during his second term. Egged on by the White House, the Special Operations Command would attempt to acquire new powers at the expense of the rest of the US military and government. Its leadership would flout the rules of the Defense Department and the Congress, on the presumption that no one would dare challenge the men who had killed Osama bin Laden. Congress eventually used its power of the purse to rein in Special Operations Command, killing the budgets for ambitious plans to extend the reach of special operations forces.

Most of the factors that precipitated this calamity could have been anticipated, and at least some avoided, had the principal players been attuned to the history of American special operations forces. That history began during the first months of US participation in World War II, when in the crucible of total war the United States formed its first units dedicated to special operations. From 1942 to 1945, the Army Rangers, the Marine Corps Raiders, the Navy Frogmen, and the special operators of the civilian-led Office of Strategic Services (OSS) executed difficult and dangerous operations that not only made them role models for future special operators, but also brought into daylight the main challenges that were to confront special operations forces ever afterward.

The history of special operations forces in World War II is so enormous in its scope and future relevance, and so compelling in human terms, that it has been accorded three chapters in this book. The first covers the Rangers and Forcemen, offspring of the US Army, who fought primarily in the European Theater and provided the inspiration for today's US Army Rangers. The second chapter covers the Raiders of the US Marine Corps and the Frogmen of the US Navy, who did most of their work in the Pacific Theater. The Marine Corps dissolved the Raiders in 1944 and avoided the reconstitution of special operations forces until 2006, when it was compelled to create the Marine Special Operations Command. The Navy, on the other hand, retained some Frogmen after the post-1945 demobilization and eventually converted them into the Sea, Air, Land Teams (SEALs). The third chapter addresses the special operations forces of the Office of Strategic Services, which differed fundamentally from the other special operations forces in composition and purpose, and subsequently inspired a very different type of outfit, the US Army Special Forces.

The first enduring challenge encountered in World War II was the involvement of political leaders who lacked understanding of the special operations forces they were creating and employing. In early 1942, Franklin D. Roosevelt ordered the formation of special operations forces based on the recommendation of his son James, a captain in the Marine Corps Reserves whose enthusiasm for special units derived from an eccentric officer with a credulous reverence for Mao Zedong's guerrilla armies. President Roosevelt disregarded the objections of generals who, unlike his son, perceived the unintended consequences that were likely to ensue. Several subsequent presidents, most notably John F. Kennedy, would champion the special operations forces based more on the popular glamorization of these units than on sober analysis of their military utility.

The problem of ill-informed politicians also manifested itself in repeated decisions to withdraw political top-cover to special operations forces once the thrill was gone. Toward the end of World War II, the fading of Roosevelt's interest in special operations forces facilitated the dismantling of most of the units. Half a century later, the Black Hawk Down debacle in Mogadishu ended President Bill Clinton's honeymoon with special operations forces and led him to make those forces a scapegoat for the failed mission, undermining their standing within the government for the remaining seven years of Clinton's presidency.

The second fundamental challenge to come to light in World War II was the mutability of special operations and the forces that conducted them. The core activities of the Army, Navy, and Air Force have been etched in granite by geography. The Army will always enjoy primacy for military operations on land, the Navy for operations at sea, and the Air Force for operations in the air. Special operations forces lack a realm upon which they can lay indisputable claim. The roles and missions of special operations forces have changed frequently, based on the perceptions of political and military leaders of the tactical and strategic environments. During World War II, special operations forces were reinvented several times as the war's character changed. The cycle of reinvention has repeated itself over and over again since 1945 in accordance with changes in leadership and circumstances.

The third enduring challenge to emerge from World War II was disputation over the value of special operations forces. Champions of special operations forces have often succeeded at convincing politicians, the press, and the public that the forces deliver results of exceptional tactical value, and in some cases even strategic value. But numerous skeptics, many of them inside the military, have just as often questioned whether the tactical or strategic benefits of special operations forces outweigh the costs. They have contended that too few missions are appropriate for special operations forces, or that the missions they perform are not appreciably more important than other missions, or that regular forces are sufficiently capable of performing the same missions. On the cost side of the ledger, special units generally receive longer training and more expensive equipment than other units, and, most importantly, they receive better personnel, which dilutes the quality of other units. Arguments about the value of special operations forces have been especially fierce because they have figured prominently in decisions on the resources and tasks assigned to them—including several decisions that disbanded special operations forces in their entirety.

The fourth persistent challenge, fueled by the first three, has been intense rivalry between special operations forces and regular forces. The disregard of politicians for protests from the regular military about special operations forces has been a recurring source of friction ever since Roosevelt decided to create the first special operations forces over the objections of the military leadership. The formation of special units led recruiters to announce the need for special men for special missions and to rob regular units of some of their most productive members, both of which were also bound to antagonize. The growth in the size, professionalism, and independence of special operations forces over time increasingly made them a threat to the regular armed forces. In turn, the hostility of the regular military and the perceived misuse of special operations forces by regular commanders fostered a persecution complex among special operators, intensifying their thirst for greater power and independence. This rivalry has been the cause of innumerable conflicts over human resources, budgets, missions, and command authorities.

These four challenges serve as the backbone of this chronicle of US special operations forces. The seventy-five-year rise of special operations forces from humble origins in World War II to the present-day behemoth is, at bottom, a coming-of-age story. Special operations forces began as unwanted stepchildren, and they languished in that status for more than four decades. From time to time, they found supportive stepfathers in Washington, but for the most part they were left at the mercy of jealous stepbrothers. In 1986, the creation of the Special Operations Command in Tampa and its accompanying bank account set SOF loose like an eighteen-year-old who just moved out of the house, prone to naïve ambitions and unwise choices. In the first decade of the twenty-first century, special operations forces came into their own, growing into a force of 70,000 troops with help from a president and Congress desperate for weapons to wield against Islamic extremists. Champions of special operations called for the transformation of SOF from a secondary weapon that supported conventional forces to a primary weapon that could take the place of their conventional counterparts. But then success went to the heads of special operations leaders and caused them to reach too far, leaving the Department of Defense strewn with wreckage whose pieces are still being picked up today.

Like any good coming-of-age story, the story of special operations forces is interwoven with a colorful cast of characters. Most special operators volunteered for what they knew would be unusually difficult and dangerous duty, and thus the pantheon of special operations forces brims with men of exceptional talent, courage, dedication, and selflessness. These same special operators, being mortals, have at times succumbed to folly, narcissism, or fear. For some, the acquisition of elite status helped turn confidence into hubris, with all the attendant troubles one might expect. Brilliance has been mixed with bad judgment, in no small part because of the need to make decisions quickly, under stress, and without sleep. The story includes first crushes, rites of passage, harrowing action scenes, falls from grace, and redemption. As a story of war, it has more than its share of suffering, glory, and death.

This book is intended to retell the drama of America's special operations forces and, at the same time, to confer the historical understanding that enhances wisdom and informs sound decisions by today's leaders. Despite a profusion of books on particular individuals or events, the history of special operations forces as instruments of military power has lagged behind other fields of military history. Today's special operators want and need a deeper understanding of their own history. Personnel in conventional forces, who now must work with SOF more than ever before, also have much to gain from learning about the history of special operations forces, which is bound up with that of the rest of the military. The need for historical understanding is most acute among the civilians within the US government, who under the Constitution determine how military forces are formed, prepared, and employed. Whereas military personnel are often well versed in military and other history, the civil side of the government is populated mainly by individuals educated in disciplines like law, public administration, economics, political science, and engineering, which for the most part have discarded or marginalized history in favor of theoretical abstraction and mathematical computation.

This history provides the familiarization required to avoid the errors to which the historically deprived are especially prone, such as relying excessively on one's own intellect, leaping at the first historical analogy to rear its head, and grasping at facile theories drawn from dubious historical interpretations or abstract reasoning. By providing a record of successes and failures, this history may stimulate insights into new environments, and illuminate pitfalls in paths that would otherwise seem free of peril. As the first comprehensive account of America's special operations forces, it delineates the traditions of which special operators are justifiably proud, while demonstrating the need to build on those traditions in ways that harness tradition without being harnessed by it.

CHAPTER 1

RANGERS AND FORCEMEN

Elevated 150 feet above Sicily's southern shoreline, the city of Gela holds a commanding view of the Mediterranean, like the central parterre overlooking the stage of an opera house. Colonized by the Greeks in 688 BC, Gela was once a proud city-state of 100,000 residents, with its own coinage and a steady influx of tax revenue from the grain farms of the native Sicels. The first coins to be minted bore a horseman, commemorating the city's vaunted cavalry and its medals in the equestrian competitions at Olympia. From Gela, enterprising Greeks established colonies at Syracuse and Agrigento, which in their maturity would turn against their progenitor, spurring repeated spasms of violence among Sicily's city-states.

During the Peloponnesian War, a conference of Sicilian noblemen at Gela ended with a peace agreement among all the city-states, in recognition that continued conflict would invite conquest by external powers. Invasion by outsiders would nevertheless become a recurring problem for Gela and the other Sicilian city-states. In the period following the Peloponnesian War, large empires gained power in the Mediterranean at the expense of the city-states, which resulted in the transformation of Gela from one of the sea's predators into one of its prey. The Carthaginians sacked Gela in 405 BC, and Mamertine mercenaries of the Campanians caused such devastation in 282 BC that the city was abandoned. For the next 1,500 years, the terra cotta tiles and stone pillars of its once-proud

Greek temples eroded under sun and wind, while the surrounding farmland came under the successive dominion of the Romans, Goths, Byzantines, Arabs, and Normans.

In the early thirteenth century AD, the Holy Roman Emperor Frederick II resuscitated Gela as part of a grandiose project to make Sicily the heart of a modern European empire. Building Gela new city walls and a castle within, he repopulated the city with Normans and Greeks. The revitalized Gela would bow to a succession of Mediterranean powers—Aragon, Spain, Austria, and Naples—until finally in 1861 the Italian general Giuseppe Garibaldi annexed all of Sicily to Italy at the point of a bayonet.

In July 1943, Gela was home to 32,000 Italian civilians, along with hundreds of soldiers from the Italian Army's 429th Coastal Battalion. Vineyards and olive groves framed the town, and beyond lay expansive fields of golden wheat. A winding road led from the city down to the crescent-shaped beach, whose 1,000 yards of seafront were bisected by a steel jetty that protruded three hundred yards into the clear blue sea.

In the early morning hours of Saturday, July 10, most of Gela was sleeping off Friday evening's pasta and wine, unaware that the newest aspirants to the control of Sicily were steaming across the Mediterranean toward Gela and twenty-five other beaches on the island's southern coast. The invasion fleet of 130 warships and 324 transport vessels bristled with arms and men possessed of the training and desire to use them. The eastern half of the flotilla carried the forces of General Bernard Montgomery's British Eighth Army, while to the west were ships bearing General George Patton's US Seventh Army, to include the forces destined for Gela—the 1st, 3rd, and 4th US Army Ranger battalions.

For the Rangers, Friday evening had involved neither good food, nor good wine, nor good cheer. As the Anglo-American armada was crossing the Mediterranean, a forty-mile-per-hour gale whipped the seas, conjuring waves the height of a two-story building. With stomachs wrenching and vomit besmirching the decks, the Rangers cursed what one wag had dubbed the "Mussolini wind."

The Rangers received several missives from General Patton during the journey. One explained that "in landing operations, retreat is impossible.

We must retain this tremendous advantage by always attacking, rapidly, ruthlessly, viciously, and without rest." Another, intended for the Italian Americans under Patton's command, stated, "There are thousands of soldiers of Italian descent who will be storming ashore with Seventh Army. However, bear in mind that the real courageous Italians who loved liberty and who had the true pioneering spirit left Italy to come to the country of freedom where they have become good citizens. Those who were left behind were the cowards and weaklings who allowed Benito Mussolini to come to power. Against them I know you as an American soldier will not fail in your duty."

As the US ships neared the Sicilian coastline, not long after midnight, the Mussolini wind abated. By the time the Rangers climbed from the big ships into the little landing boats, the water was "almost mirrorlike," in the words of Randall Harris, a twenty-eight-year-old sergeant from Pocahontas, Iowa. Guided by amphibious scouts toward Gela's pristine beach, the Rangers kept noise and light to a minimum so as not to draw the attention of the city's garrison.

Ranger hopes of catching the enemy by surprise were dashed by the sounding of a sentry's alarm at 2:40 a.m., when the lead boats were still seven hundred yards from Gela's shore. At the city's edge and on the beach, searchlights popped on, their white beams crisscrossing and bouncing off the water. Engineers detonated explosive charges that had been placed on the jetty in case of an Allied landing, throwing twisted sheets and chunks of metal in all directions.

The sea was done further injury by Italian mortar rounds, several of which struck American landing craft. One of the boats capsized, and twenty of its passengers drowned. Another boat ran aground on a sandbar, making it a particularly inviting target for the Italian weapon crews, although in the end its only casualty was the canteen of a medical officer, which had been filled with liquor that was officially designated "personal medicinal alcohol."

Most of the landing craft reached the shallow waters unscathed and safely disgorged their passengers, whose fear of death was intermingled with relief at setting foot on immovable ground. Italian soldiers had constructed pillboxes along the beach for the purpose of machine gunning invaders such as these, but the first Rangers to land were able to flank the pillboxes before most of the gunners were ready to fire. Ranger grenades left several Italian machine-gun crews entombed in concrete, and other crews surrendered to avoid the same fate.

With the pillboxes neutralized, the beach appeared to be safe for the hundreds of Rangers now streaming ashore. Photographs taken by Allied reconnaissance aircraft in recent weeks had shown fishermen and fishing vessels on the beach, leading Allied intelligence analysts to conclude that the beach was free of mines. Having been apprised of that conclusion, the Rangers charged across the beach without fear of what might lie beneath.

The analysts turned out to have been mistaken. The first Ranger to trip a mine was Lieutenant Walter Wojcik. A tall, soft-spoken physiology instructor from Minneapolis, Wojcik had demonstrated such courage, leadership, and intellect in the North African campaign as to earn command of a company at the age of twenty-three. The mine Wojcik triggered was a German S-Mine, known among the Americans as the "bouncing betty" because it shot up to the height of a man's waist before spraying two kilograms of shrapnel in a 360-degree arc.

Sergeant Randall "Harry" Harris had been running close behind when the mine exploded. He saw the blast tear Wojcik's chest open. "I've had it, Harry," Wojcik gasped to Harris as he fell to the ground. Stricken with horror, Harris could only watch as Wojcik's exposed heart convulsed in its final pumps.

Mines killed four other Rangers and blinded a fifth. Shrapnel from one mine hit Harris, who felt as though someone had swung a baseball bat into his gut. The metal pierced his Mae West life vest, a frontally inflating device named in honor of the actress's sultry bosom. The vest self-inflated and then shriveled with a hiss as air leaked from the perforation. Looking down, Harris saw that the hot metal had cut open his stomach, and that his intestines were spilling out.

Given the severity of the injury, no one would have faulted Harris had he lain down on the beach and awaited medical attention. But he chose instead to lead other Rangers in the charge up to the city. Pushing his intestines back in with his cartridge belt, he guided men out of the minefield and into the riptide of Rangers that was flowing up the bluff.

The Rangers coursed into the city so quickly that they could see Italian soldiers who were still running from their quarters toward fighting positions. Taking aim at anyone wearing blue fatigues, the Rangers shot some of the Italians dead in the streets. Lieutenant Colonel William Orlando Darby, commanding officer of the three Ranger battalions, was at the front, shouting directions to his Rangers as they surmounted the crest.

Once the Rangers had secured a foothold beyond the top of the bluff, they organized attacks on Italian strongpoints. Darby sought out the sections of town where the Italians were putting up the stiffest resistance. Finding a group of Rangers in a spirited gunfight against Italian soldiers who were barricaded in a schoolhouse, Darby cobbled together every nearby Ranger into a makeshift assault force. Among those whom he enrolled in the mission was his driver, Carlo Contrera. As Darby briefed the men on the scheme of attack, he noticed that Contrera was quivering.

"What are you shaking for?" Darby asked. "Are you scared?"

"No, sir," Contrera replied. "I'm just shaking with patriotism."

Darby led the assault force into the schoolhouse. Fighting the Italians from one room to the next, the Rangers began by tossing in grenades and then bolted in with submachine guns, spraying in all directions to finish off the survivors. At the end, a triumphant Darby emerged with a group of Italian prisoners in tow, the remaining members of what had been an Italian headquarters with fifty-two officers.

In midmorning, the Italian Army counterattacked at Gela with Renault tanks. The Rangers had no armor of their own, but they had come prepared with an array of light antitank weapons, including the recently developed "bazooka." A shoulder-fired rocket launcher with a muzzle velocity of two hundred miles per hour, the bazooka could penetrate three inches of armor plating at seven hundred yards. Lieutenant Stan Zaslaw was getting ready to fire his bazooka at one of the Italian tanks when he saw Lieutenant Colonel Darby riding on top of the vehicle, trying to open the hatch so as to throw a grenade inside. On another occasion, Darby was seen taking charge of a 37mm antitank gun and using it to knock out a Renault.

The Rangers had a tougher time against the German Tiger tanks that descended on Gela at noon. Incapable of piercing the Tiger's thick armor with the bazookas or any of the other weaponry they had carried ashore, the Rangers radioed the tank locations to US cruisers and destroyers. Drawing in close to the coast, the ships unloaded salvo after salvo of four-inch and six-inch shells, which turned the heavy tanks into burning hulks and hurled their supporting infantry into the air. Americans could hear the screams of burning Tiger crewmen from half a mile away. At 2 p.m., the German command called off the counterattack and the surviving German forces withdrew northward.

By this time, the skill and size of the Ranger force had convinced most of the Italian defenders of Gela to surrender. Ranger logs recorded nearly 1,000 Italian prisoners taken on July 10. Darby's staff tallied up the day's results in one of Gela's restaurants, which had been commandeered as the Ranger command post. A staff officer from higher headquarters arrived in the evening to declare that his commander would be making the restaurant into his headquarters, so the Rangers obligingly packed up their maps and papers and took them away, along with the cases of cognac and champagne they had found in the restaurant's cellar.

DARBY'S RANGERS HAD been in existence barely a year when they landed on the southern coast of Sicily, infants in comparison with the US, British, and Canadian battalions on their flanks, some of which could trace their lineage back to Napoleon's Peninsular War. They had something of an American precedent in Rogers' Rangers, a light infantry unit that had habitually trounced French and Indian antagonists during the Seven Years' War of 1756 to 1763, though the Americanness of the lineage was suspect, since that force had served under the British Empire and its leader had sided with the British when the American colonies declared their independence in 1776. The principal role model for Darby's Rangers was a much newer outfit, and one fully British. Like their role model, the new American Rangers were intended for a different type of warfare than the one they were fated to wage, ensuring that the US Army's first incarnation of special operations forces would be fraught with controversy.

The idea of forming US Army Ranger battalions had been born in the dark gloom of April 1942, when the Germans were running circles around the Soviet Red Army on the Russian steppes and the Japanese were expunging the remnants of American resistance in the Philippines at Bataan and Corregidor. It was conceived in the head of General George Marshall, the US Army chief of staff, during a visit to the British Commando Training Centre in the Scottish highlands. Forged in response to the unprecedented traumas of World War I, the British Commandos were the special operations force that would become the archetype for most of the special operations forces of the Western world.

Following Adolf Hitler's lightning-quick destruction of France in May 1940 and the evacuation of British troops from Dunkirk, Winston Churchill had decided that Britain needed to devise ways to fight Nazi Germany without sending a whole generation of young men to their deaths on the continent as it had done in World War I. He would have to find ways that did not require much heavy equipment, since the British Army had, in its haste to escape at Dunkirk, left most of its equipment in France. Churchill decided to focus on ground raids on the Axis periphery while at the same time maintaining air and naval superiority, letting the Soviets do most of the fighting against the Germans, and convincing the United States to join the anti-Axis coalition. The Commandos became the primary raiding weapon in Churchill's arsenal.

General Marshall arrived at the British Commando Training Centre believing that Western Europe had to be invaded with overwhelming force, rather than merely poked at the edges as Churchill preferred. The visit did not disabuse him of that conviction. It did, however, spark his interest in the Commando program. Since the Commandos were the most active of British forces at the time, American collaboration would provide a vehicle for putting Americans into combat and gaining badly needed experience. Marshall promptly ordered Colonel Lucian Truscott, the US Army's liaison to the British Combined Operations Headquarters, to find a way to involve Americans in Commando training and operations.

Truscott in turn instructed General Russell P. Hartle, commander of the 34th Infantry Division, to form an American battalion that would train and operate with the Commandos. It would be called the 1st Ranger Battalion, and its men the Rangers. "Few words have a more glamorous connotation in American military history," Truscott said in explaining his choice of name. Contributing to that glamor was the 1940 film *Northwest Passage*, in which the swashbuckling Robert Rogers, played by Spencer Tracy, led his Rangers to victory against all odds.

In appointing a commander for the Ranger battalion, Truscott and Hartle might have been expected to search for a lieutenant colonel in his early forties, the typical profile of a US Army battalion commander at the time. Instead, they chose a man two ranks lower and a decade younger, thirty-one-year-old Captain William Orlando Darby. The fact that Darby was serving as Hartle's aide gave reason to wonder whether Truscott and Hartle had simply grabbed the closest officer they could find. Time, however, would show Darby to be a superb pick.

Raised in Fort Smith, Arkansas, William Darby was the son of Percy Darby, who owned a printing business and, on the side, a thirty-piece orchestra that performed accompaniments to silent films. As a teenager, William played the clarinet and saxophone in the orchestra. He was often absorbed in reading, devouring books of high adventure, such as those in the Horatio Alger, Rover Boys, and Tom Swift series, and frequently paging through a multivolume encyclopedia called the *Book of Knowledge*. His high forehead and blue eyes made the girls in his high school swoon. Martha Knapp, a neighbor who had a crush on young Darby, believed that he had "the most beautiful complexion you've ever seen."

After reading a series of articles in *Mentor* magazine on the virtues of West Point, Darby applied for entrance into the academy. His congressman ranked him the second alternate in the district, but the recommended candidate and first alternate dropped out, allowing Darby to enroll in 1929. William H. Baumer, a West Point classmate, recalled that Darby "was known as a charming, persuasive, extremely likeable person. He had lots of energy and was always willing to jump in and do a job." As a cadet, Darby demonstrated natural leadership talents, good manners, a love for fun, and meticulous attention to personal appearance. One peer observed that Darby wore a uniform "like it had been poured on." In terms of academic work and military skill, however, Darby did not stand out, finishing with a class rank of 177 out of 346.

Upon commissioning as a second lieutenant, Darby was assigned to the 82nd Field Artillery of the 1st Cavalry Division, the only horse artillery unit left in the US military. He spent the next eight years in the threadbare peacetime army, marrying Natalie Shaw of El Paso in 1935 while serving at Fort Bliss and divorcing four years later. In November 1941, he received orders to Hawaii, but Pearl Harbor was attacked before he departed, resulting in his redirection to Hartle's 34th Division.

Truscott saw in Darby many of the qualities for which the Rangers would later extol their commander. In Truscott's estimation, Darby was "outstanding in appearance, possessed of a most attractive personality," and "keen, intelligent, and filled with enthusiasm." Confident in Darby's capabilities for independent action, Truscott vested in him full responsibility for filling the 1st Ranger Battalion with volunteers. Truscott and Hartle did impose some minimum requirements, though. Ranger candidates had to possess 20/20 vision, good hearing, and normal blood pressure. Men were automatically disqualified for heart defects, night blindness, inferior reaction time, and dentures. Restrictions were waived in some cases, such as that of Corporal Gerrit Rensink, who convinced the medical staff that his dental bridgework would not rattle during operations whose success depended upon complete silence.

To solicit volunteers, Darby posted flyers on US Army bulletin boards in Northern Ireland, where the 34th Division and other newly arrived US units were based. He delivered speeches and set up recruitment booths in areas heavily trafficked by US soldiers. Two thousand young men volunteered in short order. Darby interviewed all of the officer volunteers and many of the others, which allowed him to size up each man's character as well as his physical shape. He looked for officers and noncommissioned officers who, in his words, possessed "leadership qualities of a high order with particular emphasis on initiative and common sense." For the junior enlisted ranks, Darby targeted men between eighteen and twenty years of age who appeared physically and mentally capable of performing the most arduous of military tasks.

Aware that some Army commanders were encouraging their problem children to volunteer for the Rangers, Darby made a point of "weeding out the braggart and the volunteer looking for excitement but who, in return, expected to be a swashbuckling hero who could live as he pleased if only he exhibited courage and daring in battle." Darby could not, however, reject every man who did not conform to Army norms, for the toughness, independent thinking, and ability to improvise that Darby prized were often accompanied by a penchant for barroom altercations, curfew violations, and general disdain for the regimentation of Army life. Darby's interest in rough-hewn and unorthodox men was reflected in the diverse backgrounds of those who made it through the screening. The first group of selectees included coal miners, cowboys, railroaders, farmhands, steelworkers, truck drivers, morticians, boxers, and stockbrokers. There was a lion tamer, a bullfighter, a church deacon, and the treasurer of a burlesque theater.

In July 1942, Darby and his Rangers commenced training at the British Commando Training Centre. Located between Loch Lochy and Loch Arkaig in the western Scottish highlands, the center lay on the grounds of the Achnacarry castle, which had been rebuilt in 1802 after arsonists of the Jacobite Rising torched the original structure. All trainees were required to undergo tests of courage, and those who failed were sent back into the regular Army. Among the scariest was the so-called "death slide," a cable tied at one end to the top of a forty-foot tree and at the other to the ground on the far side of the frigid Arkaig River. Trainees were required to climb the tree, throw a toggle rope over the cable, and hope that their grip would not slip before they crossed the froth of the rushing Arkaig.

Ranger trainees also had to prove their mettle in a grueling regimen that included speed marches over rugged hills, log-lifting, obstacle courses, weapons training, patrolling, night operations, and small-boat handling. Sixteen-mile hikes thickened the callouses on the men's feet, so that after a time they were immune to blistering. Rangers learned how to sneak up on sentries and kill them silently, and how to destroy enemy pillboxes from the front, rear, and side. They practiced bayoneting dummies and shooting targets at close distances.

Rangers who passed the basic Commando training course moved to Argyle, on Scotland's western coast, for training in amphibious landings. Riding small craft onto beaches at all times of day and in all weather conditions, they conducted mock assaults on coastal fortifications and towns. Scottish townsfolk played French or Italian citizens in the exercises, and served cakes and sandwiches to the famished Rangers afterward.

On August 19, 1942, fifty of Darby's Rangers took part in the raid on Dieppe, a coastal port in German-occupied France that Churchill had designated the latest target of his raiding campaign. The Rangers were parceled out between the 2nd Canadian Division, which would land at the central beach, and two British Commando battalions, which were responsible for destroying German weapons on the beach's flanks. Among the Rangers chosen for the mission, the elation of participation in so bold a raid did not survive first contact. German torpedo boats intercepted the boats carrying one of the Commando battalions, preventing most of its men from making landfall. Canadian tanks that were supposed to charge into the town of Dieppe found the beach's exits blocked by German obstacles, leaving the Canadian division exposed to a vortex of German artillery and automatic weapons fire. Of the division's 5,000 men, nearly 3,400 became casualties in the one-day operation. The Commandos lost 247 of 1,000 men, and the Rangers 11 of 50.

The Dieppe debacle did much to discredit the idea that coastal raids could inflict more than flesh wounds on the Nazi empire. Large raids were discontinued after Dieppe, and resources were redirected toward amphibious landings in North Africa and Italy that prefaced sustained invasions. The original purpose of Commandos and Rangers—coastal raiding in service of a strategy of peripheral jabbing—was thus rendered obsolete. As the planners of the North African and Italian invasions recognized, however, these units were well-suited for the new types of campaigns, as the amphibious invasions were certain to involve difficult offensive missions on the coast.

For Operation Torch, the code name for the Allied invasion of North Africa in November 1942, the 1st Ranger Battalion was charged with taking the Algerian port of Arzew. Ranger training in stealth and night operations made the battalion a particularly attractive choice for this undertaking. If the Rangers could sneak ashore and seize the two Vichy French forts, they would spare Arzew from a massive shore bombardment, and hence preserve its much-needed port facilities. They would also minimize Vichy French casualties, an important consideration at a time when the United States was seeking to pry the Vichy French away from the Nazis.

Sailing aboard three British passenger ships that had originally been employed on the Glasgow-Belfast ferry line, the Rangers landed undetected at Arzew on November 8 shortly after midnight. They silently dispatched the few sentries they encountered en route to the town's two forts, Fort de la Pointe, at the harbor's edge, and Batterie du Nord, atop a nearby hillock. At Fort de la Pointe, they needed only a few minutes and a few gunshots to overwhelm the defenders. They took sixty prisoners, including the wife of the post's adjutant. At the Batterie du Nord, Vichy French lookouts espied the Rangers using wire cutters to slice through the eight-foot-high barbed wire surrounding the fort. French machine guns opened fire, compelling Darby to pull his Rangers back and call in rounds from Ranger mortar tubes, which had been set up nearby for such an eventuality. Eighty mortar shells crashed into the fort, quieting the guns of the defenders. Most of the garrison took shelter in the fort's magazine when the mortar barrage commenced, in the belief that Allied aircraft were bombing the fort.

Entering the fort against minimal opposition, the Rangers issued a surrender ultimatum in French to the men bunched inside the magazine. The Frenchmen rebuffed the ultimatum. When, however, the Rangers pushed grenades and a Bangalore torpedo into the ventilators, the garrison came out with hands held high. The Rangers took sixty prisoners here as well, including the battery commander, who had scampered to the magazine in such a hurry that he was still in his pajamas and bed slippers.

All told, the Rangers suffered a mere two dead and eight wounded at Arzew. Darby took control of the town as interim mayor while thousands of soldiers from the US 1st Division arrived over the beach and longshoremen unloaded supplies from American ships at the harbor. Darby had to figure out how to keep water, electricity, and other public services going, though he had a much easier time of it than Americans in areas of the North African coast where shore bombardment had wrecked purification plants and power grids. Other matters that demanded his attention included the town's brothel, whose prostitutes had wasted little time in advertising their wares to the invaders.

On February 1, 1943, the 1st Ranger Battalion flew to Tunisia in thirty-two C-47 transport planes, its mission to conduct raids against German and Italian forces retreating from Algeria and Libya. In the Tunisian countryside, the Rangers camouflaged themselves by day and marched by night, using colored flashlights and radios to stay organized. On February 13, the Rangers overran a position held by the 10th Bersaglieri Regiment, a light infantry formation of the Italian Royal Army. The Rangers killed seventy-five Italians and captured eleven while suffering one killed and twenty wounded. On March 20, the 1st Ranger Battalion marched six miles at night over mountainsides and gorges into the backside of the El Guettar Pass, which had been left unguarded by the Italian unit at the pass in the belief that no enemy could scale the steep slopes. The bewildered Italians surrendered without a fight, permitting the Rangers to net over 1,000 prisoners at the cost of a single American casualty.

Ranger successes in North Africa generated enthusiasm in the upper ranks of the US government for additional Ranger battalions. But recommendations to expand the Rangers provoked stiff opposition from a number of senior leaders in the Army, including Lieutenant General Lesley J. McNair, a curmudgeonly workaholic who headed Army Ground Forces within the War Department. As McNair saw it, special units were likely to sit unused for long periods of time for want of suitable missions, or else they would participate in "unprofitable missions" for the sake of demonstrating their ongoing relevance. Diversion of high-quality officers to Ranger units, McNair warned, "will seriously handicap the selection and training of leaders who are so essential in the present training program" of the regular Army. Thus, it would be better to provide special training and equipment to existing infantry units as needs arose.

McNair occupied a high rung on the Army ladder, but there were other men of different opinions who stood on rungs still higher, and they decided to overrule him. In May 1943, the Army formed two additional Ranger battalions, the 3rd and 4th, putting both under Darby, who was given six weeks to obtain and train the necessary personnel. Darby employed recruiting methods he had used in the past, and he devised new techniques as well. Two of his roughest sergeants strutted into bars frequented by American servicemen and announced that they were ready to fight any and all comers. Those who stepped forward for fisticuffs were signed up as Rangers. Darby also scoured the centers where the Army sent newly trained troops prior to unit assignment, seeking out, in his words, men who "were young, usually of medium size, and rugged looking."

AFTER THE LANDING at Gela, the Rangers participated in two other major operations in Italy. The first began with an amphibious landing on September 9, 1943, at the resort village of Maiori, near Salerno, as part of a broad offensive by the US Fifth Army toward Naples. The Rangers met no opposition when they stepped from the royal blue waters of the Amalfi Coast onto Maiori's black-sand beach. Marching six miles up a steep road that snaked through orchards of lemon trees, they drew on months of hard conditioning to bear their heavy packs and equipment at a steady pace. They reached the Chiunzi Pass, 4,000 feet above sea level, in just five hours. No Germans were to be seen.

The absence of Germans was testament to the Rangers' speed and achievement of surprise, rather than to any lack of German concern about the Chiunzi Pass. Overlooking Naples, Mount Vesuvius, and Highway 18, the pass was perfectly situated for sighting German military traffic and strongpoints. Darby's Rangers trimmed the chestnut trees to facilitate observation, then marked the coordinates of targets and radioed them to warships sitting off the coast, whose guns sent massive shells screaming over the Tyrrhenian Sea and the Italian countryside.

Germans soon showed up at the Chiunzi Pass to give battle. Too few in number to pose a serious threat, the German soldiers were easily thrown back by Darby's Rangers. "We are sitting pretty," Darby radioed to the Fifth Army headquarters.

No one else in the Fifth Army, however, could say the same. Difficult terrain, German resistance, and Allied disorganization conspired to slow the advance of most American units, giving the Germans time to organize a slew of counterattacks. Several of the counterattacks took place at the Chiunzi Pass, each of which the Rangers stymied with the assistance of reinforcements that included an infantry battalion, a field artillery battalion, a medium tank battalion, and a company of combat engineers. The Rangers lost twenty-eight killed, nine missing, and sixty-six wounded in ten days of conventional battle. German counterattacks at other locations proved more effective, and at one point the Germans came very close to overrunning the Allied beachhead at Salerno; only the enormous projectiles of Allied warships and the bombing and strafing of Allied aircraft averted utter ruin.

After failing to deprive the Allies of a foothold, the German Tenth Army withdrew northward from Salerno to what became known as the Winter Line, where fortified hills and passes afforded superb defensive positions. General Mark Clark, commander of the US Fifth Army, split up the Ranger battalions, attached them to larger units, and sent them to breach the Winter Line. Thus, rather than loitering or dreaming up "unprofitable missions," as General McNair had prophesied, the Rangers would be fighting conventional battles alongside the regular infantry.

The decision to employ the Rangers as standard infantry attracted its own set of detractors, which included many of the Rangers themselves. Ranger officers objected to the use of their troops in this manner, on the grounds that it squandered the specialized capabilities they had toiled months, if not years, to develop. Instead, they recommended, the Ranger leadership should determine the missions of Ranger units. These objections made no impression on General Clark, who believed that keeping special units in reserve until the need for special missions arose was a luxury that he could not presently afford. His need for infantrymen had reached such proportions that he was pulling musicians from division bands to plug holes on the front. Clark discerned, moreover, that opportunities for creeping up on the enemy and putting a dagger into his back had become scant now that they were fighting tough and canny Germans who held stout defensive lines, rather than the dispirited Frenchmen or disorganized Italians of the campaigns in North Africa and Sicily.

Bitter mountain combat at the Winter Line would expose the Rangers to German conventional military power as never before. Over a period of forty-five days, 40 percent of the Rangers became casualties. The stresses of failure and the death of comrades debilitated men's minds such that some of the bravest Rangers had to be sent to the medical area, two hundred to five hundred yards to the rear of the rifle pits, for a week or more of mental convalescence. The attrition of experienced Rangers led, in addition, to an influx of green troops who had not been selected or trained with the same care as in the past, causing Ranger units to commit errors that would have been unthinkable with the original members.

While Darby's Rangers were trying to wrest the Germans from their mountaintop redoubts, another elite force arrived at a different section of the Winter Line to try its hand against the Germans. The First Special Service Force, a combined unit of US and Canadian soldiers, had been formed in July 1942, but had not yet had a taste of battle. Created originally for Operation Plough, the force had been expected to enter the war in circumstances far different from those prevailing in southern Italy. But fighting somewhere was better than fighting nowhere, in the opinion of most Forcemen, who were itching to put more than a year of training to real use.

Operation Plough was the brainchild of Geoffrey Pyke, an English scientist whom the British government had hired in its quest for alternatives to blood-soaked infantry campaigns on the European continent. Averse to bathing and personal grooming, entirely devoid of social graces, Pyke irritated most of his professional colleagues and most of the other people he met in life. Those very quirks, however, led several men of great influence to see in Pyke a mad genius. Pyke convinced Lord Louis Mountbatten, the British chief of combined operations, to enlist him as an idea man by showing up at Mountbatten's office and declaring, "Lord Mountbatten, you need me on your staff because I'm a man who thinks." Pyke and Mountbatten, in turn, convinced Churchill and Marshall that Pyke's imaginative schemes deserved to be funded.

As conceived by Pyke, Operation Plough would revolutionize warfare by exploiting a new domain: snow. "Our studies of the strategic situation have led us to the concept of snow as a fourth element—a sea which flows over most of Europe each year," Pyke posited. "We must obtain mastery of the snow as we have of the sea." According to Pyke, the Allies should airlift snow commandos and motorized snow-sleds into Norway, Romania, and the Italian Alps to conduct precision strikes on power plants, factories, and oil fields. Pyke predicted that the snow forces would wreak such havoc on Nazi Germany's military and economic production that Hitler would have to divert half a million or more troops to contend with the menace.

Great Britain, the United States, and Canada invested hefty sums of treasure and manpower in the transformation of the mad scientist's vision into reality. Studebaker designed a snowmobile prototype, with treads resembling a tank's on the lower half and an open seating bay on the upper half. The prototype would eventually be developed into the M29 Weasel, a two-ton, four-passenger vehicle capable of traveling up to thirty miles per hour in snow at an average of five miles per gallon of gasoline. The Canadians contributed eight hundred of their finest soldiers to the initial snow commando unit, the First Special Service Force, a commitment the Americans matched in quantity but not in quality. The Forcemen received special training in the use of the snowcraft as well as skis, and parachutes.

By the time the Weasel was ready for mass production, however, the plan for Plough had come under fire from the Royal Air Force, which doubted the value of diverting its premier bomber, the Lancaster, to the lugging of the snow-sleds across Europe. The Norwegian government-in-exile raised objections to Operation Plough, as it did not consider destruction of the country's power facilities to be in the nation's long-term interests. Nor were Allied military planners able to find satisfactory solutions to essential logistical problems that to Pyke had seemed mere trifling details, such as how to refuel and repair a vehicle in a country where the enemy controlled all the gas stations and owned all the facilities capable of servicing tracked vehicles. In the fall of 1943, more than one year after the creation of the First Special Service Force, the idea of using the Forcemen as snow commandos was pitched into the dustbin.

The crushing of Pyke's dreams stimulated talk of dissolving the First Special Service Force and sending its personnel to regular US and Canadian units. But the force's enterprising commanding officer, Colonel Robert T. Frederick, skillfully reconfigured the unit to make it attractive as an all-purpose assault force. Removing snow-sleds and skis from the unit's table of organization and equipment, he obtained flamethrowers, mortars, machine guns, and bazookas. Frederick made emotional pleas to American and Canadian generals, asserting that retention of the unit would promote a spirit of cooperation between the United States and Canada. His efforts ultimately paid off with a one-way ticket to the Italian front for the entire First Special Service Force.

General Clark, in his desperation for combat troops, had gladly accepted the 1,600 men of the First Special Service Force into the Fifth

Army. From his headquarters at Caserta's cavernous Bourbon palace, Clark ordered the newly arrived Forcemen to enter the Winter Line fighting at the hill mass of Monte la Difensa–Monte Maggiore. The mission was ideally suited for an elite infantry unit, as this terrain demanded physical fitness of a higher grade than anywhere else on the Winter Line. From Monte la Difensa, with an altitude of 3,120 feet, and the adjacent Monte la Remetanea, at 2,948 feet, the Germans had repulsed and slaughtered several Allied assault forces that General Clark had sent in their direction. The plan now was to send the Forcemen via a different route, up the western face of La Difensa, the top 1,000 feet of which ascended at a seventy-degree pitch.

Walking toward Monte la Difensa in daylight on December 2, the Forcemen had to step over the bodies of men killed in prior attacks on the peak. That evening, a reconnaissance team left the rest of the force at the base of the mountain and headed up La Difensa to identify the best marching routes and string the cliffs with ropes for the use of the main body of the force. Allied air and artillery bombarded the mountain, striking on all sides with white phosphorous and high-explosive rounds to prevent the Germans from discerning the direction from which the attack would come. "It looked like the whole mountain was on fire," remembered Bill Pharis, a former roustabout from the oil fields of Texas.

The lead battalion began the upward march several hours before midnight. The paths charted by the reconnaissance teams had been well chosen, and the ropes deftly placed. At 5 a.m., the foremost Forcemen reached a position just one hundred meters from the summit. From there, they ascertained that the Germans had not ruled out the possibility of an attack up the steep mountainside, as they had posted several sentries near the top of the cliff face. The Forcemen used double-edged stilettos to kill these sentries, shoving their free hands into the mouths of the victims to muffle the screams.

Resuming the climb, the Forcemen planned to keep going in silence until 6:30 before opening fire with their rifles and machine guns, in order to allow more men and weaponry to come up the cliff. But their presence was discovered at 5:30 when several Forcemen slipped on loose stones, which the Germans had positioned near their emplacements to give warning of intruders. One man who slipped kicked the helmet off a man below him, causing the helmet to clatter down the mountain. Germans sprang to their weapons and a German flare gun went into action, shooting a green flare first, then a red one, then two magnesium flares that lighted the whole mountain.

American and Canadian hopes that the preparatory air and artillery strikes had killed off much of the German force proved to be unfounded. By sheltering in the mountain's caves or in concrete pillboxes, most of the Germans had remained alive. From positions looking down on the face, Germans shot at the Forcemen while awaiting reinforcements from other sections of the perimeter, who needed time to bring their heavy weapons over.

Taking advantage of an early morning fog to obscure their movements, Forcemen hurled grenades at the enemy defensive positions on the upper face. Several of these positions went silent, opening corridors through which the Forcemen quickly scrambled. Americans and Canadians poured into the bowl-shaped mountaintop before the Germans could haul their machine guns near the cliff. Colonel Frederick, one of the first Forcemen up the mountain, dashed from place to place across the bowl to shout instructions and exhortations.

The Germans receded slowly before the onslaught of the Forcemen. Two hours after the battle had started, the surviving Germans fled the mountaintop, leaving behind seventy-five comrades who had perished and forty-three who had been taken prisoner. The Forcemen clapped each other on the back for taking the bastion so swiftly, and for surviving their first brush with battle.

The enemy, however, robbed them of time to savor the victory or ponder the ephemeral character of human triumph. While retreating from La Difensa, the German survivors had sent word of their departure to their higher headquarters, which directed artillery and mortar crews to plaster the summit. If the German gunners had made a prayer to the heavens to lift the fog, as the Greeks had done on the plains of Troy, the prayer was soon answered. With the fog gone, the Germans could adjust their fire, guaranteeing that the peak and the troops packed atop it would incur the full hatred of the German shells.

Frederick immediately ordered the Forcemen to take refuge in German pillboxes. He himself, however, continued to stand and move about in the open without concern for the incoming fire. "There were times when a heavy barrage of mortar fire would send us scurrying for cover only to come back and find him smoking a cigarette—in the same sitting position and place we had vacated in a hurry," recalled Captain Dermot O'Neill. Other officers were less fortunate. One was killed while scanning for Germans through binoculars. A mortar round killed the entire command group of the 1st Battalion, 2nd Regiment, the first battalion up the mountain. Many Forcemen rued the death of the battalion's commander, Lieutenant Colonel Tom MacWilliam, a "fearless officer" who "always demonstrated superior qualities in everything he undertook," in the description of the regimental commander.

To Frederick's surprise, the German infantry did not counterattack the mountaintop. Unbeknownst to the Forcemen, the recent flooding of valleys and rivers in the German rear had weakened German supply arteries to such an extent as to render further combat in the region exceedingly precarious. The Germans did, nevertheless, find other ways to hurt the Forcemen. On the night of December 3, German forward observers caught sight of the First Special Service Force's 1st Regiment, which had been held in reserve. The night sky erupted with the howls of German howitzers and a new weapon that the Germans called the *Nebelwerfer*. A rocket launcher with six barrels, each six inches in diameter, the *Nebelwerfer* could fire thirty-six high-explosive rockets per minute. The English-speaking Allies would soon refer to the dreaded projectiles as "screaming meemies." War correspondent Ernie Pyle, who was at La Difensa during the battle, described it thus: "The gun didn't go off with a roar, but the shells swished forward with a sound of unparalleled viciousness and power, as though gigantic gears were grinding. Actually, it sounded as though some mammoth man were grinding them out of a huge machine."

Robert Shafer, a Forceman in the 1st Regiment, was one of those who survived the experience of watching the German bombardment blow apart the once-orderly bivouac. He saw German shell fragments slice so deeply into one man's arm that it barely remained attached. Peering down at the expensive watch on his dangling limb, the man pronounced, "I don't suppose I'll wear the watch on that hand again." Shrapnel sheared a chunk of flesh off the shoulder blade of another man, whom Shafer knew to be a star baseball player. "He was worried about it affecting his pitching arm," Shafer recorded. In the space of an hour, the Germans killed or wounded 40 percent of the regiment, a sobering demonstration of the reality that elite units could be shattered as easily as any other units when operating near the front lines. The losses upped the total of First Special Service Force casualties at La Difensa to 532.

The capture of La Difensa dealt the Germans a significant tactical setback, but it did not yield the strategic windfall that the Allied leadership had prognosticated. During the preparation for the attack, the II Corps commander, Major General Geoffrey Keyes, had told the Forcemen that if they took the mountain, they would so unhinge the German defenses that the Allied armies would be able to roll into Rome within two to three weeks. In the days after the battle, however, the Germans kept the Allies from exploiting the penetration of La Difensa by engaging the Forcemen and nearby Allied forces in jousts lasting long enough for most German forces to withdraw northward and occupy newly fortified positions in advantageous terrain. Rome was to remain in German hands for another six months.

Keyes's forecast had led the Forcemen to expect a sumptuous reward in return for taking La Difensa, such as an extended leave to a beachside resort. General Clark, however, decided on a different sort of recompense, notifying the Forcemen that he would give them "bigger and better hills to climb." Clark sent the Forcemen to Mount Sammucro, whose 4,000-foot peak gazed down upon icy precipices and slopes. Attacking on Christmas Eve and again on Christmas Day, the Forcemen drove a German unit from the mountain at a cost of sixty-five North American casualties.

THE REALITY THAT small stabs could not bring down the German dragon was on the minds of leaders in London, Washington, and Ottawa at this very moment. Over the course of December 1943, the Allies devised a plan to circumvent the rock-hard defensive lines that the Germans kept laying across the Italian boot. An amphibious landing in the German rear would be the means, and the port of Anzio would be the place. Located just thirty miles south of Rome, Anzio was best known as the city from which Coriolanus had launched his rebellion against the Roman Republic in 491 BC. If Allied forces could secure a beachhead at Anzio and drive rapidly north, they would cut the supply lines and escape lanes for the German divisions arrayed along the Winter Line.

Among the units assigned to the Anzio landing was the recently formed 6615th Ranger Force. Commanded by Darby, who had been promoted to colonel on December 11, the 6615th consisted of the three Ranger battalions, the 83rd Chemical Battalion, a Cannon Company, and a headquarters element. Invasion planners surmised that German units garrisoned in Anzio would put up a fierce fight at the water's edge, so they wanted a crack unit at the spear tip of the invasion force, and the 6615th Ranger Force was the most obvious candidate. Darby received orders to storm Anzio's beach and then seize the harbor and port facilities.

The Ranger Force landed at Anzio early on the morning of January 22, 1944, disembarking near the Art Deco domes of the Paradiso sul Mare casino. The dreaded German beach defenses turned out to consist of two men, both of whom the Rangers shot on sight. Hustling straight through the beach and up the street leading to the Paradiso sul Mare, Darby and his headquarters staff set up a command post inside the casino. The Ranger battalions moved into the center of the town, where they caught the German garrison by complete surprise. The Rangers broke into one German headquarters while officers were in the midst of breakfasting on sardines and Danish bacon, gunning down several Germans before the remainder could escape.

The Germans had only two understrength coastal battalions in the vicinity of Anzio, precluding a quick counterstrike that could pin the invasion force to the coast and crush it on the beaches. The Allies, it appeared, had a promising opportunity to cross into the interior and cut off the enemy forces on the Winter Line. But Major General John P. Lucas, the commander of the Anzio invasion, adopted the more cautious approach of keeping units in a shell around the small beachhead in anticipation of eventual German counterattacks, of the sort that had nearly wiped the Allies off the map at Salerno, while bringing more forces and supplies into the port. The Anzio salient, shaped like a half moon, had a radius of only ten miles after the first week.

Lucas's caution permitted the Germans to shift infantry, armor, artillery, aircraft, and U-boats toward Anzio, threatening the beachhead and simultaneously building a protective wall between Anzio and the lifelines connecting the Winter Line to Rome. To Allied leaders who had envisaged a swift rampage through the German rear, the passage of precious days without forward movement was maddening. "I had hoped we were hurling a wild cat on the shore," groused Winston Churchill, "but all we got was a stranded whale."

On January 28, Lucas received orders to get off his duff and push aggressively toward the highways. He directed the 3rd Division, commanded by Major General Truscott, to head eastward into "Jerryland"—slang for German-held territory—and seize a series of population centers and roads. The first objective would be Cisterna, a manufacturing town four miles beyond the Anzio beachhead. General Truscott in turn assigned the mission of taking Cisterna to Darby's Ranger Force, which had recently been attached to the 3rd Division. Truscott told Darby to send two of the three Ranger battalions to Cisterna, while the third cleared a nearby road for the benefit of two infantry regiments that would soon follow.

Darby, who was no doubt flattered that Truscott had selected the Rangers for such a difficult and important mission, thought that an attack of this size was certain to succeed. That conclusion seemed to be reflected in the selection of the code name for Cisterna—EASY. The German forces near Anzio appeared to be less aggressive than in the past, which was attributed to the increasing number of Poles in German units. Intelligence and reconnaissance reports, moreover, showed no signs of large German concentrations near Cisterna.

On the afternoon of January 30, the Rangers gathered in a pine forest on the fringe of the beachhead. Unfurling their bedrolls on the soft pine needles, they took turns napping. In the evening, they rolled up the bedrolls and stacked them on a tent canvas alongside their barracks bags, which would remain under the vigilant watch of cooks and truck drivers while the fighters visited Jerryland. The Rangers filed out of the bivouac singing Al Dexter's hit song "Pistol Packin' Mama."

Near midnight, the 1st Ranger Battalion left the point of departure, advancing in darkness along a deep canal that would take them straight toward Cisterna. The 3rd Ranger Battalion followed at 1:15 a.m. The 4th Ranger Battalion, which was responsible for securing the road, departed at 2 a.m.

Wading through murky water that came up to their knees, the 1st and 3rd battalions did their best to avoid splashes and any other noises that might reach the ears of German sentries. The canal took them near two German *Nebelwerfer* batteries, so near that they could hear the Germans talking with one another. The Rangers chose to bypass the batteries so as not to reveal their presence. Closer to the objective, the Americans saw a number of German patrols pass in front and to the side, but the Germans did not appear to detect the marauders.

Because of the number of units now under Darby's command and the multiple prongs of advance, Darby oversaw the operation from a house near the line of departure, rather than from the front as in earlier days. The first piece of bad news reached him at 0248, when four radio operators from the 3rd Ranger Battalion reported that they had gotten lost. Darby called it the "god-damnedest thing" he had "ever heard of." Then, halfway to Cisterna, the 3rd battalion became separated from the 1st. After another half mile of marching, three companies from the 1st battalion lost contact with the battalion's other three companies. These were the sorts of mistakes that Darby's original Rangers, selected and trained without the haste demanded by mid-campaign operational schedules, almost certainly would not have made.

The 4th Ranger Battalion, advancing along its assigned road, walked into a German ambush at 3 a.m. The first German to see the Americans opened fire with his machine pistol to mark their location, and then the night lit up with blotches of muzzle flashes. From rifle pits and farm buildings, the Germans raked the Rangers and an accompanying column of vehicles as they tried to get off the road. American efforts to drive armor through the kill zone were thwarted by a makeshift German roadblock of wrecked jeeps and trucks. When Ranger companies attempted to charge the Teutonic tormentors, they were shredded by German munitions. Three of the 4th Ranger Battalion's company commanders perished in the futile assaults.

At the cusp of dawn, the 1st and 3rd battalions reached a flat field on the southern side of Cisterna. Triangular in shape, the field measured roughly 1,000 yards on each side, with roads running along two legs of the triangle and a hodgepodge of irrigation ditches bounding the third. Seeking to put the open terrain behind them before losing the cloak of darkness, the Rangers made a run for the town. After dashing four hundred yards, they came upon a German bivouac, full of sleeping soldiers. The Rangers set upon the Germans with bayonets and knives, hoping to kill the whole bunch before anyone could let out a peep, but one German emitted a loud scream as his throat was cut. At the sound, other Germans sprang out of their blankets with weapons in hand, and rifle shots and grenade explosions filled the air. The ill-prepared and outnumbered Germans did not last long against the Rangers, but they had cost the Rangers the element of surprise as well as precious seconds of darkness.

German reconnaissance forces had already alerted the German headquarters in Cisterna of advancing Americans, and now the headquarters learned that the Americans were in the big field on the edge of town. The headquarters happened to command an entire German division, the elite Hermann Goering Division, which had deployed to Cisterna the previous evening in preparation for a massive German counteroffensive against the Anzio beachhead. The personal creation of Nazi Vice Chancellor Hermann Goering, the division possessed some of the finest officers and most powerful tanks in the German armed forces.

After butchering the Germans in the bivouac, the Rangers started running across the field again. When they were two hundred yards from the edge of Cisterna, with the first rays of sunlight edging the roof lines of houses and shops, the town erupted with a diabolical cacophony of German weaponry. Recognizing that no man could survive an attempt to cross the final two hundred yards to the town, the Rangers scrambled for cover in drainage ditches and the few farm buildings in the vicinity of the field. Many were cut down before they could get off the killing field.

Shortly after the German broadside commenced, the Rangers heard the creaking of tank treads to their rear. Relief and celebration broke out within the Ranger ranks at what was presumed to be the arrival of American armor from the 4th Battalion. As the tanks came close, however, a sharp-eyed young man noticed that they bore the German Iron Cross. Driving around the flanks of the 1st and 3rd Ranger battalions, the tanks of the Hermann Goering Division had surrounded both American units in their entirety.

The Germans brought forward flak wagons—wheeled vehicles mounted with antiaircraft artillery—to fire straight into the Ranger positions at short range, while large-caliber artillery pounded the Rangers from longer distances. The Rangers destroyed a number of German tanks and flak wagons by firing antitank rockets from bazookas or running up to the hulls to affix adhesive antitank grenades. Those who had been able to occupy stone houses used the thick walls as protection from the German heavy weapons while returning fire with the much lighter weapons in their own possession. Some of the Rangers attempted to break out of the encirclement, but the Germans stopped them cold with showers of metal from all manner of weaponry. With bigger guns, more troops, and larger supplies of ammunition, the Hermann Goering Division had time on its side.

When news of the fighting at Cisterna reached Darby, he directed the 4th Ranger Battalion and two Army regiments to move to the rescue of the trapped battalions. All three units found German forces blocking their paths. Half of the 4th Ranger Battalion would be killed or wounded before day's end. Darby's Cannon Company attempted to reach Cisterna in half tracks, but in each of four attempts it had to turn back after German antitank weapons shattered its lead vehicles. A reconnaissance force of forty-three men, sent toward Cisterna in jeeps, drove into a machine-gun ambush of such deadliness that only one man returned to tell the tale.

By midmorning, the attrition of Ranger officers at Cisterna had left a lone captain in charge of the 1st and 3rd Ranger battalions. While talking with Darby on the radio, the young captain began weeping, so Darby told him to put Sergeant Major Robert E. Ehalt on the phone. The sergeant, a twenty-eight-year-old stalwart from Brooklyn, told Darby calmly, "Some of the fellows are giving up. Colonel, we are awfully sorry." Amid the din of bursting German shells, Ehalt continued, "They can't help it, because we're running out of ammunition. But I ain't surrendering." Ehalt had to interrupt his analysis of the Rangers to report the arrival of German infantry, stating, "They are coming into the building now."

Darby's subsequent dialogue with Ehalt was not included in the detailed account of the battle that Darby dictated soon afterward, but an eyewitness made a record of Darby's side of the conversation. "Issue some orders but don't let the boys give up," Darby said. "Who's walking in with their hands up? Don't let them do it! Get the officers to shoot. Do that before you give up. We're coming through. Hang on to this radio until the last minute. How many men are still with you? Stick together and do what is best. You're there and I'm here, unfortunately, and I can't help you. But whatever happens, God bless you."

Shortly after 12 p.m., with American relief forces still unable to break through, Ehalt radioed his last message. "They're closing in on us, Colonel," the sergeant major said. "We're out of ammo—but they won't get us cheap! Good luck . . . Colonel."

In the early afternoon, the Germans marched twelve Ranger prisoners toward the remaining elements of the 1st and 3rd Ranger battalions, demanding that the Americans surrender. Rangers shot two members of the German party, at which point the Germans killed two of the prisoners and continued to move forward. Again, Ranger diehards shot two Germans. The Germans bayoneted two prisoners. At this point, approximately seventy more Rangers decided to surrender.

The Germans then announced that they would kill the eighty American prisoners if the Ranger holdouts did not surrender. Several Rangers opened fire on the Germans who were guarding the prisoners, inadvertently killing a number of Americans in the process. German weapons raked the hapless clump of prisoners and the Rangers who had been shooting into it. On the heels of this baleful turn of events, a flock of inexperienced Rangers dropped their weapons in panic and came out with their hands up. A few veteran Rangers shot these young Americans as they rushed to surrender, in an attempt to stop the others, but it was to no avail. For a few minutes more, the most hard-bitten Rangers kept fighting, until they ran out of ammunition, at which point they, too, laid down their arms. Of the 767 Rangers from 1st and 3rd battalions who had marched on Cisterna, 761 ended up dead or in captivity.

Sergeant Carlo Contrera, Darby's driver, recalled that when the annihilation of the battalions could no longer be doubted, Darby "put his head down on his arm and cried." Another man who was with Darby, Les Kness, attested, "I watched a great man break down. I saw defeat within a soul of one for whom I had great respect and admiration. I have never seen a person so dejected and defeated, to the point that he lost his reasoning and his drive to keep control."

The demise of two and a half Ranger battalions at Cisterna swept away in one stroke the high confidence in the Rangers that had built up among the US military leadership during the preceding year and a half. The mystique of stealthy elite soldiers, the aura of invincibility attained through victories unending, had been shattered outside a small Italian town in the span of a few hours. Concluding that superior fitness of mind and body could not compensate for lack of heavy weaponry, the high command dispensed with special operations in the Italian Theater and turned the theater's remaining special operations forces into regular light infantry. The 504th Parachute Regiment took charge of the remnants of the 4th Ranger Battalion and set them on the line alongside its other battalions. William Darby was reassigned to the command of conventional infantry forces, serving in Italy until April 30, 1945, two days before the armistice, when he was killed by a German artillery shell.

A similar repurposing was in the offing for the First Special Service Force. Following the Cisterna battle, the Hermann Goering Division joined several other German divisions in a ferocious offensive against the Anzio beachhead, keeping the Allied forces near the coast for four months while the German units on the Winter Line executed an orderly retreat. The First Special Service Force was assigned to guard a relatively quiet sector of the Allied perimeter during this period, along the Mussolini Canal, which allowed the Forcemen to conduct shallow probes and reconnaissance missions into Jerryland. Even under these relatively auspicious conditions, the force sustained crippling losses, with 114 killed, 702 wounded, and 65 missing in the four-month period.

The need to replace fallen men became so desperate that the Forcemen were officially redefined as "infantry shock troops," which permitted them to take in new men who had not received specialized training. In the middle of February, Colonel Robert T. Frederick notified Fifth Army headquarters that combat effectiveness had plummeted because of casualties, the influx of replacement troops who were "not specially trained," and the arrival of replacement officers who had not been "indoctrinated with the spirit and combat methods of this command." He concluded that "the combat strength of the force has been so reduced that the force cannot again take any major part in an operation."

The commander's lamentations notwithstanding, the First Special Service Force was ordered to take part in the breakout from the beachhead in late May. The Forcemen spent the first day assaulting Cisterna, where they lost 39 men as a bevy of German Tiger tanks pulverized the American Sherman tanks accompanying their advance. In the two-week thrust to Rome, the Forcemen sustained casualties close to those suffered during the four months at Anzio, with 127 killed and hundreds more missing or wounded. As the Allies pressed into Rome's outskirts, the Germans pulled back to yet another fortified defensive line, the Trasimene Line, once again ensuring that the Allies would not cut off German troops or sever German supply lines. The Forcemen were among the first to enter the city of Caesar and Augustus on June 4, and at last they got some real rest, occupying hotel rooms and sleeping in actual beds for the first time in more than a year.

Depleted of personnel and deprived of special missions, the First Special Service Force was dissolved in November 1944. Higher authorities reassigned its remaining men to other units, where they would serve out the war as regular infantrymen. Colonel Frederick received command of an airborne task force and then the regular 45th Infantry Division, which he led into Germany in the war's final months.

On the day that Rome fell, a new cast of Rangers boarded ships for Operation Overlord, the Allied invasion of Normandy. The 2nd and 5th Ranger battalions, formed at Tennessee's Camp Forrest in September 1943, were among the 156,000 troops assigned to the amphibious D-Day landings. While the Cisterna cataclysm had discredited the use of Rangers in raids during sustained land campaigns, the Overlord planners believed that the special training and superior physical prowess of the Rangers made them the preferred option for some particularly difficult operations at the start of the invasion. The 2nd Ranger Battalion received the most daunting mission on the entire fifty-mile invasion front, the capture of Pointe du Hoc.

A promontory overlooking both Omaha Beach and Utah Beach, Pointe du Hoc was shielded from amphibious invaders by cliffs one hundred feet tall. In the months leading up to the invasion, Allied recon-naissance had spotted six 155mm howitzers in thick concrete casemates atop the cliffs. These guns could inflict severe damage if fired continu-ously at American landing craft, potentially causing such a mess of sunken vessels as to prevent the invasion forces from advancing past the beaches into terrain where they would be less vulnerable to German firepower and more capable of harming Germans.

Allied aircraft and battleships had pounded Pointe du Hoc for weeks, plastering it with more than ten kilotons of ordnance—comparable in ex-plosive power to the atomic bomb dropped on Hiroshima. Waves of heavy bombers from the US Eighth Air Force and the British Royal Air Force Bomber Command hit the promontory in the predawn hours of June 6, and then the battleship USS *Texas* assailed it with dozens of fourteen-inch shells. The firing did not abate until the landing craft carrying the 2nd Ranger Battalion were just a few hundred yards from Pointe du Hoc.

For a few moments, all was quiet, giving rise to hopes that the coastal defenses had been obliterated by the colossal maelstroms of bombs and shells. The American boats were nearly to the narrow shale beach in front of Pointe Du Hoc when the shore exploded with fire from German ma-chine guns. The 7.92mm bullets took the lives of some Rangers before they could get out of the boats. Others struck down Rangers as they clam-bered into the surf or ran across the shallows.

Using forty-eight rocket launchers, the Rangers shot ropes and rope ladders toward the clifftops, aiming for surfaces where the grapnels at the ends of the ropes were most likely to catch. Several of the ropes and rope ladders were too waterlogged to reach sufficient height, bouncing off the cliff face and falling onto the beach. Others were unable to hook into the bomb-blasted earth on top of the promontory, so that one tug from the Rangers below brought them tumbling down. About twenty of all the hooks caught. German defenders pulled out some of these hooks or cut the ropes, flinging them down at the beach in defiance. But a few hooks held fast, and up these ropes platoons of Rangers were soon climbing.

Some of the Rangers who reached the shale beach intact made the as-cent with extension ladders, consisting of sixteen-foot sections that linked together. One man, Staff Sergeant William Stivison, mounted a motorized extension ladder that had been obtained from Merryweathers Ltd. of London, a manufacturer of firefighting equipment. As the ladder increased in length, Stivison fired the twin Lewis machine guns that had been fastened to the top rungs. When the ladder reached a height of ninety feet, however, it swayed so violently in the wind that it had to be retracted.

Germans threw grenades down at the Rangers who were trying to scale the cliffs. They fired rifles and machine pistols straight down and at angles. Nevertheless, enough Rangers made it up the cliffs within the first hour to push the Germans away from the clifftops. Breaking into the huge gun casemates, the Rangers discovered to their dismay that the howitzers had been removed and telephone poles inserted in their places. The pre-invasion bombardment had, at some point, convinced the Germans to tow the guns to another location.

Two Ranger sergeants, spotting tire marks leading away from the casemates, followed the tracks to a camouflaged position. To their amazement, the Rangers saw before them the six howitzers, stacks of unused ammunition at their sides, with no Germans anywhere to be seen. The two sergeants attached thermite grenades to the howitzers' traversing and elevation mechanisms, which aimed the barrels. Generating heat of 4,000 degrees Fahrenheit for half a minute, the grenades melted the devices into worthless hunks of metal, rendering the mighty weapons useless.

The ineffectiveness of the Germans in protecting the promontory and the guns led the Rangers to suspect that the Germans' reputation for martial prowess was a fiction. They were quickly disabused of that notion, however, by the competence of the ensuing German counterattacks at Pointe du Hoc. During the next twenty-four hours, German officers led a series of concerted charges on the 2nd Ranger Battalion, whistling and shouting commands to the Germany infantry. Taking advantage of their familiarity with the terrain and its entrenchments, the assault troops overran many of the clifftop foxholes that the Rangers had occupied. German soldiers took foxholes to the rear of other Rangers, blurring the battle lines and leaving some of the Americans isolated, like single checkers near the opponent's end of the board. "The Germans had an awful lot of underground storage with interconnecting tunnels for shells and food," explained Lieutenant Charles "Ace" Parker. "The Germans would pop up anyplace. They were very, very annoying. You'd see the dirt move aside and a German would pop up out of the bottom of a shell hole. It would be necessary to shoot him on the spot."

Captain Walter "Doc" Block of Chicago, the battalion's medical officer, set up shop in an underground chamber containing sixteen bunks that still had the smell of the Germans who had slept in them the night before, a distinctive odor that GIs attributed to the German diet of sausage and cheese. Block's work would be immortalized by the reporting of Lieutenant G. K. Hodenfield, a *Stars and Stripes* correspondent who had been notified three days before D-Day that he would accompany the battalion tasked with assaulting the most formidable German redoubt. Block "worked all night with a flickering candle and sometimes a flashlight," Hodenfield wrote in his dispatch. "At times there were so many patients that men had to lie in the command post until, maybe, one of the other patients would die or could be patched up well enough to go back out."

In the early morning of June 7, the Germans took their biggest swing at the 2nd Ranger Battalion. Infiltrating the American lines in the dark, they surrounded an entire Ranger platoon and took its men captive. Well-coordinated German assaults breached several sectors of the Ranger perimeter, putting the whole battalion in danger of dismemberment. Officers at the Ranger command post were discussing the possibility of retreat when a Ranger from E Company burst in. "The Germans have broken through," he panted. "We couldn't hold 'em. My God, there's guys gettin' killed everywhere!" A short time later, another Ranger reported that D Company had been wiped out. German fire was homing in on the command post.

The officers conferred briefly. A Ranger lieutenant emerged from the conclave to pass the word that the entire battalion would pull back immediately if the Germans launched another attack.

"Do you mean not even try to fight them off?" complained Private William Petty. "Some Ranger outfit we are!" A young man who had disdained authority from his early childhood, Petty had not endeared himself to the officers during the battalion's brief history. Had they been conducting an exercise, the lieutenant might merely have been irritated, or even amused. With their lives on the line, however, he had no patience for such carping.

"You've had a couple of years of college, so you should know what 'immediately' means," snarled the lieutenant. "I mean just that—no heroics; withdraw the moment that they hit."

"How does one prepare for withdrawal?" Petty persisted. "That wasn't included in Ranger training."

"You're the self-appointed leader out there," the lieutenant yelled back, his face flushing crimson. "Figure it out yourself, damn it!"

As feared, it was not long before the Germans initiated a new attack, heralded by a torrent of whistles, yells, and machine pistol fire. The speed and ferocity of the onslaught so unnerved some of the Rangers that they surrendered. Most of the others pulled back, save for a dozen Rangers who did not get the withdrawal order in time. Unaware that a dozen Rangers were stranded, the Ranger battalion commander called upon the US Navy to lay waste to the field that the Germans had just repossessed. The battleship *Texas* obliged with its mammoth fourteen-inch guns, the shells creating holes twenty feet wide and five feet deep. Lieutenant George Kerchner, one of the dozen men who had survived the German infantry assaults and was now attempting to survive the American barrage, pulled the Catholic prayer book from his pocket. Huddled in a ditch, he thumbed the pages and prayed to God to spare him from the earthshaking, man-destroying explosions. "I read that prayer book through from cover to cover, I suppose, half a dozen times, and I prayed very sincerely for protection," Kerchner recollected. "I've been so ashamed to ask for anything since then. I figure I used up all I had coming to me."

As in the case of many of the Allied amphibious operations in Italy, naval gunfire kept the Germans from completing the annihilation of their American adversaries. After two days of intense battle, the Germans retreated from Pointe du Hoc into the Norman hedgerows. Much additional bloodshed awaited the Americans in those hedgerows, but the 2nd Ranger Battalion would not be among the units that would bleed there, for the invasion's first two days had chewed up the battalion so badly that it was pulled out of combat for an extended rehabilitation. Seventy percent of its Rangers had been killed, wounded, or captured.

In another notable similarity to the Italian Campaign, Ranger units in France would end up participating routinely in regular infantry operations once the Allied invasion forces pushed out of the D-Day beachhead. The 5th Ranger Battalion, which sustained 114 casualties during the Normandy landing, took part in the battle for the citadel at Brest in the late fall, a close-quarters struggle in which the combatants resorted to the use of scaling ladders, grappling hooks, and other instruments of medieval warfare. The 5th Rangers took 137 casualties at Brest, and 131 more during infantry battles in December. By February 1945, the sum of the casualties it had incurred in France was close to its remaining strength of 398 Rangers.

On February 23, the 5th Ranger Battalion finally received an opportunity to conduct the type of raid for which it had been designed—though even this operation would ultimately devolve into conventional warfare. To support the advance of the US 10th Armored Division into the German heartland, the battalion was ordered to cross the Saar River and occupy a position along the Irsch-Zerf road, four miles in the enemy's rear. A major route of German supply and reinforcement, the Irsch-Zerf road would be critical for German forces attempting to disrupt the American armored penetration. The Rangers were told they would need to hold the area for forty-eight hours, until a regular infantry unit relieved them.

At 8 p.m., the Rangers arrived at a pontoon footbridge that American engineers had hurriedly built across the roaring Saar. Water splashed up onto the ten-inch planks of the footbridge, but fortunately the frosty air was not cold enough to form ice on the stepping surface. When Rangers reached the river's edge, they were told, "Don't fall in, as nobody will attempt to rescue you."

Six companies of Rangers crossed the bridge and treaded into German-held territory. During the march toward Zerf, they scarfed up a total of eighty-five German prisoners. Upon reaching the Irsch-Zerf road, the Rangers discovered a collection of empty pillboxes in an adjacent field. They took up residence in the concrete fortifications, then seeded the road with antitank mines. Training their machine guns and bazookas on the road, the Rangers lay in waiting for German military traffic. They did not have to wait long for a heavy vehicle to trip the first mine.

Once the German high command realized that a thorn had been placed in its rear, it dispatched nearby combat units to pluck it out. German artillery pounded the field occupied by the Rangers, followed by infantry assaults. By this date, however, five and a half years into the war, German infantry units were a far cry from the formations that had once overrun most of Europe. To replace the skilled and combat-hardened men who had fallen in the prime of life in Russia, North Africa, Italy, and France, Hitler was now conscripting boys and old men and throwing them into battle with minimal training, alongside Poles and Austrians who evidenced little zeal for the Nazi fatherland. The Rangers easily repulsed the first attacks with small arms and artillery.

The 5th Ranger Battalion appeared to have the situation well in hand, until word came that the American replacement forces would not be coming in forty-eight hours as originally promised. The Rangers had brought supplies to last only a few days, and as the Germans sent larger and better units to assault the field, the Rangers exhausted most of their ammunition and had to request a resupply by air. The first supplies dropped by air to the Rangers missed their mark, falling into German hands. On the second day of air-dropping, however, the Rangers received enough ammunition and food to last the nine days it would take their replacements to arrive.

The German attacks continued apace. On a few occasions, the Rangers deemed the German infantry's chances of success so high that they called American artillery on their own position, in the knowledge that it would kill more Germans than Americans since the Germans were moving in the open while the Americans were crouching in pillboxes and foxholes. Sergeant Joe Drodwell recalled that after one American artillery shower, "I never saw so many dead Germans in my life. The area was just literally covered with bodies. Some of our guys got killed, too, but nothing like the Germans." During its time on the Irsch-Zerf road, the 5th Ranger Battalion sustained 90 casualties while killing an estimated 299 enemy and taking 328 prisoners.

One other Ranger battalion, the 6th, staked its claim to fame in early 1945. Lieutenant General Walter Krueger, commander of the US Sixth Army in Brisbane, Australia, had formed the 6th Ranger Battalion after hearing of the successes of Darby's Rangers in the European Theater. During the fall of 1944, the battalion had participated in the initial American invasion of the Philippine archipelago, spearheading the invasion of several Japanese-held islands. When General Krueger received word in late

January 1945 that the Japanese were holding Americans prisoner in central Luzon, near the city of Cabanatuan, he ordered a company from the 6th Ranger Battalion to bound past the rest of the advancing American forces to raid the prison. The facility was thirty miles from the nearest American position, a frightfully long distance for a small raiding force that would be moving on foot, but for Krueger the risks of waiting were even greater. On December 14, 1944, the Japanese had slaughtered 150 Allied prisoners in the Philippine province of Palawan, and they might choose to do the same at Cabanatuan when the US Sixth Army came near.

Commanding the 6th Ranger Battalion was Lieutenant Colonel Henry Mucci, an ebullient Italian American whom the troops had nicknamed "Little MacArthur" because of the pipe that constantly hung from his mouth, and perhaps also because of his imperious bearing. Mucci entrusted the mission to his C Company, on account of its commander, Captain Robert Prince, whom Mucci rated the best of his company commanders. The son of a Washington State apple distributor and a graduate of Stanford University, Prince was the quiet type—analytical, unexcitable, and cool under pressure. He was only twenty-five years old, and had never seen combat.

Like many of the Ranger operations in Europe against retreating Germans, the raid on Cabanatuan could not wait for prolonged planning and rehearsal. Lieutenant Colonel Mucci and Captain Prince had only a few hours for initial planning, which they devoted to the long march to the prison. Bereft of information on the prison and its guards, they would not draw up the assault plan until they neared the camp and consulted with a small group of American reconnaissance soldiers who would be sneaking to the camp ahead of the Rangers.

On the afternoon of January 28, 1945, 121 Rangers began the march toward Cabanatuan. Dressed in fatigues without insignia or rank, the Rangers wore soft caps rather than helmets on orders from Mucci, who thought the helmets weighed too much, made too much noise, and reflected too much light. Wherever possible, the column marched through high elephant grass or bamboo groves to elude the eyes of the Japanese and their spies. Philippine guerrilla allies joined forces with the Rangers along the way, and they eventually outnumbered the Rangers by two to one.

Mucci and Prince linked up with the reconnaissance personnel on January 29. From the scouts they learned that an estimated 7,000 Japanese soldiers were currently located in the city of Cabanatuan, four miles from the camp, and 1,000 were bivouacked in bamboo thickets just one mile away. Mucci prevailed upon Philippine guerrillas to take up blocking positions on the two roads that the neighboring Japanese units would use to reach the camp in the event of an alarm. As soon as the guerrillas heard the Rangers open fire on the prison, they would blow the nearest bridge and engage any Japanese soldiers attempting to relieve the prison's garrison.

The prison camp sat in the middle of an open plain of rice paddies, which offered the Rangers no concealment whatsoever. The assault force would have to crawl through the open paddies for a mile and hope that the Japanese soldiers manning the watchtowers were not vigilant enough to see them. The crawl began on the evening of January 30 at 5:45 p.m.

Digging their fingernails into the muck, the Rangers clawed their way forward for an hour and forty-five minutes. In the dimming twilight, none of the Japanese guards caught sight of the crab-like advance of the Ranger company. By the time the Americans reached the prison perimeter, night had descended.

Creeping up to the prison fences, the Rangers took aim at the Japanese pillboxes, guard posts, and towers, locating sentries by the orange glow of their cigarettes. At the signal of a lone gunshot, Ranger weapons erupted in a concert of bullets, maintaining a steady fortissimo for fifteen seconds. None of the defensive positions had been thickly fortified, and none of their occupants survived the Ranger fusillade. Busting open the lock on the main gate, the Rangers stormed inside, losing just one man in subduing the remainder of what had been a Japanese force of more than 200.

The liberators found 511 American prisoners. They were unable to locate the camp's lone British prisoner, Edwin Rose, an absent-minded fellow of sixty-five years who had been in the latrine during the raid and had apparently fallen asleep in spite of all the gunfire. The Rangers rushed to evacuate the prisoners, carrying the sickly and malnourished back across the rice fields and through the elephant grass to a squadron of wooden carts. The able-bodied loaded the infirm into the carts, which were then pulled by water buffalo toward the American lines. The 6th Ranger Battalion emptied the camp in just half an hour and escaped its smoking carcass before any Japanese reinforcements could arrive.

THE RANGERS AND Forcemen came into existence because of support at very high levels of the US government, but not at the highest level. The lack of presidential paternity was one of the principal differences between these forces and the other American special operations forces of World War II. General George Marshall, the Army's chief of staff and the most influential American military officer of the war, formed these units primarily as means of bolstering partnerships with key allies. The merits of such forces on the field of battle were of much less concern at the time of their creation.

The Rangers and Forcemen were recruited and trained for missions that required exceptional degrees of fitness or skill, and in several cases these attributes enabled them to accomplish tasks that were beyond the capabilities of average Army units. At Monte la Difensa and Pointe du Hoc, where the special operations forces had to surmount extreme terrain obstacles, ordinary units likely would have come up short. At the Algerian port of Arzew, where the need to minimize destruction and bloodshed demanded stealth and cunning, the Rangers succeeded where others might well have failed.

Opportunities to exploit the superior capabilities of these units, however, proved to be few. Sneaking up on enemy forces or scaling mountains often yielded success against the Vichy French and the Italians, but such feats were much more difficult to pull off, and much less consequential, against large concentrations of German troops. Contrary to the visions of men like Winston Churchill and Geoffrey Pyke, Hitler's Reich was not to be defeated through raids on the periphery. Its dominions had to be invaded in overwhelming strength and its conventional units worn down in bloody contests of attrition, a task for which elite forces were not much better suited than regular forces, and for which they were nonetheless routinely employed for lack of alternative missions. Under these conditions, concentrating officers in elite units sucked talent away from units that needed talent just as much, and exposed talent to concentrated slaughter, as occurred most spectacularly at Cisterna.

The Rangers and Forcemen often antagonized conventional military forces by touting their elite status or by acting as if they were above the law. Disregard for regulations and standard operating procedures, which could give the special units decided advantages on the battlefield, rankled others in the military, especially those individuals who saw meticulous shoe shining and unquestioning adherence to rules as the chief marks of a good military man. One official Army historian observed that Ranger indulgence in rowdiness, barroom brawling, and hectoring of military policemen "tended to confirm the suspicion of those line troops who were more than ready to view the Rangers as prima donnas and hooligans."

For the Forcemen, the adventures and hardships of World War II were confined to the mainland of Italy. The Rangers cast a much broader shadow, fighting in Algeria, Tunisia, Italy, France, Germany, and the Pacific islands. The Rangers took part in all the major campaigns of North Africa and Europe, but they were latecomers to the Pacific, Cabanatuan being something of a swansong for special operations in the Pacific Theater. That swansong had little in common with the songs that had been sung before it in the war between the United States and Japan. An entirely different set of forces, belonging to the US Navy and Marine Corps, accounted for nearly all of the special operations in the Pacific. The island warfare of the Pacific Theater presented challenges much different from those encountered in the great land campaigns of North Africa and Europe, and hence special operations took on a different character. Many of the lessons learned by the Navy and Marine units would nevertheless bear remarkable similarity to those learned by the Rangers and Forcemen.

CHAPTER 2

RAIDERS AND FROGMEN

Following the Pearl Harbor attack, Americans put aside political, regional, and personal differences to unite in the cause of national defense, their spirit of solidarity knowing no rival in US history. At the recruiting offices of the armed forces, the nation's plowmen, stevedores, investment bankers, and professional athletes waited in line for hours to volunteer for service. American families grew fruits and vegetables in backyard Victory Gardens so that more food could be shipped to troops overseas, and they purchased war bonds to fund the production of battleships, tanks, and aircraft.

The groundswell of patriotic fervor did not, however, banish all petty rivalries, and nowhere was this more true than in the one place where one might have most expected to find unity, the leadership of the armed forces. On the critical question of who would run the war in the Pacific Theater, the Army recommended the appointment of General Douglas MacArthur, commander of US Army forces in the Far East. The Navy objected strenuously to MacArthur, lobbying instead for Admiral Chester Nimitz, commander of the US Pacific Fleet. Both sides tried to convince President Franklin D. Roosevelt that they were in the right, and neither was willing to compromise.

In the end, Roosevelt settled on a solution that appeased both services, albeit in a manner that did injury to the principal of unity of command

and ensured future friction and disputation. The president split the Pacific into two regions: the South West Pacific, under the command of MacArthur, and the Pacific Ocean Areas, under Nimitz. Most of the Army units in the Pacific Theater went into MacArthur's region, while the Navy and the Marine Corps were concentrated in Nimitz's area of responsibility. The development of Navy and Marine special operations forces, therefore, would take place under the aegis of Admiral Nimitz.

The US Marine Corps, like the US Army, was to develop special operations forces based on the model of the British Commandos. These Marine units, like the Army Rangers, would be attended by unforeseen changes in environment and purpose, and hence by profuse allegations of waste and inefficiency. The Navy would beget a very different type of special operations force, one addressed more directly to immediate operational needs, and hence less at the mercy of the vagaries of war.

THE PUSH FOR Marine Corps special operations forces originated with Captain James Roosevelt. The eldest son of the president, Captain Roosevelt had at first been vaulted to the rank of lieutenant colonel by his father, but he had chosen to take a reduction in rank and undergo standard Marine Corps officer training. He owed his interest in commando operations and guerrilla warfare to a mentor in the Marine Corps, Major Evans Carlson, who had witnessed Mao Zedong's guerrillas firsthand while serving in China during the 1930s. Enamored of Mao's forces, Carlson advocated replication of not only their guerrilla tactics, but also their ideological indoctrination.

Shortly after Pearl Harbor, the younger Roosevelt expressed his thoughts on special operations forces in a letter to the Marine Corps commandant, Lieutenant General Thomas Holcomb, under the heading, "Development within the Marine Corps of a Unit for Purposes Similar to the British Commandos and the Chinese Guerrillas." Drawing upon Carlson's theories, the president's son recommended employment of this special unit in the Pacific islands against the Japanese. General Holcomb replied to Captain Roosevelt with the politeness that a letter from presidential progeny demanded, but he did not refrain from criticizing the letter's contents.

He took particular issue with the proposed creation of a specialized "Commando" unit within the Marine Corps. "The term 'Marine' is sufficient to indicate a man ready for any duty at any time," Holcomb wrote. "The injection of a special name, such as 'Commando,' would be undesirable and superfluous." Holcomb and other senior Marine Corps leaders were of the view that Marine Corps infantry battalions could do everything British Commando battalions could do. In their estimation, the Marines were already elite forces, and they worried that forming an elite within the elite would merely concentrate resources disproportionately in a few units and antagonize the rest.

To Holcomb's dismay, President Roosevelt found the arguments of Captain Roosevelt more persuasive than those of the senior officer of the Marine Corps. Holcomb had no choice but to comply when Admiral Nimitz asked the Marines to form two commando-type battalions in January 1942. Merritt Edson was selected to command the 1st Raider Battalion, and Evans Carlson to command the 2nd. Carlson made Captain Roosevelt his executive officer.

As Holcomb had forewarned, the Raiders quickly made enemies among the rest of the Marine Corps. In a service that prized humility, the Raiders unabashedly advertised themselves as a cut above everyone else. Some Raiders even referred to themselves as "Supermarines." Granted permission to recruit whomever they pleased, the Raiders conducted their first raids on the human resources of other Marine units, infuriating commanders who watched their best Marines depart.

Raider training, like Ranger training, was patterned after that of the British Commandos. In anticipation of strenuous raiding and campaigning, it emphasized hiking and fast marching. Trainees spent long hours in the water, day and night, to practice amphibious landings. Raiders also received extensive instruction in the use of weapons, with particular attention to the employment of knives and bayonets.

Carlson's 2nd Raider Battalion launched its first raid in August 1942. Its target, the Makin Atoll in the Gilbert Islands, had more psychological than military value. Ransacking the lightly defended atoll would give the Americans a morale-boosting victory. It would also divert Japanese attention from areas of the Pacific where the United States had greater ambitions.

Departing from Pearl Harbor on August 8, a total of 222 Raiders traveled aboard the submarines USS *Argonaut* and USS *Nautilus*. Space was extremely tight, with Raiders crammed into bunks stacked four high and twelve inches apart. Enclosed in stale air with nowhere to bathe, the men spent most of the ten-day voyage sweltering like overdone sausages in a hot kitchen.

The Raiders were therefore surprisingly cheerful when they learned that they would be disembarking from the submarines in a torrential rain. Neither the twenty-foot swells that rocked their rubber boats during the nighttime boarding nor the fouling of boat engines by splashing saltwater during fueling could stem the excitement. Once the boats had parted ways with the submarines, Raiders in the foul-engined boats paddled their way to Makin's shore.

Scampering onto an empty beach with only the moon offering any light through the dark rain, the Raiders sought out landmarks they had seen on maps or aerial photographs. They whispered directions to one another as they felt their way toward their preplanned attack positions. Wilfred S. Le Francois, a forty-one-year-old lieutenant who had worked his way up through the enlisted ranks, recounted, "Once in a while, the fellows guiding me whispered a wisecrack, and it aggravated me to think they were thoroughly enjoying this adventure, which could easily mean our complete annihilation."

The element of surprise was lost when Private First Class Vern Mitchell accidentally fired his rifle. At the sound, Carlson cursed for what was reported to be the only time in his career. Japanese soldiers jumped out of bed, the machine-gun crewmen moving into camouflaged nests while snipers climbed into coconut trees. Japanese officers lined riflemen up for a bayonet charge.

Catching sight of approaching Japanese riflemen, the Raiders let the enemy draw near and then swept their automatic weapons back and forth, until everyone in the Japanese line had either fallen to the ground or fled. The Raiders stopped a second charge in like fashion. The Japanese snipers, however, kept the Raiders occupied for hours, and the Raiders had few hours to spend on the mission before they would have to return to the submarines. Lieutenant Le Francois saw Corporal I. B. Earles running around in a frenzy after receiving a hit from a sniper's bullet. "Blood ran from his mouth and the men kept begging him to lie still," Le Francois recollected. Earles, his rage mounting, shouted, "I'll get those heathens by myself! Show me where they are!" The corporal sprinted into a thicket and started shooting every Japanese he could find, whether dead or alive, until he himself was killed.

Carlson chose not to send any Raiders to destroy the island's radio facilities or military installations, which had been designated the battalion's primary objectives, for fear that it would expose the Marines to ambush by superior forces. Reports from local inhabitants suggested that the Japanese might have large groupings of men elsewhere on Makin, and Japanese aircraft had begun bombing and strafing the atoll after the Japanese garrison radioed news of the raid. Convinced that the killing of some Japanese soldiers would be enough to declare the operation a victory, Carlson kept the Raiders focused on eradicating the snipers. In the afternoon, he informed the men that they would return to the submarines in the evening.

Raiders began departing the shore at 7:30 p.m., one boat at a time. Despite the vigorous paddling of exceedingly fit young men, the boats struggled to distance themselves from the shore, shoved back by one large wave after another. Swells crashed over the gunwales, forcing some Raiders to set down their paddles and bail water while the remainder stroked ever more frantically. Boats overturned and disgorged their men, who struggled against the burdens of gear or wounds to swim to safety. An unknown number of men drowned, and at least one was eaten by a shark.

The overturning of boats and the exhaustion of paddlers compelled some of the Raiders to return to the beach, where they rested for a few minutes before trying again. With paddles torn from men's hands or lost as the result of a capsize, a growing number of Raiders had to row with palm fronds or bare hands. "We paddled and paddled and paddled," Private First Class Ray Bauml recalled. "My muscles were aching. You could see them almost popping out because they were so strained." Sergeant Kenneth L. McCullough said that the ordeal in the water was "the toughest thing I'd ever done." After four or five attempts to reach the submarines, the arm muscles of the men were so spent that they gave up trying and collapsed on the beach.

Eighty of the Raiders were able to reach the submarines, mostly by churning through pockets of water where the tide was less strong and then heading toward the colored lights on the submarines' conning towers. Lieutenant Oscar Peatross, one of the first Raiders to make it back to the submarines, described the arrival of the men who followed: "This was no longer a team, but a group of humanoids held together only by the boat they rode and their individual wills to survive. Some had their eyes fixed in a thousand-yard stare and seemed almost catatonic, paddling like automatons."

Carlson and Roosevelt were among 120 Raiders whose boats were unable to reach the submarines that night. After the last arm muscles had been drained, Carlson conferred with the other officers on the beach. One man thought it best that they surrender, pointing out that they had little in the way of weapons or ammunition and it was possible that the submarines would depart that night to avoid Japanese aircraft and ships. By some accounts, Carlson accepted this advice and sent a note of surrender to the Japanese, which never arrived because a Raider shot the Japanese soldier to whom the note had been entrusted. Other witnesses, Roosevelt among them, would claim that Carlson never had any intention of surrendering. The Raiders ended up bedding down for the night in the hope of reaching the submarines the next day.

Lieutenant Le Francois, who had been shot in the shoulder during the fighting, lay down to sleep under the cover of bushes with other wounded Marines. At dawn, he awoke to see a beach filled with what he described as "the most disheartened, forlorn, bloody, ragged, disarmed group of men it had ever been my experience to look upon." He concluded that "despair had frayed their spirits." The mood brightened considerably, however, at the sight of an American submarine on the horizon. Despite the very real threat of attack by Japanese aircraft or ships, Commodore John Haines, the task force commander, had decided to keep the submarines offshore to retrieve the remaining Raiders. When asked later why he had left the submarines at risk in the waters off Makin, Haines said matter-of-factly, "I didn't want to go back to the United States, be taken directly to the President, and tell him why I left his son on the island."

Attempts to paddle from Makin to the submarines had resumed shortly before dawn. Several boats, including one carrying Captain Roosevelt, reached the submarines in good order. Carlson deemed the risk of exposure to Japanese aircraft too dangerous to continue the evacuation in broad daylight, so he ordered the remaining Raiders to a lagoon on the other side of the atoll, where the ocean was considerably calmer, for an evening departure. Sending out patrols during the morning, Carlson learned that few members of the Japanese garrison remained alive. The Raiders therefore spent the day blowing up the radio stations and military facilities that they had come to destroy in the first place. Industrious search crews found a general store, from which they confiscated men's silk underwear, Japanese beer, and American corned beef. The Raider medical staff took possession of Japanese medical supplies, including high-quality surgical instruments of German manufacture that were put to immediate use on the wounded. The most impressive prize, at least in the judgment of the Raiders, was the samurai sword of the dead Japanese commander. Search parties also located the bodies of eighteen Raiders killed in action the previous day, whose burial they outsourced to the local police chief in exchange for American weapons and fifty US dollars.

By evening, the Raiders had tied together the four remaining rubber boats and attached two engines that the most mechanically gifted men had managed to bring to life. Loading up the wounded and the booty, they headed out from the lagoon at 8:30 p.m. Not far from the shore, one engine sputtered out, and for a time progress was so slow as to suggest that they would never reach the submarines. The Raiders in one of the four boats thought it would be better for all concerned if they separated from the other three and paddled manually. Carlson consented.

The lone boat and its crew would never reach the submarines. Accounts from Makin's inhabitants indicate that the boat eventually returned to the atoll, and that its occupants were subsequently apprehended and beheaded by the Japanese. The separation may, however, have been the decisive factor in the progress of the other three boats. With one less boat to propel, the remaining engine and the paddlers eventually delivered the Raiders to the waiting *Nautilus*.

Lieutenant Peatross witnessed this arrival as well. "Never before or since have I seen such a motley looking group of humans or such an outlandish looking craft as that which came alongside the *Nautilus* that night," Peatross testified. "In comparison, the Raiders who came out the first night would have looked healthy." Peatross described Carlson as "a walking skeleton." In the forty-three hours that had elapsed since the arrival at Makin, Carlson "seemed to have aged at least ten years."

After all heads had been counted, it was determined that a total of thirty Raiders were dead or missing. Many more had been injured, of whom the most serious cases would undergo surgery in the fetid confines of the submarines. Commodore Haines, convinced that staying longer to search for the missing boat was not worth the risk, ordered the submarines to dive beneath the waves and make a course for Hawaii.

Fourteen hundred miles to the southwest, in the Solomon Islands, Merritt Edson's 1st Raider Battalion undertook its first raid on August 7. A native of Chester, Vermont, Edson was the polar opposite of Carlson in most respects. Carlson's intellectual flamboyance, his love of guerrilla warfare theory, his cavorting with the press and the president's son, all earned the scorn of Edson. Hard-bitten, laconic, and humorless, Edson had little concern for the opinions of journalists or any other human beings. Carlson's admiration for the Chinese Communists was a dangerous delusion in the eyes of the conservative Edson, who himself had seen radicals firsthand in Nicaragua during the 1920s while leading Marines against Augusto César Sandino's leftist rebels.

The combat correspondent Richard Tregaskis observed of Edson: "His eyes were as cold as steel, and it was interesting to notice that even when he was being pleasant, they never smiled." Edson had passion, but it became evident only at times of great peril, at which point it overwhelmed the passions of other men. Whereas the surrender discussion at Makin Atoll had caused subordinates to question Carlson's toughness, no one ever doubted Edson's desire to fight. Some of his men would later complain that he was altogether too eager to lead his unit into peril, attaching to him the sobriquet of "Mad Merritt the Morgue Master."

The island of Tulagi, where Edson's first raid was to take place, measured just 1,000 yards wide by 4,000 yards long. The Japanese had occupied the small island in May 1942, and they were now in the process of constructing a seaplane base in the harbor. Edson's Raiders and a regular Marine battalion boarded landing craft in the dark for a dawn landing. To minimize the chances of encountering Japanese soldiers on the beach, where the team playing defense would hold the greatest advantages over the team on offense, the Marines landed at a beach abutting the most densely vegetated section of the island.

Finding no one at this beach, the Marines chopped through the greenery in the direction of the harbor. At 11:30 a.m., Edson fired a green flare to signal the beginning of an attack on the island's garrison. The Japanese forces, consisting of 350 crack troops from the Special Naval Landing Forces, stoutly resisted the Marines from machine-gun nests and trees, in much the same way as the defenders at Makin. Here, too, the Marines found it particularly difficult to find and kill snipers perched in coconut trees. "We thought that coconut trees would not have enough branches to conceal snipers," said Major Justice Chambers, a company commander. "But we found that the Japs were small enough to hide in them easily and so we had to examine every tree before we went by."

In the afternoon, the Raiders fought their way up the island's spinal ridge, seizing the clubhouse of a golf course that had been built by British colonial authorities. Their advance bogged down in a former British cricket field, which was located in a ravine surrounded by limestone walls. Japanese troops, firing from holes dug into the limestone, held the Marines at bay into the evening.

At 10:30 p.m., the Japanese counterattacked. Cutting off one of Edson's companies from the others, they pressed toward the battalion headquarters. Edson described the night's action to Tregaskis in his customary manner. "The Japs worked their way along the ridge, and came to within fifty to seventy-five yards of my command post," Edson narrated. "The Nips were using hand grenades, rifles and machine guns. We suffered quite a few casualties, as our men fought hard to hold the Japs back. One machine-gun company lost 50 percent of its non-commissioned officers. Finally, the enemy was thrown back."

On the following day, the remaining Japanese soldiers stayed on the defensive, shooting at the Marines from caves or bunkers. Marines methodically inserted grenades, satchel charges, or Bangalore torpedoes into these cavities, one by one. Enough Japanese soldiers survived the day to organize a feeble and futile counterattack that night, the garrison's last offensive gasp. Over the course of three days, the Marines killed all but 3 of the 350 Japanese defenders, at a cost of 38 Marines killed and 55 wounded.

Edson's battalion next headed to the nearby island of Guadalcanal. On September 8, they conducted an amphibious landing behind Japanese lines at the village of Tasimboko, where the Japanese had left only a small number of soldiers to guard a major supply depot. Concerned that Japanese forces would rush to Tasimboko upon learning that Americans had seized their logistical hub, the Raiders did not haul away most of what they found, but instead destroyed it. Splitting open thousands of bags of rice, they burned the grains or threw them in the surf. Marines bayoneted tins of crabmeat and cans of beef, although only after each man had taken as many tins and cans as he could carry on his person. They also hauled off 21 cases of Japanese beer and 17 flasks of sake. Only 2 Raiders perished and only 6 were wounded before the battalion made its escape.

Tasimboko was just the kind of raid that Edson and other Raider proponents had been hoping to execute. Edson's biggest accomplishment on Guadalcanal, however, would come during conventional combat against regular Japanese infantry. After Tasimboko, the 1st Raider Battalion was posted on a coral ridge overlooking Henderson Field, an airstrip vital to supplying and defending Guadalcanal. To protect Henderson Field against a sneak attack from the adjacent jungle, the 1st Raider Battalion and 1st Marine Parachute Battalion established a perimeter extending from the hogback-shaped coral ridge onto the flat ground between the ridge and the jungle.

On the night of September 12, Japanese soldiers struck the sector of the perimeter held by Edson's Charlie company. Sneaking inside the Raider perimeter undetected, the Japanese began the battle with simultaneous attacks on Charlie company's foxholes from every side. Several of the company's platoons attempted to withdraw in order to avoid complete destruction. "People were crawling in all directions," said Joseph M. Rushton, a Browning Automatic Rifle man in Charlie company. "It wasn't long before they were overrun by the swarming attackers of the main charge. It was horrible and frightening hearing our small group of overrun Raiders screaming as the bastards bayoneted and hacked them with their Samurai swords." Raiders formed a new defensive line behind the area that had belonged to Charlie company. The remainder of the night was largely quiet save for the shrieks of captured Raiders whom the Japanese were torturing.

In the morning, Edson attempted to push the Japanese off the ground they had taken, but the Japanese parried his lunge. In anticipation of another Japanese night attack, Edson moved more Marines onto the hog-backed ridge during the afternoon, thinning out the lower positions into little more than tripwires. With the arrival of darkness, nervous Marines on the perimeter scanned the jungle for any possible sign of Japanese troops. "It is amazing what you think you are seeing to the front at night," recounted Sergeant Frank Guidone. "Outlines of the brush take on the shape of a figure and if you stare long enough it will move." Guidone kept thinking to himself, "Is this the ending of my life? Eighteen years—ending up in a dark jungle as a corpse."

The edginess of the Marines was sharpened at 9 p.m. by salvoes from Japanese destroyers, which forced the Marines to crawl into their foxholes as far as humanly possible. The expectant silence that followed the bombardment ended abruptly with a surge of Japanese troops through the tripwires. Marines fell back on the slopes while American artillery rounds soared in and the Marines on the ridge spewed bullets and grenades at rows of advancing Japanese infantry.

Enough Japanese survived the American outpouring to organize an assault up the ridge. A Japanese battalion commander drew his sword and rushed forward, followed by riflemen howling "Banzai!" and "Death to Roosevelt!" From foxholes across the ridge, the Raiders and paratroopers mowed the attackers down with crisscrossing fire. The Japanese soon conceded failure, and the survivors ran back into the jungle.

Next came a second, more powerful assault. After peppering the ridge with smoke grenades to impair American vision, two Japanese battalions stormed onto the slopes. The Marines responded with small arms and a deluge of highly accurate artillery, littering the ridge with dead and dying

Japanese. The Japanese battalions nonetheless breached the Marine lines in several places along the center of the ridge. Raiders and paratroopers in those sectors attempted to pull back, which in the dark proved to be chaotic and counterproductive.

Edson, standing ten to twenty yards behind what remained of the Marine defensive line in the center, hollered directions and encouragement with a complete indifference to personal safety, which did much to stiffen the resolve of the discouraged and convince the retreating to return to their foxholes. "The only difference between you and the Japs is they've got more guts!" Edson yelled. "Get back!" When Marines from the parachute battalion wavered for what appeared to be reasons of inadequate leadership, Edson took the extraordinary step of relieving his fellow battalion commander and replacing him with a parachute officer whom Edson deemed a better man for the job.

As the Japanese assault came nearer his command post, Edson mounted the highest point on the ridge. "Raiders, parachuters, engineers, artillerymen, I don't give a damn who you are," he thundered. "You're all Marines. Come up on this hill and fight!"

Raider casualties in the center reached such alarming proportions that Edson decided to notify Lieutenant Colonel Merrill Twining, the operations officer of the 1st Marine Division, that the enemy could plow through his center "like shit through a tin horn." If Edson's center broke, the Japanese would be free to overrun the division command post and advance on Henderson Field.

At this, the 1st Division committed its reserve battalion to the ridge. Fresh Marines arrived in time to patch holes left by the fallen and reconstitute the center of the line. The Marines hung onto the ridge until daybreak, at which time US aircraft arrived to strafe and bomb the remaining Japanese. Crippled by the night's combat, the Japanese quit the battlefield.

In the three days of battle on what became known as Edson's Ridge, the Raiders sustained 135 casualties. The 1st Marine Parachute Battalion incurred 128 casualties, and other US units took 53. An official Japanese report put Japanese casualties at roughly 1,200, though other Japanese sources suggest that the total may have been much higher. By saving Henderson Field from capture, Edson's Raiders and the other Marine combatants ensured that enough American reinforcements would arrive on Guadalcanal to finish off the Japanese in the months ahead.

Among those reinforcements would be the 2nd Raider Battalion, which set foot on Guadalcanal at the beginning of November 1942. Carlson intended to lead his battalion on a prolonged raid in the enemy's rear, marching into one Japanese flank and out the other. It would be a highly risky endeavor, as the battalion would be far removed from any friendly forces and dangerously close to large concentrations of enemy soldiers. Keeping the Raiders resupplied would be exceptionally difficult, so difficult that Marine skeptics predicted confidently that the Raiders would run out of food and ammunition in the middle of the operation.

Carlson's Raiders set out on November 6 with four days' worth of food. The primary staple was rice, which they would boil in their helmets. Other provisions included bacon, raisins, and tea. Carlson planned to rely on local guides for resupply until they were deep into hostile territory, at which time low-flying US aircraft would drop them hundred-pound bundles.

Once inside the jungle, the Raiders quickly acquired an intimate acquaintance with Guadalcanal's liana vines. Laced with barbs, the vines slashed through clothing and lacerated flesh as effortlessly as a razor blade through a peach, leaving Raiders spotted with bleeding and festering sores. Infernal heat and the stench of sweaty clothes were nearly as oppressive as they had been during the submarine expedition to Makin, though these torments were relieved from time to time by the fording of rivers.

Patrolling and scouting in small detachments, Carlson's Raiders engaged in intermittent combat with Japanese troops, most of whom were caught unawares and in small numbers, since Americans were not supposed to be so far behind the front lines. Some of the Japanese soldiers, however, proved to be vicious and implacable foes. After the Japanese tortured one Raider, castrated him, and stuffed his testicles into his mouth, the Americans dispensed with all thoughts of taking prisoners.

Although the Raiders shed a good deal of weight during the raid, they received air-dropped food consistently enough to keep going for the thirty days it took to complete the mission. Disease, wounds, and exhaustion proved to be greater scourges, turning the evacuation of Raiders into a routine occurrence. As the days accumulated, what had once been extraordinary feats of strength and endurance were no longer possible, and what had once been ordinary marches were now extraordinary and desperate exertions upon which their lives depended. "Everybody was getting pretty beat," Private First Class Jesse Vanlandingham said in describing the latter days of the raid. "There was an awful lot of jock itch. We had one guy in our squad covered with it. I don't know how he could wear any clothes it was so painful. We all had it to a certain extent. We'd had the same underwear on for thirty days." When Carlson's Raiders reached the end of the 150-mile trek on December 4, only 57 of the original 266 Raiders stepped across the finish line. Seventeen Raiders had been killed, an equal number had been evacuated for wounds, and the rest had been evacuated for disease or exhaustion.

Carlson would tout the raid as a major success, which it undeniably was. According to the battalion's records, the Raiders killed 488 Japanese during the month-long operation. Navy Seabees who later searched the area counted 700 Japanese bodies. The Raiders also destroyed hundreds of Japanese weapons, including "Pistol Pete," a set of howitzers that had been a constant menace to the Marines at Henderson Field.

News of the long raid met with great enthusiasm in the United States, at a time when the nation badly needed battlefield successes and heroes. "Carlson's boys," reported *Newsweek*, were "America's first trained guerrillas, whose boast was that they 'know how to do anything,' and could prove it." The periodical explained that "the Raiders took 'graduate work' in military mayhem, at camps and for periods which still remain a strict secret." Journalist Wesley Price likened Carlson to Abraham Lincoln and Gary Cooper, asserting that "Lt. Col. Evans Fordyce Carlson writes books, kills Japs, plays the harmonica and speaks Chinese. He can deliver polished lectures on Asiatic problems, swim an ice-flocked river naked and exist on a half-sock of rice a day." Executives at Universal Studios commissioned a feature film on the exploits of Carlson's battalion, with Randolph Scott playing the role of Carlson.

The publicity surrounding the Raiders encouraged Admiral Nimitz to request two more Raider battalions, the 3rd and 4th. General Holcomb, the Marine commandant, again raised objections. First, he said, the Marine Corps did not have enough men to form additional Raider units while still maintaining three Marine Corps divisions. Second, special units deprived regular units of the leaders they needed and deserved. Third, raiding operations were not "sufficiently profitable to justify the organization of special units." Fourth, all Marine infantry battalions could conduct raids.

As before, Holcomb's protestations did him no good. Bowing to the will of higher authorities, the Marine Corps formed the 3rd Raider Battalion at Samoa, and the 4th Raider Battalion at Camp Pendleton.

In July 1943, the 4th Raider Battalion joined forces with the 1st Raider Battalion and two US Army battalions in the invasion of New Georgia, the largest of the western Solomon Islands. Landing unopposed, they trudged across eight miles of swamp, jungle, and river, their misery magnified by a driving rain. Their reward was the surprise and defeat of a Japanese force at Enogai, whose commander had thought it impossible for anyone to attack through the terrain that had just been traversed.

After the Raiders had taken their initial objective, higher headquarters sent them on conventional infantry assaults against other elements of the Japanese garrison, who were now aware of the American presence in their neighborhood and were preparing accordingly. The Marines would blame the woes that followed on the micromanagement of Rear Admiral Richmond Kelly Turner, the commander of Amphibious Forces South Pacific. Lieutenant Colonel Twining of the 1st Division derided Turner for "playing soldier," adding for good measure that he was "a loud, strident, arrogant person who enjoyed settling all matters by simply raising his voice and roaring like a bull captain in the old navy."

On July 20, the 1st and 4th Raider battalions marched two miles from Enogai to Bairoko, a Japanese redoubt on the opposite side of the Dragon's Peninsula. After the Enogai raid, the Japanese commander at Bairoko had built additional fortifications outside the town, forming four concentric defensive rings. The Raiders penetrated the two outer rings, which consisted mainly of log and coral bunkers, but they lacked heavy weapons to break down the concrete fortifications of the inner rings, from which Japanese machine guns sawed through Raiders whenever they tried to approach. A requested air strike did not occur, and the jungle canopy prevented the Raiders from using mortars. The two Raider battalions abandoned the attack after sustaining 250 casualties.

Across the Pacific, as across Europe, the increasing size of offensive operations was diminishing the opportunities for raids and other nonstandard operations. By 1944, the mass production of large landing craft in US shipyards and the decline in Japanese air and naval power had led American commanders in the Pacific to concentrate on conquering bigger and more heavily fortified islands, which were better suited to multi-division landing forces—complete with Sherman tanks and heavy artillery—than to lightly armed battalions. The United States increasingly embraced the approach that had produced victory in the Civil War and World War I: deploying ground troops and materiel in overwhelming numbers to grind down a numerically inferior enemy.

Numerous Marine officers came to share General Holcomb's view that the Raiders had siphoned off too much talent for raids that were not especially valuable and could have been performed by other units. According to Colonel Alan Shapley, the second commander of the 2nd Raider Battalion, both he and Edson of the 1st Battalion decided that "there wasn't much a Raider battalion could do that a good Marine battalion couldn't do." Admiral Nimitz, an early proponent of the Raider concept, decided in the end that regular Marine units were fully capable of conducting raids.

One other major experiment in raiding forces was to take place in the Pacific during World War II, in the form of the 5307th Composite Unit, known popularly as "Merrill's Marauders." At the Quebec Conference of August 1943, the British convinced President Roosevelt to create an American raiding unit in Burma to team up with the Chindits, a force of British, Gurkha, and Burmese guerrillas that was wreaking havoc on the Japanese. The organizers of the 5307th Composite Unit sought volunteers, but also asked US infantry commanders to provide personnel, prompting some commanders to offload their least desirable men. "We've got the misfits of half the divisions in the country," one officer in the new unit lamented.

Merrill's Marauders took their nickname from their titular commander, Brigadier General Frank D. Merrill. As it turned out, though, Merrill would be absent from the field for long spells, being evacuated twice in the middle of military operations after suffering heart attacks. His deputy, the able Colonel Charles N. Hunter, took charge of operations in his absence. The assignment of missions, meanwhile, was the prerogative of the cantankerous theater commander, General Joseph "Vinegar Joe" Stilwell.

In early 1944, Stilwell assigned the motley Marauders to a multinational offensive in northern Burma. They and the Chindits were to conduct raids in the Japanese rear while British and Chinese regulars took on the main Japanese forces. To evade detection, they would steer clear of roads and trails. Embarking on February 24, the Marauders cut through dense jungles swarming with malarial mosquitos, waded across jungle rivers that left a man coated with leeches, and climbed steep mountains made slick by the monsoon rains.

As events would have it, the Marauders bumped into large Japanese forces early in the campaign. Stilwell, lacking other forces nearby, ordered the Marauders to stay where they were and fight as conventional infantry in order to shield the Allied flank. Having been lightly equipped to give them superior mobility, the Marauders ended up fighting heavily equipped Japanese forces in battles where mobility counted for less than big weapons.

During this campaign, Stilwell failed to keep adequate food supplies flowing to the Marauders, with the result that the men lost an average of thirty-five pounds before it was over. He issued senseless orders, demanding blanket transfers of wounded Marauders from hospitals to the front, where they often collapsed from their injuries or fatigue. Indifferent to the plummeting of morale, Stilwell avoided speeches to the troops, decoration ceremonies, and the other tools used by commanders since time immemorial to buoy sagging spirits. In their dejection, the Marauders referred to Stilwell and his staff as "stuffed baboons," and worse.

Within the first few months of the campaign, half of the Marauders became casualties. Under most circumstances, such losses would have led to the unit's rotation to the rear for physical and mental recuperation, but Stilwell refused to pull the Marauders off the line. He did have a valid strategic rationale: because the Marauders were the only US force in the theater, their removal would have undermined American exhortations to the Chinese and British to continue fighting. Eventually, 2,400 of the original 3,000 Marauders were lost to injury, illness, capture, or death.

WHILE THE TRAVAILS of the Marauders were reinforcing doubts about organizing infantrymen into discrete raiding units, a different kind of special operations force, specializing in amphibious warfare, was eliciting a crescendo of praise. In 1942, the US Navy had begun experimentation with forces recruited and trained for niche roles in amphibious warfare, principally in the fields of reconnaissance and demolitions. In August of that year, a joint amphibious reconnaissance school opened in Little Creek, Virginia, midway between Norfolk and Virginia Beach. Much of the school's initial trainee cohort came from the Navy's Physical Training Program, a repository of college and professional athletes under the leadership of boxer Gene Tunney, former heavyweight champion of the world. The amphibious reconnaissance school's graduates, labeled the Scouts and Raiders, deployed to the Atlantic and Pacific to reconnoiter beaches, guide landing craft during amphibious operations, and set flares for naval gunfire.

At this same time, the US Navy began systematic training of underwater demolition specialists. To meet the demands of the Allied campaign in North Africa, the first volunteers were rushed through training, making their first appearance in Morocco in November 1942. The demolition men succeeded in destroying the boom and net blocking the Wadi Sebou River in the face of thirty-foot waves and enemy machine-gun fire.

The Navy subsequently formed Naval Combat Demolition Units for employment in the amphibious landings in Italy and France. Despite rumors that the new organization would be a "75 percent casualty outfit," plenty of volunteers showed up for training at Fort Pierce, Florida, in June 1943. With the Sicilian invasion only a matter of weeks away, the officer in charge of the new program, Lieutenant Draper L. Kauffman, accelerated preparation by condensing the physical training regimen of the Little Creek program into a single week. A grueling sequence of running, swimming, diving, boat-handling, detonating, and mock attacking, with almost no sleep and little food, it was dubbed "Hell Week." Between 30 and 40 percent of this and ensuing classes of volunteers washed out of the program by week's end.

Jerry N. Markham, who gave up his draft-exempt job at a Jacksonville, Florida, paper mill to join the Navy, volunteered for the Naval Combat Demolition Units because it seemed far more exciting than the water purification job for which the Navy had been grooming him. Markham had been interested in deep-sea and shallow-water diving since boyhood, his love for the sea fueled by Jules Verne's *Twenty Thousand Leagues under the Sea*. After months of demolition training at Fort Pierce, Markham moved to the Welsh city of Swansea for exercises tailored to the invasion of Normandy. As Operation Overlord approached, Markham learned that he would take part in the clearing of a 50-foot-wide by 350-foot-long section of mines and obstacles at Omaha Beach.

On June 3, 1944, Markham's six-man demolition team boarded an amphibious landing craft that was carrying tanks and towing a 50-foot boat that the team would board when they neared the coast of France. They slept on the steel decks, crawling under the hulls of tanks to escape the rains that assailed the ship during its amble across the English Channel. On the night of June 5, Markham and his teammates climbed into the small landing boat, which took its place in the endless lines of American boats queuing up for D-Day.

Just as the boat arrived at its predetermined section of Omaha Beach and lowered its ramp, German machine guns opened fire. Heavy bullets hit men in the boat as well as those who sought refuge in the water. A German mortar round landed squarely on a nearby boat, blowing it to pieces. Moments after Markham's team entered the water, a mortar round killed the team's commanding officer and blew the head completely off another teammate.

Markham, as the next in line to command the team after the officer's death, directed the surviving members to move from one obstacle to the next and attach charges. The crisscrossed steel bars of German "hedgehog" obstacles provided enough cover to give the men some hope of surviving and accomplishing the mission, though not enough to shield a man's entire body. They connected the charges with Primacord, a newly developed waterproof cable that looked like yellow clothesline. By linking a long string of charges with Primacord, a demolitioneer could blow them all simultaneously by time fuse or remote-command detonator.

Short on team members and harried by blistering German fire, Markham's team had not yet detonated any charges when the first wave of US infantry neared the shore. Some of the infantrymen's boats were impaled on hedgehogs that should have been blown up already. No detonations occurred before the arrival of the second wave of infantry-laden boats, which piled up behind the first like cars behind a highway accident. Next, bulldozers and jeeps on crawler trailers plowed into the landing area, tearing the Primacord from obstacles before the charges could be blown.

Eventually, Markham's team and other demolition teams at Omaha Beach were able to detonate some of the obstacles, the pace quickening as American infantrymen eliminated German machine-gun and mortar positions. Only half of the obstacles intended for demolition were destroyed by day's end, and only five of the sixteen channels on Omaha Beach were fully cleared. Still, it was enough to get US troops on shore in the numbers required to secure the beach and establish a bridgehead in occupied France. Of 175 demolitioneers, thirty-one were killed and sixty wounded.

In the Pacific Theater, the Navy expanded its demolition capabilities after the November 1943 Battle of Tarawa, where coral reefs had sliced open American landing craft and sent Marines and tanks to the bottom. Establishing a new training center at Waimanalo, on the Hawaiian island of Oahu, the Navy formed Underwater Demolition Teams, whose "Frogmen" numbered 3,500 by the end of the war. In 1944 and 1945, as US amphibious warfare in the Pacific reached its zenith, the Frogmen swam along island coasts to chart terrain and prepare demolitions. Using fish lines to take soundings at twenty-five-yard intervals, reconnaissance teams determined where vessels could pass safely, and where coral or other obstacles needed to be destroyed. On demolition missions, the Frogmen typically arrived by high-speed boat the night before a landing, jumped into the water, and swam to the obstacles with haversacks of explosives and Primacord.

One of the greatest successes of the Underwater Demolition Teams took place at Guam. Annexed by the United States after the Spanish-American War, Guam had fallen to the Japanese on December 10, 1941, and hence the island was a point of national pride, as well as the largest prize in the Marianas. The Japanese had garrisoned the island with 19,000 troops, who had enjoyed plenty of time to get ready for the return of the Americans. To block amphibious landing craft, the Japanese had filled hundreds of wire cribs with rocks and put them on coral reefs near the shoreline. Japanese engineers had constructed fortified defensive positions on the beaches and crowded the sand with obstacles.

In the week preceding the invasion, Underwater Demolition Teams swam to the reefs and beaches to undo the Japanese handiwork. Piling boats high with blocks of the explosive tetrytol, they sailed close to shore and then waded through the water to reach their targets. Slowly, blast after blast, they chiseled channels through the coral and pathways across the beaches. By the date of the invasion, July 21, 1944, the US Navy was fully confident in its ability to land 60,000 troops on Guam. The landing craft encountered few troubles in delivering American ground forces, and those ground forces met with little difficulty in passing through the beaches. The Americans destroyed the Japanese garrison and reclaimed the island in just twenty days.

The amphibious reconnaissance and demolition men received widespread praise as the end of the war approached. Rear Admiral Turner pronounced that their contributions at Guam "fully justify the extraordinary efforts which have been made to organize, train and equip the Teams." Admiral Nimitz asserted, "Assault operations in the Marianas would have been far more difficult, if not impossible, on some beaches without the capable and courageous work of the Underwater Demolition Teams."

FRANKLIN ROOSEVELT'S INSISTENCE on the creation of the Marine Corps Raiders in January 1942 marked the beginning of presidential tinkering with special operations forces. In founding the Raiders, President Roosevelt took the advice of his novice son over the objections of the Marine Corps commandant—objections that subsequent events were to vindicate. Roosevelt approved the creation of Merrill's Marauders in the interest of meeting a request from an ally, without considering the practical factors that would influence the ultimate roles and effectiveness of the units. Such factors received much greater attention in the formation of the special operations forces that were not objects of high-level political fascination—the Navy Frogmen—which had much to do with the fact that the Navy Frogmen played a more significant military part in the war, and the fact that they outlived the presidentially fathered forces, which ultimately fell victim to a loss of presidential interest.

The Marine Raiders, like the Army Rangers and Forcemen, put their special capabilities to effective use on occasion. Stealth and physical fitness were critical to the success of Edson's landing on Tulagi and Carlson's month-long raid on Guadalcanal. But in the Pacific Theater, as in the European Theater, the Axis enemy was too strong and vigilant to be overwhelmed by raids or other light infantry operations. Heavily equipped infantry and armor would be required to snuff out the Japanese island garrisons.

In the Pacific, as in Europe, the limitations and negative perceptions of the special operations forces led to the dissolution of most units before the war ended. The Marine Corps converted its Raider battalions into a regular Marine regiment, the 4th Marines, in February 1944. Six months later, the US headquarters for the China-Burma-India Theater merged the battered remnants of Merrill's Marauders into the 475th Infantry Regiment. The Army deactivated the 6th Ranger Battalion and the few remaining Ranger battalions in Europe shortly after the war ended. The only special operations forces still in existence at the end of 1945 were a select number of Underwater Demolition Teams, owing to their proven effectiveness in amphibious warfare.

The fact that special operations forces played almost no role in the final defeat of Germany and Japan reinforced the belief among conventional military officers that such forces were an unnecessary and wasteful sideshow. For the next few years, the US military leadership would pay little attention to special operations forces, as it was preoccupied with the postwar decommissioning of military equipment and personnel and the accompanying problems of readiness. When the next war came, those interested in resurrecting special operations forces would have to compete with desperately impoverished conventional forces for coins from the national treasure chest. When that war came far sooner than expected, it ensured that criticism and resentment of special operations forces would still be fresh in military minds.

CHAPTER 3

OSS

Of the twenty-one students who entered Columbia Law School in 1905, the one destined to climb highest on the mountain of earthly power arrived already bearing the name and lineage of the nation's standing president. Born on the 110-acre Springwood estate in the Hudson Valley, Franklin D. Roosevelt had spent his youth shuttling between Springwood, a New York City town house, and an eighteen-room summer cottage on Campobello Island. He took an early liking to the sea, spending countless days learning to sail and fish aboard the family's fifty-one-foot yacht and a flotilla of lesser boats. Among the family's retinue of servants could be found a housekeeper, several maids, a butler, a nurse, a gardener, a horseman, and a team of farmhands. For his education, Franklin's parents relied on private tutors until the time came for high school, at which point they sent him off to the nation's premier boarding school, Groton. In 1900, he entered Harvard College, where he earned "Gentleman C's" in most of his courses.

For someone of Roosevelt's social class, gaining entrance to Columbia Law School was not considered an exceptional accomplishment. The mediocrity of his undergraduate record testified to the modesty of the admission standards that scions of the northeastern elite had to meet. Roosevelt certainly did not treat his admission to Columbia as a cherished privilege, as evidenced by grades that were even worse than those on his undergraduate transcript. Failing several of his courses, he would end up leaving the school without a degree.

Franklin Roosevelt could scarcely have differed more from the member of his law school class who would become its second-most-famous luminary, William J. Donovan. For Roosevelt, the future president, accolades and privileges appeared spontaneously, demanding no exertion strenuous enough to dampen his tailored shirt or disrupt his elaborate social calendar. For Donovan, the future head of the Office of Strategic Services, everything had to be earned by rolling up his sleeves and toiling into the night. Yet the acquaintance begun at Columbia between the unlikely duo was to be the genesis of the third type of special operations forces of World War II, a type burdened by the same troubles as most of the others, but one with a more robust legacy.

The son of poor Irish immigrants, Donovan was raised in the waterfront district of Buffalo, New York, where the lowest of the city's lower classes resided. James Quigley, a Catholic bishop who saw promise in the boy, used funds from the Buffalo diocese to pay for Donovan to attend a Catholic high school and Niagara University. Donovan enrolled at Niagara with aspirations to enter the priesthood, but both he and the faculty soon decided that he was not a good fit for the clergy. In 1903, he transferred to Columbia College to complete his undergraduate degree before entering law school.

For Donovan, admission to Columbia Law School was his golden ticket out of poverty and into the upper middle class. Donovan worked hard during law school, though a substantial amount of his labor went into part-time jobs that helped finance his education. He did not perform particularly well on written assignments and examinations, and hence his grades were undistinguished, but he excelled in oratory and debate. One of his law professors, the renowned Jackson E. Reynolds, recalled that whereas Roosevelt was "not much of a student and nothing of a lawyer afterward," Donovan was "a good student, industrious, quick and alert, his work practical, adaptable to any problem."

Donovan had a gift for social interaction, and in time would show that he could endear himself to the world's wealthiest with the ease of a Viennese grand duke. At Columbia, however, he did not mingle with Roosevelt or the other blue bloods. Roosevelt, as the son of a prominent Episcopalian family and a product of Groton, socialized with the children of railroad tycoons, not those of poor Irish Catholics. "I would meet Franklin Roosevelt walking across the campus almost every day, but he never once even noticed," Donovan remembered years later. "His eyes were always fixed on some other object."

The paths of Donovan and Roosevelt diverged after Columbia. Following a brief foray into the world of law, Roosevelt entered politics. In 1913, when he was a mere thirty-one years of age, Roosevelt received an appointment from President Woodrow Wilson to the position of assistant secretary of the Navy. Donovan went to work for the Buffalo law firm of Love & Keating, then formed his own practice two years later. During World War I, Donovan went off to Europe to lead troops of the 69th "Fighting Irish" Regiment, an outfit of 3,000 Irishmen from New York City. He found that he enjoyed combat, informing his wife that it thrilled him like "a youngster at Halloween." Displaying exceptional courage and poise under fire, Donovan earned the nation's highest military awards, the Congressional Medal of Honor and the Distinguished Service Cross.

The trajectories of the two men crossed back over in 1932, when Franklin Roosevelt ran his first presidential campaign. Roosevelt's decision to vacate the office of Governor of New York, to which he had been elected four years earlier, convinced Donovan to make a run for the governorship. Capitalizing on his war record and his more recent triumphs as assistant attorney general of the United States, Donovan secured the nomination of the Republican Party. In the swirl of the gubernatorial campaign, the conservative Donovan denounced his Democratic opponent as a "Siamese twin" of the liberal Roosevelt, intent on continuing Roosevelt's big-government policies. Donovan also inserted his mouth into the presidential contest, publicly denouncing Roosevelt as a "faker" whose claims to represent the lower classes belied the fact that he was a "new kind of red, white and blue dictator" with "delusions of grandeur."

Roosevelt parried the insults with words of conciliation. In one speech, he asserted that he had been friends with Donovan in law school. Donovan, sensing that Roosevelt's fronds of grace were but cover for poisonous berries of condescension and self-promotion, retorted, "I was a youngster earning my way through law school, and he never knew me."

That November, Roosevelt won the presidency by eighteen percentage points, and Donovan lost the race for the New York governorship by eighteen percentage points. Donovan went back to the private sector, but he maintained a foot in politics, with a particular eye toward foreign affairs. Traveling abroad with the frequency of a diplomat and the fervor of a pilgrim, Donovan used his war record and ingratiating charm to gain audiences with foreign leaders. In the late 1930s, as the Axis powers built their armies and swallowed territories, he demanded preparedness for looming conflict. "In an age of bullies," he pronounced in November 1939, "we cannot afford to be a sissy."

Donovan's support for the cause of Britain and France in their war with Nazi Germany was to bring him back into Roosevelt's orbit. Eager for Republican allies in galvanizing the nation against the Axis, and willing to overlook Donovan's prior affronts, Roosevelt sent Donovan on a secret mission to London in the summer of 1940. He asked Donovan to determine how, if at all, the United States could help the British stay afloat in the aftermath of Germany's crushing conquest of France. British officials, desperate to show that their country could keep fighting the Germans with American help, gave Donovan a reception fit for a chief of state. He received audiences with Prime Minister Winston Churchill, King George V, and all the leading military and intelligence figures. Legions of British experts briefed Donovan on British industrial production, ship and aircraft design, food supplies, and anything else that might make a favorable impression on the American.

Upon his return to the United States, Donovan delivered his findings to Roosevelt during an overnight ride on the eight-car presidential train and a cruise aboard the presidential yacht *Potomac*. The British, Donovan reported, could repulse a German invasion, but to do so they would need a massive infusion of US military aid. The items most desperately needed were destroyers, bombers, and the newly developed Sperry telescopic bombsights. Energetically delivered and rich in detail, Donovan's findings revitalized Roosevelt's resolve to support the beleaguered island kingdom.

Donovan then took his hopeful message to the rest of the country, which at the time was crawling with doubts about supporting a British empire that seemed destined to fall to the Nazi juggernaut. Donovan did Roosevelt, and the country, a great favor by dissipating popular gloom and building support for aid to Britain. Columnist Walter Lippmann observed that Donovan's trip report "almost single-handedly overcame the unmitigated defeatism which was paralyzing Washington."

In the coming months, Donovan further developed his relationship with top British intelligence officials, who were keen to cultivate this curiously Anglophilic Irish-American and obtain his assistance in convincing Roosevelt to establish a central intelligence service. In the spring of 1941, Donovan and the British jointly advised Roosevelt to create a new agency that would generate intelligence, wage psychological warfare, and employ commandos in raids and guerrilla operations. Donovan recommended modeling the intelligence component on the British MI-6, which had been in the espionage business since the sixteenth century, and the special operations component on the British Special Operations Executive, which Churchill had formed in July 1940 to foment resistance activities in Axis-held territories.

Donovan's proposal encountered stiff opposition from a host of Washington bureaucrats, who in the main were worried that the new organization would intrude upon their organizational turf. Roosevelt, however, was receptive. Since his days as assistant secretary of the Navy, Roosevelt had been infatuated with espionage, absorbing spy novels and demonstrating a schoolboy's love for fantastic chicanery. During World War I, he had ordered a series of investigations into alleged German conniving inside the United States, to include a scheme by German Americans to buy an aircraft in New Hampshire and bomb the Portsmouth Navy Yard. After claiming to have uncovered several improbable German plans to assassinate him, he had carried a revolver to and from work.

Roosevelt was taken in by Donovan's limitless confidence in unorthodox methods of warfare and by the effervescent ideas that seemed to spring eternal from Donovan's head. The president reveled in his chats with Donovan, finding them a delightful contrast to his interactions with other government officials, most of whom bored him terribly. Donovan, for his part, was amiable enough when speaking with the president, though he was distinctly less enthused by his conversation partner. To one friend, Donovan confided that Roosevelt was "a conceited man whose moods resembled those of a young girl: they were liable to sudden changes."

In July, the president signed off on the centralized intelligence service conceived by Donovan, and he made Donovan its first director, with the privilege of reporting directly to the commander in chief. Dubbed the Coordinator of Information, Donovan received his own secret funding account. Taking advantage of this slush fund and an exemption from civil service salary caps, Donovan plunged into the task of recruitment in his usual manner, with a terrier's verve and a bulldog's tenacity.

Few Americans had experience in espionage, so Donovan sought out talented individuals who could be sculpted into intelligence specialists. One veteran of the organization recounted that Donovan "concentrated on recruiting talent wherever he could find it—in universities, businesses, law firms, in the armed services, at Georgetown cocktail parties, in fact, anywhere he happened to meet or hear about bright and eager men and women who wanted to help." With promises of indispensable secret missions, offers of high salaries, and solemn utterances of "I'm counting on you," Donovan drew a startling array of high flyers into his new organization. Four of his junior recruits were to become directors of America's Central Intelligence Agency—Allen Dulles, Richard Helms, William Colby, and William Casey. Even more impressive was Donovan's success in recruiting people who had already risen to greatness in other pursuits, such as movie director John Ford, poet Archibald MacLeish, Rhode Island governor William H. Vanderbilt III, Harvard historian William Langer, and travel writer Eugene Fodor.

Acquiring talent and setting up an organization on the scale that Donovan envisioned would take close to one year. At the time of the Pearl Harbor attack, the Coordinator of Information had yet to coordinate anything, let alone conduct operations or generate intelligence products. During the organization's formative period, Donovan placated Roosevelt's craving for skullduggery by concocting amazing plots for undoing the Axis powers, which he presented to the president with the aplomb of a jeweler bringing out his finest diamonds from the safe. Among the most imaginative was the slipping of female hormones into Hitler's carrots and beets to cause his mustache to fall out and his voice to rise to a soprano pitch. Donovan's contrivances for countering enemy propaganda included inundating German territory with leaflets containing, in his description, "pictures of succulent appetizing dishes that would make a hungry person go almost mad with longing."

Roosevelt egged Donovan on with his unveiled delight and his own outlandish suggestions. At one point, he asked Donovan to look into air-dropping bats over the Japanese homeland for the purpose of "frightening, demoralizing and exciting the prejudices" of the Japanese people, who reportedly abhorred bats. Donovan convinced the curator of the mammalian division of the American Museum of Natural History to help organize experiments in which transport aircraft released bats at high altitude. The project had to be abandoned after the bats repeatedly froze to death.

During Donovan's first year as intelligence chief, he herded a wide assortment of activities into his organizational corral—espionage, intelligence analysis, research, special operations, and psychological operations, to name the most important. In the stampede of bureaucratic expansion, Donovan and his lieutenants often paid scant heed to the bureaucratic toes they trampled. Donovan had his operatives pose as military attachés overseas without obtaining the consent of the military. His propaganda division espoused US foreign policies at variance with the State Department's official line. A bitter rivalry emerged between Donovan and Federal Bureau of Investigation director J. Edgar Hoover after both tried to burglarize the Spanish embassy at the same time. In April 1942, Assistant Secretary of State Breckenridge Long observed that Donovan "has been a thorn in the side of a number of the regular agencies of the government for some time. . . . He is into everybody's business—knows no bounds of jurisdiction—tries to fill the shoes of each agency charged with responsibility for a war activity."

The most problematic of Donovan's rivals was the War Department, the leadership of which had fought in vain against the creation of his organization. Donovan's initial attempts to form special operations forces fell victim to the bureaucratic gatekeeping of the head of military intelligence, Major General George V. Strong, known as "George the Fifth" for his haughty demeanor. Strong refused to give Donovan access to the military's manpower pools, which were teeming with men whose prior training could allow them to become commandos in relatively short order.

The military's stinginess nearly starved Donovan's organization to death in the spring of 1942. Recognizing the danger, Donovan executed a cunning change of course, employing the full measure of his persuasive powers to reach the intended destination. Cozying up to generals and admirals who had tried to stifle the infant organization, Donovan lobbied with them to move him and his staff under the umbrella of the War Department, which would gain him access to military resources and shield him from the tentacles of jealous civilian agencies. He persuaded the military leaders to go along with this plan by explaining that they could prevent the sullying of the hands of their military personnel by leaving certain messy jobs in the hands of Donovan's civilian operatives. On June 13, 1942, Roosevelt signed an order redesignating Donovan's organization the Office of Strategic Services (OSS) under the Joint Chiefs of Staff. Army Chief of Staff George Marshall then granted the OSS permission to create guerrilla and commando forces using US military personnel.

DONOVAN'S FIRST SIGNIFICANT success in special operations would come in Asia. He began his Asian ventures by entreating the principal US commanders in the Pacific, General Douglas MacArthur and Admiral Chester Nimitz, to permit cloak-and-dagger activities in the Pacific islands. Both men refused. He next turned to General Joseph Stilwell, who as commander of the China-Burma-India Theater was a pauper in comparison with the other Pacific Theater commanders, desperately short on US personnel and other resources. Given his dearth of manpower, Stilwell was willing to entertain any proposals that put more Americans under his command.

In April 1942, Stilwell accepted an offer from Donovan to create a new special operations unit for service in the China-Burma-India Theater. The unit was to be called Detachment 1. Then, however, someone pointed out that this name would disclose to enemies and allies alike the extremely embarrassing fact that the Americans had only one unit. The unit was hence renamed Detachment 101.

Stilwell, in one of his many questionable decisions as theater commander, handpicked Carl Eifler to command Detachment 101. No one who met Eifler, it was said, would ever forget him. His appearance was often likened to that of a mastodon. In comportment, he demonstrated certain beast-like tendencies, though he also manifested a surprising degree of intelligence. Lieutenant Commander James C. Luce, a medical officer assigned to Detachment 101, described Eifler as "a tremendous man with a florid countenance and a voice that would dwarf a circus barker into insignificance. I never heard him talk in any other than maximum volume." Stilwell, having commanded Eifler's reserve unit during the 1930s, knew all of the man's idiosyncrasies, and subsequent events would suggest that Stilwell chose Eifler precisely because he wanted someone who would not inscribe the new unit into the annals of military glory.

Donovan authorized Eifler to select whomever he desired for the new unit, up to one hundred men in total. Seeking individuals with a multitude of skills and attributes that might be of use in special operations against the Japanese, Eifler went in search of investigators, electrical engineers, chemists, finance officers, radio technicians, demolition experts, locksmiths, railroad engineers, mechanics, and photographers. "The word was out now," Eifler later wrote, "that a strange new outfit was looking for some talented and unusual men."

When interested individuals showed up for interviews, Eifler opened by asking them to punch him in the stomach as hard as they could. Then he took a dagger and plunged it several inches into his desk. His displays were enough to convince some men that they had found just the right unit, and others that they had best put maximum distance between themselves and Detachment 101. Ray Peers, who later commanded Detachment 101 and eventually attained international acclaim for his investigation into the My Lai Massacre during the Vietnam War, counted himself among those initially put off by Eifler's bravado and theatrics. He agreed nevertheless to join the unit after Donovan gave him a much more sober and sophisticated explanation of the unit's purpose.

Following several months of training in the United States, Detachment 101 headed to the extreme eastern reaches of India, where the British had retreated in May 1942 after the Japanese overran most of Burma.

Eifler and his men had not been there long when they ran afoul of regular US Army units stationed in the vicinity. Resenting the detachment's unorthodox mission and chain of command, regular officers believed that the unit ought to be stuffed into the box of Army conformity, complying with standard Army tactics and operating under a regular Army headquarters. Several Army organizations attempted to take control of the unit's personnel, but Eifler and his superiors were able to fend them off.

In September 1942, Eifler reported that his men were ready for duty. Stilwell directed him to commence sabotage operations against the Japanese in Burma, as an opening gambit in Stilwell's long-term plan to reopen the Burma Road, a critical supply artery into China. "You have ninety days for me to hear booms from the jungle," Stilwell informed Eifler. Peers considered Stilwell's directive to be "utterly fantastic," for "we had no trainees, no radios, it was over three hundred miles away through some of the world's worst jungles, and there were less than three months to do it in." Eifler suspected that Stilwell had given him a mission that he thought stood no chance of success, because of a conventional officer's doubts about the effectiveness and legality of irregular units. In a message to OSS headquarters, Eifler alleged that Stillwell would relish his failure, because it "will be the end of operations and the verification of his belief."

Knowing that Americans could not pass for natives of Burma, Eifler and his staff decided to recruit Burmese personnel to produce the prescribed booms in the jungle. Detachment 101 men fanned out to refugee camps and army installations in India to find men of Burmese or Anglo-Burmese descent. Eifler set up a training base on the Assam Tea Estate, a large plantation near the Indian town of Nazira. Fearing that the Japanese had spies in the area, Detachment 101 spread rumors that the Americans were using the plantation to conduct research on malaria.

Eifler organized the recruits into six groups and trained all of them for long-range penetration operations. The amount of time required to recruit and train the saboteurs prevented Eifler from meeting Stilwell's ninety-day deadline; the groups would not set off for the Burmese jungle until February 1943. Burma's western jungles were too dense and expansive to permit overland marches from India to Burma, so agents would have to be inserted and resupplied by sea or air.

Five of the six groups were to go down in flames. One fell into Japanese hands as soon as it landed, its whereabouts divulged to the Japanese by locals of Shan ethnicity who had seen its parachutes floating down from the sky. Japanese interrogators tortured the would-be saboteurs and then executed them. Another group landed without its equipment as a result of a ten-second delay in the dropping of the equipment chutes, and both it and the team sent to rescue it were wiped out by the Japanese. Team REX, which landed by parachute near Rangoon, disappeared and was never heard from again.

Eifler personally accompanied the team assigned for insertion near the Taungup Pass, a critical chokepoint in the Arakan Yoma Mountains of southwestern Burma. Vessels of the Royal Indian Navy carried the infiltrators across the Bay of Bengal to the Burmese coast. At the beach where they intended to land, they sighted a Japanese patrol boat and Japanese shore patrols, so Eifler directed them to move farther along the shoreline to find an undefended stretch. Pressure mounted as daylight approached, for the landing party needed to get ashore before sunup if it wished to evade Japanese air patrols.

Near dawn, they found a section of the coast that appeared to be undefended. High swells thundered into the wall of rocks that formed the coastline, sending plumes of white foam jetting into the air. Eifler instructed the Burmese team members to swim ashore through a break in the rocks, with the first man tying a rope around his waist for the others to use as a guide. The spectacle of big waves smacking the rocks, however, had convinced the Burmese that the task was entirely too dangerous. They refused to go.

At this point, Eifler could have taken the whole entourage back to port, returning another night to find a more auspicious location. But, like many of his American colleagues, he held the opinion that an officer should not order an action that he was unwilling to undertake himself. Looping the rope around his torso, Eifler jumped into the sea and swam toward the shore. His huge arms churning through the water like propellers, he crossed two reefs and passed through a gap in the rocks unscathed before reaching land. Sheepishly, the Burmese operators followed the rope to the shore. Within fifteen minutes, the entire Burmese team was on land, along with 1,500 pounds of supplies.

Eifler shook the hands of the team members one at a time, warning each man to avoid getting captured alive. He then headed back toward the ships of the Indian Navy. On the way, a large wave caught him and threw him headfirst into one of the mammoth rocks, opening a nasty gash on his head. Dazed and unable to hear from one ear, he nonetheless summoned the strength to resume swimming, albeit at a considerably slower pace. The Indian sailors were about to give Eifler up for lost when they saw him clawing through the surf toward the vessel. Grabbing the bleeding hulk like fishermen hauling in an enormous tuna, they were able to pull Eifler onto the deck.

Back on the shore, the landing force made haste to leave the beach and get under cover before sunup. In the commotion, someone dropped one of the dry-cell batteries that powered the radios. After daybreak, a local fisherman found the battery lying in the sand. The Burmese in this area, like those in many other parts of the country, had supported the Japanese invasion of Burma as liberation from the British, and were happy to help them ward off any intruders, the likes of which might be presaged by so peculiar an object as a dry-cell battery. The fisherman took the battery to the Japanese authorities, who immediately launched a manhunt across the region. The local population joined in the search, and their tips to the Japanese proved critical in finding the would-be saboteurs. The Japanese and their local friends hunted down the Detachment 101 men and killed them in groups of one or two until none were left.

The only group that did not fail utterly was the one that infiltrated by parachute near Myitkyina in northern Burma. Landing undetected, the group split into three teams and set out to destroy three bridges on roads that fed into a Japanese air base. They planned to blow the bridges simultaneously, in order to achieve maximum surprise. One team, however, blew its charges before the others, triggering alerts at the other two bridges. The Detachment 101 teams at those bridges had to flee with their tasks unfinished. One OSS man was captured, but the others escaped to Fort Hertz, the one British base in Burma that had not fallen to the Japanese.

These men had survived because the local population did not betray them to the Japanese and instead helped them hide. The residents of this part of Burma, the Kachins, detested the Japanese and were fond of the

British, for the British colonial authorities had treated the Kachins well and given them autonomy, in one of the innumerable divide-and-conquer ploys with which the small island nation had come to dominate much of the world. The activities of British and American missionaries had further contributed to the population's favorable disposition toward English-speaking white men.

The ancestry of the Kachins could be traced back to Mongol tribes that had migrated from the Himalayas several centuries earlier. Most Kachins lived in the Himalayan foothills, their bamboo huts perched on hilltops to afford maximum protection against the ravenous tigers that stalked the Kachin territories. Farming for subsistence, the Kachins grew rice, beans, and corn and raised chickens and pigs. All adult males carried a sharp sword called a *dah*, which they decorated with jewels and other ornaments. Their reputation as mighty warriors owed not only to their prowess with weapons and their passion for battle but also to their mastery of the jungle. Their ability to find their way through dense flora and detect the presence of others from long distances would astound their American friends and Japanese foes, for whom the jungle was merely an endless sea of green.

After the Japanese had driven the British from Burma, they attempted to subdue the Kachins by despoiling the small number of Kachin villages in the lowlands. Japanese soldiers burned down huts, skinned men alive, raped women, and castrated boys, in the belief that Kachins who survived the bedlam would pass word of Japanese ferocity to their highland brethren and advise them to bow to Japan's will. The highland Kachins chose instead to take up arms against the Japanese. Some Kachin communities organized independent guerrilla forces, while others joined units organized by the British. Armed with ancient muzzle-loading flintlocks, along with a number of weapons of more recent vintage, including Enfield rifles, Bren guns, and shotguns, the Kachins sprang out of nowhere to ambush Japanese columns on jungle trails, then melted into the jungle as invisibly as they had come.

The more Eifler and Detachment 101 learned about the Kachins, the more they wanted to sponsor a Kachin guerrilla force. In the summer of 1943, word reached the Americans of a Kachin leader in the snowcapped

Kumon Mountains named Zhing Htaw Naw, who was reputed to have inflicted fearsome losses on Japanese forces. At the end of August, Captain Vincent L. Curl left Fort Hertz on an expedition to find Zhing Htaw Naw, taking with him nine OSS men, several Kachin guides, and a group of porters who had agreed to haul heavy loads in exchange for opium.

Curl's band trekked through undulating foothills and valleys toward the Kumon range, obtaining directions from Kachin travelers as they went. It took a month to reach the place where Zhing Htaw Naw had established his latest headquarters, a village etched high upon the shoulder of a mountain. As the voyagers approached the village, a party of men sallied out to greet them.

"You are friends, but you cannot see the *duwa*," said a young Kachin, using an honorific term for their leader. After the Americans pressed for an explanation, the man said, "The *duwa* is sick."

"I can cure him," Curl replied. The American officer actually had no idea what afflicted Zhing Htaw Naw, but he hoped that the medical supplies in his pack would contain something to remedy the illness. Persuaded by Curl's sincerity, the Kachin guides agreed to take him to see Zhing Htaw Naw while Curl's companions stayed at a nearby camp.

The man to whom Curl was brought seemed anything but a mighty warrior. Huddled next to a fire, the slight man agonized in a half-conscious stupor. Curl offered Zhing Htaw Naw a greeting in the local tongue, then said in English, "I can help you."

Zhing Htaw Naw's symptoms were consistent with malaria, an illness that Curl knew to be endemic to the area. Removing a bottle of quinine from his backpack, Curl gave a strong dose to the sick man. To induce a sweat, Curl wrapped the patient in a bedroll, fed him warm soup, and kept him near the fire. Soon beads of sweat were trickling down Zhing Htaw Naw's body as it purged the malarial fever. Then he fell into a peaceful sleep, his head cool and his face serene. Curl lay down nearby and also went to sleep.

When they awoke the next morning, a reinvigorated Zhing Htaw Naw took an immediate liking to the white man who had exorcised his misery. With the help of an interpreter, he and Curl became fast friends. Eager to join together in fighting the Japanese, they promptly cemented a partnership in which the OSS would equip and supply Kachin guerrillas. Curl radioed Eifler a request for weapons to arm 250 men, and several days later a C-87 Liberator Express showed up to air-drop cases of rifles, shotguns, Tommy guns, and ammunition.

Word of the new alliance spread across the Kachin lands. Within a few months, the alluring combination of Zhing Htaw Naw's leadership and American arms induced more than 1,000 more men to volunteer for what the Americans now called the American-Kachin Rangers. Curl and Zhing Htaw Naw established two new forward bases, with an airstrip at each, to which weapons for the new volunteers were flown.

American and Kachin leaders formed the new recruits into units of fifty to sixty men. The Americans trained the Kachins in the use of the weapons, while Zhing Htaw Naw and his lieutenants provided instruction on guerrilla warfare. The Americans were amazed by the tactical expertise that Zhing Htaw Naw's men already possessed. Ray Peers likened their painstaking preparation of an ambush site to the work of an architect planning a building. They set up positions in dense foliage without breaking a branch, making a footprint, or providing any other indicator that something was out of the ordinary. In undergrowth where Japanese soldiers were most likely to jump when attacked, the Kachin guerrillas planted bamboo *pungyi* sticks that had been sharpened with knives and hardened with fire.

The Americans found the execution of the ambushes to be equally stunning. When a Japanese column entered the kill zone, the guerrillas ambushed it at multiple points simultaneously, their gunfire knocking some men down and causing others to jump into the undergrowth, where they were impaled on the *pungyi* sticks. If the Japanese were able to counterattack, the Kachins reconcentrated at strongpoints a short distance back, from which they would inflict additional carnage. If any Japanese withstood the mauling and were still capable of attacking, the Kachins withdrew to a prearranged meeting point miles away, employing their superior knowledge of the terrain to lose any pursuing Japanese.

While Detachment 101's men in the field were causing the Japanese more trouble than anyone had ever imagined, the unit was suffering from troubles of its own at headquarters. The head injury that Eifler had sustained on the Burmese coast had left him with severe and recurring pain, which he attempted to ease by consuming profuse quantities of alcohol and injecting himself with morphine. The toxic mixture of pain, alcohol, and drugs drove Eifler into bouts of rage and petty tyranny. On one occasion, he grabbed the front of an officer's shirt, lifted him off the ground, and shook him like a rag doll. To a newly arrived man, he sneered, "What do you do? I can walk seventy-two hours without sleep or drink." Eifler attempted to resolve heated disputes with other officers by slamming his hand into a table and cleaving it in two.

Word of Eifler's behavior eventually reached Donovan. On December 8, 1943, the OSS chief arrived at Eifler's headquarters to see matters for himself. After speaking with Eifler and others in the headquarters for several hours, Donovan ordered Eifler to return to the United States. In an account published years later, Eifler claimed that Donovan had sent him to the United States temporarily, in order to tell the American people about the successes of Detachment 101, and wanted him to return to Burma afterward. Whether Donovan ever characterized Eifler's departure as temporary is doubtful, given the lack of corroborating evidence, the fact that Eifler would never return to the unit, and the implausibility of Eifler's memories of the ensuing events. In Eifler's retelling, the OSS ultimately chose not to send him back to Burma because it needed him for a series of daring strategic missions, among which were the assassination of Chiang Kai-shek, the abduction of Germany's leading nuclear scientist, and a submarine invasion of Korea that would be followed by a direct penetration of Japan. In each case, the plans were on the verge of execution when they somehow had to be aborted.

Following Eifler's departure, Ray Peers took command of Detachment 101. A native of Stuart, Iowa, Peers differed from Eifler in most every way. One Detachment 101 man explained that if the task were to demolish a building, Peers "would carefully remove each brick and end up with neatly stacked piles, whereas [Eifler] would get a Bull Dozer and level it." Rather than try to do everything at the same time, as Eifler had done, Peers focused the organization on a few carefully selected tasks in order to perform them with an artisan's skill. Peers extricated Detachment 101 from the unprofitable business of long-range penetration operations and concentrated on building up the short-range intelligence and guerrilla operations with the Kachins.

To beef up assistance to the Kachins, Peers inserted more American personnel into Burma. He gave meticulous attention to the selection of Americans for these missions. At first, he assumed that men who had been raised on farms would be the best, owing to their familiarity with outdoor life. Over time, however, he discerned that some city boys could perform quite well, particularly those who had spent time in the unit learning the ropes from others. Peers also found that an individual's upbringing and boyhood activities were strong predictors of success. "A boy who had stayed with scouting and had attained a high rank, up to Eagle Scout, almost invariably was well equipped for the job," Peers observed. "On the other hand, the sheltered boy, the mama's boy, was almost useless until the mama could be taken out of the boy and he could become one of the group. We salvaged several such boys, but under hostile conditions it was very costly in training time and effort." Peers added, "Another type of individual we learned to treat cautiously were the braggarts. When alone in the thick jungle they tended to become tense and panic. They needed companionship to buoy their spirits."

The spectacular battlefield successes of the American-Kachin Rangers caught the attention of Stilwell's headquarters at Chungking. In early 1944, Stilwell gave Detachment 101 additional equipment and manpower to expand the number of Kachin guerrillas to 3,000. With news of Zhing Htaw Naw's victories reverberating across the Kachin hill country, Detachment 101 had no trouble raising additional Kachin troops. Stilwell then directed Peers to employ the expanded force in support of a new Allied offensive against Myitkyina, in which Merrill's Marauders and Chiang Kai-shek's National Revolutionary Army were to provide the conventional muscle.

As the offensive unfolded, the American-Kachin Rangers collected information, served as guides for the conventional Allied forces, and harassed the Japanese. Too lightly equipped to fight toe-to-toe with regular units, they steered clear of the front lines and instead struck in the enemy's rear areas, where troops were thinly spread in small groups. Flitting through the jungle like phantoms, the Kachins routinely provided advance warning of Japanese troop movements, which enabled the Marauders and the Chinese to counter Japanese thrusts and exploit Japanese weaknesses. Kachin reports on enemy troop locations provided the best information available to the Allied bombers prowling the skies over Myitkyina. Lieutenant Colonel Samuel V. Wilson, the top intelligence officer in Merrill's Marauders during the offensive, later said that "without the assistance and support of the Kachins, we would have been licked before we even got started."

The contributions of the American-Kachin Rangers to the Myitkyina offensive led Stilwell to authorize a further increase in the strength of the Kachin guerrillas, to 10,000. The additional American men he sent to Detachment 101 to undergird the expansion brought the number of Americans in the detachment near 1,000. As the Allies pushed to the south and east during the final year of the war, the Rangers provided their special services to Chinese, British, and American units.

By the time of their disbandment in July 1945, the American-Kachin Rangers had recorded 5,447 confirmed kills of Japanese soldiers. According to OSS estimates, they had killed or seriously wounded another 10,000 of the enemy. Air strikes for which Detachment 101 had provided targeting information killed an estimated 11,225 more. The gains had come at the remarkably low cost of 270 Burmese killed or missing and 15 Americans killed.

IN THE EUROPEAN Theater, OSS special operations forces began in the same manner as the rest of the OSS in Europe, as a caboose hitched onto the long train of British secret activities. Winston Churchill had created the Special Operations Executive (SOE) in the summer of 1940 with an injunction to its chief to "set Europe ablaze." In its first years, though, the SOE had set only a few brushfires, most of which were stomped out by the black boots of fascism. Efforts to support French resistance fighters had run up against French resentment stemming from the Dunkirk evacuation in June 1940 and the Royal Navy's annihilation of French ships at Oran the following month, as well as the effectiveness of German and Vichy authorities in hunting down subversives. German intelligence smashed the main French resistance network in 1942 after one of its members fell asleep on a train with a briefcase containing the names of the network's 250 leading members. A German Abwehr agent swiped the briefcase and passed it on to his superiors, who tracked the 250 individuals for several months before rounding them up in one fell swoop.

Donovan wanted to parachute OSS commandos into France right away, but he was rebuffed by the British, who feared that inexperienced Americans would, in their overconfident and overeager manner, inadvertently tear through the fine webs of espionage and resistance that the Special Operations Executive had been spinning across France. Donovan's first effort to support anti-Nazi resistance would take place in French North Africa, where anti-British sentiment made US involvement a more attractive option. During the run-up to the Operation Torch landings, the OSS did not yet have any military forces aside from Detachment 101, so Donovan assigned the task of resistance support to his intelligence chief for the region, William Eddy.

Born in Syria to American missionaries, Eddy had lost a leg in World War I as a Marine, then had joined the English Department at the American University in Cairo, where he distinguished himself by introducing the sport of basketball to the Egyptian people. To find Frenchmen willing to risk their hides in support of the Allied invasion, Eddy maneuvered among French exiles and Vichy French officers in North African bistros and bordellos. Securing promises from a variety of senior French leaders, he became convinced that French military officers in Algeria and Morocco would turn against the Germans en masse on the eve of Torch. Eddy assured Lieutenant General Dwight D. Eisenhower, commander of the invasion, that these turncoats would allow US forces to seize much of French North Africa unopposed.

When the Allied invasion forces came ashore on November 8, 1942, most of the expected antifascist resistance failed to materialize. Pro-Allied Frenchmen seized only two facilities, a military headquarters and a communications complex in Algiers, and both were quickly retaken by Vichy French officers loyal to the Germans. As news of Eddy's failure filtered in from North Africa, Donovan attempted to stave off defeatism among the headquarters staff by pointing to times in US history when even more severe setbacks had not precluded ultimate success. At daily staff meetings, he read aloud from a history of the War of 1812, ending each recitation by shutting the book and pronouncing, "They haven't burned the White House yet."

After Torch, Donovan shifted his attention to southern Europe. Using 1,100 newly acquired Army personnel, he formed a small number of commando-type forces, which he named Operational Groups. Composed of four officers and thirty noncommissioned officers who were fluent in European languages, the groups received training in parachuting, sabotage, and guerrilla warfare. Donovan planned to insert an Operational Group into Sicily to organize an antifascist uprising ahead of the Allied invasion, but invasion commanders aborted his plan as the invasion date neared out of concern that it would tip off the enemy about the main invasion. The only OSS man to land in Sicily on the invasion date was Donovan himself, who managed to scrounge a ride on a landing craft that took him to Gela just a few hours after Darby's Rangers had stormed the mine-strewn beach. Donovan convinced General Theodore Roosevelt Jr. of the 1st Army Division to order a staff officer to drive him toward the front, and then Donovan talked that officer into approaching Italian forces, upon whom he could fire the jeep's machine guns. "Donovan got behind the machine gun and had a field day," the officer recalled. "He was happy as a clam when we got back."

Donovan's efforts to put an Operational Group ashore ahead of the Salerno landings likewise fell victim to the caution of four-star generals, but he was able to land a twenty-man group at Salerno on the first day of the invasion. To the dismay of Donovan, who again found his way onto the beach on opening day, the OSS team evidenced more concern about requisitioning fancy cars and other luxury items than organizing resistance fighters. The group leader commandeered the finest hotel in the area and compelled the wait staff to serve him seven-course dinners in black tie. One OSS veteran attributed the problems to the presence of "too many prima donnas who were driven by ambition without the sterner stuff which is a prerequisite for success." The Operational Groups redeemed themselves to a degree in subsequent raiding operations on Italian islands and the Italian coast, blowing up rail-track and machine-gun emplacements to draw German troops away from the Winter Line.

When Donovan was read in on the plans for the invasion of France, he beseeched high authorities for permission to insert OSS special operators into Normandy in support of the conventional forces. The Supreme Headquarters Allied Expeditionary Force consented to the use of the Operational Groups and the Jedburghs, the latter a joint venture between the OSS and SOE, in helping the French resistance blow up bridges and railroads and otherwise discombobulate German efforts to reinforce the Normandy defenses. Resistance operations were one of three delaying instruments that the Allied high command would employ, the other two being deception and aerial bombardment. By Allied estimates, the Germans had thirty-one divisions that could reach Normandy by the twenty-fifth day of the offensive. They could throw the invasion force back into the sea if they could get just fifteen of those divisions to Normandy by the sixtieth day.

Of the hundreds of OSS operators whom destiny was to toss into occupied France, none would be more significant to the history of special operations than Aaron Bank. One day in the spring of 1943, as a young railroad training officer at Camp Polk, Louisiana, Bank was strolling by the adjutant's tent when a recruiting notice on the bulletin board caught his attention. His pulse quickened as he read that volunteers with foreign language skills were needed for special missions. Bank had been looking for a chance to escape Camp Polk and the Louisiana swamplands, having been subjected daily to wet heat, oversized mosquitos, snakes that slithered into sleeping bags, and a boring job. He knew German from speaking with his grandfather, and French from conversing with his mother, whose wealthy Russian family had sent her to high school in France before their emigration to the United States. During the 1930s, he had spent time in France as a lifeguard and swimming instructor at one of the private beaches of Biarritz. While presiding over aquatic recreation on the Bay of Biscay, he had practiced his languages with wealthy tourists, both French and German.

Bank contacted the recruiting office at once. The captain who interviewed him began by testing his fluency in French. It became clear immediately to both men that Bank's French was superior to the captain's, so they quickly dispensed with that part of the interview. The captain then asked, "Would you volunteer to operate behind the lines in uniform or civilian clothes?"

So nervous was Bank that he blurted out an answer before thinking the question over. Yes, he said, he would be willing to volunteer for those operations.

That was it. The captain told Bank that he would receive reassignment orders within the week. Bank recollected that upon hearing the news, "I was in a state of euphoria, floating on a cloud, eagerly awaiting my release from an unpleasant assignment."

Bank received orders to report to Washington, DC, in civilian attire. When he arrived in the nation's capital, an OSS duty officer directed him to the Congressional Country Club in Bethesda, Maryland. Depleted of members by the Depression, the club had come to such dire financial straits that its board had decided to lease the club's 406 acres and facilities to the OSS for the modest sum of $4,000 per month. The fairways of the golf course had been converted into obstacle courses and rifle ranges, the sand traps into demolition beds. In the early-Italian clubhouse, the ballroom now served as a hall for lectures on the arts and sciences of modern war. The dining room, once the place for Maryland's well-heeled to take their families for a prime rib dinner or a Sunday brunch, was now a military mess hall where cooks dished up mass-produced meats and starches.

Bank and the other volunteers began with a battery of physical and mental tests aimed at weeding out those unfit for the highly dangerous and unusual missions that lay ahead. Instructors ran them for hours on the obstacle course and cross-country trails to measure their stamina. Under the observation of clipboard-toting psychologists, sleep-deprived candidates took part in guerrilla exercises that subjected them to high stress levels and compelled them to essay impossible tasks. As a means of assessing resourcefulness and creativity, they were required to solve difficult problems, such as moving a large object that was too heavy for a man to carry.

Those who passed these tests underwent a training regimen similar to that of the British Commandos. They learned raiding and ambushing, and they practiced the destruction of bridges, culverts, railroads, canal locks, and electric transformer stations. To hone their physiques, they climbed ropes, performed pushups with packs on their backs, and punched out five-mile runs.

From the Congressional Country Club, the recruits were taken to Area B, a secret training site in the Catoctin Mountain Park. Chestnut, hickory, and black birch trees shaded the site's log cabins, which were only one ridge away from the airy presidential retreat that Franklin Roosevelt called Shangri-La, later renamed Camp David by Dwight Eisenhower. At Area B, the trainees learned hand-to-hand combat from William Ewart Fairbairn, a thirty-year veteran of the Shanghai police. Fairbairn demonstrated how to strike a man's nerve centers and pressure points with fists, elbows, and knees, and how to break a man's bones with a rapid strike from the side of the hand. During knife exercises, he trained them in the severing of arteries and the piercing of vital organs.

Bank was one of the trainees deemed worthy of participation in the Jedburgh program. He and the other selectees traveled to Britain for advanced training at a series of specialized schools, culminating in final exercises at a site that in classified correspondence was called Area D or ME-65. Located in the flatlands of Peterborough ninety miles north of London, it was an Elizabethan manor whose real name was Milton Hall. The manor's massive gray castle, built of stone walls measuring three feet in thickness, was surrounded by a 500-acre park of gardens, terraces, and fields, and beyond lay 20,000 acres of forests and pastures.

The Jedburgh candidates were housed among the castle's fifty rooms, whose oak-beamed ceilings overlooked collections of Cromwellian armor and swords. In the sunken gardens and rose-bordered terraces, the Jedburghs practiced wrestling and martial arts, while the snapping of small arms fire could be heard from the croquet court. A climbing wall, built onto a corner of the castle, served as the training ground for scaling operations. Instructors taught the trainees how to dress like Frenchmen, and required them to memorize the multitudinous uniforms of German and French military and police forces. Bank filed every facet of the experience into his memory, where all of this knowledge was to remain until, nearly a decade later, he would draw upon it in forming a new organization on the Jedburgh pattern, the US Army Special Forces.

Despite the rather comfortable conditions of Milton Hall, morale sagged during Bank's first weeks. The British commanding officer was a strict disciplinarian, better suited to whipping teenaged enlisted men into shape than cultivating maverick officers in their twenties and thirties. When no other activities were scheduled, the martinet refused to let the aspiring Jedburghs leave Milton Hall, instead forcing them to participate in inane drills and roll calls, or subjecting them to long and boring monologues about his own service in India years ago.

American and French trainees groused about the British food. The Americans found the British to be snobbish and the French to be petulant, while the Europeans bemoaned the crudeness of the Americans. After an inebriated American spouted off in the presence of foreign officers, the British lodged an official complaint against the offender for "violently insulting and abusing the British people, their army, and their part in our mutual war effort."

By February 1944, the atmosphere had become so toxic that Bank and another officer went to the London headquarters of the OSS to plead for intervention. The Americans at Milton Hall, they reported, were on the verge of mutiny. The OSS leadership took the matter up with the Special Operations Executive, which acted promptly to rectify the situation. Jedburgh trainees were given weekend passes to London, where they could drink pints of strong English ale at the pubs of Covent Garden or dance with English girls at the Palladium Ballroom. Frenchmen were ushered into Milton Hall's kitchen to add flair to the cuisine. The trainees were assigned batmen, who tended to all of their laundry, ironing, boot shining, housekeeping, and gear cleaning. Soon, men of all nationalities were gathering together at the castle's drawing room for evenings of song, drink, and good cheer.

The planners for Operation Overlord decided that the Jedburgh teams would consist of three men, with one French officer, one American or British officer who spoke French, and one enlisted radio operator. Because the Yanks and Brits heavily outnumbered the Frenchmen, the French officers were allowed to pick the members of their teams. Like suitors seeking the hands of the princesses with the largest family fortunes, American and British officers courted the Frenchmen who seemed the most likely to stay alive in occupied France. Bank went after a small French lieutenant, Henri Denis, paying for extravagant weekends in London's finest hotels and restaurants to seal the deal.

Bank's team, and most of the other Jedburgh teams, would not parachute into France until well after D-Day. As with the Italian landings, Allied leaders worried that inserting large numbers of special operators ahead of the invasion would put the enemy on alert that something large was afoot. Allied planners also anticipated, correctly as it turned out, that few French civilians would assume the risks of backing the resistance until the Allied invasion force had firmly established a foothold on the continent and begun to roll the Germans back.

Most of the OSS men to enter France, like most who had entered Italy, would arrive long after their organization's leader. General Marshall and Navy Secretary James Forrestal had notified the invasion commanders that under no circumstances was Bill Donovan to be permitted ashore at Normandy. They had not been amused by Donovan's appearances in Italy, which had posed a grave security risk, since Donovan had knowledge of the Allies' most vital secrets. The wily Donovan nonetheless wormed his way aboard the flagship of one of Overlord's top naval commanders, who happened to be an old friend. The admiral had the good sense to prevent Donovan from disembarking until the second day of the invasion, after large sections of the Norman shoreline had been secured. Donovan hitched a ride to the shore on a Duck amphibious truck, taking with him the head of the OSS London station, David Kirkpatrick Este Bruce, a former state legislator who was married to the daughter of banker Andrew W. Mellon.

Once on land, Donovan led Bruce toward the sound of the guns. They reached an American antiaircraft battery, whose commanding officer was astonished by the appearance at the front lines of an old man wearing the Congressional Medal of Honor. Before them lay a large open field in which three French peasants were digging up vegetables. Intent on getting even closer to the fighting, Donovan gave the battery commander the preposterous story that the peasants were his French agents. They were expecting him, Donovan continued, so he needed to move forward without delay to glean vital information. The artillery captain warned Donovan against stepping any farther, stating ominously that Germans lay not far ahead. Paying him no heed, Donovan proceeded toward the French peasants.

The peasants disappeared when they saw Donovan and Bruce approaching. The two American spy chiefs then headed to a hedgerow at the edge of the field. German machine guns opened fire, forcing them to dive into the nearest shrubs.

Turning to Bruce, Donovan intoned, "David, we mustn't be captured. We know too much."

"Yes, sir," replied Bruce.

"Have you your pill?" Donovan inquired. He was referring to the suicide pill that OSS officers carried in case they fell into enemy hands.

Bruce admitted that he was not carrying the pill. He had not expected to be anywhere near German forces.

"Never mind," Donovan grunted, "I have two of them." Donovan dug into his pockets to retrieve the pills, but he could not feel them. In frustration, he began to empty the pockets. Out came several hotel keys, a passport, newspaper clippings, travel orders, photographs of grandchildren, and currencies from various countries. The pills were nowhere to be found.

"We can do without them," Donovan said finally, with the resignation of a miner who has dug in every direction without finding quarry. "But if we get out of here," the OSS boss continued, "you must send a message to Gibbs, the Hall Porter at Claridge's in London, telling him on no account to allow the servants in the hotel to touch some dangerous medicines in my bathroom."

The German machine-gun fire continued. Donovan whispered to Bruce, "I must shoot first."

"Yes, sir," Bruce responded, "but can we do much against machine guns with our pistols?"

"Oh, you don't understand," Donovan said. "I mean if we are about to be captured I'll shoot you first. After all, I am your commanding officer."

Fortunately for the two men, Allied forces arrived and put an end to the German gunfire. Donovan and Bruce were able to return safely to the beach later in the day, and by evening, they were back on a US warship, enjoying a hot meal.

Aaron Bank's team parachuted into occupied France at the end of July. They were met at the drop site by a motley group of Frenchmen toting Sten submachine guns, which had been smuggled in previously by the British. After the Jedburghs provided a secret password to confirm their identity, the greeting party loaded them and their equipment bundle onto a charcoal-fueled truck that emerged from its camouflaged position beneath a cluster of trees. Driving to a local farmhouse, the resistance men delivered Bank, Denis, and their radio operator to a local chief of the Maquis, as the resistance was known.

The Maquis leader, who referred to himself as Commandant Raymond, briefed the Jedburghs on the local situation. His nationalist resistance forces had not yet attacked the Germans, he explained, because they first wanted to receive more Allied weaponry and an explicit authorization from the Allied high command to commence guerrilla warfare. Raymond also filled them in on the activities of the French Communists in the area, who were running a separate resistance organization. The Communists were hijacking his supply trains, and they had stolen supply drops intended for his forces.

Bank and Denis wanted to work behind the scenes and keep their presence hidden from the local population, which was certain to contain enemy informants. They insisted that their parachutes be buried, as otherwise the Maquis would give the fabric to their wives or girlfriends, who would spin it into garments of such striking composition as to arouse suspicions. Their efforts to maintain a low profile were quickly sabotaged when some of the resistance members leaked word of their presence to local villagers. With a mixture of delight and dread, the Jedburghs were feted in village after village with champagne toasts and chants of "Vive les Américains!"

The nationalist resistance fighters in Bank's area of operations had all served in the French Army and thus already possessed basic military skills. Bank nevertheless insisted that they receive training in guerrilla tactics, explosives, and firearms before guerrilla warfare commenced. "I explained to Commandant Raymond that the organization should be trained properly and achieve reasonable strength before we started needling the enemy," Bank recalled. Bank and Denis trained the resistance leaders, who then gave the training to their rank and file while the Jedburghs went on to the next group.

By the time these resistance forces were ready, the Germans had abandoned hope of retaining Normandy and were retreating eastward toward their homeland. Resistance forces therefore sought to trip up the Germans and help advancing Allies smash them before they could get away. Raymond's fighters began with several hit-and-run attacks, including an ambush of a twenty-vehicle German convoy. The Germans responded with counterinsurgency tactics that would have garnered plaudits from Genghis Khan. Descending upon the town nearest to the guerrilla attack, they hauled out a dozen men and executed them on the spot.

In the interest of protecting innocent men from reprisals, several mayors urged the resistance to stop ambushing the Germans. Denis notified the mayors that "sacrifices had to be made if they wanted France liberated." The resistance fighters "would be considerate," Denis maintained, but "we would not reduce the activities we consider necessary."

Commandant Raymond was apparently more sympathetic to the views of the mayors, for he reduced guerrilla activities for a time. The resistance stepped up its attacks when German forces began a full-scale evacuation of the area in the face of the advancing US Seventh Army. Rebels ambushed German convoys, built roadblocks across avenues of retreat, and hunted down German stragglers. Traveling to see friends and relatives near the front lines, they obtained information on German troop dispositions and passed it on to Bank and other Allied officers. Their efforts did little, however, to impede the departure of the main German force in the area, the 11th Panzer Division.

Once the Germans had completed their withdrawal from Bank's operational area, the usefulness of the French resistance forces fell sharply. With no Germans left to bother, resistance groups busied themselves fighting one another. The nationalists clashed with the Communists, who had proven more intent on seizing towns abandoned by the Nazis than on harassing the withdrawing German forces.

The life-span of resistance operations was similarly short in most of the other areas of France where the Allies sent men and materiel. Still, even a few weeks of interference with German movements could contribute meaningfully to the Allied campaign, and many of the Jedburghs and Operational Groups did help the Maquis reach that level of achievement. General Eisenhower, now the Supreme Commander of Allied Forces in Europe, was sufficiently impressed with the results attained by the OSS in supporting the resistance that he decided, in late summer, to give the OSS more personnel, aircraft, and supplies for the mission.

Casualties among the Jedburgh teams and Operational Groups were surprisingly light. A significant minority of teams, however, fell into German hands, a misfortune that usually involved torture and ended in death. Several groups landed in the wrong place. Others were betrayed by French collaborators. One French spy notified the Germans when Marine Operational Group Union II entered the village of Montgirod in the company of French guerrillas. The Germans killed several of the guerrillas, along with a number of residents of the village, but the OSS men managed to escape. On their way back to the limestone plateau where the local Maquis were based, they ran into a German column of two hundred soldiers. The Germans chased the OSS team to a nearby village, encircling the community after the Americans took refuge in its houses. Residents begged the Americans to surrender in order to spare the village from annihilation by the Germans, whose reputation for draconian punishments had preceded them. Surrounded and outmanned, the Americans laid down their weapons. Their surrender may have contributed to the fact that the Germans sent them to POW camps instead of putting them to death.

The Jedburghs and Operational Groups were also constrained in their effectiveness by the small size of the two programs. Only 9 Jedburgh teams dropped into France during the first 19 days of the Normandy invasion. Between June 25 and the end of July, another 15 teams entered France, and 50 more arrived during August and early September, bringing the total number of Jedburghs to 222. A total of 20 Operational Groups, with roughly 640 men, dropped behind German lines. By comparison, the British Special Air Service, a unilateral British special operations force, inserted 1,574 personnel into occupied France during the same period.

The Allied resistance support effort, of which the OSS contribution was only a small fraction, was itself but a small fraction of the Allied disruption of the German reinforcement of Normandy. Although the Maquis caused some delay to German force movements by sabotaging rail lines and miring German forces in counterinsurgency operations, the other two tools for keeping German divisions away from Normandy—deception and bombing—figured far larger. Operation Bodyguard, an extraordinary deception plan involving dummy aircraft, ghost armies, and false disclosures to double agents, convinced Hitler to keep several dozen divisions in north-central France and Norway to contend with invasions that never materialized. American and British bombing of logistical targets in France did much more than the Maquis to slow the transit of German reinforcements toward Normandy, a point conceded even by the greatest OSS advocate, Donovan. The impact of Maquis depredations on the subsequent German retreat from France was similarly modest. Resistance forces accounted for the liberation of only 2 percent of France's 212 urban centers.

As the end of the war approached, with Allied thoughts turning from the defeat of the Axis powers to the future political landscape, the Jedburghs and other OSS special operators found themselves enmeshed in a multitude of struggles between nationalist and communist resistance movements for control of the postwar world. The OSS men seldom had the knowledge or the experience to influence events to the advantage of the United States. As one British officer lamented, the OSS demonstrated a "capacity for blundering into delicate European situations about which they understand little," not to mention a "permanent hankering after playing cowboys and red Indians."

In Yugoslavia, OSS Major Louis Huot threw American support behind Josip Broz Tito after concluding, quite erroneously, that "Tito was planning no Communist revolution for his country" and was instead "working out the pattern of a new and democratic popular front movement which would embrace all the elements in his community." In Italy, the OSS unwittingly abetted Communist guerrillas through the indiscriminate distribution of weapons to resistance groups. The OSS men handed out firearms to all Italian factions equally on the presumption that they would use the weapons solely to dislodge the Nazis, when in actuality the Communists used their weapons more against nationalist rivals than against the Germans.

The British, who were considerably more attuned than the Americans to the perils of communist resistance organizations, choked off assistance to communists and bolstered nationalists in key European countries during the war's last months. This foresight may ultimately have saved France, Italy, and Greece from falling into Moscow's orbit after the war.

The British were unable, however, to prevent OSS bungling from facilitating communist subversion in parts of the Far East. The most serious consequences were to be felt in French Indochina.

Like Major Huot in Yugoslavia, the OSS men who parachuted into Indochina in July 1945 took at face value Vietnamese Communist professions of commitment to an inclusive postwar government. Communist leader Ho Chi Minh assured the young OSS officers that his Viet Minh guerrillas needed American weapons only to defeat the Japanese. Yet the Viet Minh made little use of the duly provided weapons until the Japanese surrender, at which time Viet Minh troops brandished them in seizing Hanoi ahead of Vietnamese nationalists and the French. That seizure made possible Ho Chi Minh's establishment of a Marxist-Leninist dictatorship in northern Vietnam, leading to a prolonged war between France and the Viet Minh, and an ensuing war between the United States and North Vietnam.

As the death knells began to toll for the Axis powers, William Donovan embarked on a campaign to write the OSS into the federal government in permanent ink. Even in times of peace, he argued to Roosevelt, and after Roosevelt's death to Harry Truman, the nation would need a strategic intelligence agency and an arm for covert and clandestine operations. Donovan convinced friends in the media to write positive stories about the OSS, in some cases leaking classified documents on sensitive operations to showcase the organization's triumphs. A number of heavyweights weighed in on the side of the OSS, the heaviest being Eisenhower, who declared that in Europe the value of the OSS "has been so great that there should be no thought of its elimination."

Other men of influence, however, lobbied for the abolition of the OSS. Principal among them were individuals whom Donovan and his lieutenants had antagonized in recent years, mainly through intrusions into their perceived bureaucratic territory. J. Edgar Hoover and John Grombach of Army intelligence deluged President Truman and the press with allegations of incompetence and scandal within the OSS, sprinkling a good bit of fiction in with the incriminating facts. Truman received a scathing report on the OSS written by Colonel Richard Park, who had served as Roosevelt's military aide, in which it was alleged that "poor organization, lack of training and selection of many incompetent personnel has resulted in many badly conceived, overlapping and unauthorized activities with resulting embarrassment to the State Department and interference with other secret intelligence agencies of this government."

At war's end, Truman decided to close the OSS down. He transferred select pieces of the OSS to the State Department and War Department, but most, including the special operations forces, were buried *in toto* in the OSS graveyard. The influence of the harsh critiques on the decision remains something of a mystery. Truman had other reasons to shutter the agency, foremost among them the tide of demobilization that was sweeping away most of America's machinery of war.

THE SPECIAL OPERATIONS forces of the OSS ended as they had begun, their fate determined by larger presidential decisions on the centralized intelligence agency conceived by William Donovan. The OSS owed its birth at least as much to Roosevelt's fascination with the secret and the sensational as to his appreciation of the strategic value of intelligence and special operations. As in the cases of most other special units of World War II, many of Donovan's special operations forces ended up playing roles very different from what he and other senior leaders had originally envisioned, after circumstances had compelled them to redefine themselves.

The OSS experience in special operations would be remembered mainly for its successes, in particular the tactical achievements of the Jedburghs and Detachment 101. OSS proponents would at times overstate the organization's strategic impact, whether through express assertion or disregard of the relative size of OSS contributions. That remembrance would benefit a number of future endeavors in special operations, yielding new special operations forces with the permanence and usefulness that Donovan had sought. Selective memory of OSS special operations would also obscure obstacles and shortcomings, which would lead special operators and their masters to repeat the mistakes of the past.

Unlike the military's special operations forces, the OSS men in both the Pacific and European theaters operated almost entirely in the enemy's rear, which provided geographical and organizational distance from the

US military's conventional forces and hence limited friction with them. Even under these conditions, though, the special operators had cause for complaint. Detachment 101, during its early phase in India, had to swat away the paws of conventional military forces that wanted to dismantle the unit. It then had to withstand the leadership of a theater commander, General Stilwell, who seemed intent on causing it to fail. Over time, its successes gained the respect of conventional officers, including the theater commander, which led to more resources and larger missions.

In Europe, the Jedburghs and the Operational Groups were too small to register concern in the minds of conventional commanders who oversaw divisions, corps, and armies. While senior leaders gained an appreciation for the capabilities of the special operators in supporting the French resistance groups, it was akin to the appreciation of a gladiator for the mosquitos that pester his hulking adversary. The OSS special operators had accumulated a few weeks' worth of glory in the summer and fall of 1944, and then faded from view before their personnel were put back into the armed services and their command structure dissolved, along with so many other makeshift structures that Roosevelt and his lieutenants had erected in wartime haste. Had anyone predicted that the direct descendants of those forces would one day endanger the core of the world's greatest army, the prediction would have been laughed off as the wildest flight of fancy.

CHAPTER 4

THE FORGOTTEN WAR

The Korean War was nearly two months old when a young lieuten-
ant named Ralph Puckett Jr., of Tifton, Georgia, arrived at Camp
Drake. A former Japanese Army base twenty miles outside Tokyo,
Camp Drake had been rechristened by the Americans after Colonel
Royce A. Drake, who had fallen in battle against Japanese forces in the
Philippines in 1944. The US Army was now using the base as a way station
for the vast caravans of men traveling toward Korea as fast as the gears of
American bureaucracy could take them. Each man who arrived at Camp
Drake from the United States spent three days passing through adminis-
trative wickets before boarding a transport ship destined for South Korea.

Puckett had entered West Point near the end of World War II as a tall
and slender young man who dreamed of becoming a pilot in the Army
Air Forces. He had changed his mind about occupational specialty after
an infantry officer gave the cadets a presentation on the infantry, which
included a World War II film showing US Army infantrymen in mortal combat with Nazi soldiers. In reaction to the imagery of men struggling and falling in battle, Puckett asked himself, "Do I have the guts
and brains, do I have the intestinal fortitude and courage to become an
infantry leader?"

While Puckett had changed course for the infantry in expectation of
a future land war, most Americans were at this time convinced that war

had become outmoded. Reflections of that conviction could be found in the government's mothballing of battleships and its return of combat veterans to the civilian labor force. During Puckett's years at West Point, the number of men in the US armed forces plummeted from 12 million to 1.5 million, and it would sink to 600,000 by 1950. Populated mainly by the young and inexperienced, the US armed forces were woefully ill-prepared to deal with the North Koreans when their tanks rolled into South Korea on June 25, 1950.

Seeing the South Korean Army buckle beneath the weight of the initial North Korean onslaught, the United States had rushed troops into southern Korea to prevent the red flood from engulfing the entire Korean Peninsula. The first US combat forces to enter the fray, short on equipment, ammunition, and leadership, were routed time and again by the well-prepared North Koreans. By the time of Puckett's arrival in Japan, US and South Korean forces had been squeezed into the southeastern corner of the Korean Peninsula and were in danger of being pushed into the sea.

Near the end of Puckett's third day at Camp Drake, just a few hours before his scheduled departure for the 24th Infantry Division, the camp's PA system crackled alive with an order for Lieutenant Ralph Puckett to report to the headquarters building. Upon his arrival, he was escorted into an office in which an impressive-looking lieutenant colonel was seated behind a field folding desk. Puckett gave the lieutenant colonel a crisp salute. When told to stand "at ease," Puckett remained in a rigid parade rest, petrified to be scrutinized by a man of such rank and distinction.

"I'm selecting volunteers for an extremely dangerous mission behind enemy lines," Lieutenant Colonel John H. McGee told the young lieutenant.

"Sir, I volunteer," Puckett said.

Surprised at the short-circuiting of his pitch, McGee asked, "Don't you want to know what the mission is?"

"Yessir," Puckett responded, "but I volunteer."

Lieutenant Colonel McGee probed Puckett with questions about his background and character. He seemed especially interested in Puckett's captaincy of the West Point boxing team. Later, Puckett would learn that McGee himself had been on the West Point boxing team in his day.

Puckett's recent completion of jump school, a mark of superlative physical fitness, also appeared to make a positive impression on the lieutenant colonel. At the end of the interview, McGee said he had to do some more thinking about whether Puckett could join the Rangers, adding that he had already selected the lieutenants for the Ranger company.

"Sir," Puckett pleaded, "I want to be a Ranger so badly that I volunteer to take a job as a squad leader or a rifleman if you'll take me into that Ranger company."

Puckett was dismissed. For several hours he awaited the decision that could change, and possibly end, his life.

That evening, McGee informed Puckett that he had been selected to command the entire Ranger company, designated the 8th Ranger Company. Command of a company was normally reserved for a captain, but McGee was so impressed by the eager lieutenant that he rated him above all the captains he had interviewed. The two other lieutenants whom McGee selected for the new company, also recent West Point graduates, became the leaders of the unit's two platoons.

Puckett was given responsibility for finding enlisted men to fill out the unit, with the stipulation that he could not take riflemen from other units. Riflemen were in short supply, and senior infantry officers were in no mood to surrender any of them to an upstart unit commanded by a boyish lieutenant with no combat experience. Puckett fished for volunteers among the clerks, cooks, typists, and mechanics who were transiting Camp Drake. Screening personnel records, he tracked down the most promising men and interviewed those who showed an interest in the Rangers. Each interview began with the statement, "If you are not willing to volunteer for anything dangerous, you are free to leave the room now." One-third of the interviewees left at that point. From those who stayed, Puckett culled seventy-three enlisted men.

Lieutenant Puckett gave the volunteers a crash course in soldiering before the company was attached to the 25th Infantry Division in Korea. Joining the division in October 1950, they became the first Rangers to set foot on the Korean Peninsula. By this time, the North Korean Army was reeling from General Douglas MacArthur's surprise landing at Inchon, and the forces of the United Nations Command were driving into northern Korea. For its first big mission, the 8th Ranger Company would serve as an advance infantry element of the US Eighth Army in MacArthur's "Home by Christmas" offensive, scheduled for late November.

MacArthur had concluded that North Korean forces were in such sorry shape that a new offensive would wipe them from the North Korean map in a month's time. Unbeknownst to him and the rest of the UN high command, Mao Zedong had begun pouring Chinese Army forces into northern Korea to save his Communist allies from annihilation. Moving men and equipment at night, the Chinese Army had eluded the American reconnaissance aircraft that were flying back and forth over North Korea. US forces had captured soldiers who resembled and spoke like natives of China, but MacArthur and his staff decided that the Chinese Army had sent only token forces, if any at all. Some surmised that the Chinese captives belonged to the Chinese immigrant communities of North Korea. "We should not assume that Chinese Communists are committed in force," said Lieutenant General Walton W. Walker, the commander of the Eighth Army. "After all, a lot of Mexicans live in Texas."

In actuality, Mao had committed 200,000 men of the Chinese Thirteenth Army to northern Korea. Their mission was to launch an offensive against the forces of MacArthur's United Nations Command, scheduled to begin at the same time and in the same area as MacArthur's "Home by Christmas" offensive. The Chinese Thirteenth Army and the US Eighth Army were on course to collide along the Chongchon River.

A broad waterway running from the Rangrim Mountains in central Korea into the Yellow Sea, the Chongchon had long ago been the site of an epic battle between imperial China and the Korean kingdom of Goguryeo. In AD 612, China's Sui Dynasty sent an army of 1 million troops into the Korean kingdom to compel its submission to imperial authority. While the Chinese hordes were wading across the river, the Goguryeo opened a dam, unleashing a flood that swept away every man and horse in its path. An estimated 300,000 Chinese men drowned or were cut down by Goguryeo cavalry during the consequent retreat.

Of the eighty-five men in the 8th Ranger Company treading toward the Chongchon on November 25, 1950, none was aware that he was headed for one of Asia's most historic battlefields. Nor did any of them realize that this same strip of water would that night become the fault line for another great clash of empires. The fear of imminent maiming or death, the surging adrenaline of mortal combat, the witnessing of ghastly wounds, all were presumed to be a few days distant.

During the afternoon of the twenty-fifth, the Rangers approached Hill 205, their main objective for the day. A sudden zipping of bullets revealed it to be guarded by a small contingent of hostile soldiers. Although the resistance took the Rangers by surprise, they did not flinch or recoil, but instead pressed forward in methodical attack. The Rangers became entangled in a vicious struggle with men who were more numerous than they had at first appeared, and who were as intent as the Rangers to kill before being killed. Nearly half of Puckett's men suffered injury or death in a period of a few hours.

A more cautious commander might have broken off the attack after sustaining losses of such magnitude, but Puckett was not the type to relent on account of unanticipated difficulty. It would be the Chinese, late that afternoon, who decided to quit the battlefield. Ascending the hill, Puckett ordered the evacuation of the wounded and directed the remaining forty-seven Rangers to occupy the hill for the night. The forty-seven young men, buoyant from surviving and passing their first major test, carved foxholes into the frozen tundra.

With a commanding vista of the Chongchon's shallow waters, Hill 205 would be a key terrain feature in any contest for control of the river. No American, however, expected the Chongchon to be the main battleground, so the Eighth Army had sent no one but the lightly armed Ranger company to hold the hill, and it dispatched no reinforcements toward the Rangers after the debilitating afternoon skirmish with the Chinese. The thirty-eight casualties sustained by Puckett's unit might have seemed high to the 8th Ranger Company, but at army-level headquarters it was penny ante.

The Chinese Thirteenth Army, which was planning to make the Chongchon the place of decision, valued Hill 205 much more highly. Peering through the twilight from concealed positions, Chinese scouts counted the unsuspecting US soldiers as they shoveled dirt from the hillside. The scouts quickly sent their findings to a nearby headquarters, where staff officers were already making final preparations for the seizing of the

Chongchon. The Chinese commander directed a battalion of six hundred soldiers to take up attack positions around the hill after dark and then assault it frontally.

At 10 p.m., a cacophony of drums, bugles, and whistles penetrated the dark silence on Hill 205. Like a brisk autumn wind pulling leaves from their branches, the sound carried a wave of Chinese soldiers up the hill's forward slope. Lieutenant Puckett immediately called for flares, while dozing Rangers bolted awake and pointed their weapons toward the ruckus. Soon the sky was alight with flickering white incandescence, and on the ground could be seen bunches of Chinese figures scrambling up the hill. As the Rangers fired their small arms into the enemies nearest at hand, Puckett directed artillery fire onto the approaches to the hill. Chopped up by the American weaponry, the assault force soon lost its momentum, and within fifty minutes it had stalled out.

The Chinese attacked the Rangers again at 11 p.m. After the first thrusts faltered, Chinese reinforcements joined the attack. In the hillside foxholes, the former cooks and typists of the 8th Ranger Company held their ground, with few casualties. Puckett spent most of his time darting from one foxhole to another to talk with the Rangers. "I saw that my main task was encouraging my soldiers, giving them what I call a lot of 'atta-boys,'" Puckett recalled. "We can do it," he would tell the young men. "We're depending on you." A few members of the Chinese assault force came within grenade range of the Rangers, but none survived long enough to rupture the Ranger perimeter.

In the early morning, the Rangers repulsed the third and fourth attacks. The base of the hill was now crowded with dead soldiers of the Chinese People's Liberation Army. But the Chinese commander, calculating that the Rangers would run out of ammunition before he ran out of men, ordered yet another attack. Commencing at 2:45 a.m., the fifth assault was the most intense yet, with more Chinese mortar rounds and grenades finding the hill than in any of the preceding onslaughts.

Puckett, who was crouched inside a two-man foxhole with one of the platoon commanders, picked up the radiophone. Wrapping his hand around the mouthpiece to muffle the booms and shrieks of exploding ordnance, he called the artillery fire-direction center and requested another dose of howitzer shells.

"We're firing another mission," an officer replied to Puckett. "We'll give it to you as soon as we can."

"We really need it now," Puckett countered. "We've just got to have it." Before the conversation proceeded further, two mortar rounds landed in Puckett's foxhole. The blasts killed the platoon commander and left Puckett with severe wounds in both of his feet and his left shoulder and arm.

The fifth Chinese wave failed to evict the Rangers from the hill, but by its end the Rangers were desperately low on ammunition. In the dark quiet that followed, somebody hollered, "Fix bayonets and prepare for counterattack."

At 3 a.m., before any counterattack could take place, the Chinese initiated their sixth assault. Puckett, still capable of talking, told the artillery officer that the Chinese were coming in from two directions and the Rangers needed artillery immediately. The officer replied that the guns were still fixed on another sector where Americans were under attack. Peering over the lip of the foxhole, Puckett saw Chinese soldiers inside the perimeter. He asked the artillery officer to pass word that the Rangers were being overrun.

Exhilarated that the American defenses had at last been breached, Chinese soldiers swarmed over the hill, bayoneting and shooting Rangers in their holes. Once the hopelessness of the situation became clear, the remaining Rangers fled off the hill in the direction of the American rear. One Ranger picked up Lieutenant Puckett and carried him to a small draw. Too tired to carry Puckett farther, the Ranger dragged the company commander down a ravine with the help of another man, reaching the bottom of the hill at daybreak. Other Rangers took Puckett to an aid station, from which he resumed the direction of artillery fire onto Hill 205.

Headcounts determined that only twenty-one of the forty-seven Rangers returned from Hill 205 alive. Seventeen of the twenty-one survivors had been wounded. Eleven men were missing, their bodies never recovered.

THE US ARMY had begun the Korean War devoid of special operations forces and any other forces trained in what were commonly considered special operations. President Truman did not share Roosevelt's fascination with special units or secret warfare, and even had he shared it, he would have been handicapped by want of manpower and funds in a period of mass demobilization. Special operations forces came into existence in Korea because of tactical requirements identified by military commanders, requirements that in some cases would disappear before they could be met. As in World War II, special units would have to contend not only with enemy forces, but also with friendly forces who doubted that the returns justified the investment.

The impetus for the creation of Puckett's 8th Ranger Company, and the other Ranger companies that followed it, had its roots in the opposing side. During the North Korean Army's summertime advance, fifteen-man teams of North Korean commandos had disguised themselves as civilian refugees and infiltrated behind South Korean lines to ambush convoys, raid command posts, and demolish bridges. The effectiveness of these commandos convinced a number of well-placed Americans that the United States needed similar forces.

Among those Americans was Lieutenant Colonel John H. McGee, who at the time was serving on the Eighth Army staff. McGee had been captured in the Philippines in 1942, then had escaped when a US submarine torpedoed the Japanese ship that was moving him to a new camp. Swimming from the sinking ship to the nearby island of Mindanao, McGee was found in a bedraggled state by curious natives. They took him to Colonel Wendell Fertig, an American engineer who had eluded the Japanese at Corregidor and organized guerrilla forces on the island. McGee joined the guerrilla effort, gaining on-the-job training and experience that would make him one of the few men in the Eighth Army in 1950 who knew much of anything about special operations.

McGee advised his Eighth Army bosses to create Ranger units in Korea in order to give the North Koreans a taste of their own behind-the-lines medicine. His proposal caught the attention of Army Chief of Staff J. Lawton Collins during a visit to Korea in August. An approving Collins directed the Eighth Army to form a Ranger company "to infiltrate through enemy lines and attack command posts, artillery, tank parks, and key communications centers or facilities." McGee promptly traveled to Japan to find leaders for the first Ranger company, the one that Puckett was to command.

While Puckett was whipping his enlisted men into shape, General Collins ordered the creation of a Ranger training center in the United States to generate additional Ranger companies. Established at Fort Benning, Georgia, the new center was staffed by World War II veterans who had served in the Rangers, the First Special Service Force, or Merrill's Marauders. The new Rangers were required to be airborne qualified, so recruiters sought volunteers mainly from the 11th and 82nd Airborne divisions, with preference for those who had scored well on intelligence tests, demonstrated initiative, or excelled at hand-to-hand combat. Trainees were put through fifty-mile speed marches, and any man who failed to keep pace was taken away in a white-flagged jeep. The course had a "Hell Week," during which the trainees parachuted at low altitude, maneuvered in small groups across a forty-nine-square-mile area, and performed acts of sabotage.

The revival of Ranger training captured the imagination of the home front. Newsmen catered to the public's fascination with elite units, in a manner certain to nauseate other military personnel. In one article on the Rangers, dated November 12, 1950, the *Ledger-Enquirer* of Columbus, Georgia, asserted, "Each is a one-man gang who can sneak up to an enemy sentry, chop off his head, and catch it before it makes noise by hitting the ground."

On the very day that the Chinese attacked six times up Hill 205 against Puckett's Rangers, the troop ship USNS *C. G. Morton* left the United States for Korea carrying the 1st Ranger Company and a variety of other military units. Soon after the ship left port, a voice announced over the ship's loudspeaker that the North Koreans were on their last legs and the war would be over by the time the ship reached its destination. A large number of US servicemen cheered and clapped each other on the back in celebration. The Rangers, however, sat in quiet gloom, distraught that fortune had stolen their chance to prove their mettle and add their names to the nation's registry of heroes. Several days later, after the unexpected guests from the Chinese Thirteenth Army had thrown back the Americans at the Chongchon River and spoiled the "Home by Christmas" offensive, the loudspeaker of the *C. G. Morton* shared the news that the Chinese had entered North Korea in force, and thus the war would be longer than anticipated. Now the Rangers jumped for joy while other soldiers moped about in dejection.

Fort Benning churned out a total of six Ranger companies for deployment to Korea, all of them reaching the Korean peninsula between December 1950 and March 1951. Each was attached to a division and assigned missions by the leadership of the division or its subordinate regiments. By the time these Ranger units reached the front, the huge north-south shifts in the location of the battle line had come to an end and the war had settled into a stalemate, with the combatants squaring off from trenches near the 38th parallel. Several major offensives were still to follow, but the resultant swings in the battle line were limited by the fact that both sides had built up several layers of defense, so that front-line penetrations were usually contained by secondary and tertiary lines of defense.

The Chinese and North Korean forces were deployed so densely near the battle line that infiltrating Rangers into the enemy's rear unnoticed was nearly impossible. Once detected, a Ranger company was likely to be engaged by bigger and more heavily equipped enemy forces, which would compel American division commanders to send their regular units to bail them out. As a consequence, conventional commanders rarely ordered their Ranger companies to conduct the behind-the-lines raids for which they had been created.

While great time and effort had been invested in the airborne capabilities of the men who joined the Rangers, and many men had been injured or killed practicing their jumps, only once did the Rangers make use of their airborne training, in Operation Tomahawk. That operation, in which two Ranger companies were attached to the 187th Airborne Regimental Combat Team, largely failed in its intended purpose of trapping and destroying large enemy forces. The minor clashes between American and enemy forces during the operation, claiming just nineteen Ranger casualties, were less eventful than the preceding air drop, during which eighty-four Rangers were injured.

Only once did the Rangers make use of their amphibious capabilities, in the 4th Ranger Company's assault on the Hwachon Dam. In April 1951, the 1st Cavalry Division sent the Rangers to the dam to close the gates and destroy the hoists after the Pukhan River, which twisted through bridges, military headquarters, and supply depots in the UN's rear, rose seven feet in a three-hour period. During the black of night, the Rangers crossed the reservoir at the top of the dam by boat and marched to within half a mile of the gates, at which point a Chinese machine gun opened fire. The bullets punctured two Rangers and convinced the others to dive to the earth. Ranger forward observers called in mortar and artillery fire while Lieutenant Michael D. Healy and five other Rangers slipped around the enemy's flank. Healy's team, designated the company's "killer" element, knocked out enemy heavy weapons and reached the summit with a speed that astonished the other Rangers. Before the Americans could go farther, however, several hundred Chinese soldiers attacked. The Rangers repulsed the onslaught, but by the time the Chinese relented, the Rangers had exhausted most of their ammunition, necessitating the termination of the raid short of its objective.

American division and regimental commanders assigned a miscellany of regular infantry missions to the Ranger companies. Because the Rangers had been handpicked for their combativeness, smarts, and physical prowess, commanders often assigned them the most difficult infantry missions, such as spearheading an assault or defending an especially vulnerable point. Other common uses of the Rangers were patrols and ambushes in the no-man's-land between friendly and enemy lines. The Rangers were better prepared than other units for most of the tasks they performed, but they were tasks that regular units could perform nonetheless. As Ranger units accumulated casualties in conventional clashes, complaints mounted among Ranger officers that the Rangers were being misused, their special capabilities squandered. The complaints seldom went anywhere, for the Ranger units were led by captains and lieutenants who lacked the rank, combat experience, and resources to hold sway on matters that were decided by generals.

More influential than Ranger officer complaints about this state of affairs were conventional officer complaints about it. In the spring of 1951, several division commanders concluded that the tactical benefits arising from occasional exploitation of the Rangers' behind-the-lines capabilities were not commensurate with the harm to regular units arising from the diversion of human capital to the Rangers. They recommended dissolving the Ranger companies and sending their men back to regular units.

To buttress the point, conventional officers cited US Army historian S. L. A. Marshall's landmark 1947 study *Men Against Fire*, which had found that less than 25 percent of US infantrymen in World War II had actually fired their weapons. If only one-quarter of infantrymen were tough enough to shoot, then taking men out of the infantry for elite units was liable to tear the martial spirit out of the regular Army. "In each squad, you may have only one man who really wants to fight," one general remarked. "You need him there to influence the other men." With "that one man volunteering to be a Ranger," it "leaves that squad bare of inspiration to fight."

Such arguments resonated with General Matthew Ridgway, the US Army airborne officer who assumed command of all UN forces in Korea in April 1951 after Truman sacked MacArthur. One month into his tenure, Ridgway informed the Army that the Ranger units in Korea were not providing enough tactical bang for the buck that they were costing the rest of the Army. He recommended the deactivation of all Ranger units in Korea.

As THE RANGERS were sputtering out, a different set of special operations forces was taking shape in Korea. These forces were like a younger brother to the Rangers, as they, too, were sired by Lieutenant Colonel John H. McGee. In character, though, they bore greater resemblance to a more distant relative, the OSS special operations forces, for they had support of resistance movements as their primary mission.

North Korean resistance fighters had been waging guerrilla war against the North Korean government even before the Korean War erupted in June 1950. The resistance was concentrated in Hwanghae, a coastal province whose fishermen provided North Korea's population with much of its protein. Culturally, the 1.8 million residents of Hwanghae were closer to the residents of South Korea than to those in the North. In October 1950, word arrived in Hwanghae that the US Eighth Army was pressing north toward the province, inciting a wave of violence against Communist Party officials and policemen. Communist security forces responded with bitter reprisals across Hwanghae in which hundreds of rebels and their supporters perished. A cycle of atrocity and counter-atrocity followed, until finally the steamroller of the Eighth Army induced the North Korean policemen, soldiers, and apparatchiks to pack their suitcases and flee northward.

Anti-Communist organizers ran local affairs in Hwanghae for just a few months before the massive counterstroke of the Chinese Thirteenth Army sent them fleeing to islands off the coast. On January 8, 1951, the US Eighth Army learned that 10,000 North Korean guerrillas had gathered on the islands adjacent to Hwanghae. A South Korean Navy report described the refugees as "desperate, hungry, poorly armed, and mad as hell." McGee convinced Eighth Army headquarters to create a new organization for supporting the resistance forces, which was called the "Attrition Section." Becoming the organization's first commander, McGee sent American officers to the islands to train the partisans along with American weapons and ammunition to provision them.

The partisans began raids on the coast of Hwanghae in March 1951. Inserted by boat, the first team advanced on foot to villages known for their hatred of communism, where they recruited some of the male population into their ranks. They scored an early success with an attack on a police station where Communist Party leaders had convened for a meeting. While the officials were discussing party business, the guerrillas cut the telephone line to the building and placed small blocks of C3 explosive at the windows and doorways. Detonating the explosives simultaneously by means of Primacord, they then threw grenades into the building before storming inside to kill anyone who was not yet dead.

Over the next four and a half months, the partisans killed a reported 280 Communist officials and several hundred North Korean security personnel. They blew bridges, severed telephone wires, and plundered enemy supply warehouses. In response, the enemy beefed up security forces in the region from 2,000 to 30,000.

Encouraged by the early returns, the Attrition Section sent more partisan units to raid coastal Hwanghae. To deposit partisans ashore inconspicuously, the Americans put them in fishing junks, which were outfitted with hidden diesel engines to enable a quick getaway. Radio antennae were concealed inside masts, and recoilless rifles inside collapsible walls.

On paper, the American officers were only "advisers" to the partisans. In practice, they were commanding officers. The first Americans assigned to lead the partisan units knew little about Korea or its people, so their ability to lead depended heavily on their aptitude for understanding new circumstances and cultures. The culture of Hwanghae proved different from American culture in a multitude of ways, some highly pertinent to the development of resistance forces. Adviser Archie Johnston developed a list of five rules he considered vital to American leadership of the partisans: "1. Never allow the partisans to question an order from an Advisor. 2. Never ask a Korean to do anything; tell him. 3. Never lie to a Korean. 4. Never get drunk in front of a Korean. 5. Never make a 'pass' at a Korean woman."

In September 1951, the Communists extended their tentacles toward the islands where the partisans were based. US ships and planes had shot up most of the seacraft in North Korea, so the enemy decided to cross on foot at low tide, when the islands were connected to the mainland by a mud landbridge for several hours. American officers, having anticipated such sallies, had directed the partisans to seed the landbridge with mines and booby-trapped napalm drums. Using railroad ties and sandbags, the partisans had built bunkers facing toward the coast and stocked them with machine guns and crates of bullets. The first North Koreans who attempted to cross the mud were obliterated by streams of machine-gun rounds and orange blossoms of napalm. The partisans reported burying 286 North Korean corpses. After another foiled North Korean attack, US Air Force photos corroborated a partisan claim that 3,000 enemy soldiers had died. The enemy kept up the attacks in the months to come, and in a few cases were able to take islands by sheer numerical superiority, but partisan counterattacks ensured that the resistance retained control of its main island bases.

In March 1951, the Attrition Section started parachuting Korean partisans and American officers into North Korea. Many of the men disappeared immediately. Most North Korean civilians were less supportive of the anti-Communists than were the residents of Hwanghae, and hence more likely to report infiltrators to the authorities. A few of the airborne teams, the most successful of the lot, were able to sabotage railroad tracks for a short period before the partisan headquarters stopped receiving radio transmissions from them. The largest team to be inserted by air had ninety-seven men, it being one of two teams whose purpose was to establish a permanent base area in North Korea. For six months, this group maintained intermittent radio contact, but under circumstances that suggested it had been compromised early on. None of its men ever returned.

The disappearance of American officers during the first airborne missions led the Attrition Section to discontinue the parachuting of American personnel, leaving only Koreans to participate in subsequent airborne drops. The fact that Caucasians stuck out amid the Korean population and could not speak the language were the main reasons cited for the new policy, though this explanation came increasingly into question as more and more Koreans disappeared without any interruption in the program. Of the 389 partisans parachuted by the Attrition Section and its successor organizations into North Korea over the course of the war, only a handful came back.

In the business of fomenting resistance in enemy-held territory, the Eighth Army's Attrition Section faced stiff competition from the Central Intelligence Agency. Breathed into life by the National Security Act of 1947, the CIA laid claim to most of the functions that had formerly belonged to the Office of Strategic Services, including not only intelligence collection and analysis but also covert operations. General MacArthur, wary as ever of intrusions into his theater, was no more inclined to cooperate with the CIA in Korea than he had been with the OSS in the previous war, and therefore the Army avoided providing the military assets the CIA wanted and needed for operations behind North Korean lines. The CIA returned the favor by paying off US Army personnel clerks at Camp Drake to divert Americans with resistance experience to the CIA.

The CIA found the other armed services distinctly more receptive to its requests for assistance. Marines and Navy Frogmen helped train the CIA's Korean personnel and, in some cases, led them ashore on coastal raids. Air Force aircraft dropped hundreds of the CIA's Korean operatives behind enemy lines. The survival rate of those men was not much better than that for men parachuted in by the Attrition Section. As word spread that few of the operatives were making it back, the Air Force began equipping cockpits with a switch that dumped out the entire cargo compartment, parachutists and all, in the event that second thoughts kept the men from jumping at the appointed hour.

The Korean partisans controlled by the US Army claimed to have inflicted 69,000 casualties on the enemy. In addition, the partisans gave themselves credit for the sinking of 195 boats, the dropping of 80 bridges, the destruction of 3,800 tons of food, and the ruination of 2,400 farm animals. A large percentage of the reported tallies came from operations for which Americans were not present, encouraging the view among American officers that the partisan numbers were grossly inflated. A study conducted by the Johns Hopkins University Operations Research Office shortly afterward concluded that "the figures for casualties inflicted probably are 3 to 10 times too high, and further, many of the killed and wounded were civilians."

The partisan operations never caused the Communists serious supply problems, for 94 percent of operations took place in western and southern Hwanghae Province, far to the west of the main enemy supply routes. Partisan operations did exert some strategic influence by compelling the Communists to divert forces to deal with the partisans and guard against the possibility of seaborne invasion that their presence might portend. Between 20,000 and 50,000 enemy troops were tied down on the western coast at any one time. In a war where the combined strength of North Korean and Chinese forces reached 1.5 million men, such a diversion could not be strategically decisive, but neither was it insignificant.

For the South Korean government of Syngman Rhee, the US Army's management of the partisan units engendered more concern than contentment. South Korea's leaders were skeptical about the value of guerrilla operations in North Korea, and wary of dealing with an autonomous armed force over the long term. As a result of their opposition, the United States halted recruitment in February 1953, by which time the partisans had grown to 22,000 men, and at war's end Rhee's government persuaded the Americans to evacuate the partisans to the south of the negotiated armistice line, which was well below Hwanghae.

Few members of the resistance were especially eager to pull out, given that they had been seeking the liberation of a province that was now being conceded to North Korea. During a meeting of top resistance figures, one man was adamant that they should stay, but several others recommended withdrawal as the most pragmatic solution. They asked the lone American attendee to leave so they could continue the discussion in private. As the American was cooling his heels outside the tent, the Korean voices grew louder and angrier. Then the American heard a gunshot. A few minutes later he was invited to come back in. The man who had opposed withdrawal was no longer present. "We are now unanimous," said one of the remaining men. "We will withdraw."

It was during the Korean War that Army special operations forces entered into marriage with Army psychological warfare. In early 1951, the Army formed the Office of the Chief of Psychological Warfare at Fort Bragg, North Carolina, under the command of Brigadier General Robert A. McClure, to improve the Army's capabilities in what was variously termed psychological warfare, information warfare, and propaganda. Hiring artists, journalists, and technicians from the private sector, McClure organized a Loudspeaker and Leaflet Company for deployment to the front lines in Korea. The unit fielded vehicle-mounted and man-pack loudspeaker systems that blared carefully scripted messages at the trenches of the North Korean and Chinese armies. Dubbed "bullet magnets" by the grunts, the loudspeakers attracted enemy attention that their crews did not want, but that combat commanders found useful in locating enemy weapons.

McClure did not receive ownership of the Ranger companies or the Eighth Army units that worked with the Korean partisans, but the Army did authorize him to form a new Special Warfare Division, to be focused primarily on guerrilla warfare. This arrangement derived from the quite tenuous argument that guerrilla warfare undermined the enemy's will and thus was a component of psychological warfare. McClure filled the upper ranks of his Special Warfare Division with veterans of World War II special operations, including Colonel Aaron Bank of the OSS, Lieutenant

Colonel Marvin Waters of Merrill's Marauders, and Colonel Wendell Fertig and Lieutenant Colonel Russell W. Volckmann of the guerrilla campaigns in the Philippines.

Once the new staff had arrived, McClure informed them that he intended to create a new and permanent organization for special operations. Volckmann proposed a "Special Forces Command," which would include the Rangers and all other special operations forces. McClure liked Volckmann's concept, and was inclined toward filling the prospective command with Ranger or Ranger-like light infantry units. The Army's familiarity with the Rangers, McClure reasoned, would make the top brass more amenable to these units than to other special units, such as those resembling OSS forebears.

Colonel Bank argued for the creation of a different type of special operations force patterned on the Jedburghs. Called Special Forces, they were designed for supporting guerrilla forces in Europe in a future war with the Soviet Union. As Bank saw it, these forces should avoid involvement in raids, amphibious landings, and other types of operations associated with the Rangers, because those operations were less valuable strategically and could be undertaken by infantry units whose cultivation was less costly and time-consuming.

General Maxwell Taylor, who had attained worldwide fame as the commander of the 101st Airborne Division in World War II and who was now the US Army's chief of operations, convened a meeting on August 23, 1951, to determine the future of Army special operations forces. The meeting began with Taylor and his staff remarking upon dissatisfaction with Rangers among the senior commanders in Korea. They noted that lack of language capabilities and the nature of the conflict had restricted the Rangers to shallow penetrations of enemy lines. Bank and McClure, seated in the audience, relished each jab at the Rangers. Every negative word increased the likelihood that the Army would shut down the Rangers, thereby freeing up troop spaces for new special operations forces and bolstering the case for omitting Ranger-type operations from their repertoire.

When Taylor's staff raised the question of employing special units in deep-penetration operations and guerrilla warfare, McClure nudged Bank and whispered, "Here's your golden opportunity. Go to it!" Bank came forward to present his Special Forces concept. He explained that the new forces would be modeled on the Jedburghs and Operational Groups of the OSS, emphasizing the achievements of the OSS special operators to show that he was not just floating in abstract theory. The Special Forces units would have fifteen men apiece, and each unit would be capable of organizing indigenous guerrilla forces of up to 1,500 men.

At the end of the meeting, General Taylor decreed that all Ranger units would be deactivated. The Ranger training center, he said, would be turned into a component of the US Army's infantry school and would train select members of the regular Army in infiltration, scouting, and raiding skills. Taylor gave a nod to Bank's proposed Special Forces and authorized a training center for psychological warfare and special operations.

As McClure contemplated how he would set up this new training center, Lieutenant Colonel Volckmann urged him to separate special operations from psychological warfare. According to Volckmann, the conventional military looked down upon psychological warfare as a repository for untrustworthy "longhairs" who were prone to exaggerating the impact of leaflets and radio broadcasts, and Volckmann did not want this "stigma" to "rub off on Special Forces." Furthermore, Volckmann worried that the "longhairs" would dominate the leadership of the center and drag the special operators along by the collar.

Colonel Bank brushed off Volckmann's worries with the airy confidence of an old deckhand counseling a sailor's apprentice. "We'll supersede those longhairs, you watch," Bank assured Volckmann. "They'll have a few Psy War units there amounting to perhaps 150 men. Compared to what we hope to have, that'll be peanuts."

McClure decided to keep special operations within the Psychological Warfare Center. The umbrella of psychological warfare, he recognized, would reduce the visibility of special operations and hence tamp down opposition from conventional military men who distrusted special operators but merely ridiculed psychological warriors. Some observers would credit his cloaking of special operations beneath the psychological warfare umbrella with averting the elimination of the Special Forces in their infancy.

Activated in May 1952 at Fort Bragg, the Psychological Warfare Center consisted of two departments—Psychological Warfare and Special Operations. They were not to be the most harmonious of partners. Some officers in both departments doubted that the two fields had enough in common to warrant inclusion in the same center. Because of classification concerns and the desire to minimize scrutiny from the regular Army, most of the publicity given to the new center accentuated Psychological Warfare rather than Special Operations, giving rise to complaints from the Special Operations department that it was not getting its share of the limelight. Special operators also groused that the school's student handbook was "slanted heavily toward Psychological Warfare to the detriment of Special Forces," and that "the Special Forces student, therefore, will look upon himself as a 'country cousin' to the Psychological Warfare Center."

On June 19, 1952, the US Army formed the first Special Forces Group at Fort Bragg. It was designated the 10th Special Forces Group, to make the Soviets think another nine were sneaking around somewhere, and placed under the command of Colonel Aaron Bank. The 10th Group's stated purpose was to wage guerrilla warfare behind Soviet lines in tandem with indigenous resistance organizations. The workhorse of the Special Forces Group was the fifteen-man Operational Detachment Alpha, called ODA or A-team for short, each having a captain as commander, a first lieutenant as executive officer, and thirteen enlisted personnel. The Special Forces company consisted of ten A-teams and one B-team, the latter a headquarters element led by a major. The battalion had three companies and a C-team led by a lieutenant colonel, whose seniority would make him a more credible counterpart to senior resistance leaders.

Colonel Bank issued stringent recruiting standards in the belief that operating with indigenous guerrillas behind enemy lines "required maturity, expertise, dedication, and leadership, and only the best possessed these essential qualities." Recruits were required to be at least twenty-one years of age, with a rank of sergeant or above and a superior personnel record. They had to be airborne trained or ready to receive airborne training, and they had to express a willingness to parachute into enemy-held territory wearing civilian garb. Preference was given to those who could speak a European language.

Bank anticipated a flood of volunteers, with heavy representation from highly desirable groups like OSS veterans, Ranger veterans, airborne troopers, and foreign-born individuals who had been accepted into the US armed forces. To his dismay, the 10th Group received only a trickle of applications. The security classification of the group's activities made publicity so difficult that large numbers of soldiers knew nothing of the Special Forces or their recruitment drive. Commanders in airborne units and other Army units, worried by the prospect of losing their most enthusiastic and fit men, obstructed the distribution of applications for the Special Forces or made sure that completed applications got lost in the administrative paper shuffle. Career management officers, moreover, advised potential candidates that service in the Special Forces would reduce their chances for promotion.

Obtaining foreign-born personnel for the Special Forces proved especially problematic. Under the Lodge Bill, the Army had been authorized to recruit 12,500 aliens, but the number of applications received, not to mention the number of worthy applications, came nowhere near that sum. By mid-1952, only 5,272 men had applied for the Lodge Bill billets, of whom only 411 were deemed suitable for security clearances. Only 211 of those ended up enlisting in the Army. By late 1952, just 22 Lodge Bill men had signed up for Special Forces.

In the face of these difficulties, Bank concentrated on siphoning manpower from a few oases of suitable men. The noncommissioned officer corps of the Army Airborne became a top source of enlisted recruits. For officers, the 10th Group drew heavily on the Army Reserves, where officers were less concerned with attaining high rank and more open to unconventional assignments. Charles Simpson, one of the first men to join the Special Forces, observed that the early Special Forces officers included "freethinkers who had never adapted to the spit and polish of the peacetime, palace-guard, 82nd Airborne Division," and "innovators and imaginative people who wanted to try something new and challenging, who chafed at rigid discipline, and who didn't care what the career managers at the Pentagon said or believed." The oases did not, however, satisfy all of the needs of the 10th Group, and in the end the group took in some men who were special only in the sense that no one else in the Army wanted them.

Bank saw to it that the training regimen of the 10th Special Forces Group resembled the Jedburgh training he had received during World War II. Trainees learned techniques of guerrilla warfare, sabotage, and espionage as well as the Fairbairn style of hand-to-hand combat that had been taught to OSS trainees. At Camp Carson in Colorado, they marched, patrolled, climbed, and made camp in the snow of Pike's Peak and the Garden of the Gods. Language training and area studies took place at forward locations in Europe.

While Bank concentrated on preparing the Special Forces for World War III in Europe, several dozen members of the Special Forces were shipped off to the war of the here and now, arriving in Korea during the spring of 1953 for the conflict's final months. Americans who encountered the newcomers generally came away less than impressed. Officers on the staff of the Combined Command Reconnaissance Activities Far East faulted the Special Forces personnel for their lack of training in Korean culture and skills like foreign weapons, small boats, and supply. A high percentage of the Special Forces arrivals failed a basic map-reading test.

Some individuals who witnessed the Special Forces in Korea contended that "not enough attention had been given in the initial selection of candidates, particularly in respect to temperamental, psychological, and intellectual factors." At the UN headquarters responsible for partisan forces, staff members reported that a number of Special Forces soldiers "were too young and immature" and had shown up with mistaken hopes that they would all get to jump out of airplanes. Certain Special Forces personnel were said to be "contemptuous and hostile toward the Koreans," and they appeared "to have had no desire toward achieving a better understanding of another culture."

In June 1953, mass protests against the Communist authorities in East Berlin triggered a decision in Washington to send the 10th Special Forces Group into Germany to support the opposition. East German and Soviet security forces crushed the uprising before the 10th Group could get near, but the event did lead to the deployment of the 10th Special Forces Group to the Bavarian town of Bad Tölz. Bank and his men took up residence in a compound that the Nazis had used to train soldiers, which they found a vast improvement over the Spartan barracks they had inhabited at Fort

Bragg. Bachelor officers occupied a requisitioned hotel while married officers and men lived in requisitioned houses. Single enlisted men stayed in "private" rooms, which meant that only six men occupied each room. The compound had a soccer field, an outdoor track, a large mess hall, and a sparkling kitchen replete with modern electric appliances. Training exercises made use of the compound's airstrip, indoor swimming pool, and finely appointed gym, and the nearby mountains and forests provided excellent grounds for the practice of guerrilla war.

Only half of the 10th Group ended up deploying to Bad Tölz, the other half remaining at Fort Bragg to become the nucleus of a new Special Forces Group, the 77th, redesignated the 7th Group a few years afterward. In 1957, the 1st Special Forces Group took shape at Japan's Camp Drake, birthplace of Puckett's Rangers. Opposition to special units among the regular Army prevented the Special Forces from attaining the rapid growth that McClure and Bank had envisioned. By the end of the 1950s, the three Special Forces Groups had a total of just 2,000 men.

Although the relatively modest pace of expansion left the Special Forces as Lilliputians in the land of the big green Army, it did allow the special warriors to surpass the psychological warriors in numbers. As Bank had predicted, numerical superiority enabled the Special Forces to shake the psychological warfare yoke. In 1956, the Psychological Warfare Center was renamed the Special Warfare Center and School, and at the Pentagon, the Office of the Chief of Psychological Warfare became the Office of the Chief of Special Warfare. The Army's psychological warriors thereafter were the indisputable "country cousins."

Other rivalries, though, would present the Special Forces with more formidable and lasting problems. Because supporting resistance movements in Europe was the raison d'être of the new Special Forces, Bank and McClure were intent on obtaining information concerning Europe's potential resistance groups. No one in the Army possessed that information, so they turned to the one organization that did, the CIA. When pressed by McClure for information on such groups, the CIA stonewalled, claiming bureaucratic privilege like a colonial viceroy waving off meddlesome visitors from the ministry of colonies. General Walter Bedell Smith, the CIA director, notified the Army in March 1952 that his agency was not meeting McClure's requests "because the information requested impinges directly upon secret operations in which we are currently engaged and for which, at this time, we are solely responsible."

The Air Force, which in 1947 had been split off from the Army into a separate service, piqued McClure by attempting to elbow its way into a bigger position in "unconventional warfare," the newest moniker for the support of armed resistance movements. Air Force officers contended that their service's insertion of Korean operatives into North Korea for the CIA and its resupply of CIA-sponsored guerrillas showed that the Air Force occupied a seat of prominence and distinction in the court of unconventional warfare. McClure lobbied with the Joint Chiefs of Staff to compel the Air Force to transfer all aircraft currently supporting the CIA to the mission of supporting his Army special warfare branch, but to no avail.

The Air Force went so far as to form an Air Resupply and Communications Service dedicated to the conduct of unconventional warfare. Colonel Bob Fish, who was summoned to Washington in 1951 to help develop the new organization because of his World War II experience in clandestine air operations, later described the whole Air Force effort as an exercise in amateurism. "There was a small group—a clique, you could call it—in the Pentagon at the time that was trying to grab off a great big mission that didn't really belong to the Air Force," Fish said. "They figured, if they could swing it, it would mean promotions for them and all that kind of good stuff. They really hadn't thought the thing through very well."

The commander of the Air Resupply and Communications Service, Brigadier General Monro MacCloskey, attempted to make the unit permanent as the end of the Korean War approached. Foreseeing stiffer bureaucratic competition for resources, he ordered his subordinates to execute Operation Think, which consisted of brainstorming for peacetime missions for the unit to perform. The results of Operation Think failed to impress the postwar budget cutters. After the Korean armistice, the Air Resupply and Communications Service was deactivated and the Air Force's involvement in unconventional warfare restricted to providing air transport at the request of the Army and CIA. Because of those decisions, Air Force special operations forces would be constrained in their subsequent acquisition of missions and in their organizational divergence from the rest of the Air Force, setting them on a profoundly different course from Army special operations forces.

PRESIDENT HARRY TRUMAN, unlike his predecessor, displayed no particular interest in special operations forces. The revival of special operations forces during the Korean War was driven solely by military leaders and guided mainly by officers' remembrances of World War II. The scarcity of involvement from the political leadership spared the special operations forces from the meddling of the uninitiated, though it did not avert a good many other decisions that ultimately undermined the cause of special operations forces, such as the initial emphasis on Ranger units and the focusing of the Special Forces on Europe.

During the Korean War, SOF again struggled to find missions that justified the resources invested in them. The Rangers found few opportunities to operate behind enemy lines or to use their special airborne and amphibious capabilities. This problem led ultimately to the dissolution of the Rangers, which in turn opened the door to the creation of the Special Forces—whom the nation would never end up using in their original core activity of supporting resistance movements in Europe.

Geography, time, and the size of the opposing armies made it impossible for special operations forces to alter the Korean War's strategic momentum. At times, the Rangers made outstanding tactical contributions by performing particularly difficult infantry tasks, which explains why some conventional commanders welcomed them. Those contributions, however, were largely offset by the reduction in quality of the other US ground forces resulting from Ranger absorption of superior personnel. In the case of the Korean partisans whom US special operations forces supported, resistance activities compelled the enemy to divert troops from the main battle line, which provided some tactical advantages but had only modest strategic impact.

For conventional officers who were inclined to think ill of special units, the brief and problematic history of the Rangers in Korea confirmed that special operations forces were a wasteful diversion of talent. The poor results of the deployment of Special Forces into Korea provided them further ammunition. Thanks in part to the subsuming of special warfare under psychological warfare, the Special Forces managed to work their way onto the scene without attracting much notice from the regular Army, but conventional officers consistently obstructed their efforts to recruit men away from conventional units.

By the end of the 1950s, the outlook for special operations forces appeared bleak. The Rangers were gone. Early historians of the Korean War were treating special operations forces much like the historians of World War II had—as minor sideshows. Within a war that was to acquire the nametag of "the Forgotten War," the special operations forces were to become some of the most forgotten units. The recently minted Army Special Forces had not grown to the extent their champions had desired, and the sole war-zone deployment on their resumé, during the last months of the Korean War, had been a shambles. The special operations forces of the Navy and Air Force were even smaller and more obscure. Their existence under siege, the special operations forces entered the 1960s anticipating renewed struggles to keep the conventional forces from swallowing them up, with the odds heavily favoring the sharks over the minnows.

CHAPTER 5

VIETNAM

Within the pantheon of America's special operations forces, the bust of William J. Donovan is rivaled in prominence by only one other, that of another son of Irish immigrants, John F. Kennedy. Born in the Irish mecca of Boston one month after the United States entered World War I, Kennedy grew up in a country that looked down on Irish Americans as second-class citizens, much as it had thirty-five years earlier during Donovan's boyhood. In terms of social status and upbringing, however, Kennedy was closer to Franklin Roosevelt than to Donovan. Born into the Irish American nobility, he was the son of Joseph Kennedy, a fabulously wealthy financier, and Rose FitzGerald Kennedy, daughter of Boston mayor John Francis FitzGerald. Attending the Choate School and Harvard, long the bastions of Anglo-Saxon Protestants, young John Kennedy used his charisma and charm not just to fit in but to gain entrance to exclusive institutions such as Harvard's Spee Club and Hasty Pudding.

After graduation from college, on the eve of Pearl Harbor, Kennedy joined the US Navy. In August 1943, a Japanese destroyer rammed his torpedo boat in the middle of the night, breaking the boat asunder and dumping its crew into the ocean. Kennedy and most of the other sailors swam through shark-infested waters to a nearby island, where they drank coconut milk for six days until their rescue. Joseph Kennedy, as part of his life-long campaign to propel his son to high office, arranged for a Hollywood studio to turn the episode into a feature film.

In 1946, John F. Kennedy gained election to the US House of Representatives at twenty-nine years of age, and six years later he won a seat in the US Senate. An ardent anti-Communist, Kennedy chided the Eisenhower administration for shrinking America's land armies and relying on nuclear deterrence to protect America's overseas interests. In Kennedy's view, the United States needed to enlarge its ground forces, including its special operations forces, so that it had the option of intervening militarily in limited conflicts, rather than having to choose only between nuclear brinksmanship and capitulation. Of special concern to Kennedy was the subversion of third-world governments by Communist insurgencies, which the Soviet Union and China were promoting in order to spread the global revolution without massive invasions that could incite US intervention, as had occurred in Korea in 1950.

By the time of Kennedy's narrow victory over Richard Nixon in the presidential election of November 1960, Communist insurgents were gaining ground in Laos, South Vietnam, Colombia, and Venezuela, and other countries seemed on the verge of joining the list of insurgent hotbeds. The Soviets and Chinese had initially sought to conceal their support for third-world Communist rebels, most of whom were posing as independent nationalists to attract supporters and deceive the antibodies of anticommunism. But on January 6, 1961, two weeks before Kennedy was sworn in, Soviet premier Nikita Khrushchev made plain the Communist bloc's use of insurgency as a Cold War weapon. The world was progressing toward communism, Khrushchev said in a globally publicized speech, and the Communist powers would hasten the progress by supporting "wars of national liberation" in the third world.

On the date of the presidential inauguration, a sunny but bitterly cold day in Washington, Kennedy called upon Americans to devote themselves to a crusade against the Communist scourge. "In the long history of the world, only a few generations have been granted the role of defending freedom in its hour of maximum danger," Kennedy averred. "The energy, the faith, the devotion which we bring to this endeavor will light our country and all who serve it—and the glow from that fire can truly light the world." Kennedy proclaimed that "we shall pay any price, bear any burden, meet any hardship, support any friend, oppose any foe, in order to assure the survival and the success of liberty."

Kennedy came into the Oval Office less concerned about pushing through a raft of domestic legislation than about combating the nation's foreign enemies. Throwing himself and his administration into the business of national security, he would waste no time in beefing up the military, with extra emphasis on the special operations forces. For the special operators, a period foreseen as a swim through a shark tank would instead become one of explosive growth, in both size and activities, with profound implications for the strategic impact of special operations forces and their relations with conventional forces.

Kennedy set out to bolster the nation's capabilities for counterguerrilla warfare—defined as military operations against guerrillas—and counterinsurgency—defined as civil and military operations against insurgents supported by local populations. By his decree, all military schools, from the service academies to the war colleges, had to teach these subjects. The president also required senior military officers and civilian officials to take counterinsurgency courses, and he brought them to the White House to lecture them personally on the importance of defeating insurgency in underdeveloped countries.

Kennedy gave unprecedented attention to special operations forces because they were integral to his counterinsurgency agenda, and also because the president and his brother, Attorney General Robert F. Kennedy, revered the Special Forces. The Kennedy brothers were fascinated by the mystique and gadgetry of the Special Forces, in much the same way as Franklin Roosevelt had been fascinated by the contrivances of William J. Donovan's OSS. Michael Forrestal, a Kennedy administration official and the son of former secretary of defense James Forrestal, bemusedly likened the Kennedy brothers to "Boy Scouts with guns." With encouragement from the White House, the Defense Department's Advanced Research Projects Agency (ARPA) developed James Bond–like technologies for special operations, such as toothpick-sized nylon rockets that could kill a man, and explosives that could pass for soap.

Kennedy inflamed most of the Army by authorizing the Special Forces to wear the green beret, a symbol of elite status that the Army leadership had previously banned. Stoking the fire further, the president encouraged the publicizing of the Special Forces, which had heretofore largely avoided publicity. White House adulation spurred the Special Forces, or the Green Berets, as they now called themselves, to engage in a number of publicity stunts that were to become the objects of scorn and ridicule among the rest of the armed forces. At the 1962 annual meeting of the Association of the United States Army in Washington, DC, Special Forces soldiers rappelled six stories down the side of the Sheraton Park Hotel. To lure tourists to Fort Bragg, the Green Berets created a demonstration area where they showed off skills such as how to catch and skin snakes.

The Kennedy brothers had little idea of the practical realities of special operations forces, the mundane details that put limits on what could actually be achieved. "Why can't we just make the entire Army into Special Forces?" Robert Kennedy once inquired. Soon after entering the White House, President Kennedy asked Congress to increase the Army Special Forces to 10,500 men over five years in order to enlarge the 1st, 7th, and 10th Special Forces Groups and form the 5th Special Forces Group. What Kennedy did not fully grasp was the downside of so precipitous an expansion. To meet Kennedy's growth targets, recruitment standards had to be lowered and training shortened. In the next few years, the attrition rate at the Special Warfare Center fell from 90 percent to 30 percent. Proficiency in technical skills declined, as did the ability of Special Forces troops to withstand the stress of prolonged deployment in isolated and dangerous camps.

Kennedy's emphasis on counterinsurgency led the Special Forces to expand their expertise beyond the resistance-support activities of "unconventional warfare" to a new category entitled "special warfare," which encompassed counterinsurgency and psychological warfare as well as unconventional warfare. Whereas in the past the Special Forces had concentrated on bolstering guerrilla insurgencies in enemy territory, they would now focus on defeating guerrilla insurgencies in friendly nations. Kennedy chose to spread the Special Forces across the world, which put substantial numbers into locations where there was no obvious need for special warfare. In these places, they trained conventional military forces, or latched onto sundry tasks that even charitable observers found difficult to characterize as worthwhile. "We were accepting any mission that came to the 10th [Group], or that we could dig up," recalled a company commander in the 10th Group. "The value to long-range U.S. foreign policy was often doubtful."

Kennedy pressed the Air Force and the Navy to create new special operations forces for use in counterinsurgency and unconventional operations. In April 1961, the Air Force activated a new special operations unit, the 4400th Combat Crew Training Squadron, code-named Jungle Jim. Manned entirely by volunteers, Jungle Jim deployed a detachment to Vietnam in November 1961 with a fleet of upgraded World War II aircraft, including the B-26 Invader and the T-28 Trojan. In what was termed Operation Farmgate, the squadron's pilots and South Vietnamese trainees flew together in American planes painted with South Vietnamese markings. The Americans were supposed to serve only as instructors, and the Kennedy administration claimed publicly that they were not engaged in combat, but in practice the American pilots often flew the aircraft and fired their guns while their South Vietnamese counterparts observed the proceedings from the passenger seats.

The Navy answered Kennedy's summons for special operations forces with the Sea, Air, Land (SEAL) teams. According to Navy planning documents, the SEAL teams were to engage in intelligence collection, raids, sabotage, counterinsurgency, and advising of partner forces. Unlike the Frogmen of the Underwater Demolition Teams, which generally stayed in coastal waters, the SEALs could operate as far as twenty miles inland.

Composed of volunteers from the Underwater Demolition Teams, the SEAL teams underwent the same basic training course as the Frogmen, a course that was renamed Basic Underwater Demolition / SEAL Training (BUD/S). SEALs also took courses in advanced subjects like High Altitude, Low Opening parachuting and Ranger operations. Many of the early volunteers struggled with terrestrial skills that distinguished the SEALs from the Underwater Demolition Teams, such as advising foreign allies, and were returned to their original units.

The first Navy SEALs to deploy to Vietnam arrived on March 10, 1962. Setting up a training program similar to BUD/S, they trained South

Vietnam's naval commandos, the Lien Doan Nguoi Nhai, whose name means "soldiers who fight under the sea." Four-man SEAL detachments advised Vietnamese units on planning, tactics, and equipment and accompanied them into battle, where their main duty was the direction of naval gunfire and other supporting assets.

The number of SEALs in Vietnam was small in comparison with that of the Special Forces, and it would remain so throughout the war. Deployed to Vietnam on a limited basis since June 1957, the Special Forces increased their presence in Vietnam exponentially in 1961 as part of a huge increase in US troops ordered by President Kennedy. Unlike the Special Forces assigned to other countries, they had no trouble finding useful missions, for the South Vietnamese government faced a formidable Communist insurgency in the Viet Cong and needed help in a multitude of counterinsurgency tasks.

During the fall of 1961, soldiers of the 5th Special Forces Group began staffing a CIA paramilitary program in South Vietnam's central highlands. The Vietnamese Communists coveted this region because it offered base areas for conventional warfare and contained hidden roads and trails that could be used to slip men and materiel from Laos and Cambodia into South Vietnam. The principal residents of the region's remote mountains were the Montagnard tribes, who were readily distinguished from the ethnic Vietnamese majority by their dark skin, loincloths, and slash-and-burn agriculture. Driven long ago from the coastal lowlands by the swords of the ethnic Vietnamese, the Montagnards had little affection for either the South Vietnamese government or the Vietnamese Communists.

The CIA program originated with a visit by a small group of Americans to the Montagnard village of Buon Enao. Through offers of US weapons, military training, and medical supplies, the Americans convinced the Montagnards to build a fence around the village and declare loyalty to the South Vietnamese government. Seven Green Berets trained Montagnards at Buon Enao and organized them into units, called Civilian Irregular Defense Groups (CIDGs), and soon Montagnard men from forty nearby villages were coming to Buon Enao for training. When the Special Forces were not teaching the Montagnards the arts of war, they were building schools and dispensaries, administering medical care, stocking ponds with fish, or repairing roads and bridges.

The Americans learned that the Montagnards did not care to practice marksmanship with the M-1 carbines and other surplus US firearms they received, much preferring to spray semiautomatic bursts in haphazard fashion. American carping on such matters often had little effect. Nevertheless, the Americans appreciated the work ethic and straightforward devotion of the Montagnards, seeing in those virtues a pleasant contrast to the stubborn evasiveness of the ethnic Vietnamese. The Montagnards took a liking to their American advisers and welcomed them not merely as trainers but as leaders. "The American Special Forces soldier loved the Yards," observed Henry Gole, employing the affectionate nickname that he and other Green Berets affixed to the Montagnards. "In addition to a winning innocence and child-like sweetness, the Yard was tough, brave, and loyal. The fact that he treated his Special Forces leaders like royalty was a nice bonus."

The early successes of the Montagnard program in mobilizing villages against the Viet Cong led the United States to invest in a breakneck expansion. To increase the number of American personnel, Washington transferred control of the program from the overstretched CIA to the Special Forces and boosted the strength of the Special Forces in Vietnam to 126 officers and 544 enlisted men. By late 1963, the Special Forces had trained and armed 62,000 Montagnards.

Several years of improvement in South Vietnam's counterinsurgency capabilities ended abruptly at the beginning of November 1963 with the assassination of South Vietnamese president Ngo Dinh Diem. The US ambassador in Saigon, Henry Cabot Lodge, had instigated the coup in disregard of White House objections because of his conviction that someone else could lead the country better than the autocratic Diem. The generals who took over, however, soon set upon each other like Byzantine noblemen, leading to a series of purges that decimated the government's rural administration and security forces.

The North Vietnamese responded by moving beyond their strategy of low-intensity insurgency, implemented by guerrillas and political cadres in black pajamas, to one of high-intensity conventional warfare, fought by battalions of uniformed North Vietnamese soldiers wielding heavy machine guns and 75mm pack howitzers. During 1964, Hanoi enlarged and improved the Ho Chi Minh Trail, a collection of routes in Laos and Cambodia used by North Vietnamese vehicles and soldiers to skirt the demilitarized zone between the two Vietnams. The widening of roads and strengthening of bridges for truck traffic enabled the North Vietnamese to quadruple the amount of supplies shipped to the South. In November 1964, Hanoi for the first time dispatched an entire North Vietnamese Army Division to South Vietnam.

Three weeks after the assassination of President Diem, an assassin's bullet claimed the life of John F. Kennedy, thrusting Vietnam and the nation's other problems suddenly into the hands of Lyndon B. Johnson. A blustering career politician from the Texas Hill Country with none of Kennedy's glamor or charm, Johnson had served in the Navy during World War II, though his only brush with combat occurred during a passenger trip aboard a B-26 bomber. When Japanese Zeroes chased after the bomber, Johnson did little but hang on and pray that the aircraft would make it back safely, yet he subsequently convinced military authorities to award him a Silver Star for the flight. Johnson later regaled journalists with stories about how he had flown months of combat missions over the Pacific during the war, claiming that his exploits had earned him the sobriquet "Raider" Johnson.

Unlike Kennedy, Johnson cared much more about domestic issues than foreign affairs. Preoccupied with an expansive legislative agenda and the looming presidential election, Johnson wanted to keep Vietnam off the front pages during 1964. Thus, when presented with proposals from Secretary of Defense Robert McNamara to initiate covert attacks against North Vietnam in early 1964, Johnson authorized a lengthy slate of operations as a low-visibility way of fending off the North Vietnamese in the near term.

McNamara was convinced that the Defense Department could wage covert warfare in North Vietnam more effectively than the CIA, which in recent years had lost 85 percent of the agents it had inserted into the North. He formed the Studies and Observations Group (SOG), manned primarily by Special Forces soldiers, to initiate covert activities in North Vietnam and neighboring countries. Captain Bill Murray, a naval officer in the Pentagon who worked with SOG in its formative stages, recounted that "the people assigned to SOG were in general undisciplined, wild-eyed Army Special Forces people . . . who believed that the whole of Southeast Asia could be conquered by a handful of Green Berets." He lamented that "for a considerable period of time, McNamara also believed this myth."

The first Special Forces officers assigned to SOG advocated the organization of resistance forces in North Vietnam. The fact that organizing resistance forces had been the foundation stone of the Special Forces no doubt had something to do with their position. But the idea also had merit in its own right. North Vietnam's Catholics and tribal minorities had a history of taking up arms against Communists, and individuals from these groups who had fled south after the division of Vietnam were offering to return to their home areas if the Americans would underwrite resistance organizations.

President Johnson, however, opted against resistance operations, for fear that they would provoke North Vietnam or its ally China. This line of argument was the cause of bewilderment and derision among US military officers, who had been watching North Vietnam provoke South Vietnam and the United States for years by running a large resistance movement in the South. The White House restricted SOG's activities in the North to insertion of intelligence agents, a business in which the Special Forces had much less expertise.

The first adverse consequence of this decision was the snubbing of SOG by northern Catholic and tribal refugees, who accurately predicted that operations into the North would fail without resistance movements that could assist SOG's personnel. The Vietnamese individuals who ultimately entered North Vietnam for SOG were, by and large, poorly educated young men of lackluster spirit and aptitude whose principal motive was monetary. The Vietnamese Special Forces assigned some of their personnel to the operations, but the cream of the Vietnamese Special Forces had been skimmed off and discarded during the purges that followed the November 1963 coup.

Although McNamara and the Green Berets had denigrated the CIA's agent operations in North Vietnam, SOG could not come up with better ideas on how to carry out the operations and ended up relying on the same methods that the CIA had employed. After undergoing SOG training, small teams of Vietnamese agents parachuted into North Vietnam with instructions to melt into the population, make contact with relatives, and develop networks of informants. No Americans were permitted to accompany the teams.

Some of the inserted teams disappeared immediately and were never heard from again. Others began broadcasting messages on their radios, but in a disturbingly consistent pattern. In the first few days after insertion, these teams sent a large number of short messages, usually on basic administrative matters, then went silent for a spell. After that, they came back on line with messages explaining the silence, most often citing equipment malfunctions. The teams would request supplies and equipment, including luxury items for bribing Communist officials, such as Salem cigarettes, Seiko watches, and pistol silencers. When pressed to carry out intelligence or sabotage missions, they invariably came up with excuses as to why such missions could not be performed.

Once the Americans began to suspect a systemic compromise of the SOG teams, they changed security procedures. But the pattern continued. Of the nearly 250 agents whom SOG inserted into the North between April 1964 and October 1967, not one returned. None of the teams ever provided information of significant value, and only one known act of sabotage took place, the total effect of which was to blow a leg off a footbridge.

The abysmal failure of agent operations into North Vietnam elicited much pointing of fingers. SOG leaders laid blame on America's civilian leadership for refusing to authorize resistance movements that could have protected SOG's recruits from North Vietnam's internal security apparatus. Whether North Vietnamese resistance organizations could have prospered in the face of fierce Communist countermeasures is not certain, but at minimum they would have compelled the North Vietnamese to divert resources from the war in the South. Others in SOG criticized high officials in Washington and Saigon for continuing the missions after the folly had become obvious. "We were all amateurs," asserted Lieutenant Colonel

Jonathan Carney, head of SOG's Airborne Operations Section. "We had no business sending brave young men on missions which had almost no chance of success."

Marginally more successful than the agent insertions were SOG's raids on the North Vietnamese coast. During 1964, at McNamara's direction, American speedboats carried South Vietnamese commandos to the coast to conduct acts of sabotage and general harassment. Their demolitions felled bridges and scalded buildings, but the successes came at a heavy cost in commando lives. As the raids mounted, the North Vietnamese wised up and thickened their coastal defenses, further diminishing returns for the raiders. Escalation of the war in 1965 and 1966 caused the United States to strike coastal targets overtly with aircraft and large warships, which could do much more damage and with considerably less risk, reducing the SOG raids to insignificance.

The Special Forces' CIDG program, by contrast, remained significant after the 1963 coup, both because it mobilized friendly populations and because senior American leaders adapted it to new military realities. In response to Hanoi's intensification of the war in 1964, General Paul Harkins and his successor as the top US military commander, General William Westmoreland, integrated the Montagnard fighters of the CIDGs into a new strategy for thwarting Hanoi's designs. This strategy sent conventional South Vietnamese units into the wilderness to hit big enemy units before they could reach South Vietnam's population centers, in order to maintain the initiative and buy time for the civil government to get back on its feet. Pursuant to this strategy, the mission of the CIDG program shifted from defense of the Montagnard population to reconnaissance and offensive operations against North Vietnamese troops infiltrating into South Vietnam.

American construction teams built new CIDG camps in unpopulated areas near South Vietnam's borders with Laos and Cambodia, flying in pallets of sandbags and railroad ties to fortify them against large North Vietnamese assaults. The Special Forces formed some of the Montagnards into mobile strike forces of battalion size, which could be used to relieve camps under attack. They even experimented with "mobile guerrilla forces," company-sized units that operated in enemy base areas for weeks at a time, receiving periodic supply drops by air, though that effort was terminated after the enemy brought large forces to bear on the mobile guerrilla units with unexpected frequency.

Air Force special operations did their part in defending remote CIDG bases by developing the AC-47 fixed-wing gunship, the first US aircraft unique to special operations. Built upon the frame of the World War II–era C-47 transport aircraft, the AC-47 sported three electrically driven miniguns, each of which had six barrels that rotated around a central axis and could fire 100 rounds per second. Executing pylon turns at an altitude of 3,000 feet, the AC-47 could concentrate fire at a target roughly one mile away, putting the slow-moving aircraft beyond the reach of enemy machine guns.

At CIDG outposts, the defenders built large wooden arrows to guide the fire of the AC-47s. Swiveling the arrows in the direction of hostile forces, they lit flares to indicate the distance, with one flare representing one hundred meters. Many an American and Montagnard would owe his life to the torrential fire that the AC-47 brought onto the pith helmets of the North Vietnamese assault forces. Grateful American foot soldiers nicknamed the aircraft "Puff the Magic Dragon."

Some of the special operators and their advocates were to argue that the shift in CIDG activities represented the victimization of the program by a conventional US Army establishment that simply did not understand the importance of protecting the population in counterinsurgency. But protecting the population was the overriding problem only so long as the enemy's forces operated solely as guerrillas. By 1964, the Vietnamese Communists had acquired formidable conventional military capabilities, fielding heavily armed regiments of 1,500 men apiece that could execute the final phase of the revolutionary warfare espoused by Mao Zedong, in which conventional forces destroyed the enemy's army and conquered its cities. To ignore those regiments was to allow the enemy to concentrate where and when he pleased, an invitation to defeat in detail.

The accommodation of the Special Forces to the comprehensive US military strategy ensured that their tactical achievements would serve a larger strategic purpose. It did not, however, entirely spare them from aspersions by conventional officers about their tactical and strategic effectiveness. General Harold K. Johnson, the Army chief of staff, faulted the Special Forces for anchoring the CIDGs to fortified bases instead of keeping them active in the field. The Special Forces claimed to be "highly mobile, disdainful of fixed installations, innovative, not requiring organized logistical support," Johnson groused, but "what they did was build fortifications out of the Middle Ages and bury themselves with concrete." Other critics noted that the Special Forces camps did not prevent the enemy from moving large numbers of troops through their areas of operation. A number of senior military officers, moreover, disputed the notion that peculiar attributes of the Special Forces accounted for the successes of the Montagnard units, asserting that Special Forces soldiers were, on average, no better than other Americans at advising the South Vietnamese.

Some of the units did indeed show a tendency to spend inordinate amounts of time inside their camps. But even had all the CIDGs kept as active as Stonewall Jackson's Army of the Valley in the Shenandoah, they were spread out too far to stop the infiltration of the North Vietnamese Army. With sixty-three strike force companies at eighteen border sites, the CIDGs could, at best, assign one platoon for every twenty-eight miles of border, and it was a border consisting mainly of jungles and mountains that were particularly conducive to surreptitious movement. Their patrolling and summoning of air strikes did, nevertheless, cause the enemy some harm and irritation—enough to make the CIDG camps targets of frequent North Vietnamese onslaughts.

On July 6, 1964, eight hundred Communist troops assembled in the darkness of a remote South Vietnamese valley near the Laotian border. The Special Forces had recently established the Nam Dong CIDG camp in the valley by fortifying an old French installation and expanding its defenses outward. At 2:30 a.m., Viet Cong mortar tubes spewed a barrage of white phosphorus shells at Nam Dong. Exploiting information from an informant inside the camp, the Communist mortar crews made quick work of the command post, supply facility, and dispensary. Viet Cong infantrymen rushed forward, hurling grenades toward the perimeter foxholes while machine guns raked the camp's breastworks. Breaking through wire fences, the attackers overran the section of the camp held by the strike force. Of the three hundred men in the strike force, one hundred were wounded or killed. Most of the strike force survivors fled to a shanty town one kilometer away, where their family members were housed.

The assault force then turned its attention to the other section of the camp, the original French fort, defended by a Special Forces team and sixty South Vietnamese guards of the Nung ethnic minority. Although heavily outnumbered and without air support, the Americans and Nungs repulsed repeated Viet Cong attacks on their perimeter, in some cases shooting down the Viet Cong at point-blank range with shotguns and rifles. Directing the whole defense was Captain Roger Donlon of Saugerties, New York, the Special Forces team leader, who ran indefatigably from one defensive position to another to observe the enemy, give directions, buoy spirits, and direct fire. Witnesses saw him pick up grenades thrown by the Viet Cong and toss them back. At one point in the battle, Donlon braved heavy enemy fire to drag a wounded sergeant, several heavy weapons, and crates of ammunition to safety.

Holding the enemy at bay until dawn, the Americans and Nungs bought sufficient time for US aircraft to reach Nam Dong. Chastened by the sight of America's chariots of the air, the Viet Cong commander knew that daylight would allow US aircraft to locate and pulverize his exposed troops. He ordered a retreat. The Viet Cong departed in such haste and disorder that they left behind fifty-four of their dead. Nam Dong's garrison suffered a total of fifty-five dead, of whom two were Americans, along with sixty-five wounded. Donlon, who had been hit four times but kept going to battle's end, would be awarded the Congressional Medal of Honor for his efforts, becoming the first recipient of that award for actions in Vietnam.

During 1964, the Americans encouraged Vietnamese Special Forces officers to take charge of the CIDGs, of which they were the titular commanders. But the debilitating purges of the Vietnamese Special Forces following the 1963 coup and ethnic animosity between the Vietnamese and Montagnards necessitated that the Americans remain the de facto commanders. So confident of US backing did the Montagnards become that in September 1964 they staged a revolt against the Saigon government and sought American recognition of their independence. Seizing four CIDG camps and assailing a South Vietnamese Army garrison in Darlac Province, they killed several South Vietnamese soldiers.

The American embassy had long implored the Saigon government to improve its treatment of the Montagnards, but it had no appetite for Montagnard secession. US and Australian advisers pleaded with the Montagnards to end the mutiny before South Vietnamese reinforcements arrived and the bloodletting really got into swing. Colonel John F. Freund, an American with a natural affinity for persuading the Montagnards, talked some of the rebels into laying down their weapons. He induced the others to relent by pointing his pistol at the head of a recalcitrant mutineer.

When US Army and Marine Corps combat divisions arrived in the middle of 1965 to help a weakened South Vietnamese Army stave off a North Vietnamese Army offensive, the CIDGs entered into partnerships with American units, to the benefit of both parties. Possessing air mobility and firepower unprecedented in the annals of war, the US forces came to the aid of beleaguered CIDG camps and patrols with remarkable dispatch. The Montagnards and their Green Beret mentors, for their part, conducted long-range reconnaissance missions to sniff out prey for the big American units. The CIDGs also participated in large operations orchestrated by conventional US forces, in some cases performing unusual missions that exploited their special capabilities, in others serving as regular infantry. The Green Berets bemoaned conventional commanders who employed the Montagnard units as infantry, emphasizing that the CIDGs lacked the heavy armaments to put them on a par with the conventionally equipped North Vietnamese battalions.

As the American military colossus berthed in South Vietnam, SOG expanded its covert war into Laos to contend with mounting North Vietnamese infiltration through that country. Because of the feeble results of reconnaissance operations manned exclusively by Laotian tribesmen, SOG received authorization in September 1965 to send US reconnaissance personnel into Laos. Code-named Shining Brass, this new reconnaissance program undertook 8 insertions in 1965 and 137 in 1966.

Shining Brass belonged, at first, to Colonel Arthur D. "Bull" Simons. As a Ranger in the 6th Ranger Battalion during World War II, Simons had garnered a reputation as one of the toughest, meanest, and craftiest officers in the whole US Army. Gray of hair, with hands twice the size of a normal man's, he had the look of a middle-aged ox. Simons was also known for his love of artifacts. A collector by instinct, he owned a potpourri of antique Vietnamese spittoons, chamber pots, snuffboxes, and dragon heads, as well as a collection of historical firearms so large that fellow officers joked it could equip an invasion force big enough to take Cuba.

Simons would have been content to spend all his time in Laos hectoring the North Vietnamese, but circumstances forced him to divert much of his energy to bureaucratic battles with the State Department. The US ambassador to Laos, William Sullivan, restricted Shining Brass to two small boxes near the South Vietnamese border, and limited the size of SOG units to small teams. A larger program, Sullivan contended, would undermine the Laotian government, and it could provoke stronger reactions from North Vietnam, China, or the Soviet Union. Simons and other military officers thought it preposterous to hold down US involvement so strenuously in a country whose neutrality had been so thoroughly violated by the enemy. Month after month, Simons pressed for expansion of Shining Brass, and each time Sullivan and his State colleagues shot down his proposals. The professional dispute became personal, with Sullivan airing his condescension openly and the SOG officers expressing most of their contempt out of Sullivan's earshot. One SOG commander told his subordinates that the State Department was full of "shoves." When asked for clarification, he said, "A cross between a shit and a dove."

Most of the American manpower for Shining Brass came from the Special Forces, with members of Vietnamese or Laotian ethnic minorities accounting for the bulk of indigenous team members. To conceal the identities of Shining Brass personnel, SOG issued them plain uniforms that bore no rank or unit insignia. Their weapons included 9mm Swedish K submachine guns, Belgian Browning 9mm pistols with serial numbers that could not be traced, and 6-inch knives that had been manufactured in a secret factory in Japan.

Based out of CIDG camps along South Vietnam's western frontier, the Shining Brass teams flew across the Laotian border by helicopter, usually near dusk. After disembarking at preselected landing zones, they set up night ambushes around the insertion point in case the enemy had sighted their arrival. Moving out in the morning, they hacked, scratched, and clawed through dense jungle vines while laboring to avoid making noises that would give away their position. Oftentimes they advanced only a few hundred yards before their machetes had been dulled and their muscles exhausted.

The reconnaissance men watched roads to see the magnitude of enemy traffic and the types of materiel moving through, snapping photographs with pocket cameras when possible. They searched for truck parks, arms depots, storage facilities, and other targets vulnerable to bombing. Communicating by radio with forward air controllers flying overhead in propeller-driven aircraft, they could summon an Air Force jet to a target within thirty to forty minutes. SOG communications specialists eavesdropped on North Vietnamese field telephones with state-of-the-art electromagnetic couplers that could retrieve conversations through induction without having to splice into the line.

The cross-border missions lasted anywhere from one day to several weeks. Certain men thrived in prolonged isolation in enemy territory and were eager to go on missions again and again. Others were worn down by boredom or fear. "There are some people that once they hear the helicopters go off in the distance, their ass gets so tight they can't breathe," commented Captain Jim Storter, a SOG veteran. "When it gets quiet and you're on your own, a lot of people can't handle it."

Reconnaissance was always the most common type of mission for Shining Brass teams. The team members, though, also participated in pilot-rescue operations under the code name Bright Light. One of the most famous episodes in SOG's history took place in October 1966 when Sergeant Dick Meadows led a team into North Vietnam to rescue Lieutenant Robert D. Woods.

Countless special operators could have been the protagonist in a Horatio Alger novel, but few were as qualified for that distinction as Meadows. Born on the dirt floor of a moonshiner's cabin in West Virginia, he had enlisted in the Army in 1947 at age fifteen, having prevailed upon his mother to lie about his age. Many of the young men who entered the Army with Meadows disliked the regimentation and privation of basic training, but for him the living conditions surpassed anything he had ever experienced. He was astonished to receive three meals every day along with all the milk he could drink.

Entering the Airborne, Meadows fought in Korea with the 187th Regimental Combat Team, and in 1952 joined the 10th Special Forces Group. His meticulous planning and rehearsal, his creativity, and his ability to make every task fun for his subordinates caused the young sergeant to stand out among the noncommissioned officers. Within the 10th Group, he became known as the man who always succeeded.

On October 12, 1966, North Vietnamese antiaircraft fire hit the A-1 Skyraider flown by Lieutenant Woods, forcing the young pilot to eject. His parachute came down on a jungle-covered ridge thirty miles from Hanoi. Using a survival radio, Woods sent word of his hiding spot, which was located twenty meters from the intersection of a downed tree and a dirt trail. Meadows and his team of Americans and Nungs were flown to the USS *Intrepid*, an aircraft carrier that was prowling the South China Sea. After reviewing aerial photographs of the area, Meadows selected an insertion point eight hundred yards from the pilot's reported location.

At dawn on October 15, Navy Sea King helicopters ferried the rescue team from the deck of the *Intrepid* into the North Vietnamese jungle. Landing without incident, the team headed toward Lieutenant Woods. When they were within one hundred yards, the Nung pointman froze, then motioned for the others to halt. The team hid behind the flora next to the trail and lay still, guns at the ready, wondering whether the pointman's instincts were correct.

After fifteen minutes, they heard voices speaking an alien tongue, and then four North Vietnamese soldiers appeared on the trail, walking in their direction. When the North Vietnamese reached the stretch where the Americans and Nungs had chosen to halt, they caught sight of Meadows and went for their weapons. Before they could fire, Meadows sprang forward from the brush and gunned down all four of them with his Swedish K submachine gun.

Moving forward, Meadows and the rest of his team began calling for Woods by name. Their voices drew the attention of other North Vietnamese soldiers, who were likewise looking for the American airman. The jungle erupted with the sound of North Vietnamese bugles, vectoring the North Vietnamese search teams toward the rescue party.

Meadows, whom no one had ever accused of excessive caution, concluded that the North Vietnamese had so many men in the area as to render the risks prohibitive. They would have to forget about Woods and try to avoid capture themselves. Meadows radioed for an emergency extraction from the original landing zone. Racing back to their point of arrival, the Americans and Nungs rendezvoused with two Sea Kings and clambered aboard before the pursuing North Vietnamese soldiers could put any bullets in them.

As the Sea Kings arose from the landing zone, North Vietnamese antiaircraft shells gouged one of the helicopters. The pilot was able to fly the chopper to the sea, but it did not have enough strength left to reach the *Intrepid*. Gently setting the Sea King on the water's surface, the pilot was able to spare the passengers from injury. The helicopter rolled onto its side and began taking on water, whereupon the crew and passengers donned life vests and jumped into the cool blue of the Tonkin Gulf. The destroyer USS *Henley* sped to the location and dispatched a motorboat, which recovered all of the men.

Lieutenant Woods was taken prisoner and incarcerated in a North Vietnamese jail until March 1973, when he was released under the terms of the Paris Peace Accords. That the futile operation to rescue him went down as one of the most renowned special operations of the war had much to do with the valor of the participants and their suspenseful encounter with the enemy. It also resonated with American veterans because it was a microcosm of the war as a whole—the struggle of brave and skillful men against overwhelming odds in a place the American nation would eventually write off.

While SOG and the CIDG advisory effort were the largest and most famous Special Forces programs in Vietnam, the Army's psychological operations branch also carved out a large niche. Equipped with high-speed printing presses, the four battalions of the 4th Psyop Group spent most of their time producing leaflets for aircraft to disgorge over areas trafficked by the enemy. The leaflets contained propaganda messages on such subjects as the inevitability of North Vietnam's defeat and the superiority of life in South Vietnam. Some promised good treatment to Communist soldiers who brought the leaflet along when they surrendered to the South Vietnamese government. The 4th Psyop Group also dropped thousands of transistor radios into enemy base areas, each one pretuned to a 50,000-watt radio station that served anti-Communist fare.

American psychological operators often took an active role in crafting the propaganda messages because of Vietnamese apathy or incapacity. But few of the Americans had the deep familiarity with Vietnamese culture required to create messages that would press the right psychological buttons and avoid the wrong ones. As a consequence, they defaulted to messages suited to American audiences, often to the befuddlement of the Vietnamese. One group of American propagandists wrote a comic strip based on an old American yarn about bullying, with only the superficial details tailored to the Vietnamese context. In the comic strip, a Vietnamese peasant put a brick on the ground and covered it with a hat that he had inscribed with an anti-Communist slogan. When a Viet Cong bully saw the hat, he kicked it, breaking his toe. The Americans were surprised to find that no Vietnamese found the comic strip funny. When they asked what could be done to improve it, one Vietnamese man replied that they should put a hand grenade under the hat.

Officers in conventional US military units were a good deal more skeptical than psyops officers about the impact of psychological operations. They noted that although thousands of Vietnamese Communist soldiers deserted or defected while bearing leaflets promising good treatment, interviews of prisoners suggested that their defections resulted mainly from unremitting pounding by potent American weaponry. Other critics faulted psychological operations units for an unimaginative, bureaucratic mentality. "Psychological operations were essentially defensive in nature," remarked Colonel Francis J. Kelly, who commanded the 5th Special Forces Group in Vietnam in 1966 and 1967. "Opportunities or suggestions for offensive psychological operations were usually buried in the useless and meaningless statistics of numbers of leaflets delivered or broadcasts made."

Few of the American special operators in Vietnam served in elite strike teams of the sort for which SOF would later become famous. The principal exceptions were to be found among the Navy SEALs, who in 1966 began using fourteen-man SEAL platoons for raids and ambushes. Operating mainly in the shallow waterways of the Mekong Delta, they flitted to and fro on specially designed boats, such as the Light SEAL Support Craft, a twenty-four-foot vessel powered by twin Ford V8 engines and Jacuzzi water-jet pumps.

The independent SEAL platoons were freed from the problems that went with working alongside local nationals—the poor marksmanship, the lack of noise discipline, the barriers of language and culture. But the SEALs discovered that independence had its drawbacks. The absence of partner forces who spoke Vietnamese kept them from obtaining information from the population, and few other intelligence sources were to be had. Practicing endlessly on the rifle range and loading boats to the gunwales with ammunition did little good when the SEALs could not find anyone to shoot.

A number of enterprising officers determined that the SEAL platoons needed to find South Vietnamese partner units if they wanted to find the enemy. Well-led South Vietnamese forces, of which a considerable number existed, obtained information on Viet Cong targets with an ease that astonished the Americans, principally by talking with their own family members in the villages. The SEALs were particularly drawn to the Provincial Reconnaissance Units (PRUs), the best of the South Vietnamese forces by a wide margin.

Created in 1964 for the mission of attacking the Viet Cong in their lair, the Provincial Reconnaissance Units operated under the control of CIA paramilitary officers. The CIA appointed the South Vietnamese PRU commanders and seconded American special operators and other US military personnel to serve as advisers. The key to the program's success lay in the CIA's authority over personnel decisions, for it removed the politicization of command appointments that compromised the leadership of other South Vietnamese forces.

The PRUs carried the enemy's weapon, the AK-47, and at times dressed in the black garb of the Viet Cong. The units received scraps of intelligence here and there from the Phoenix program, an intelligence-sharing program whose coordination centers fused information from different agencies. For the most part, however, they obtained targeting data from their own informants.

Numbering approximately 5,000 men, the Provincial Reconnaissance Units eliminated 10,000 or more of the enemy per year while sustaining remarkably few casualties. No other organization was as successful in targeting Viet Cong leaders. It should be noted, though, that they were far from a precise instrument, at least in comparison with the precision-strike special operations units of the twenty-first century. The Viet Cong leaders rarely lived in the villages after 1965 because of the probability of getting caught, and instead resided with military units. If the Provincial Reconnaissance Units or their US partners captured or killed a Viet Cong leader, it was usually by chance during a routine military engagement.

The year 1967 heralded a sharp intensification of SOG's cross-border activities. Operations into Laos, which were now called Prairie Fire, faced increasingly sophisticated North Vietnamese countermeasures. North Vietnamese Army units positioned sentries and listening devices along American flight paths and at open areas where US helicopters were most likely to land. Tracker dogs and one-hundred-man "hunter-killer" teams from the 305th North Vietnamese Army Airborne Brigade combed the border region for traces of intrusion. With sophisticated direction-finding equipment obtained from their Communist allies, the North Vietnamese could locate SOG teams via their radio transmissions. Once the North Vietnamese obtained a fix on a SOG team, they beat gongs or sent messages by phone or runner to summon swarms of North Vietnamese Army soldiers to the area and inform North Vietnamese antiaircraft crews where to prepare a rude welcome for American rescue aircraft.

Over the course of 1967, the SOG leadership lobbied aggressively with General Westmoreland for a loosening of restrictions on the Laotian operations, in order to increase their effectiveness and reduce their vulnerability. Westmoreland, himself distraught at the continuous cascade of enemy men and supplies through the supposedly neutral country, was sympathetic to the proposals. Whenever he attempted to obtain greater latitude for Prairie Fire, however, he was stopped at the iron gates of Ambassador Sullivan, whose contempt for the military had been calcified by prolonged arguments over the use of US ground forces to interdict the Ho Chi Minh Trail. Sullivan cabled the State Department in October that Prairie Fire "involves a gung-ho group who, by their very nature, are always attempting to exceed the political limitations of more reasonable men everywhere" and "constantly pressing . . . for more and more reckless and irresponsible endeavors." Sullivan mused that the Prairie Fire controversy was "largely a problem of morale for overgrown adolescents and I certainly don't wish to disappoint their inevitable image of parental rigidity. Therefore, largely for their own good, it is wise to be most severe on Prairie Fire."

The military did achieve a breakthrough on Cambodia in the spring of 1967, after years of fruitless complaints to Washington about North Vietnamese exploitation of Cambodian territory for sanctuary and logistics. The White House authorized SOG to commence ground reconnaissance on Cambodian territory in May, under the code name Daniel Boone. Like Prairie Fire, Daniel Boone labored under severe restrictions on its size and activities, with the teams permitted to enter and leave Cambodia only on foot and to go no farther than twenty kilometers past the border.

SOG's activities in Laos and Cambodia caused the enemy more trouble than Ambassador Sullivan and other detractors recognized at the time. The targeting data provided by SOG teams greatly improved the accuracy of American air strikes. Damage inflicted by SOG-directed strikes undoubtedly figured prominently in the North Vietnamese decision to assign 40,000 men to the security of the Ho Chi Minh Trail in Laos and Cambodia during 1967. No amount of SOG activity, however, could have choked the trail to the extent required to starve the North Vietnamese forces in South Vietnam. Only the presence of US infantry units could have had such a strategic effect, and Lyndon Johnson was unwilling to deploy infantry into Laos or Cambodia.

In 1967, SOG also undertook a new type of ground operation into North Vietnam, in grudging recognition by the White House that prior operations had come up empty. On direction from Washington, SOG infiltrated Short Term Reconnaissance and Target Acquisition (STRATA) teams of between five and fifteen Vietnamese men into the North Vietnamese panhandle. Dressed in North Vietnamese Army uniforms, the teams were to install seismic wiretap devices, observe road traffic, locate enemy installations, and acquire targets for air strikes.

Two STRATA teams entered North Vietnam in 1967, only one of which made it back out. But the mere fact that one escaped was celebrated as a major victory, in light of the failure of all previous infiltrators to return. Twenty-four STRATA teams entered the North in 1968, with the average mission lasting thirteen days and a significant number of teams returning home. The teams obtained intelligence of only modest value and caused little trouble to the North Vietnamese, provoking accusations from American advisers that the Vietnamese personnel were inordinately preoccupied with coming back alive. Captain Roy Meeks, the assistant chief of staff of operations for the STRATA teams, complained, "I got the feeling that every time we inserted them, they found a hole to hide."

SOG's operations into North Vietnam ended in October 1968 because of President Johnson's decision to discontinue the bombing of North Vietnam after three and a half years of intermittent, slowly escalating strikes. Cross-border missions into Laos and Cambodia, however, increased in number during the subsequent period, peaking in 1969 with more than 400 operations. SOG personnel strength also reached its apex that year, with over 1,000 Americans and several thousand Vietnamese, Cambodians, Thais, and Laotians.

In 1969, SOG operations received a major boost from the introduction of the newly developed AC-130 Spectre. Based upon the C-130 transport aircraft platform, the AC-130 was bigger, faster, tougher, and deadlier than the AC-47. Outfitted with a weapons suite that the Air Force called "Surprise Package," featuring 40mm Bofors antiaircraft guns and 20mm Gatling guns, the AC-130 could fire from higher altitudes than the AC-47, reducing its vulnerability to North Vietnamese antiaircraft guns. The Air Force, which had kept the AC-47 out of Laos since 1966 following the loss of four gunships to antiaircraft fire, decided to send the new gunship into the Laotian gauntlet to see if it could make it back.

The sudden appearance above the Ho Chi Minh Trail of hundred-foot-long gunships that could lay down sheets of projectiles for minutes at a time came as a nasty surprise to the North Vietnamese. The antiaircraft weapons positioned along the trail could not shoot the AC-130s down, and Hanoi was unable to send new weapons that were up to the task. For North Vietnamese truck drivers and porters, the Spectre became the devil of the sky, its appearance instantly instilling fear. In 1970 and 1971, the AC-130s of the Air Force's 16th Special Operations Squadron destroyed 2,432 North Vietnamese trucks, accounting for more than 60 percent of all trucks destroyed by American air power.

During SOG's last years in Laos and Cambodia, as the North Vietnamese regime further beefed up the defenses of the Ho Chi Minh Trail for fear of incursions by the hardnosed President Richard Nixon, teams routinely bumped into large concentrations of North Vietnamese Army troops. The average operation lasted only two days, down from an average of six days in 1965, and many teams had to be pulled out after only a few hours. When on the run from tens or hundreds of North Vietnamese soldiers, SOG teams were often extracted with "McGuire rigs," six-foot slings tied to hundred-foot ropes that dangled from helicopters into the jungle canopy. Of the 481 total US personnel assigned to Prairie Fire in 1969, 19 were killed, 199 were wounded, and 9 disappeared.

Recon Team Colorado, entering Laos in January 1971 on one of SOG's last cross-border operations, had been on the ground for three days when it made contact with the North Vietnamese. The first member of the team to catch wind of the North Vietnamese was Sergeant David Mixter. An athletic young man from a prominent New England family, the six-foot-six Mixter towered over his teammates, who had nicknamed him "Lurch" after the butler of *The Addams Family*. One fellow Green Beret said that Mixter "was a soft-spoken gentle giant who laughed easily but rarely made anyone else laugh. Practical jokes, rubber barf, and gags were more his style. His virtue was generosity. He would give you the shirt off his back. Mix would share his last buck with you and was always good for a short-term loan."

While the team was on a rest break, Mixter heard what he suspected to be North Vietnamese soldiers. He alerted team leader Pat Mitchel and radio operator Lyn St. Laurent, who passed word of the danger to the team's Montagnards. Soon enemy soldiers came into Mixter's field of vision. Sighting them in his crosshairs, he opened fire.

The clanking of AK-47 shots that answered Mixter's weapon came with such rapidity as to indicate that the enemy had at least two squads. More could be on the way. With the North Vietnamese already holding a much superior number of pieces on the chessboard, Mitchel decided on flight over fight. Sergeant Mixter laid down fire while the other Americans and the Montagnards pulled back. He then rejoined them under their covering fire.

"Got bad guys all around us," Sergeant St. Laurent radioed. He requested immediate air strikes. Mixter, from the inside of a bomb crater, flashed a mirror to show airmen the team's position. The reconnaissance men rejoiced at the appearance of two F-4 Phantoms, jet fighter-bombers capable of flying at twice the speed of sound.

Unbeknownst to Recon Team Colorado, the North Vietnamese had detected the team's presence the previous day, and during the night had encircled the team with 37mm antiaircraft guns. Opening fire at the sight of the F-4s, the guns revealed themselves to be so close to the recon team's position that the US jets could not bomb the North Vietnamese without a high risk of harming the Americans and the Montagnards. As the F-4s backed away, North Vietnamese infantrymen pressed in from all sides.

Trading fire with the North Vietnamese, Recon Team Colorado sought to hold them off long enough for US helicopters to arrive for an emergency evacuation. A well-aimed rocket-propelled grenade exploded near Mixter, killing the big man instantly and injuring St. Laurent. At this calamity, the Montagnards decided that the team was doomed and ran away.

Mitchel and St. Laurent, aware that they could not fight off multiple squads of North Vietnamese by themselves, resolved to take Mixter's body to a new location from which they would be extracted by helicopter. But with St. Laurent wounded and both of them much smaller than Mixter, they were unable to carry the body. Back on the radio, St. Laurent contacted John Plaster, who was coordinating action from an OV-10 Bronco overhead, to say that they intended to stay with Mixter until they could be picked up. Plaster could see large bunches of North Vietnamese in nearby positions, who would surely shoot apart any helicopter that landed near the spot where Mixter lay dead—if they had not already killed Mitchel and St. Laurent by the time a helicopter was ready to retrieve them. Plaster told St. Laurent that he and Mitchel needed to move, even if it meant leaving Mixter behind. "It's OK, Lurch would understand," Plaster radioed. "We have to think about the living right now, partner. Now get moving."

US aircraft would attempt to suppress the North Vietnamese while the two men made a run for it. To get a bead on enemy forces that might interfere with the escape, Plaster directed St. Laurent to prepare a white phosphorous grenade. "I'll give you a countdown," Plaster yelled over the din, "then I want you to throw it and give me an azimuth and distance to the enemy." As Plaster's turboprop Bronco dove toward the ground, he started the countdown. When St. Laurent's grenade burst into sizzling white streaks, the enemy mistook it for a rocket from the aircraft and concluded that an American pilot had already zeroed in on them. Most of the North Vietnamese dove into their bunkers, alleviating the pressure on Mitchel and St. Laurent and giving them a fighting chance of slipping away.

Leaving Mixter behind, the two men dashed through the smoke from the white phosphorous grenade and broke out of the encirclement undetected. The nearest clearing was four hundred yards away from the Americans, next to a road running toward the east. As Cobra gunships and propeller-driven A-1 Skyraiders arrived on the scene with their vicious automatic cannons, Plaster directed the SOG men to run toward the clearing as soon as the aircraft were in position to shoot up the surrounding area.

Upon receiving the signal, Mitchel and St. Laurent sprinted toward the open ground, coming up onto the road. During the final stretch, as they were moving between the road and the clearing, Plaster radioed, "Stop! Get back on the road! There are people in that field!"

The Cobras and Skyraiders turned their metallic fury onto the field, scattering the North Vietnamese soldiers who had congregated there. Other aircraft strafed the road to prevent North Vietnamese trucks from shuttling reinforcements to the field. A Huey helicopter flew toward Mitchel and St. Laurent, banked hard, and set down on the ground. Scurrying aboard in the glowing ecstasy of survival, the two men watched the ground pull away until the North Vietnamese were the size of ants and the helicopter leveled off for the flight eastward toward safety.

THE MOST FAMOUS special operation of the war, the Son Tay raid, involved neither SOG nor the CIDGs, but rather a separate force created for the sole purpose of conducting the operation. During the latter part of the 1960s, US forces had raided dozens of suspected POW camps in Cambodia, Laos, and South Vietnam, but in nearly every case they had come away empty-handed. In the first forty-five raids, only one prisoner was retrieved, and that individual died a short time afterward from wounds that his captors had inflicted just before his liberation.

An opportunity of unprecedented promise arose in May 1970, when US reconnaissance aircraft photographed a highly unusual building compound at Son Tay, twenty-three miles west of Hanoi. In the courtyard, laundry had been hung in a pattern that to an overhead observer spelled the American code letters for search and rescue. Brigadier General Donald B. Blackburn, the special assistant for counterinsurgency and special activities, proposed a nighttime rescue operation, in which US special operations forces would fly in, scoop up the prisoners, and get out within thirty minutes. American planners estimated that thirty minutes was the minimum time required for the nearest North Vietnamese Army troops to pile into trucks and drive to the camp.

It came as little surprise that a president nicknamed "Tricky Dick" approved planning for the operation. Nixon relished the prospect of rescuing American captives while at the same time delivering a kick to the nettlesome North Vietnamese on the outskirts of their own capital. He expressed concern, though, that landing US troops in North Vietnam would stir up the antiwar movement at home, as the incursion of US forces into Cambodia had done earlier in the year. "Christ, they surrounded the White House, remember?" Nixon remarked. "This time they will probably knock down the gates and I'll have a thousand incoherent hippies urinating on the Oval Office rug. That's just what they'd do."

Blackburn's choice to lead the rescue force was Brigadier General Leroy J. Manor, commander of the Air Force's Special Operations Force, which in 1968 had supplanted the Kennedy-era Air Force Special Warfare Center as the central node of Air Force special operations. For second-in-command, Blackburn selected Bull Simons. Manor and Simons handpicked the pilots and the ground troops from large pools of experienced men, assembling a team that included Dick Meadows and numerous other all-stars.

Because of internal debates and pressing international matters, the White House waited until November—six months after the sighting of the laundry—to launch the operation. During the long waiting period, Simons rehearsed the ground assault at a mock-up of the camp up to three times a day and three times a night, more than 170 times in all. He modified the scenario on each iteration so that the members of the raiding party could think through all potential hiccups and opportunities. At the end of each rehearsal, Simons examined the cardboard silhouettes that signified enemy guards and counted the number of bullet holes in each. If the cardboard men had not been sufficiently perforated, he made the men go through the whole rehearsal again.

During the final days of preparation, the Pentagon received aerial photographs and other intelligence suggesting that the prisoners had been moved out of the Son Tay camp, together with other information suggesting that they were still there. In a meeting with the chairman of the Joint Chiefs of Staff, Defense Intelligence Agency director Donald Bennett held aloft a large stack of photos and cables in one hand and pronounced, "I've got this much that says 'They've been moved,'" then lifted a stack of comparable size in his other hand and asserted, "I've got this much that says 'They're still there.'" Even if the odds of success were much less than fifty-fifty, as some intelligence analysts believed, the chance to rescue American POWs for the first time seemed worth a shot in the minds of most of those involved. On November 18, Nixon decided that the mission was a go.

The raiding party of fifty-six Special Forces soldiers took off from the Royal Thai Air Force Base in Udorn, Thailand, on the night of November 20. Flying in six assault helicopters into the world's densest air defense system, they winnowed through holes in North Vietnamese radar coverage that had been located by analyzing the motions of radar dishes. Fifty-one other Air Force aircraft flew in support of the mission, including five F-105 Wild Weasels with radar-homing Shrike missiles and ten F-4 Phantoms that could intercept any North Vietnamese aircraft that had the audacity to take off. Fifty-eight US Navy aircraft from the carriers *Ranger*, *Oriskany*, and *Hancock* staged a fake attack on Haiphong Harbor, dropping flares and simulating the mining of the harbor, to draw North Vietnamese attention to the east coast while the assault force intruded from the west.

One part of the raiding force landed four hundred yards south of where it was supposed to land, its navigator having mistaken another building compound for the prison camp. US intelligence reports had previously identified this compound as a school. The compound was, in actuality, a barracks full of North Vietnamese troops. Scrambling out of bed, the North Vietnamese shot at the Americans from windows and doors. The errant landing actually worked to the advantage of the Americans, for it enabled them to engage this unanticipated hostile force before it could get organized. In an astonishing display of marksmanship, the twenty-two Americans who landed outside the barracks killed an estimated one hundred to two hundred North Vietnamese soldiers in five minutes without the loss of a single American life. Then they put the barracks to the torch, incinerating the dead and dying North Vietnamese in a bright orange pyre.

The primary breaching force, thirteen men under the leadership of Dick Meadows, touched down at the intended destination. Toting a bullhorn, Meadows announced, "We're Americans. Keep your heads down. We're Americans. This is a rescue. We're here to get you out. Keep your heads down. Get on the floor. We'll be in your cells in a minute." As the Special Forces swept through the facility, they shot forty-two North Vietnamese soldiers. But they could find no sign of prisoners.

Shocked by the initial reports of vacant prison cells, Meadows told his men to search the cells again. After ten more minutes of futility, Meadows radioed, "Negative items," meaning no prisoners. It was later learned that the North Vietnamese had moved the prisoners from Son Tay on July 14, probably because of heavy summer rains that had flooded the nearby Black River.

Twenty-seven minutes after arrival, the rescue team took off. Only two members of the raiding force were wounded during the entire operation, one sustaining a broken ankle, the other a gunshot wound. Every one of the more than one hundred aircraft that participated in the operation survived the flight out of North Vietnam's dreaded air defense system. Although the Americans had been unable to retrieve any hostages, they could take some satisfaction that they had displayed exceptional skill and had lost neither a man nor an aircraft.

One month after the Son Tay raid, the CIDG program was dissolved in conformance with "Vietnamization," Nixon's multiyear drawdown of US forces. The Special Forces had spent nearly a decade supporting the CIDGs, whose strength exceeded 50,000 for most of the program's life-span, making it by far the largest and most significant program in the brief history of the Green Berets. The South Vietnamese government integrated

15,000 of the CIDG members into units operating in the country's western border regions, which were seeing as much North Vietnamese traffic as ever.

On March 31, 1972, by which time no US ground forces remained in South Vietnam, SOG shuttered its doors. The organization went into retirement laying claim to an extraordinary record of efficiency. According to SOG statistics, enemy casualties resulting from SOG operations were more than one hundred times the friendly casualties.

When a conventional North Vietnamese offensive vanquished South Vietnam in 1975, critics of special operations forces seized upon the cataclysm as evidence that counterinsurgency and its SOF champions had doomed South Vietnam by diffusing resources that should have been concentrated on the conventional war. SOF personnel and their supporters countered that the United States had lost because hidebound Army officers had adopted a conventional military strategy against an unconventional adversary, misusing SOF in the process. That both of these interpretations were erroneous did not prevent them from proliferating.

In the years immediately following the war, the opponents of counterinsurgency held the upper hand within the US Army. At a time of dwindling defense budgets, they made sure that the Special Forces felt much of the pain. The number of Special Forces groups fell from seven to three, with the total strength of the Special Forces tumbling from a peak of 13,000 in 1971 to 3,000 in 1974. Budgets for Special Forces training and equipment suffered larger cuts than those for conventional units. Navy leaders delivered similar blows to the SEALs, slicing the number of SEAL teams in half. Opposition to the SEALs among the rest of the Navy ran so high in the mid-1970s that they likely would have been disbanded had they not enjoyed the protective shield of the chief of naval operations, Admiral Elmo Zumwalt.

No US PRESIDENT, before or after, gave as much attention to special operations forces as John F. Kennedy. His insistence on expansion of special operations forces drove the Navy and Air Force to birth new forces and the Army to multiply its Special Forces. His emphasis on counterinsurgency ensured that the armed services put those forces to use in Vietnam. Without Kennedy's actions, special operations forces might forever have remained the small sideshow of the 1940s and 1950s, if they managed to survive at all. The rapid growth he fathered, however, would necessitate a lowering of SOF standards and a shortening of SOF training, to the detriment of the quality and reputation of special operations.

Lyndon Johnson, who did not share Kennedy's interest in special operations forces, saw in them a means of jabbing North Vietnam inconspicuously at a time when he wished to keep Vietnam out of the newspapers. By exploiting the secrecy surrounding special operations forces for personal political gain, he set a perilous precedent. His insistence on avoiding support for resistance movements barred SOF from the type of work for which they were best prepared, and ensured that the North Vietnamese would wipe out the small teams that SOG sent north. For reasons of both politics and policy, Johnson relied on SOG for covert operations into Laos and Cambodia instead of positioning large conventional forces across the Ho Chi Minh Trail, which would have been far more effective at obstructing enemy infiltration. That decision, moreover, set the State Department and special operations forces against one another, sparking a rivalry that would grow in the coming decades.

Kennedy's advocacy of counterinsurgency broadened a SOF repertoire that hitherto had been limited to the tunes of unconventional warfare. The CIDGs began as a counterinsurgency program, though over time they became closer to an unconventional warfare program, as the Montagnards executed guerrilla operations against the North Vietnamese Army in the no-man's-lands of South Vietnam's jungles and mountains. SOG drew the Special Forces into agent insertion, compelling them to copy CIA methods that worked no better for the glamorous Green Berets than for the anonymous CIA. SOG's reconnaissance operations into Laos and Cambodia, the advising of the CIA's Provincial Reconnaissance Units, and the employment of SEAL strike forces were all new missions. Beyond Vietnam, the thrusting of the enlarged Special Forces into new environments caused them, by improvisation and necessity more than by design, to latch on to the objective of training foreign security forces of all sorts, an activity that would become an enduring feature of the Special Forces.

The tactical and strategic effectiveness of special operations forces in Vietnam ran the gamut, and as usual the assessment of effectiveness stimulated heated disputation, much of it self-serving. During the war's early years, the CIDG program clearly achieved success in the large-scale organization of South Vietnamese tribal minorities for counterinsurgency. When the North Vietnamese Army shifted to large offensive operations in 1964, the war's increasingly conventional hue sapped the CIDGs and their Special Forces advisers of strategic influence; the South Vietnamese Army, and later the conventional US Army and Marine forces, became the lead strategic actors. Nevertheless, the CIDG program made important tactical contributions to the conventional war by collecting intelligence, assisting conventional forces, and drawing enemy units into battle.

SOG caused the enemy considerable tactical grief through its cross-border operations into Laos and Cambodia, but, like the CIDG program, it could not exert strategic sway. The air strikes that SOG guided never disrupted the flow of traffic on the Ho Chi Minh Trail enough to stymie North Vietnamese offensive operations in the South. As for SOG raids and agent insertions in North Vietnam, unalloyed tactical failure guaranteed strategic impotence.

The glamorization and meteoric growth of special operations forces during the Vietnam era enlarged the psychological gulf separating them from the rest of the military. Their elevation as a premier counterinsurgency force would come back to haunt them after the war, when critics pinned the loss of Vietnam on the special operations forces and demanded their emasculation. The special operators survived the end of the war, but they would once again have to search for new tasks to convince spendthrift lawmakers, bureaucrats, and generals to keep them afloat.

CHAPTER 6

JSOC AND SOCOM

In the depths of the post-Vietnam doldrums, special operators went about the now-customary brainstorming for new hills to climb and new dragons to slay. Tossing around ideas over coffee or beer, they followed any glimmer that might foretell the starburst, the brilliant idea that would excite individuals of influence at the Pentagon, in the White House, or on Capitol Hill. As had so often been the case, however, internally generated ideas were to gain little traction in the absence of external events and external personalities who were prepared to exploit those events.

Repeating another familiar pattern, the seminal events were to come from a direction no one had anticipated. In the mid-1970s, Islamic extremists perpetrated a spate of airplane hijackings and other attacks on Western targets as a means of punishing Western nations for supporting Israel. At the Olympian levels of the US government, the rash of incidents kindled interest in a new counterterrorism force, one that would be capable of killing terrorists with such speed and precision that no harm would come to their hostages. Over the next decade, the quest for such a force would drive the development of new special operations forces and new commands. It would forever change the face of special operations forces, influencing their employment and their relations with conventional forces far beyond the realm of hostage rescue.

IRONICALLY, THE INITIAL surge came from Army Chief of Staff General Creighton Abrams, who had long disparaged elite forces as an unwise segregation of the Army's top talent. Abrams saw a new counterterrorism force as an opportunity to improve the nation's emergency readiness, increase the Army's relevance in the post-Vietnam era, and bolster the big Army at the expense of two rivals that purported to possess rapid-reaction counterterrorism capabilities—the Marine Corps and the Army's own Special Forces. Abrams resolved to form new Army counterterrorism units separate from the Special Forces, using manpower slots that would otherwise have gone to the Green Berets. The new units would be able to rescue hijacked airplanes, secure American embassies, and conduct raids by parachute, helicopter, and boat. Rather than create an entirely unprecedented force, Abrams chose to reincarnate the Rangers, capitalizing on their storied legacy to subdue institutional resistance to the addition of forces at a time of declining budgets. In the fall of 1974, Abrams reactivated the 1st and 2nd Ranger battalions and designated them the nation's premier counterterrorism units.

Two years later, another of the Army's leading lights, General William DePuy, concluded that the Army needed an even more elite force for hostage rescue. Viewing the British Special Air Service as a model for the new organization, DePuy put the project in the hands of Colonel Charlie Beckwith, a Special Forces officer who had served a tour with the Special Air Service in the 1960s. Broad of shoulder and face, his lower lip protruding above a sharp jaw, Beckwith had the look of a man in a perpetual state of ferocious insolence. In contrast to later generations of ultra-elite warriors, for whom the ideal officer had the waist of a triathlete and the head of a monk, Beckwith was a man who let it all hang out, whether it was his expansive belly or his combustible emotions. At times, he demonstrated a lack of self-control under stress that flagrantly violated the ethos of his new organization, which demanded exceptional poise at the most stress-inducing of moments.

During his prior twenty-five years of service in the Army, Beckwith had accumulated lengthy rosters of both loyal followers and staunch enemies. In Vietnam, as an officer in the 5th Special Forces Group, he had in some eyes demonstrated an impressive tenacity in completing tough missions. In other eyes, his most noteworthy trait was a propensity for getting troops killed through impatience and recklessness. The negative version of his reputation dogged him in later years, to the extent that it caused a large number of Special Forces men to shun the new organization he was forming. Knowledge of the damning whispers about his time in Vietnam pained Beckwith, who seemed genuinely intent on atoning for his past sins.

Beckwith used his considerable smarts, as well as General DePuy's backing, to gain a bureaucratic foothold for the proposed new unit. Parrying arguments from the Rangers that another unit would merely duplicate Ranger capabilities, Beckwith contended persuasively that his unit could operate less visibly than the Rangers or anyone else. His men would move in very small groups, wear civilian clothing, and mimic the customs of the local population. Beckwith also planned to acquire specialists whose skills were unavailable in the Rangers or anywhere else, such as locksmiths, electricians, and climbers.

Beckwith did not, however, possess the gifts in oratory and salesmanship that often count for more than substance in persuading others. After hearing Beckwith drone on during a presentation about the new unit, DePuy decided that he would need someone else to brief the concept if it were to obtain the necessary signatures in the Pentagon. He brought in the most talented briefer he could find on his staff, Lieutenant Colonel John Devens. An engineer by trade, Devens knew nothing about special operations, but he quickly picked up the key facts and arguments from Beckwith. His briefings to high Army leaders in the middle of 1977, delivered with a delicate synthesis of eloquence and passion, paved the way for authorization of the unit at year's end.

The new unit, code-named Delta Force, fell under the Special Forces. DePuy put it there to give it access to the manpower and resources of the three Special Forces Groups that had survived the cuts of the late Vietnam era. Beckwith set up the unit's headquarters at Fort Bragg in what had been the base stockade, a relatively new building whose nine acres and barbed-wire fence afforded it an isolation much prized by a secretive organization. Transferring the inmates to a jail in downtown Fayetteville, Delta Force converted the maximum-security wing into a holding area for ammunition, explosives, and sensitive documents. Beckwith, who admitted to a strong partiality for roses, ordered the planting of rose gardens adjacent to the front walkway, dictating that they include every color in the rose palette. Gardeners planted French Lace, All-American, Seashell, Dainty Bess, and Lady X, and groomed them with the meticulousness of the rose coiffeurs of Versailles.

To both DePuy and Beckwith it was clear that Delta Force would draw its personnel from the Special Forces and the Rangers. Those organizations, however, pulled out every trick in the book to keep their personnel from participating in Delta's tryouts. After much pressuring from above, the Special Forces and Rangers agreed to allow men with specializations in weapons and demolitions to audition for Delta Force—thereby excluding those with scarcer and more prized skills, such as medicine, communications, and intelligence. They also found ways to keep their best weapons and demolition men from trying out. To Beckwith's chagrin, few of the initial applicants from the Special Forces and Rangers met his exacting standards.

Beckwith complained about the personnel problem to his superior in the Special Forces chain of command, Major General Jack Mackmull. Little changed. On March 8, 1978, Beckwith decided to circumvent Mackmull and take his grievances directly to General Edward "Shy" Meyer, deputy chief of staff of the Army. A member of Beckwith's staff drove from Fort Bragg to Washington to hand deliver the envelope, in order to ensure that the message would not be intercepted by an unsympathetic party or get stuck in the clogged arteries of the Army bureaucracy. In the letter, Beckwith informed Meyer that the obstructionism of the Special Forces and Rangers was preventing Delta Force from obtaining the manpower it needed to fulfill its mission. He requested that Delta be taken away from General Mackmull and placed directly under the authority of the Army chief of staff.

Undoubtedly Beckwith hoped that General Meyer would take care of the problem without involving General Mackmull. Meyer, however, was the type of leader who wanted the accuser to face the accused. Mackmull was in Korea when Meyer's office notified him of Beckwith's protest. News that a subordinate had complained directly to a higher link in the chain of command pleased Mackmull no more than it would have pleased any other leader. Cutting short his trip, Mackmull flew back immediately to Fort Bragg and summoned Beckwith to an early Saturday morning meeting.

Mackmull paid no homage to subtlety in dressing down Beckwith. "What you did the other day, Colonel, was an act of disloyalty," Mackmull steamed. "From the beginning, you have shown a reluctance to work within the system."

The flame tips of Mackmull's words had no trouble igniting Beckwith's emotional tinder. "I am not in the business, General, of getting my ticket punched," Beckwith retorted.

Turning red in the face, Mackmull shouted, "Well, Colonel, what's your game then?"

"My game is to get out of Dodge," Beckwith yelled back. "I'm gonna get this unit moved out of Fort Bragg, North Carolina."

"Well, that's not going to happen."

"We'll see."

Later that very day, General Shy Meyer showed up at Fort Bragg to settle the matter. After receiving an initial briefing, Meyer addressed the group with a forcefulness belying his curious nickname. "I want everyone but the following people to leave: General Warner, General Mackmull, Charlie [Beckwith], Dick Potter, and my two action officers, Colonels Owen and Stotser. Everyone else will leave." All smiling and joking ceased as the other attendees shuffled out of the room. Casting his eyes across those who remained, Meyer projected an air of sublime authority, so captivating in its effect that Beckwith thought it must have been comparable to King Arthur's commanding presence at the round table.

"I have the authority from the Chief of Staff of the Army to hire, to fire, and to transfer anyone in this room," Meyer intoned. Turning his head to Beckwith, he said, "Charlie, you've got to realize something. I think about you and the guys down here every day. But, I'm a busy man. I don't have time, personally, on a day-to-day basis, to run this unit." Therefore, explained Meyer, there was no alternative to keeping Delta Force under Mackmull.

Beckwith put up his hand. "Can I say something?" he asked. Rising to his feet, his voice choking up like that of a nervous high school student during a class presentation, the Delta Force commander spluttered, "How in the hell do you expect me to do my job and run this unit when that general right there told me this morning I was disloyal? How can I continue to work under that man?"

Looking Beckwith in the eye, Meyer said flatly, "I'm not interested in hearing that, so sit down." Beckwith sank back into his chair.

Meyer then addressed Mackmull. "Jack, I'm not sure in my own mind you have supported Charlie. But, I'll tell you one thing you're going to do on Monday morning; you're going to open the gates and allow anyone in the Special Forces who wants to try out for Delta to come on over." The same would go for the Rangers.

"There is to be no more bickering," Meyer continued. "Do you understand, Jack?" Meyer added that if Mackmull and Beckwith came to an impasse, Beckwith could contact Meyer's office.

With the manpower spigot now fully open, Beckwith began screening candidates in earnest. Seeking only a dozen men for the first Delta Force training class, he could be extremely selective. Any man who wished to be considered had to meet an age minimum of twenty-two years, a service minimum of four years, and an Army aptitude test minimum of 110. Preliminary screening involved trials of physical fitness, which included swimming one hundred meters in a lake while wearing fatigues and boots. Psychologists inundated the candidates with questions, such as: "Do you hear voices? Are you an agent of God? Are people following you? Are you often misunderstood? Do you have thoughts too terrible to speak about?" To identify individuals who might be suffering from ulcers or alcoholism, the questioners inquired, "Is your stool black and tarry?" The prospective special operators were asked to enumerate their weaknesses, and those who responded that they did not have any were eliminated from contention.

Individuals who passed through the preliminary filters went on to a selection course in the Uwharrie National Forest, near Troy, North Carolina. Because Beckwith prized the ability to operate alone for extended periods, the course compelled the candidates to spend days at a time navigating the wilderness in solitude. Carrying a fifty-five-pound rucksack, they traipsed through hardwood forests, scaled steep hills and mountains, and forded streams and rivers. Men who did not reach prescribed checkpoints in the allotted times were disqualified and sent back to their units. In the end, Beckwith invited the top twelve men of the first candidate class of 163 to join Delta Force. The 7 percent acceptance rate seemed shockingly low at the time, but in fact it would be higher than the rates for all subsequent Delta selection classes.

The newly inducted Delta operators proceeded to a five-month Operators Course, focused mainly on high-end tactical skills. They practiced breaching, room clearing, land navigation, hostage management, and communications. Each man learned how to climb and rappel from buildings, and how to pick a pin tumbler lock. Beckwith made marksmanship a top priority, in anticipation of stealthy raids in which operators would have to fell dozens of guards without scratching the hostages in their midst. Every man was expected to spend three to four hours a day, five days a week, shooting weapons. In a new $90,000 motion-picture facility, the Delta operators were immersed in videotaped hostage scenarios, the screens freezing the instant a shot was fired so that they could determine exactly whom the shooter had hit.

Unlike many of its special operations kin, Delta Force did not have to wait long for an opportunity to put its capabilities into use. Nor did it face any doubts about the strategic importance of the first task it was seeking to perform. The opportunity germinated on November 4, 1979, with the seizure of the US embassy in Tehran by elements of Iran's Islamic revolution. President Jimmy Carter, convinced that resort to military measures involved too much risk, initially vowed to get the sixty-three American hostages back through diplomacy.

The military, though, has a habit of planning for contingencies, particularly in situations where it doubts that the adversary is as willing to negotiate for peace as the State Department believes. The Joint Chiefs of Staff formed an ad hoc Joint Task Force to plan and organize a rescue mission, labeled Operation Eagle Claw, in case Carter's confidence in diplomacy ran out. The chiefs named Army Major General James B. Vaught the task force commander and put Beckwith in command of the ground element, which included ninety-three Delta operators and a thirteen-man Special Forces team.

Because no friendly air bases lay near Tehran, the planners devised an elaborate series of air and ground movements to get Beckwith's men into the city and get the hostages out. American C-130 transport aircraft were to rendezvous with helicopters at an abandoned airfield 260 miles southeast of Tehran, designated Desert One. The helicopters would be refueled from fuel bladders hauled aboard the C-130s, and would then take the rescue team to a dry riverbed in an area of deserted salt mines fifty miles outside Tehran. The ground operators would transfer to six Mercedes trucks and two smaller vehicles that had been staged there in advance. Accompanied by Farsi-speaking volunteers from the US military and two former Iranian generals who could talk their way through checkpoints, the force would drive into Tehran, disembarking at a street next to the embassy. The ground operators would climb over the embassy walls, shoot the guards with silenced weapons, liberate the hostages, and move everyone to a soccer stadium across the street from the embassy, where helicopters would retrieve them and fly them to Desert Two, an airstrip thirty-five miles south of Tehran. C-130s would be waiting at the airstrip, ready to take them home.

The task force began training for Eagle Claw in December 1979. To simulate the conditions expected at Desert One, they rehearsed at the Marine Corps Air Station in Yuma, Arizona, and at the secretive Area 51 in the Nevada desert. The CIA built models of the US embassy compound, exploiting detailed information on circuit breaker locations and wall thicknesses from thirteen women and black men whom the Iranians had released from custody as a gesture of their magnanimity and their contempt for the white American male. The task force practiced assaulting the mock compound so many times that they became bored, depressed even.

All of the CIA's case officers in Iran had been taken hostage, and the CIA was unwilling to assume the risks of sending in new case officers to obtain fresh information on the situation. The Department of Defense therefore infiltrated its own spies into Tehran. Dick Meadows, who had reached only the rank of major before retiring from the Army, despite his exemplary service in Vietnam, volunteered to take a small team of men into the city in disguise. Posing as Irish and German businessmen, the team snooped for facts on the embassy and nearby facilities and secured vehicles for the overland phase of the operation.

Meanwhile, the Iranians were thwarting Carter's diplomatic initiatives with the deftness one might expect of descendants of Persian rug salesmen in negotiations with a well-meaning Georgia peanut farmer. The Ayatollah Khomeini, Supreme Leader of the Islamic Republic of Iran, spurned every US envoy, even Attorney General Ramsey Clark, who had publicly voiced support for Khomeini's revolution. As Carter's goodwill soured into distrust, he began imposing economic sanctions on Iran, but the sanctions failed to sway Khomeini. Months without result drained the American public's patience and aroused a yearning for tougher action, embodied in the radio hit "Bomb Iran," set to the tune of the Beach Boys' "Barbara Ann." President Carter's approval ratings tumbled, putting his reelection bid in grave jeopardy.

In the middle of April 1980, a desperate Carter finally invited the Pentagon to present him with military options. General Vaught and Colonel Beckwith were summoned to the White House on April 16 to brief the president on Eagle Claw, which held greater appeal for Carter than did other military options, such as mining Iran's ports or bombing its oil refineries, as it appeared to involve less risk of provoking the Soviet Union or entangling the United States in a protracted war. Dressed in their formal service attire, the military men were surprised to see White House Chief of Staff Hamilton Jordan strut into the White House situation room wearing Levi's jeans. Vice President Walter Mondale showed up late in a fancy sweatsuit and sneakers. President Carter, clad in a blue blazer and gray slacks, looked more dignified than his underlings, and he looked to be calm and at ease.

Carter opened the meeting. "Dave," he said, addressing Chairman of the Joint Chiefs of Staff General David C. Jones, "I am seriously considering going ahead with the mission, but I will make a final decision only after this meeting and after I've had several days to think about it. I would like you all to assume that none of us knows anything about it and provide us with a step-by-step rundown."

Jones introduced Beckwith and Vaught, noting that "the Joint Chiefs' unanimous recommendation was for Charlie Beckwith to lead the rescue team." The military officers described the planning in detail, exuding confidence in successful execution of the operation as they stepped through the phases. Having thought through the problem for months, they quickly and effortlessly answered volleys of questions about potential complications.

Beckwith's remark that Delta Force planned to "take the guards out" at the embassy drew a question from Warren Christopher, the deputy secretary of state. "Will you shoot them in the shoulder or what?" Christopher asked.

Beckwith replied, "No, sir. We're going to shoot each of them twice, right between the eyes."

Christopher's nerves went taut. "You mean you're really going to shoot to kill?" Christopher asked. "You really are?"

"Yes sir," Beckwith said. "We certainly are."

In the middle of the briefing, Mondale leaned over to Beckwith and asked him for a set of handcuffs. A bewildered Beckwith handed the cuffs over, his amazement escalating as Mondale tinkered with them while the briefers delved into the intricate plan for snatching the prize from the center of the enemy's lair.

Carter, however, paid close attention throughout, and he came away thoroughly impressed with both the commanders and their plan. "In their meticulous description of every facet of the operation," Carter wrote in his memoirs, "I received satisfactory answers to all my many questions." His congenital aversion to force overcome, Carter ordered the generals to execute Operation Eagle Claw.

During the next week, the men and equipment of the task force converged on airfields across the United States. Transport aircraft leapfrogged to refueling sites scattered between the Azores and Germany before coming together at an abandoned Soviet airfield at Wadi Kena, Egypt, the operation's final staging area. Ahead of the task force's arrival at Wadi Kena, pallets of beer and soda were flown to the airfield and offloaded into two large refrigerators.

For the first time that anyone on the task force could remember, the US Army gave the men alcohol free of charge. Each man was allotted two beers per day, though some seemed to get their hands on considerably larger quantities. Spending several days in reinforced concrete hangars that could have passed for avant-garde sculptures in a Soviet museum of people's art, the troops relied on the beer and soda to compensate for a shortage of drinking water from the facility's overtaxed potable-water system. Once the canned beverages had run out, the medics filled the refrigerators with bags of blood.

One part of the task force flew to the aircraft carrier USS *Nimitz* in the Gulf of Oman. Already on board the *Nimitz* were the eight RH-53 Sea Stallion helicopters that would make the six-hundred-mile journey to Desert One. The largest helicopter in the US inventory, the Sea Stallion had been selected for the mission because it could haul thirty passengers and their equipment with the imperturbability of a pack mule. The rest of the task force went to Masirah, a small desert island off the coast of Oman, whence six Air Force C-130 transport planes would carry the ground element and the fuel bladders to Desert One.

The task force aircraft lifted off from the *Nimitz* and Masirah on April 24. Within half an hour, the mishaps began. The C-130s were supposed to reach the Iranian coast after dark so they would not be seen, but when the first C-130 made land there was still light in the sky. Two hours later, a warning light flashed in the cockpit of one of the Sea Stallions, signaling that the rotor blade was losing pressure. The pilot, Major Bill Hoff, landed the helicopter in the desert to verify the cockpit reading. He could not see damage to the rotors, but his years of flying Sea Stallions for the Marine Corps led him to conclude that the rotor had suffered a hairline crack, an affliction that would make the aircraft unsafe for flying. Hoff and his crew abandoned the helicopter and hitched a ride aboard another. Unbeknownst to Hoff, aluminum rotors of the sort on the Navy Sea Stallion he had been flying had never cracked, whereas the titanium rotors on the Marine Corps model had cracked thirty-one times in preceding years. Had the task force possessed dedicated air assets, instead of a hodgepodge of aircraft and pilots thrown together after the crisis erupted, the pilot would have known that the aircraft could have continued to fly.

Three hours into the mission, the airmen in the remaining helicopters were surprised to find dust storms, hundreds of miles deep and wide, swirling in their path. Because the operation had been highly compartmentalized for security reasons, the pilots did not have regular contact with weather specialists, but instead received all their weather information from an intelligence officer. Somewhere along the line, the information about the storms had been lost.

Surrounded by dust, their eyeballs overstressed by prolonged use of night-vision goggles, the air crews lost sight of the ground and their fellow helicopters. In the words of one airman, it was like "flying in a bowl of milk." The pilots had to fly on instruments for several hours, trying the mental endurance of even the most resilient of men. When the gyroscope in one of the helicopters failed, the pilot lost his only sure means of avoiding a crash into one of the region's mountains, so he had to turn back to the *Nimitz*. The number of helicopters was down to six.

The sandstorms compelled the helicopters to fly more slowly than planned, such that each of the six remaining helicopters reached Desert One well behind the appointed time in the operation's carefully scripted forty-hour schedule. The first helicopter to land was piloted by Jim Schaefer, an exceptionally skilled flyer whom the Delta operators would have most expected, of all the pilots, to triumph over adverse flying conditions. After five hours in the air, the first thing Schaefer did was walk behind his aircraft to urinate. While he was still in the act, Beckwith and other Delta officers rushed up to him.

"What the hell's going on?" demanded Beckwith. "How did you get so goddamned late?"

"First of all, we're only twenty-five minutes late," Schaefer replied. "Second of all, I don't know where anyone else is because we went into a big dust cloud."

"There's no goddamned dust cloud out here," Beckwith insisted, pointing into a sky that appeared devoid of dust.

"Well, there is one," Schaefer said. He informed Beckwith that he had never flown through such perilous weather in all his years. His helicopter might have been damaged during the flight, he said, and he was not sure that they could continue with the mission.

To Beckwith, it appeared that Schaefer's spirit had been trampled by the ordeal. "I'm going to report this thing," Beckwith growled. Slapping Schaefer on the back, Beckwith said that he and the other air crews would have to suck it up.

Beckwith counted the helicopters as more came in. When the sixth arrived, the task force men cheered and exchanged high fives, for six was considered the minimum number required for the flight to the outskirts of Tehran. Delta Force began loading gear into the bellies of the Sea Stallions.

As the men were stacking MP-5 submachine guns, ammunition boxes, and backpacks on the choppers, the helicopter flight leader informed Beckwith that one of the six remaining Sea Stallions had suffered the loss of one of its two hydraulic pumps. If the other pump failed during flight, the pilot would lose steerage of the helicopter and the resultant crash would likely kill all aboard. The flight leader recommended that the chopper not be flown.

Beckwith believed that the problem was not a mechanical one but a loss of nerve among the pilots. If any individuals deserved blame for the helicopter shortage, though, they were to be found among the aviation planners at rear-echelon headquarters. Heirs to the "Whiz Kids" of the Vietnam-era Defense Department, these planners prided themselves on the use of statistical analysis in solving difficult problems. Forecasting helicopter breakdown rates by crunching numbers from past Sea Stallion flights, the planners had decided to assign Eagle Claw only two helicopters above the minimum requirement.

The performance data that the number crunchers had used came from flights operating under normal conditions, and hence their analysis did not take into account the impact of desert heat and sandstorms on helicopter attrition. The planners also had hurt themselves by disregarding the history of heliborne operations. Over time, military practitioners had learned to include twice as many helicopters as the minimum required for mission completion, on account of the susceptibility of helicopters to mechanical breakdowns and their vulnerability to enemy fire.

The task force notified Washington that only five of the helicopters could fly. Zbigniew Brzezinski, Carter's national security adviser, sent word back that the operation could proceed if the commanders on the scene thought they could accomplish the mission with five helicopters. Beckwith, who had been saying for months that the mission could not succeed with only five helicopters, reiterated that judgment now in recommending that the operation be aborted. Secretary of Defense Harold Brown phoned the White House to relay Beckwith's recommendation. Listening to Brown on a secure phone, Carter learned that officers up the chain of command concurred with Beckwith. After a brief moment, Carter said quietly, "Let's go with his recommendation."

Rather than flying the helicopters back to the *Nimitz* through the sandstorms, the task force leadership decided to destroy the helicopters and fly everyone out on the C-130s. To make way for the big transport aircraft on the improvised desert landing strip, Jim Schaefer lifted his helicopter a few feet off the ground and steered it under the guidance of a combat controller. When the desert wind kicked up a cloud of sand, however, Schaefer did not see that the controller had stepped back. Disoriented, Schaefer flew his Sea Stallion into one of the C-130s.

The Sea Stallion's rotors caught the top of the plane, and then the helicopter's torso plunged into the cockpit of the C-130, igniting both aircraft. Men piled out of the flaming wrecks and ran as fast and far as they could, their sense of urgency fortified by the knowledge that the fuel bladders inside the C-130 could ignite at any moment. Eight men who had been injured or killed in the collision were still inside the aircraft when the fuel exploded. Casting out heat and yellow-orange light like a small sun, the wreckage burned so hot that the survivors who attempted to recover the bodies of the eight men could not get anywhere near them. The task force had to leave the dead behind.

The would-be rescuers flew back to Wadi Kena, arriving just thirty hours after they had left. As other men sat down in dejection, Beckwith erupted into a fit of rage, hurling insults in all directions. He called the helicopter pilots cowards. Learning that men had fled the two burning aircraft without taking their weapons or other equipment with them, he yelled, "You guys, as you came off, should have reached up and grabbed something. Goddamn, a lot of money burned up in there." When one officer refused to pay attention to Beckwith's ranting, Beckwith went over to him and barked, "If we ever do this damn thing again, I'll make sure people like you don't come along!"

Once Beckwith had stomped away from the scene, an angry troop sergeant went to speak with him in private. The sergeant expressed the collective belief that the men in the flaming Sea Stallion and the C-130 had not had time to think about saving equipment. No one had known how soon the fuel-laden C-130 would blow. The sergeant ultimately persuaded

Beckwith that the criticism had been unfair, and that he should issue an apology.

Beckwith soon accepted the fact that at least some of the blame lay with him. At a meeting with President Carter at Camp Peary, Virginia, a few days after the operation, Beckwith broke down at the sight of the commander-in-chief. Carter described the encounter: "His chin was quivering and tears were running down his cheeks. I opened my arms and we embraced and wept together." Beckwith said through the tears, "Mr. President, I'm sorry we let you down."

Eagle Claw dealt Beckwith's seemingly immortal self-confidence an irreparable blow. After Desert One, Beckwith "was never the same," recalled Delta Force veteran Eric Haney. "The failure of the operation seemed to completely deflate him. I never again saw a flicker of that fabulous internal fire of his. It fled his being, never to return."

For critics of SOF, Desert One proved that the special operators were not as good as advertised, and that special operations could not solve strategic problems. For proponents of SOF, it showed that the special operators had been thwarted by the military's reliance on an ad hoc organization with poor internal communications and inadequate aviation assets. A review group of six senior military officers, commissioned by Chairman of the Joint Chiefs of Staff Jones, agreed with the latter assessment, and as a remedy to the disease of ad hockery, the review team proposed the creation of a Counterterrorist Joint Task Force with permanently assigned staff and forces.

This proposal caused the service chiefs to form into a phalanx, with the aim of protecting their elite units from the clutches of the chairman of the Joint Chiefs. The regional military commanders opposed the joint task force because they thought it would operate in their areas without their knowledge or consent. Secretary of Defense Brown, who favored the proposed task force, decided to cut short the opposition of the generals by issuing an executive fiat to the service chiefs. Summoned to what they had thought would be a meeting to hear their views on the matter, the Joint Chiefs were enraged when they learned of Brown's fiat halfway through the briefing. The new organization, dubbed the Joint Special Operations Command and abbreviated as JSOC, thus became the newest entry on the list of special operations forces pushed down the throat of the rest of the military, and hence the newest to incur the resentments of the military establishment.

AT THE BEGINNING of September 1980, General Jones pulled Brigadier General Dick Scholtes from the 82nd Airborne Division to command JSOC. Establishing a new headquarters at Fort Bragg inside the Delta Force compound, Scholtes took control of Delta Force, the Army's two Ranger battalions, and the Air Force's 1st Special Operations Wing. Higher headquarters notified Scholtes that JSOC should prepare to launch another mission to rescue the hostages in Iran.

JSOC planned and rehearsed for several months. The victory of the hardline Republican Ronald Reagan in the November presidential election convinced the men of JSOC that they would be unleashed as soon as the White House changed hands. JSOC was going through the final dress rehearsal on the day of Reagan's inauguration when word came that the Iranian government had agreed to release the hostages in return for the unfreezing of financial assets.

The evaporation of a chance at redemption in Tehran left Scholtes and JSOC bereft of overseas tasks for some time. Their next challenge was internal, the result of a directive for Scholtes to take the Navy's newly formed SEAL Team Six into his brood. SEAL Team Six was conceived and commanded by Commander Richard Marcinko, a burly thirty-nine-year-old who had risen from the enlisted ranks to become a SEAL officer. Marcinko had served two tours in Vietnam, during which he had received a Silver Star and four Bronze Stars. After the war, he had worked for several high-flying naval officers, whom he so impressed that they hoisted him up the promotion ladder ahead of his peers.

The two admirals who did the most to put Marcinko in charge of SEAL Team Six were James A. "Ace" Lyons and William Crowe. Both of them eventually attained the rank of full admiral, the highest rank in the peacetime Navy, and Crowe went on to become chairman of the Joint Chiefs of Staff. According to Marcinko's autobiography, the admirals were drawn to him not only by his hard work, but also by a shared predilection for locker-room banter. Marcinko wrote of Lyons, "I found it reassuring when he called me 'asshole' and came to realize that I was making progress when that sobriquet changed to 'shithead.'" With respect to Crowe, Marcinko wrote, "Despite his courtly manner with subordinates and soft Kentucky accent, he was one of those admirals I could say 'fuck' to."

SEAL Team Six was ostensibly a maritime force like the other SEAL teams. Marcinko, however, sought to make it a super-elite unit that could do anything Delta Force could do, and more. In the manning of the unit, the Navy granted Marcinko permission to cherry-pick SEALs from the other SEAL teams. Marcinko took full advantage of this license, and did so with a bravado that twisted the knife in the psychological wounds of the SEALs whose teams were plundered.

A heavy drinker, Marcinko tested prospective Team Six members for their aptitude in the consumption of alcohol. One recruit was offered a beer at 7 a.m., and when he declined, Marcinko warned him that unwillingness to drink in the morning might make a man unsuitable for the team. SEAL Team Six seldom finished field exercises, because, in the words of the team's executive officer, "as soon as things got tough, Dick would step in, abort the exercise, and take the troops drinking." At Virginia Beach, the venue for vibrant nightlife closest to the Team Six headquarters at Dam Neck, the police department was kept busy responding to reports of drunken brawling and hijinks at the bars along the boardwalk. If junior officers objected to Marcinko's encouragement of drinking and fighting, or to anything else Marcinko did, they were kicked out of the unit. A Team Six veteran recounted that Marcinko's intolerance of dissent "brought out the worst of deadly 'group think,' a sort of collective megalomania, where a Team begins to think that they are too good to fail."

Scholtes, a creature of the regular Army, was not amused by Marcinko's fraternity house antics. The JSOC commander's forbearance was extinguished on the night of a promotion party at Marcinko's headquarters. Marcinko, unable to suppress his inveterate urge for bragging, informed the visiting Scholtes that they would be dining on Maine lobsters following the promotion ceremony. When Scholtes asked how the SEALs had obtained the lobsters, Marcinko replied, "I flew them down." Whether Scholtes was more appalled by Marcinko's use of government aircraft to fly the lobsters or by his self-congratulation was unclear. Marcinko had also arranged for the delivery of cases of alcoholic beverages, from which he and his team quaffed so tenaciously that by the end of the evening they had difficulty standing up. Scholtes watched the drunken revelry with the revulsion of the Theban King Pentheus observing his subjects debauched by the wine and carousing of Dionysus.

The next day, Scholtes called Marcinko onto the carpet. "Last night was an absolute disgrace," Scholtes barked at the SEAL commander. After enumerating the offenses, Scholtes notified Marcinko that he would receive a letter of reprimand for the escapade. Marcinko most probably would have been stripped of his command for this incident, and others that were to follow, were it not for the fact that his guardian angels in the naval chain of command protected him from afar.

Marcinko remained in his charmed position for three years, until finally his luck ran out. On a night of partying near Dam Neck, Marcinko directed his driver to take him for a spin in a Mercedes sedan that was supposed to be used solely for overseas operations. It was by no means the first time Marcinko had taken the vehicle out on the town, and it certainly would not have been the last had the driver not rear-ended a car in a manner serious enough to require the ministrations of the police. When details of the misadventure reached JSOC headquarters, Scholtes decided to issue Marcinko an unsatisfactory fitness report, a career-ruining event for a naval officer. By this time, Marcinko's friends in the upper ranks of the Navy had moved out of positions from which they could protect him. Marcinko was relieved of command of SEAL Team Six and sent to work at the Pentagon.

In his most incredible feat yet, the enterprising Marcinko managed to get the unsatisfactory fitness report removed from his personnel file. Then he obtained a promotion. When word of the promotion reached the SEAL community, however, several SEALs contacted the Naval Investigative Service with allegations of misconduct that would, if proven true, be serious enough to sink Marcinko once and for all.

The investigators who dug into Team Six's records discovered that Marcinko and others had been reimbursed for lodging at an address where no lodging had ever existed. They learned that one of Marcinko's subordinates had used bogus travel and schooling claims to buy Marcinko a Smith and Wesson Model 56 pistol with handles of elephant-tusk ivory, onto which Marcinko's face had been scrimshawed. After further probing, the Investigative Service determined that Marcinko had received a kickback of over $100,000 from a company in Phoenix that had sold the Navy 4,300 grenades on Marcinko's instructions. In March 1990, a court sentenced Marcinko to twenty-one months in prison and fined him $10,000.

Following Marcinko's departure from SEAL Team Six, the Navy decided to clean up the unit. A formal personnel selection process replaced Marcinko's personal whims and trials of beer swilling. But Marcinko's braggadocio and criminal activities left a lingering distaste for SEAL Team Six on the tongues of the other special operations units for years to come. One SEAL Team Six veteran lamented, "I came in a decade after Marcinko and I completely felt that we had the Marcinko stink on us."

WHILE JSOC WAS struggling to attach its bridle to SEAL Team Six, the Special Forces were galloping off to their next overseas conflict, in El Salvador. Cuban-backed Communist guerrillas had spread across the Salvadoran countryside in 1980 by promising to liberate the peasantry from the nation's cruel and corrupt security forces. Ten days before President Carter left office, the Communists launched what they hoped would be a decisive offensive, in the belief that Carter would be much less inclined to intervene on behalf of the Salvadoran government than would his staunchly anti-Communist successor. "It is necessary," the insurgents asserted, "to launch now the battles for the great general offensive of the Salvadoran people before that fanatic Ronald Reagan takes over the presidency of the United States."

The offensive did not attain the intended objective of overthrowing the government, but it did heighten American concerns about the state of affairs in the Central American nation. Racing to strengthen the Salvadoran security forces before the Communist rebels could overrun the cities, President Reagan authorized an increase in the small US Special Forces presence in March 1981. Beholden to the provisions of the War Powers Resolution of 1973, he could raise the number of American advisers in El

Salvador to only fifty-five, and these advisers could not accompany Salvadoran forces in the field.

The Special Forces advisers set out to reform the Salvadoran officer corps, in combination with US military instructors at Fort Benning, who trained Salvadoran officers sent on temporary assignment to the United States. Appalled by the low work ethic and lack of initiative among Salvadoran officers, the Special Forces taught them the American way by example. They advised the Salvadorans to desist from indiscriminate violence against villages suspected of harboring insurgents, in order to obtain the popular support needed to win the war.

Over a period of several years, the Americans succeeded in altering the organizational culture of the Salvadoran armed forces. Salvadoran officers replaced their forty-hour workweek with an intensive wartime schedule. Instead of waiting for orders from on high, they acted on their own initiative. Military proficiency soared, putting an end to easy insurgent military victories, and sharp declines in human rights violations eliminated the principal grievance of the rural peasantry. These improvements rescued the Salvadoran government from what had seemed like imminent defeat and set the conditions for transition from military rule to liberal democracy.

A much more intense, if also much briefer, conflict awaited America's special operators in Grenada, a 133-square-mile mound of volcanic ash in the eastern Caribbean. The island was home to 110,000 people, and to the peaks and craters of the volcanoes that had brought it out of the seafloor 2 million years earlier. In 1979, the Marxist-Leninist Maurice Bishop had seized control of the island's government by coup d'état, and thence had become a recipient of Soviet and Cuban military largesse. Although Bishop's hostility to the United States was plain, he permitted American faculty and students to remain at St. George's University Medical School, an institution established by four American entrepreneurs to serve Americans who had failed to gain admission to medical schools in the United States. Approximately six hundred Americans were at the school when the crisis erupted in October 1983.

The war, if it could be called that, sprang from a coup at the beginning of October. While Prime Minister Bishop was visiting socialist brethren in Hungary and Czechoslovakia, one of his Communist rivals, Bernard

Coard, convinced members of the Grenadian Party Central Committee to turn against him. Upon Bishop's return, the committee stripped him of his powers and put him under house arrest. Ten thousand of Bishop's supporters showed up at his house, compelling the guards to hand the prime minister over, but then a column of armored military vehicles drove into the mob and gunned their way to Bishop, whom they executed.

The new regime rounded up suspected enemies and imposed a shoot-on-sight curfew. Americans at the medical school were confined to their dormitories, their communications with the outside world severed by the snipping of telephone wires. To President Reagan, it had all the makings of another Iranian hostage crisis. Unlike Carter, whose fear of provoking others always inclined him toward diplomacy rather than force, Reagan had few qualms about responding in the way that leaders of great powers traditionally responded when challenged by an ant-sized adversary in their own neighborhood—squashing the ant under a boot heel.

Reagan directed the Pentagon to invade Grenada in just a few days' time. The ultimate objectives, the White House stated, were the rescue of the Americans and the replacement of the Communist government with a democratic one. Owing to uncertainty about the strength of the Cuban and Grenadian soldiers defending the island, American planners decided that the operation demanded more than just special operations forces. US Atlantic Command created an ad hoc organization, Joint Task Force (JTF) 120, to command an admixture of 7,300 special and conventional forces. The task force staff made a concerted effort to assign the special operators missions that capitalized on their special capabilities, tasking Delta Force with rescuing hostages, SEALs with scouting beaches for amphibious landings, and Rangers with surprise assaults on hardened targets. The "Nightstalker" airmen of the 160th Special Operations Aviation Battalion, a unit created in October 1981 to provide the dedicated air assets for special operations that had been sorely missing in Eagle Claw, were slated to make their combat debut in Grenada.

Hours before the invasion began, at the final briefing for Joint Task Force 120 commander Vice Admiral Joseph Metcalf, representatives from the State Department demanded a change to the operational plan. The task force, they said, needed to seize the island's Richmond Hill Prison during the invasion's first hour, rather than later in the day as originally scheduled. By launching the operation at the very beginning of the invasion, the diplomats explained, the United States would deny the Grenadian government time to move or harm the inmates. Under questioning by military planners, the State Department's representatives could not say who was incarcerated in the Richmond Hill facility or who was guarding it.

General Scholtes, the JSOC commander, recommended delaying the operation by twenty-four to forty-eight hours in order to gain more information on the prison. The State Department overruled him. An intelligence briefer assured the task force that the island defenders would put up little resistance, characterizing the whole invasion as a "walk in the park." They could expect that the locals would "wave at them" as they flew into the country.

Early in the morning of October 25, at an airfield on Barbados, Delta Force boarded nine Black Hawk helicopters of the 160th Special Operations Aviation Battalion for the assault on the prison. The helicopters were supposed to depart at 1 a.m. so that they could reach the target well before sunrise and take it down under cover of darkness. They did not take off until 6:30 a.m. An official government account attributed the delay to "chaotic planning, last-minute inter-service bickering at senior levels, and Air Force delays." Given the assurances about the weakness of enemy defenses, though, the delay did not seem especially important.

By the time the Black Hawks had covered the 160 miles between Barbados and Grenada, the Caribbean was glistening sapphire blue under the morning's tropical sun, and the denizens of the volcanic island were wide awake. The helicopters had nearly crossed the one mile of ground between the sea and Richmond Hill when shell bursts from ZU-23 antiaircraft guns interrupted the steady swishing of helicopter blades. From positions that American reconnaissance had not had time to locate, the Grenadian gunners hit the first six helicopters in quick succession. On board the Black Hawks, smoke billowed from damaged engines and fuel spurted from punctured hoses. One helicopter crashed in flames. In the face of this wholly unexpected resistance, the mission commander ordered the remaining helicopters to turn tail. The American special operators sustained twenty-four wounded and one killed during the abortive raid.

At this same time, two companies of Rangers were assaulting the airfield at Point Salines on the southwestern tip of the island. Their transport aircraft also encountered unexpectedly fierce antiaircraft fire, but most of the Rangers were able to leap from the aircraft and parachute safely onto the airfield. Forming into squads and platoons on the tarmac, the Rangers composed themselves before they had to fight the airfield's Cuban military construction troops. The Cuban troops were not exactly prime military specimens—many of them were overweight and over forty years of age—but they did bring to bear BTR-60 armored personnel carriers, recoilless rifles, and machine guns. With attack aircraft from the carrier USS *Independence* providing close air support, the Rangers overpowered the airfield's defenders in a few hours, taking 250 Cubans prisoner. They then rescued 138 American medical students from campus buildings near the airstrip.

Reinforcements from the 82nd Airborne Division arrived by air at Point Salines to begin the push toward St. George's, the capital city. Conventional forces took most of their planned objectives over the next two days. They were not, however, able to reach the enemy barracks at Calivigny as quickly as high authorities in Washington desired. At noon on the 27th, the Pentagon notified Admiral Metcalf's headquarters that the barracks had to be taken before dark. According to intelligence reports, the barracks served as the nerve center of the Cuban military forces on the island, and was guarded by six hundred crack Cuban troops and six antiaircraft cannons. Although the task was better suited to conventional infantry, Metcalf had to call upon the Rangers because all of the conventional infantry were tied up. The Rangers, who had been relaxing at Point Salines in expectation of an imminent return to the United States, hustled aboard Black Hawks for a late afternoon assault.

As it turned out, the much-feared barracks were empty. In the process of landing in the narrow streets, though, three helicopters were lost to collisions or faulty landings. Three Rangers were killed and nearly two dozen wounded.

Tallies taken after the nine-day war revealed that special operations forces accounted for a disproportionate share of American casualties, including thirteen of the nineteen American fatalities. General Scholtes blamed his command's losses on ad hoc organization and the misuse of special operations forces by conventional commanders. Scholtes advocated a new joint combatant command with permanent standing capabilities and authorities of sufficient size to handle a Grenada-sized crisis on its own. His arguments made a strong impression on several US senators who met with him in closed-door session.

The problems of Grenada served as ammunition for a small but influential group of officials at the Pentagon and on Capitol Hill who were campaigning to increase the size and authorities of special operations forces. Within the Pentagon, the reformers encountered the coalescence of opposition at every turn, so they eventually concentrated all of their efforts on Congress. A burgeoning "SOF Liberation Front," consisting primarily of former SOF officers in the Defense Department or on congressional staffs, pressed the case for change to sympathetic congressmen. The neglect and mishandling of special operations forces, asserted the cadres of the Liberation Front, demanded that Congress create a joint SOF command with a separate SOF funding line.

Under normal circumstances, the chances that former captains and lieutenant colonels would sway Congress against the opposition of four-star generals and admirals were about as low as the chances of retired parish deacons changing the Catholic Church in the face of objecting cardinals. But their campaign happened to coincide with a broader congressional initiative to overhaul the military, which culminated in the Goldwater-Nichols Act of 1986. Written in reaction to coordination problems among the armed services at Desert One and Grenada, Goldwater-Nichols reorganized the military into regional joint commands that compelled the services to work together. Senators Sam Nunn (D-Georgia) and William Cohen (R-Maine), two of the congressmen most favorably disposed toward special operations forces, believed that SOF reform would further the objectives of Goldwater-Nichols, and they recognized that reform legislation could gain traction by riding the act's coattails.

Nunn and Cohen, ably assisted by the clandestine information campaign of the SOF Liberation Front, convinced their congressional colleagues to pass a SOF reform package that became known as the Nunn-Cohen Amendment. The legislation created the Special Operations

Command (SOCOM), with a four-star commander responsible for training and equipping all special operations forces. Command of operational units, though, would remain in the hands of the four-star regional combatant commanders. To enhance the attractiveness of SOF in the eyes of the combatant commanders and the White House, Nunn-Cohen assigned special operations forces a discrete mission set, which consisted of direct action, strategic reconnaissance, unconventional warfare, foreign internal defense, civil affairs, psychological operations, counterterrorism, humanitarian assistance, and theater search and rescue. The amendment gave SOF a dedicated funding line, Major Force Program 11, and established the position of assistant secretary of defense for special operations and low-intensity conflict to give SOF stronger representation inside the Pentagon.

The Army, Navy, and Air Force put their special operations forces under SOCOM. The Marine Corps, however, refused to contribute any personnel. The Marine generals of the mid-1980s, like their predecessors, were loath to transfer some of their best Marines to elite units under the command of non-Marines, fearing that it would degrade the Marines as a whole. To ward off accusations that they were not playing their part in special operations, the Marines touted their newly formed "special operations capable" units. Trained in certain highly specialized operations, these units had been created by the Marine leadership to satisfy the appetite of higher authorities for SOF without surrendering control of any Marines. Special operations personnel from other services derided the program as less than special. Bickering over Marine abstention from SOCOM and over the validity of the "special operations capable" Marine units would poison relations between the Marines and special operators for the remainder of the century.

At the inaugural ceremony for SOCOM on June 1, 1987, Joint Chiefs chairman Admiral William J. Crowe Jr. entreated special operators to "break down the wall that has more or less come between special operations forces and the other parts of our military, the wall that some people will try to build higher." In the months that followed, his prophecy about building the wall higher was fulfilled by individuals on both sides. Die-hard SOF proponents argued that special operations forces should take advantage of their newfound powers to concentrate on irregular warfare, counterterrorism, and other activities in which they would be the main show, instead of activities that supported or complemented conventional forces. The Special Forces formed their own separate branch within the Army, which allowed soldiers to remain in the Special Forces to the end of their careers and extricated them from a personnel system that had treated service with the Special Forces as a temporary and career-inhibiting diversion.

Some conventional military officers and Defense Department officials were content to let the special operators go their own way, so that they were not poking their noses into the play yards of the big divisions and fleets. To limit the influence of the new Special Operations Command and distance it from its congressional supporters, the Pentagon leadership put the new organization far from Washington, at Tampa's MacDill Air Force Base. Representatives Dan Daniel, John Kasich, and Earl Hutto, three of the leading SOF proponents in Congress, denounced the Defense Department for placing SOCOM "as far away from the rest of the US government as is possible without setting sail out to sea."

The striving of the Special Forces to separate themselves from the rest of the Army did not sit well with the Army's top leaders. Acting swiftly and forcefully, they halted the addition of bricks to the wall and started knocking bricks off. Brigadier General Jim Guest, commandant of the Army Special Warfare Center and School at the time, credits the decisive action to General Maxwell Thurman, the four-star commander of the Army's Training and Doctrine Command.

"I'm tired of having to apologize for Special Forces," Thurman wrote to Guest in a letter that reverberated across the Special Forces world. "I am tired of their reputation. I am tired of having to deal with their lack of professionalism. Are they in the Army or not? If you don't do something about this, I am going to relieve you. I will run you out of the Army."

The threat had the intended effect. As explained by General Guest, the letter forced the leadership of the Special Forces to recognize that "we've got to convince the senior generals that we are professionals, that we are capable of doing special missions, and that we're not just a camp of thugs." The message also brought home the point that "we can't mess around any longer outside the Army system; we've got to do things inside it."

Guest raised the standards for incoming Special Forces personnel. He established a new two-week selection course to identify individuals who could withstand high levels of stress and ambiguity, and who could both operate on their own and serve as part of a team. Troublemakers and slackers were plucked out and recycled into the regular Army or terminated from the service. "Jim Guest did more to enhance the Special Forces and make them the significant force they are today than any other general officer," observed Brigadier General Richard W. "Dick" Potter, who was himself one of the main standard-bearers of the reform movement.

Special operations forces received an early opportunity to showcase their new capabilities and interoperability with conventional forces in Operation Just Cause, the invasion of Panama. President George H. W. Bush authorized Just Cause in December 1989 to depose dictator Manuel Noriega, also known as "the Pineapple Face" because of his acne-pitted visage, for a series of offenses that had culminated in the killing of US Marine Lieutenant Robert Paz. Joint Task Force South, which was in charge of the invasion, assigned responsibility for all US special operations forces to a joint special operations task force.

In preparation for the invasion's conventional assaults, Special Forces from the 7th Group scouted Panamanian facilities. Once hostilities commenced, twenty-four Green Berets seized a critical bridge over the Pacora River and held it long enough for reinforcements to arrive. Several other Special Forces teams descended by fast rope onto the roofs of television and radio stations and blew up the transmission equipment, putting an end to pernicious Noriega propaganda.

Replete with Spanish speakers, the 7th Group sent some of its personnel to help conventional forces goad enemy combatants into surrendering. Calling Panamanian commanders by phone, the Special Forces men told them to place their units' weapons in the arms room, line up the men on the parade field, and surrender to the US forces that were about to arrive in overwhelming strength. Almost 2,000 Panamanian troops laid down their arms as a result of these conversations.

In Panama City, Delta Force, the Rangers, and the Nightstalkers joined a conventional Army mechanized company in assaulting the headquarters of the Panama Defense Forces. Moving into blocking positions around the headquarters, M-113 armored personnel carriers pumped shells into the walls while AC-130 and AH-6 gunships, from what was now termed the 160th Special Operations Aviation Group, peppered the buildings from above. Once the main headquarters building had been beaten to a pulp, Rangers arrived to clear the facility. Nightstalker MH-6 Little Bird helicopters landed on the rooftop of the adjacent Carcel Modelo prison to drop off a Delta contingent, which blasted through the prison's roof and walls to rescue American radio operator Kurt F. Muse, whom they found huddled in his cell's bathroom.

Ranger battalions parachuted onto the country's two most important airfields to neutralize the Panamanian defenders and destroy the Panamanian Air Force on the ground. When confronted by the airborne Rangers, most Panamanian soldiers fled or surrendered. At the civilian terminal of the Omar Torrijos International Airport, however, recalcitrant Panamanian troops opened fire on the advancing Americans.

A small group of Rangers, led by Sergeant David Reeves, charged two Panamanian gunmen who had been seen retreating into a large public restroom. Jumping into the lavatory with his M-16 assault rifle at the ready, Reeves was shot in the shoulder and collarbone by a Panamanian hiding in one of the stalls. Specialist Michael Eubanks and Private First Class William Kelly crawled to Reeves and pulled him out into the hallway, then rolled grenades into the restroom. Catching sight of the grenades before they exploded, the Panamanians jumped on toilet rims and closed the stall doors. Encased in the cocoons of the commode walls, the Panamanians suffered no ill effects from the spray of grenade shrapnel.

Eubanks and Kelly then rushed into the bathroom with guns blazing. After they had shot the whole place up, Eubanks said in Spanish that it was time for the Panamanians to throw down their weapons. A man stuck his head around a corner and told Eubanks, "Fuck off!" In the ensuing scuffle, Eubanks and Kelly shot one Panamanian in the head and kicked the other out a window. The latter survived a fall of twenty-five feet, only to be shot dead by approaching Rangers when he pulled a gun on them.

In another section of the civilian terminal, Panamanian forces were intermingled with four hundred civilians from two commercial jetliners that had touched down just minutes before. Ten Panamanian soldiers searched the crowd and were delighted to find two American girls, ideal candidates for human shields. Taking the girls with them, the soldiers attempted to escape the terminal as the Americans closed in, but a Ranger security perimeter got in their way. For the next several hours, the Panamanians traded fire with the Rangers. Finally, the Americans notified the Panamanians that if they did not surrender, the Rangers would make a frontal charge with weapons ablaze. The Panamanians capitulated.

During the first three days of the invasion, Delta Force and the Special Forces launched dozens of raids against Noriega's known and suspected safe houses. Veiled by black hoods, the Americans broke into villas, houses, and huts, forcing the occupants down at gunpoint. Flex-cuffed and questioned, some of the detainees offered tips that led to raids on further sites where "the Pineapple Face" might be hiding. None of the raids bagged Noriega, though at one of his homes Delta operators did find $8 million in cash, a large collection of hardcore pornography, and an altar to Satan festooned with jars of human organs. Noriega eventually surrendered after ten days holed up in the Vatican embassy, a result that may have been influenced by the efforts of American psychological operators, who blared Van Halen, the Clash, and the Howard Stern Show from loudspeakers outside the embassy walls in an effort to unsettle him.

Although Noriega's banana republic had not subjected America's special operators to a stern test of their mettle, the brief war did function as a valuable proving ground for reconnaissance, hostage rescue, airfield seizure, and surgical strike operations. The special operations forces executed their assigned tasks effectively and, with the exception of the raids on suspected Noriega hideouts, achieved the desired outcomes. JSOC had collaborated with the other special operators of SOCOM as never before, and the special operators as a whole had interacted effectively with conventional forces.

One year later, the US military faced a far greater challenge in the sands of the Middle East, against the million-man army of Iraqi strongman Saddam Hussein. On August 2, 1990, Saddam's forces invaded the fantastically affluent Emirate of Kuwait, steamrolling its inconsequential military and hanging its officials from a gallows at Kuwait University. Declaring Kuwait to be Iraq's nineteenth province, Saddam took possession of Kuwait's oil fields. In response, the United States sent 425,000 troops and marshaled another 250,000 troops from allied countries to liberate Kuwait in what became Operation Desert Storm. Because Desert Storm dwarfed the invasion of Panama in magnitude, special operations forces hoped to receive a much larger number of missions. To their dismay, the US regional combatant command in charge of Desert Storm—Central Command—left them with considerably fewer tasks this time around.

General "Stormin'" Norman Schwarzkopf, the commander of Central Command, had never cared much for special operators. His headquarters were located down the street from SOCOM headquarters on MacDill Air Force Base, but they might as well have been based on opposite ends of the Earth. The special operators scoffed at the work habits of the Central Command staff, most of whom went home for the day by the middle of the afternoon. Around their coffee pots, SOCOM officers caricatured Schwarzkopf as a slow, unimaginative tactician, someone who might have been acceptable commanding a platoon of tanks, but not a joint and multinational force with a cornucopia of revolutionary technologies and hundreds of thousands of troops. In their view, Schwarzkopf disdained special operations out of sheer ignorance. Military officers closer to Schwarzkopf generally had a more favorable opinion of the general, noting that while he could be overbearing and thin-skinned, he was a sharp and inquisitive thinker with a deep interest in global politics.

When the US military behemoth began its five-month mobilization for the Middle East deployment, Stormin' Norman gave SOF low priority in resources and retarded their movements, allowing conventional units to snatch facilities and missions ahead of them. He permitted some latitude to special operators responsible for psychological operations and civil affairs, but he rebuffed pleas from the Special Forces, SEALs, and JSOC to participate in combat operations. According to Jim Guest, now the commander of the Army Special Forces Command, Schwarzkopf viewed SOF as a coiled cobra in a cage, and did not want to let the cobra out for fear that it would cause trouble and embarrassment.

General Carl Stiner, the SOCOM commander, flew to Riyadh on two occasions to charm Schwarzkopf into including his special operators in the offensive. In a disarming Tennessee drawl, Stiner explained that he would personally move his four-star headquarters from Tampa to Saudi Arabia to run counterterrorism operations and deep-strike missions into Iraq and Kuwait. Some of Stiner's own staff thought the idea was a pipe dream, for no four-star commander, least of all one as prickly as Schwarzkopf, was likely to welcome another four-star headquarters in his theater. But Stiner would not be dissuaded.

During the first trip, in October 1990, Schwarzkopf told Stiner that he wasn't interested in permitting commando operations in Iraq or Kuwait. They were too risky and could trigger a war prematurely. The special operators, Schwarzkopf continued, could contribute by supporting the conventional forces in such areas as reconnaissance and mine clearing. When the deflated Stiner returned to the United States, he attempted to go over's Schwarzkopf's head, pitching Joint Chiefs chairman General Colin Powell and heavy hitters at the State Department and the Defense Department on his plans for deep raids. But no one was willing to go to bat for him.

Stiner made his second trip to Riyadh in January 1991, shortly before Desert Storm was scheduled to swirl into Kuwait. Schwarzkopf was none too pleased to receive another visit from Stiner, whose four-star status was probably the only reason why he was even able to obtain an audience. Stiner's Tennessee airs and his flamboyance may have soothed some interlocutors, but they were only irritants to the CENTCOM commander. When Stiner entered Schwarzkopf's office, the general dispensed with the usual glad-handing that occurs when two four-star commanders meet. "You've got forty-five minutes," Schwarzkopf uttered coldly.

Stiner explained how he would deploy a JSOC "package" consisting of Delta Force, SEAL Team Six, Rangers, and special operations helicopters to Saudi Arabia. A second package would deploy to Europe. He spelled out concepts for counterterrorism and deep-strike operations into the heart of the enemy in what was essentially a rehash of the proposals he had presented three months earlier.

Schwarzkopf listened impassively. He was no more inclined than before to accept Stiner's offers of assistance, and he was peeved at Stiner for wasting his time by going over the same things that had been rejected before. But rather than divulge his true views to Stiner, he resorted to evasion.

"Carl, that is a really good idea," Schwarzkopf said when Stiner was through with his briefing. "I'm going to need time to look at it."

To give Stiner some forewarning that his plan was headed nowhere, and to distance himself from that outcome, Schwarzkopf added, "I'm not sure the Saudis want another American four-star in the theater."

The 5th Special Forces Group obtained permission for the relatively innocuous mission of training Kuwaiti forces-in-exile. Schwarzkopf gave the Kuwaiti forces little to do in Desert Storm, aside from a highly publicized entrance into Kuwait City after American arms had evicted the Iraqis, for the purpose of showing that Kuwaitis had helped retake the country. Other Special Forces paired up with coalition forces to provide brief training courses and coordinate their operations with US units. Years of concentration on irregular warfare had left many of the Green Berets short on the knowledge of conventional operations that those foreign conventional forces needed.

On opening day of the American air campaign, January 17, 1991, JSOC was sitting on the end of the American bench, with nothing to do and no promise from the coach of playing time later in the season. The outlook began to change, however, when Saddam Hussein responded to American bombing raids by firing Scud ballistic missiles at Israel. Several of the Soviet-built Scuds crashed into apartment complexes in Tel Aviv and Haifa, wounding dozens and causing the Israeli government to prepare for retaliation, possibly with nuclear weapons. Israeli military action against Iraq would be certain to topple the coalition of Arab nations that the United States had carefully erected in opposition to the Iraqi regime, and it could lead to a larger conflagration.

Lieutenant General Wayne Downing, the JSOC commander, knew that Stiner had alienated Schwarzkopf, so he appealed directly to the Joint Chiefs of Staff for permission to unleash Delta Force on the Scud launchers. The chiefs proceeded to ask Schwarzkopf if he would consent to Downing's proposal. Schwarzkopf refused, insisting that he could destroy the launchers with air strikes. At JSOC, indignation at this response was amplified by the news that Schwarzkopf had authorized British Special Air Service commandos to operate behind Iraqi lines against the Scuds.

President George H. W. Bush promised the Israelis that US airpower would eliminate the Scud threat within a few days. When, however, a week of American air strikes failed to halt the Scud launches, with Israeli casualties mounting and the prospect of Israeli retaliation against Iraq looming large, Secretary of Defense Dick Cheney decided to call JSOC off the bench. He asked General Powell to send word to Schwarzkopf that JSOC was to join the chase for the Scuds.

Before passing the message on, Powell warned Cheney that such a decision was liable to send Stormin' Norman into one of his tempests of rage. "You know Norm doesn't want these guys over there," Powell said.

"I don't care what Norm wants," Cheney snarled. "He's had seven days to shut this thing off and he hasn't done it. They're going."

JSOC deployed a task force of four hundred men to Saudi Arabia, the staging ground for the Scud-hunting mission. Driving into the Iraqi desert on four-wheel-drive vehicles, the ground operators roamed in enemy territory for up to three weeks at a time. By day, they camouflaged their vehicles and slept, and by night, they looked for Scud missiles and their facilities, using laser designators to direct air strikes onto suspected targets. The number of Scuds that JSOC actually helped destroy was frequently disputed and never determined, but the damage that it inflicted, together with the fear it created in the enemy, did much to diminish the threat. Scud launches fell from five per day to one per day after the uncaging of JSOC in the desert.

NEITHER JIMMY CARTER, nor Ronald Reagan, nor George H. W. Bush had a particular interest in special operations forces, but each would come to commit SOF into perilous enterprises and battles. In Carter's case, the special operators were invited to solve the nation's most pressing crisis. During the late Cold War period, in marked contrast to earlier times, the Congress, rather than the executive branch, was the most critical actor in the development of special operations forces. Members of Congress led the offensive that broke through the Pentagon's entrenchments to create SOCOM and the Major Force Program 11 funding line.

The rise in hostage taking by Islamic terrorists in the post-Vietnam era turned hostage rescue into a critical SOF mission and precipitated the revival of the Rangers and the creation of Delta Force, SEAL Team Six, and JSOC. Preoccupation with hostage rescue encouraged a focus on superlative marksmanship and meticulous planning for lightning-quick raids, skills of important but intermittent value. Because of dissatisfaction with CIA risk aversion during the Iran hostage crisis, Delta Force entered the business of intelligence collection in dangerous environments, initiating a prolonged rivalry between the nation's premier special operations force and its premier intelligence agency.

With the passage of the Nunn-Cohen Amendment, Congress codified the missions of special operations forces for the first time. The official listing of a mission set, however, did not remove the necessity of showing others in the military how SOF could contribute to larger US objectives. The special operators still had to search for new types of missions if they wished to remain near the front of the bureaucratic pack in a world of rapid change. In Panama and Desert Storm, the top US military commander employed special operations forces based on what he perceived to be his own tactical and strategic requirements. If SOF could not fulfill those requirements, then they missed out on the action and the laurels.

The most conspicuous special operation of the 1980s, Eagle Claw, ended as a national debacle. The failure of the Iran hostage rescue undermined the prestige of all SOF, even though it was merely the result of poor air planning and operations on the part of an ad hoc task force, in which special operations and conventional air personnel had been hastily patched together. In Grenada, special operators succeeded in some tactical tasks and failed in others. They helped rescue the American medical students and faculty, a task for which their speed and marksmanship made them better suited than regular forces. Hostage rescue was also the foremost achievement of the special operators in Panama. In the case of Desert Storm, where General Schwarzkopf rejected most proposals for the employment of special operations forces, the hunt for Scud missiles served as the chief special operations contribution to attainment of America's strategic objectives, helping to avert an Israeli military intervention that would have alienated America's Muslim allies.

The conventional US military leadership in Grenada made effective use of SOF capabilities, but on occasion used them for tasks that plainly were better suited to conventional infantry, thus strengthening the case for greater SOF independence that led eventually to the Nunn-Cohen Amendment. While the advent of SOCOM and Major Force Program 11 afforded the special operators new protection from conventional military commanders and Pentagon budget cutters, it also sharpened resentments among the rest of the military. Those resentments, moreover, still mattered. Any hopes that Congress had completely liberated SOF from dependence on conventional commanders for resources and missions were dashed in the Kuwaiti Desert by the miserly dispensations of Stormin' Norman Schwarzkopf.

CHAPTER 7

GOTHIC SERPENT

Lifting off from a dilapidated airfield next to the Arabian Sea, the Black Hawks flew low and fast along the coast, where the Rangers could see, between their dangling legs, the azure-blue waters splashing onto black rocks and sand. Those who kept their eyes on the beach could be forgiven for imagining themselves over the shore of a Caribbean island where the wealthy came to lounge and scuba dive, rather than on the periphery of the world's most lawless and desolate city. The Rangers had launched raids into Mogadishu on six previous occasions, but this would be the first time they would enter the Black Sea District, heart of the empire of Somali warlord Mohamed Farrah Aidid, or the Bakara Market area, which was the heart of the heart. One week before the raid, the commander of the US task force had informed Washington, "If we go into the vicinity of the Bakara Market, there's no question we'll win the gunfight, but we might lose the war."

The twin-engine Black Hawks had been stripped bare of seats and other accoutrements to accommodate the muscle-bound men and their fearsome weapons. Seated in the middle of one of the aircraft, with his back to the cockpit, Sergeant First Class Sean Watson listened to the radio chatter through a corded headset. Flanking him on either side were other Rangers clad in Kevlar helmets and desert fatigues. This Black Hawk, and each of the three other Black Hawks flying in its formation, carried a twelve-man infantry "chalk"—militaryspeak for a unit inserted by a single aircraft.

The helicopter was three minutes out when Watson heard that hostile forces had just been seen on the target. If the news had any impact on his thoughts or emotions, his face did not show it.

The Americans were intruding during the middle of the afternoon, the least auspicious time of day for battle in Mogadishu from the American point of view. They would have much preferred to arrive at night, when the sudden appearance of scores of heavily armed white men would be less conspicuous and night-vision equipment would provide the Americans a huge edge over Aidid's ragtag militiamen. Somali men were most active in the afternoon, for it was during those hours that the high from their daily ritual of chewing khat leaves peaked. US intelligence on Aidid had been scarce, however, so the Americans took targets whenever and wherever they could get them.

"One minute!"

In an effort to throw the enemy off balance, the helicopters flew past the objective and then doubled back. Banking around toward the Bakara Market, the aircraft divided into two lines. At an altitude of sixty feet, they flew along the streets where they planned to unload their passengers.

When the Black Hawks reached the drop zones, they came to a hover. Sergeant Keni Thomas, a University of Florida graduate whose squad was sandwiched on the left side of Watson's helicopter, was supposed to inform the crew chief when he had "confirmed the target building." But neither Thomas nor anyone else could see any of the structures on the ground. The helicopters had stirred up so much dust that they had surrounded themselves in a brownout. Normally, the infantrymen descended from the Black Hawks on ropes at a distance of thirty to thirty-five feet from the ground, but the lack of visibility and the accompanying risk of collision with ground structures dissuaded the pilots from descending to such altitudes.

"Ropes!" shouted one of the crew chiefs on Thomas's helicopter, signaling that it was time to kick out the nylon fast ropes. Thomas shoved his ninety-foot coil into the brown murk, and another Ranger did the same on the opposite side of the helicopter. Thirty feet of the coil was left on the helicopter when the rope thudded down on the Somali street.

"Go! Go! Go!"

As Thomas swung himself toward the rope to make the descent, the starboard crew chief, Sergeant Ned Norton, pointed at his own forehead. Norton was sporting a black visor and dust mask, which reminded Thomas of Darth Vader. The red, white, and blue sticker to which Norton's finger was directed read, "No Fear."

"Remember!" Norton yelled above the din of the helicopter. "No fear!"

Peering at Norton in disgust, Thomas thought to himself, *Fuck you, pal, you're not the one going in*. As he grasped the nylon rope, Thomas yelled at Darth Vader, "Screw you!"

Below, nothing was visible but the brown dust cloud. Thomas took a deep breath and slid down the rope, choking on dust.

When the last of Sergeant Watson's Rangers had come down, the helicopter crewmen released the ropes and the pilot took the aircraft to a higher altitude. From there, the helicopters were to watch over the infantrymen, protecting them with mighty 7.62mm miniguns if necessary. With its rate of fire of 100 rounds per second, each minigun could spew as many bullets as one hundred riflemen firing assault rifles on full automatic.

The last Black Hawk to arrive at the objective was carrying chalk number four, under the command of Staff Sergeant Matt Eversmann. The helicopter's crew had encountered more trouble than the other helicopters in finding its drop zone. "I can't see shit!" the pilot kept saying. Struggling to identify landmarks they had seen in photographs distributed hours earlier, the pilot eventually decided to drop the passengers off a short distance from the original destination, telling Eversmann that he should move his Rangers a few blocks on foot once they had landed.

Eversmann's Rangers threw down the ropes from a height of seventy feet. For reasons that were never clearly established, Private First Class Todd Blackburn lost hold of the nylon rope as soon as he brought his body over the side. Weighed down by fifty pounds of gear, Blackburn was little impeded by wind resistance as gravity pulled him to the earth.

When Eversmann's boots reached the ground, he looked over to see Blackburn lying in a crumpled heap, bleeding from the mouth, ears, and nose. Two medics were already working on the eighteen-year-old. Although Blackburn was unconscious, he was still alive, much to the surprise of his fellow Rangers.

Within a matter of seconds, Somalis were shooting at the cluster of Americans around Blackburn. Rangers responded with loud bursts from their assault rifles and automatic weapons, while the medics rushed to open Blackburn's airway and stabilize his neck. Then two Rangers picked Blackburn up and carried him behind two parked cars.

Although Blackburn was now out of immediate danger, massive internal hemorrhaging was bringing him closer to death by the minute. The medics informed Eversmann that Blackburn would have to be evacuated immediately if he were to stand any chance of survival.

FROM A DISTANCE, an American onlooker might have surmised that the Rangers were flying into central Mogadishu on the afternoon of October 3, 1993, to rescue hostages. That, after all, was the primary mission for which they had been created, and the stealth and speed with which they moved were the hallmarks of hostage-rescue operations. But these Rangers were seeking to take hostages rather than liberate them. With opportunities to save hostages few and far between, the temptation to assign hostage-rescue forces to different but similar tasks had become irresistible.

Chief among the sibling missions were surgical strikes to capture or kill enemy leaders, which, in a post–Cold War world of uncertain boundaries and challenges, appeared to be a high-growth industry. By cutting off the head of the beast, the reasoning went, these strikes could eliminate the messiness and costliness of tearing an adversary limb from limb. But the special operators did not have much experience in decapitation operations. In Vietnam, they had been frustrated by the inaccessibility of Viet Cong leaders, while in Panama a lack of timely information had prevented the nabbing of Manuel Noriega. Thus, the feasibility and strategic value of decapitation strikes were largely matters of speculation and abstract theorizing.

Since the ousting of President Siyad Barre by rebel forces in January 1991, Somalia had been devoid of centralized authority, fragmented into fiefdoms of clan warlords who vied for control over resources with the cunning and ruthlessness of their nomadic ancestors. In Mogadishu, the militias of the Habr Gidr clan, led by Mohamed Farrah Aidid, and the Abgaal clan, led by Ali Mahdi Mohamed, waged a cruel war for pre-eminence. Lobbing artillery shells into each other's neighborhoods and firing automatic weapons at crowds in the city streets, they spurned the precautions that most peoples have employed to protect civilian bystanders. Somali hospitals treated hundreds of people every day for war wounds. The warlords used food deprivation as an instrument of warfare, and when the United Nations and United States responded by flying relief supplies to Mogadishu, the warlords seized the goods on the runway at gunpoint or stole them from the warehouses of relief organizations.

By the fall of 1992, famine, disease, and war had killed somewhere between 300,000 and 500,000 Somalis. American reporters in Somalia and their editors in the United States bombarded the American people with photographs of starving women and children and unabashedly championed US military intervention as a solution to the humanitarian crisis. "It is intolerable and unthinkable to remain aloof while teen-age hoodlums impede the delivery of emergency food and medicines," the *New York Times* editorialized. "There is no alternative to the threat or use of force if food is to reach those trapped in a chaotic clan war." *Washington Post* correspondent Stephen Richburg recounted that he and other journalists advocated the application of US military force to "raise the flag for a new kind of interventionism, a benevolent, selfless interventionism with no American interest at stake other than the collective revulsion at violence and a desire to relieve suffering."

At the end of November 1992, a few weeks after losing his reelection bid, President George H. W. Bush decided to dispatch 29,000 troops, most of them Marines, to intimidate the clan leaders into submission and permit the distribution of food from the ports to the country's interior. Impressed by the American show of force, the warlords refrained from provoking the Marines or interfering with the dispensation of humanitarian aid. The UN leadership prodded Bush to commit the United States to a far more ambitious agenda, aimed at ensuring that hunger would never strike Somalia again. UN officials advocated full disarmament of the

Somali warlords, creation of new Somali national security forces, and the holding of democratic elections. The Bush administration balked, out of the conviction that Somali clans would take up arms against those seeking to impose such a fundamental transformation, dragging the United States into a costly, protracted, and quite possibly fruitless war.

Bush's successor, Bill Clinton, was more amenable to the UN's plans to reshape Somalia, and more willing to commit US troops to the execution of those plans. In March 1993, the Clinton administration transferred authority for the international task force in Somalia from the United States to the United Nations and agreed to keep 6,000 US troops in Somalia under the UN banner. Madeleine Albright, Clinton's ambassador to the United Nations at the time of the transition, announced, "We will embark on an unprecedented enterprise aimed at nothing less than the restoration of an entire country as a proud, functioning and viable member of the community of nations."

The Asian, European, and African peacekeepers who took charge of security in March 1993 did not patrol the streets as the US Marines had done. As a consequence, the clans regained control over much of the nation's territory. An emboldened Aidid resisted foreign efforts to monitor his weapons and restrict his activities, resulting in several armed clashes that claimed the lives of UN peacekeepers. In August, the killing of four American soldiers by a bomb traced to Aidid's forces convinced Clinton to take new measures against the Somali strongman. Clinton was unwilling to send more conventional forces to Somalia, owing to reservations among congressmen in his own party, some of whom were already calling for removal of all US forces from what they considered the "next Vietnam." But Clinton was open to sending special operations forces, since they were smaller and designed to maintain a low profile.

The UN special representative in Somalia, retired US admiral Jonathan Howe, advocated the deployment of Delta Force to Somalia. So did a large element of the special operations community, which saw an opportunity for the special operators to show their worth and bury the ghosts of Desert One. Among both civilians and soldiers, a considerable number of voices contended that employment of special operations forces in Somalia would prove the theory that SOF could solve big problems without the participation of conventional forces.

Much of the senior military leadership, however, opposed sending Delta Force. General Joseph P. Hoar, who as head of US Central Command was the regional military commander responsible for Somalia, warned that Delta Force had only a 25 percent chance of capturing Aidid, owing to Aidid's clan support network and his intimate familiarity with the city. In the view of Hoar and a number of other experts, suppressing Aidid's clan would require a long-term commitment of conventional forces to counterinsurgency operations, an approach that enjoyed little support in the US military or Congress.

Clinton decided in favor of sending Delta Force to Somalia. From the White House, orders went out to Fort Bragg for deployment of a Delta Force squadron to apprehend Aidid. The supporting units would include a Ranger company and a detachment of aircraft from what had grown into the 160th Special Operations Aviation Regiment. The White House leaked word of Delta Force's imminent departure to friendly journalists in order to show the world that Clinton was getting tough. In turn, Aidid undertook new precautions against capture.

The special operators flew into Mogadishu's airport on August 26, 1993. A tall, imposing man, older than the rest, stepped from one of the C-141 Starlifter transports onto the tarmac. His graying hair had been cut to the "high and tight" style of a Ranger, and he wore a Ranger uniform bearing the rank of a young man, rather than the two stars he had earned in twenty-seven years of service. A cigar hanging from his mouth, he sucked in the sweltering Mogadishu air while surveying the Soviet-era hangar where the special operations task force, code-named Task Force Ranger, would set up its headquarters.

Major General William F. Garrison, the commander of JSOC, may have looked the consummate warrior, but he had not been born one. When the Vietnam War had heated up in the mid-1960s, he had tried hard to avoid the draft. It proved to be of no avail, as he was inducted into the Army in 1966 as an infantryman. During a tour in Vietnam, Garrison discovered that the life of a soldier at war actually suited him quite well, and he chose to go back to Vietnam for a second tour before making a career of the military.

It was not difficult to see why Garrison had risen to such lofty positions. He had the combination of charisma and competence that subordinates crave. He loved his job and relished a good fight, pulsing with an infectious confidence in the face of danger. He also had a penchant for self-deprecating humor. "If you guys keep pulling this shit," he would tell his staff, "how'm I ever gonna make general?"

Garrett Jones, the CIA's chief of station, had been busy sniffing around for Aidid in the hope that he could serve Aidid's location to Garrison on a platter the moment his task force arrived. The previous month, the CIA had established a relationship with a subclan leader who enjoyed access to Aidid and was willing to betray him for a price. According to the CIA's plan, this individual would present Aidid with a hand-carved ivory cane, inside of which was a homing device. On the day of Task Force Ranger's arrival in Somalia, however, the CIA chief informed Garrison that before the subclan leader could bestow the cane, he had shot himself in the head during a game of Russian roulette.

The CIA now had to turn to communications intercepts and human informants. But Aidid, aware that the Americans would try to locate him through communications devices, scrupulously avoided using phones and radios. Finding reliable informants in Mogadishu was similarly daunting. Plenty of individuals offered to provide information for money, but most either failed to deliver or mysteriously disappeared.

Garrison and the Delta Force operators were not the type of men to lean back in the sun while waiting for the fish to bite. Dissatisfied with the information the CIA was providing during Task Force Ranger's first days in Mogadishu, Garrison pressed Jones to get more and better information. Garrison's irritation turned to rage on August 29, when Aidid's militiamen conducted a mortar attack on the task force's base, wounding five of the special operators. With the enemy now up five to nothing and Task Force Ranger having yet to swing the bat, Garrison vowed to "kick somebody's ass." Dialing up the CIA station, he informed Jones that he needed "your number-one target where Aidid has been reported."

Within hours, Garrison had the information for his first operation. Task Force Ranger set out that night for a building that was alleged to house top aides of Aidid. At 3 a.m., elements of the task force landed on the roof of the building while others broke through doors on the ground floor. The Americans found a handful of sleepy-eyed expatriates and

Somalis who claimed to work for the UN. Their story gained in credibility when someone noticed that the UN flag was flying outside the building. Delta operators handcuffed the detainees and hauled them away in helicopters, but had to release them four hours later after determining that the individuals did in fact work for the UN.

In their next operation, Task Force Ranger stopped a convoy and arrested thirty-nine Somalis. The detainees turned out to be a Somali general and his staff.

The two fiascos made the international newspapers, much to the embarrassment of the US government and its ballyhooed special operations forces. At a meeting inside the Pentagon, Secretary of Defense Les Aspin fulminated, "We look like the gang that can't shoot straight!" People on all sides were beginning to wonder whether Delta Force had been vastly overhyped.

Task Force Ranger conducted four more missions in the ensuing month, with significantly better results. They netted several important figures in Aidid's organization, and they avoided apprehending any more friendlies. Aidid himself, however, continued to elude them, flitting inconspicuously through the city's sprawling neighborhoods.

On October 3, a CIA informant reported the location of a meeting that afternoon that would be attended by two of Aidid's top men. Garrison assembled a formidable force for the raid, dubbed Operation Gothic Serpent, including a total of 19 aircraft, 12 ground vehicles, and 160 ground troops. MH-6 helicopters would carry the Delta operators responsible for securing the building and its occupants, with each helicopter holding four men on externally mounted benches. Eight Black Hawks would come next, carrying the Rangers, a small number of Delta operators, and a Combat Search and Rescue Team. A vehicle convoy would rendezvous at the objective to retrieve the raiders and their prisoners. The whole operation was expected to last about one hour.

THE FOUR RANGER chalks that landed near the Bakara Market on October 3 had been ordered to secure the intersections outside the four corners of the target compound. The Rangers formed L-shaped perimeters at the intersections, guarding against any hostile forces in the surrounding area that might entertain the idea of interfering with Delta's raid. Looking toward the chalk to his east, Sergeant Thomas saw Rangers already firing their weapons. He could not see any Somalis yet.

A short time later, bullets whizzed toward Thomas's squad, accompanied by the distinctive metallic *bang* of a Kalashnikov assault rifle.

"He's in the tree!" yelled Private David Floyd.

"Floyd!" Sergeant Watson responded. "Do you see him?"

"Roger, S'rgnt. He's in the tree. He's in the tree!"

"Well, Floyd, if you see him, why don't you shoot him!"

Many of the Rangers had wondered how Floyd, a nineteen-year-old from South Carolina, had ever made it through Ranger selection. He was far from an imposing physical specimen, weighing in at just 130 pounds. Nor did he have a natural affinity for soldiering. He was one of those Rangers who never seemed to get things right the first time and routinely required extra attention from his superiors. Rangers jokingly compared him to Barney Fife, the ham-fisted deputy sheriff on *The Andy Griffith Show*.

Recent operations had given Thomas and Watson reason to believe that their extra attention to Floyd had made a real fighter out of the young man. But Floyd had not faced a test as stern as this one before, and he was on the verge of flunking. Armed with a gas-operated M249 squad automatic weapon, Floyd had been entrusted with enough firepower to protect the entire squad, yet he appeared oblivious to his obligations.

Then, all of a sudden, something switched on inside Floyd's brain. Aiming the M249 at the tree with a newfound inspiration that perhaps even he found surprising, Floyd squeezed off half a belt of ammunition. The bullets sawed the tree in half, bringing the sniper to his end.

The compound that the Rangers had surrounded was enclosed by a high stone wall. Inside was a small courtyard and a three-story stone house with a flat roof, its facade strangely unblemished in a city where most of the buildings had been riddled with holes or reduced to rubble in the preceding two years of civil war. While the Rangers had been fast-roping onto the streets, a helicopter had inserted four Delta operators into the courtyard, and three other helicopters had offloaded Delta passengers on

GOTHIC SERPENT | 203

the adjacent streets. The Somalis inside the building caught sight of the American helicopters and scrambled for the exits, but the Americans were too quick for them. Storming the building with their gun barrels sweeping every crevice, the raiding force cut off all possible avenues of escape.

The Delta operators, or D-boys, as the admiring Rangers liked to call them, handcuffed twenty-four suspects and herded them together with rifle butts. The take included one of the high-value targets whom the CIA expected to be there, and another man who was Aidid's spokesman. Outside the compound, the D-boys began to load their catch into ground vehicles that had just pulled up to return everyone to base. Within minutes, it appeared, Task Force Ranger would be back at the hangar with a nice new feather in its cap and just a couple of wounded men.

The carefully choreographed progression was interrupted by the explosion of a rocket-propelled grenade at the tail of one of the Black Hawks. Its tail rotor destroyed, the Black Hawk spun uncontrollably, tumbling toward the earth until its belly clipped the tin roof of a stone house. The collision pushed the nose of the aircraft down, the main rotor snapping apart when it touched the ground, and then the helicopter flopped onto its side in a narrow alley.

For Staff Sergeant Eversmann, commander of chalk number four, the downing of the Black Hawk put an end to hopes of evacuating the severely injured Blackburn by air. With the chalk still pinned down one block north of its assigned position, they would need to move Blackburn on foot under fire toward the ground vehicles, putting more lives at risk. Eversmann doubted that Blackburn would still be alive by the time the stretcher bearers got through.

Eversmann, nevertheless, was willing to risk able-bodied men to give a wounded man a chance to live. He convinced the commander of the vehicle convoy to keep several vehicles at the convoy's assembly area for the evacuation of Blackburn. At Eversmann's command, two medics and two other Rangers put Blackburn on a stretcher and rushed him through the city streets while other Rangers shot at armed Somalis, forcing the gunmen to keep their heads down. The stretcher team made it through safely, and Blackburn was soon in a three-vehicle convoy heading back to base, where the doctors would manage to save his life.

Most of Task Force Ranger was still figuring out how to return to base when the crowds of hostile Somalis began to arrive in earnest. The spectacle of nineteen helicopters circling like yellowjackets over the Black Sea District in midafternoon drew Aidid's militiamen to the compound from all parts of the city. Throbbing with the stimulation brought on by chewing khat, the men nearest to the site of the raid ran straight at the American perimeter, assailing it on every side. In more distant neighborhoods, militiamen and thrill seekers piled into cars and trucks and drove in the direction of the helicopters. Surveillance cameras in the US aircraft captured thousands of Somalis converging on the D-boys and Rangers.

Women and children mingled in the throngs, looking on like spectators or actively assisting the militiamen. The Somali fighters stepped forward to shoot their weapons, then merged back into the masses of women and children. In training, the Rangers had received briefings on the rules of engagement in urban Somalia, according to which Somalis who carried weapons were not necessarily hostile, and civilian casualties had to be avoided at all costs. "You will not fire at someone unless you are fired upon," the instructors had said. But a combination of common sense and survival instinct quickly led the Rangers to toss the rules of engagement out the window. Within a few minutes, the Americans had concluded that Somalis were toting weapons for only one reason: to kill Americans. The Rangers started shooting any Somali bearing a weapon, and anyone abetting such a person.

Lieutenant Larry Perino was supervising the troops at one of the four corners of the perimeter when he saw Somali children creeping toward him. The children began pointing at the American positions, and then a Somali shooter fired his weapon at them. The Rangers threw flash-bang grenades at the child spotters, which chased them away. The next time that children came near, Perino interrupted his radio conversation to spray warning shots from his M-16. The kids scampered away again.

A woman attempted to sneak toward an M60 machine gun manned by Sergeant Chuck Elliot. "Hey, sir," Elliot shouted to Perino, "I can see there's a guy behind this woman with a weapon under her arm!"

Perino gave the order to open fire. The heavy machine gun peppered the man and the woman with large holes, dropping their lifeless bodies into the dirt.

General Garrison had prepared for the eventuality that one of the helicopters would go down. The combat search-and-rescue helicopter that was now over the Black Sea District could drop a fifteen-man team to treat the wounded and protect them until they could be evacuated. Garrison ordered the team to the crash site. Fifteen men, however, might not be able to hold out very long against hundreds of angry Somalis, so Garrison ordered all of the forces at the original target building to head to the crash site as reinforcements. Once everyone had assembled at that location, they would load up the casualties and head out. Some of the Rangers and D-boys climbed aboard the nine remaining vehicles from the ground convoy, and the others moved toward the crash site on foot.

Sergeant Thomas was preparing to move with his squad toward the crash site when he saw his squad leader, Sergeant Doug Boren, running into a building with blood gushing from his neck. Sergeant Watson followed Boren inside an improvised first aid station. Watson emerged a few minutes later to tell Thomas, "Boren's been hit. You're in charge."

"Is he all right, S'rgnt?" Thomas asked.

"He's been hit. You're in charge."

"Yeah, but what happened? Is he gonna be OK?"

"Sergeant Thomas, you're in charge!"

Thomas and his squad joined the procession of Rangers and Delta operators who were en route to the crashed Black Hawk. The pace had picked up once the Americans realized that they were in a race with swarms of Somalis who were moving in the same direction on parallel streets. As the special operators crossed intersections, they took turns firing into the Somali columns to the left and the right while others barreled across.

At an intersection a few blocks from the crash site, Aidid's militiamen were gathered in especially large numbers, flooding the crossing with streams of semiautomatic rifle fire. Specialist Mike Kurth, one of Thomas's men, saw Sergeant First Class Earl Fillmore getting in position to race across the intersection, and then saw a bullet strike him in the head. Fillmore, like the other D-boys, wore a thin helmet that looked like the headgear of a hockey player, which facilitated rapid movement but did not offer the same protection as the Rangers' Kevlar combat helmet. Fillmore's head snapped back from the bullet's impact on the front of his helmet, and a puff of red mist exited the helmet's rear.

A Delta medic went to help Fillmore, and he too was hit. Sergeant Thomas rushed over and found that the medic was still strong enough to move but Fillmore was not. Braving the hostile fire, which mounted in intensity when the Somalis saw the Americans clustered together, Thomas and the medic dragged Fillmore from the street. By a miracle, they reached cover without further injuries.

Seeing a Delta operator fall in battle was as unfathomable for the Rangers as the downing of a helicopter of the 160th Aviation Regiment. The Rangers looked up to, even idolized, the Delta operators, referring to them as "the varsity squad" and "big brother." Some of the D-boys in Task Force Ranger had taken young Rangers under their wing and taught them tricks of the trade during their spare time. Fillmore was especially popular among the Rangers because of his willingness to help out the younger men.

The brotherly fondness of the D-boys for the Rangers did not extend to the Ranger company commander, Captain Mike Steele. A former football lineman at the University of Georgia, Steele liked to do things by the book and had little patience for the unorthodox thinking of Delta Force. Steele's preoccupation with minutiae was so thorough that the D-boys were convinced that he was blind to the bigger picture. In the weeks preceding the raid, the D-boys had told Steele they had concerns about the readiness of his Rangers. Steele blew them off, believing that as part of an organization of uber-elite career soldiers they did not understand the need for basic, spit-and-polish discipline in shaping the youthful Rangers.

Fillmore was still alive, but his brain was bleeding and he needed to reach a hospital quickly if he were to stand any chance of survival. Sergeant Thomas stayed at Fillmore's side until he caught a glimpse of Captain Steele down the street. Running toward the captain, Thomas shouted, "We've got a head wound. I need to get him medevacked now!"

With a wave of his hand, Steele indicated that he was tied up in a conversation on the radio. He and other officers were trying to untangle the movements of the ground forces, which had run into a number of unforeseen complications. The Rangers and D-boys who had gone on foot toward the crash site had become separated from the ground vehicles, and those vehicles were now lost. Officers in the helicopters were trying to provide directions to Lieutenant Colonel Danny McKnight, the convoy commander, but they could not figure out where he was.

"We don't know where the Humvees are," Thomas heard Steele say over the radio. "They can't find us."

Specialist Kurth waited for a break in the radio conversation to recommend an aerial medevac. "This guy has a serious head injury, and if we don't get him out right now, he's probably not going to make it," Kurth warned Steele.

"Negative," Steele replied. "The area is still too hot for the birds to land."

Fillmore died a few minutes later.

The first group of Rangers to reach the crash site arrived just before the combat search-and-rescue team. The Black Hawk's pilot and co-pilot had been killed on impact, and one of the passengers, Staff Sergeant Daniel Busch of Delta Force, had been mortally wounded fighting off the first Somali scavengers to arrive, but the other men inside the shattered helicopter were still alive. The Rangers and D-boys shooed away Somalis, established a perimeter around the survivors, and prepared to evacuate the site.

McKnight's ground convoy, however, was still lost, its fighting strength dwindling as its vehicles and soldiers staggered under the blows of the Somali gunmen who lined every street. Ammunition supplies were running low, and the medics were saying that if they did not get the wounded back to base soon, several men would likely die. At 5 p.m., McKnight decided to head back to the hangar to deliver the casualties and replenish the vehicles with ammunition before making a run back into the city.

In the meantime, General Garrison had assembled a second emergency convoy at the Task Force Ranger headquarters by cobbling together the men who had brought Blackburn back and by soliciting volunteers among the cooks, ammunition handlers, communications technicians, intelligence analysts, and other support troops. By the time this convoy was ready to depart, though, Garrison had an even more urgent problem than retrieving the Rangers and D-boys. Just before McKnight's decision to return to base, a rocket-propelled grenade had hit the tail of a second Black Hawk, compelling pilot Mike Durant to crash-land the helicopter in the middle of the city. With no friendly forces near this crash site, Garrison decided to send the makeshift convoy of Humvees and trucks to rescue Durant and his crew.

Sergeant Jeff Struecker, a twenty-four-year-old Ranger from Dodge City, Iowa, led the convoy from the front vehicle as it drove out of the base. Eighty yards into the journey, they ran into a Somali ambush. Lacking armored vehicles and short on combat soldiers, the convoy was likely to receive a horrendous drubbing if it tried to push through. Struecker decided to turn the convoy around and seek a different route.

The next route brought the convoy face to face with a Somali roadblock. The Humvees might have been able to roll over the rubble and furniture and trash that the Somalis had heaped together to form the roadblock, but for the convoy's trucks it was impassable. Beyond the roadblock was a concrete wall that none of the vehicles could surmount or destroy. When Struecker radioed this information to headquarters, he was told that the only other option was to drive all the way around the city and come in from the back side. Struecker said he would go that way.

The convoy was in the process of making its third attempt to reach Durant's helicopter when McKnight's convoy came rumbling into Struecker's view. In light of the time it would take Struecker to reach Durant's helicopter and the deterioration of McKnight's casualty-laden vehicles—they were riding on flat tires and broken differentials—Garrison decided to have Struecker help McKnight's convoy return to base. Casualties were transferred into Struecker's vehicles, and then they drove back together. Struecker's convoy joined McKnight's on the list of forces that could not help Durant and his crew.

Garrison had one more option for rescuing the men at the two crash sites. Phoning Lieutenant General Thomas Montgomery, the senior US military commander in Somalia, Garrison requested a relief force from the US Army's 10th Mountain Division, the repository of America's remaining conventional forces in the country. Montgomery obliged, sending an infantry company in the only vehicles in his inventory, Humvees and trucks. When the 10th Mountain's convoy neared the danger zone, it came under heavy attack from AK-47s and rocket-propelled grenades on both sides of the street. The soldiers dismounted and traded fire with the Somalis for the next thirty minutes. So numerous were the grenade launchers in the enemy's possession that the convoy commander decided that his thin-skinned Humvees and trucks would be slaughtered if they attempted to press farther. Turning the convoy around, he took the vehicles back to their base.

Several other assets that could have been used to save the isolated Americans were absent from Somalia on October 3. When the Rangers had deployed to Somalia, Secretary of Defense Aspin had chosen to withhold a platoon used during rehearsals as a reserve, a platoon that now could have been flown to Durant's crash site. The Defense Department had also prohibited the Rangers from bringing along the AC-130 Spectre gunships with which they had been rehearsing, depriving the task force of a weapons suite that could have annihilated anyone approaching a downed helicopter for a good many hours.

Of the assets withheld by the Pentagon, the one that would draw the most attention and recrimination was armor. In September, following Somali ambushes of US combat engineers and Pakistani forces, General Montgomery had sent a request to the Pentagon for four M-1 Abrams tanks and fourteen Bradley Fighting Vehicles. Either of those vehicles could have bowled through Somali roadblocks, ridden over them, or cut them apart with blade devices. Aidid's rocket-propelled grenades would have been as useless as Ping-Pong balls against Abrams tanks and Bradleys. The CENTCOM commander, General Hoar, and the chairman of the Joint Chiefs of Staff, General Colin Powell, had backed the request. But Secretary of Defense Aspin had turned it down, on the grounds that the United States was trying to downsize its military presence in Somalia and increase its reliance on diplomacy.

The only Americans to reach Durant's helicopter would arrive by air. One of the remaining Black Hawks, piloted by Chief Warrant Officer Mike Goffena, flew to the scene in time to drive off the first Somali sallies toward the downed helicopter. A Black Hawk, however, could not hold back a concerted onslaught on a ground target for long, as an AC-130 could, and the surging of Somalis toward the crash site indicated that such an onslaught would not be long in coming. Two Delta snipers in the Black Hawk, Sergeant First Class Randy Shughart and Master Sergeant Gary Gordon, volunteered for insertion on the ground. Their first two requests for permission to insert were denied. Their third was granted, after it had become clear that none of the ground convoys were going to make it through.

Goffena's helicopter descended into a small field surrounded by huts and shanties, fifty yards from the crash site. Most of the structures withstood the rotor wash, convincing Goffena to come to a hover five feet above the ground rather than landing. As Shughart attempted to climb down the skids, he became entangled in the tether connecting him to the helicopter and had to be cut free. Gordon slipped and fell while running for cover. Disoriented by the mishaps, Shughart and Gordon waved their arms at the departing helicopter to request guidance on the crash site's location. Goffena brought his helicopter back down and gestured in the direction of Durant's helicopter, while a crew chief threw a smoke grenade to mark the way. The two D-boys put their thumbs up and moved off toward the smoke.

Employing their world-class powers of evasion, Shughart and Gordon reached the crash without making contact with hostile forces. They found that all four of the helicopter crewmen were alive, but all had suffered severe injuries, which ruled out moving them back to the insertion point for extraction by helicopter. The six of them would have to hunker down and fight off the hordes until reinforcements arrived. Pulling the injured crewmen from the helicopter, the Delta operators placed them in covered positions, distributing firearms to those capable of shooting. Durant recalled, "They acted as if they were in no particular rush, and they raised me up gently, as if they were handling an ostrich egg." Shuffling around the perimeter, Gordon and Shughart shot down attackers with single shots from their sniper rifles. When Somalis gathered in larger numbers, the machine guns in Goffena's Black Hawk subjected them to showers of bullets.

The two D-boys had been on the ground for ten minutes when a rocket-propelled grenade struck Goffena's helicopter. The blast blew out the windshield, knocked the copilot unconscious, riddled the number-two engine with shrapnel, and severed the leg of a gunner. The cockpit filled with flashing lights and horns that signaled equipment malfunctions and danger conditions. Recognizing that the aircraft could not stay aloft much longer, Goffena headed toward the sea and crash-landed at the airfield.

Following the departure of Goffena's Black Hawk and its automatic weapons, the sky over the crash site was empty. Gordon and Shughart fought off the burgeoning attackers for nearly an hour. When they ran out of rifle ammunition, they fired their pistols. When they ran out of pistol ammunition, Somalis swarmed into the perimeter and killed them. The Somalis butchered the injured helicopter crewmen, too, except for Durant, whom a Somali militia commander thought would make a useful bargaining chip.

At the first crash site, the Rangers and D-boys were settling into an L-shaped perimeter, having been told that the arrival of ground forces had been delayed again. They set up fighting positions inside houses and established four casualty collection points, where medics labored to save limbs and lives. Captain Scott Miller, the commander of the ground element, sent word that they had casualties in need of urgent evacuation, one of whom was certain to die if he was not evacuated by helicopter. Colonel Jerry Boykin, who as Delta Force commander was overseeing the operation from the task force's headquarters, decided that it was too dangerous to try landing another helicopter. "Scotty, we can't send another helo in there and get it shot down," Boykin told Miller. Boykin later called it "the most agonizing decision I have ever had to make."

Night would soon arrive. Under most circumstances, the Rangers and D-boys relished night combat in the third world, because the Americans had night-vision equipment and third-world adversaries did not. But the Americans had left all of that equipment at their base, never imagining that they would still be in the middle of Mogadishu at nightfall. They were running low on ammunition, water, and medical supplies, whereas Aidid's militias enjoyed immediate access to all manner of supplies.

Captain Miller kept receiving reports that a relief convoy was coming. One was said to be half an hour away. Then, after forty-five minutes, a voice announced that it would arrive in one hour. At approximately 8:30 p.m., the most seriously injured Ranger, Corporal Jamie Smith, bled to death.

A rescue convoy composed of 10th Mountain soldiers, Task Force Ranger volunteers, and 4 tanks and 28 armored personnel carriers borrowed from Pakistani and Malaysian forces finally arrived at around 2:30 a.m. The survivors of Task Force Ranger were taken to a soccer stadium, where they saw American dead and wounded lying on stretchers all over the grass.

Specialist Kurth was shocked to see so many American casualties. Fellow Rangers informed him that his two best friends had been killed. One man from his platoon, whose eyes showed the signs of prolonged sobbing, kept mumbling, "They're all gone, Ruiz, Smith, Joyce, Pilla, Cavaco, Alphabet—they're all dead." Kurth smoked a cigarette that he had bummed off some 10th Mountain soldiers, then put his head down on a Humvee and started to cry.

US helicopters flew into the stadium in shifts to pick up the wounded. They would be flown to medical facilities at the airport and the US embassy, and the more serious cases would be moved on to the United States. As Sergeant Randy Ramaglia was loaded aboard a helicopter, a medic leaned over to him to say, "Man, I feel sorry for you all."

The sergeant replied, "You should feel sorry for *them*, 'cause we whipped ass." No precise count was ever made of Somali casualties, but most put the Somali dead at or above 1,000, with several thousand more wounded. According to US intelligence reports, the casualties devastated morale among Aidid's allies and caused some of them to pull out of the city. A number of Somali warlords were even telling the Americans they would depose Aidid if the Americans would stop killing people.

Task Force Ranger suffered a total of 16 killed and 57 wounded. For the 10th Mountain Division, the casualty count came to 2 dead and 22 wounded. Ninety-seven casualties was a modest sum in comparison with what the American nation had suffered at Shiloh, Salerno, or Hue City, but the United States had not paid so steep a price in more than two decades. For that reason, Operation Gothic Serpent was certain to draw attention from the American public.

The battle's impact on the public, however, would be shaped as much by press imagery as by the casualty list. At the site of Durant's crash, Somalis dragged the naked bodies of dead Americans through the streets while onlookers cheered and snapped photographs. The images, which quickly reached every newspaper and newscast in the world, convinced Americans that the situation in Somalia had spiraled out of control, and that the Somalis were repaying American kindness with barbarity.

President Clinton might have been able to avert complete strategic failure had he resolutely explained to the American people what had happened, and had he ramped up offensive military operations in Somalia, as General Garrison and UN Special Representative Howe were now recommending. But Clinton had never possessed much of an appetite for military action, and the public disgust with the dragging of the dead Americans multiplied his unease. Clinton therefore chose to disengage, and to duck responsibility.

A few days after Operation Gothic Serpent, Clinton ordered an end to offensive operations against Aidid. All US combat forces, he announced, would leave Somalia by March 31, 1994. "We cannot leave immediately because the United Nations has not had an adequate chance to replace us, nor have the Somalis had a reasonable opportunity to end their strife," Clinton remarked. "Moreover, having been brutally attacked, were American forces to leave now we would send a message to terrorists and other potential adversaries around the world that they can change our policies by killing our people. It would be open season on Americans."

But ending the hunt for Aidid and setting a withdrawal date for US forces were changes to America's policies, ones that future terrorists like Osama bin Laden would cite as evidence of the value of killing Americans. Most of the Americans who had participated in the Battle of Mogadishu were appalled by the president's dissembling, as well as by his new policies. According to Mark Bowden, the foremost chronicler of Operation Gothic Serpent, the prevailing sentiment among the men was, "If it had been important enough to get eighteen men killed, and seventy-three injured, not to mention all the Somalis dead or hurt, how could it just be called off the day after the fight?" When the Rangers were told they would soon be heading home, Sergeant Struecker remembered, "we exploded in a volley of anger and frustration. Guys threw equipment across the hangar, cursed, and pounded their fists."

Even more infuriating to the veterans were statements from the Clinton administration conveying the impression that the president had known nothing of the US military's hunt for Aidid—the hunt that he had personally deployed Task Force Ranger to carry out. In one public speech, Clinton averred that the hunt for Aidid "never should have been allowed to supplant the political process that was ongoing." Secretary of State Warren Christopher explained that policy in Somalia had been managed by the Deputies Committee, one level below the Cabinet, and for that reason, top officials "were not sufficiently attentive." Later, when Clinton met with families of the Americans killed in Mogadishu, he said the raid had taken place because he did not want to micromanage the military.

Members of Congress called for the firing of Aspin, and the press reported that some of the Joint Chiefs of Staff wanted Aspin fired, too. When it became public knowledge that Aspin had rejected General Montgomery's request for armor, Aspin went on ABC's *This Week* to explain that "the request was never put in terms of protecting troops; it was put in terms of the mission of delivering humanitarian aid."

Someone promptly leaked a copy of Montgomery's request to journalist Barton Gellman, who duly revealed its contents in the *Washington Post*. The heading of Montgomery's message, Gellman reported, was "Subject: U.S. Force Protection." Within the main body, Montgomery stated that the "primary mission" of the armor "would be to protect U.S. forces," and asserted that the vehicles would "provide a critical roadblock clearing capability for our vulnerable thin-skinned vehicles."

Clinton stood behind Aspin for a few months. Then, with the outcry against Aspin becoming ever louder, he accepted Aspin's resignation.

Garrison was permitted to stay on as JSOC commander. The fallout from Operation Gothic Serpent, however, prevented him from obtaining a third star and moving on to a higher position. For veterans of the battle, the Clinton administration's unwillingness to promote Garrison was an act of scapegoating, and yet another instance of the prioritization of political self-interest ahead of honor and dignity. "Garrison is the finest general officer I ever worked for," asserted Dan Schilling, an Air Force combat controller, in 2003. "It wasn't just a shame that his career was derailed after our deployment; it was a criminal act committed by political cowards."

On October 23, 1993, a physician at Walter Reed Medical Center who was treating men wounded in Gothic Serpent telephoned the White House. Patched through to a member of the White House staff, the doctor said in an angry tone that the injured men had been at the hospital for three weeks and yet no one from the White House had paid any attention to them. Upon receiving the complaint, Clinton decided to visit the hospital the following day. No reporters were permitted into the hospital during his visit. The wounded were told ahead of time that if they had negative opinions of Clinton, they should keep those opinions to themselves.

According to hospital officials who accompanied Clinton, the president was shocked by the sight of the severely injured men. "Clinton was visibly moved," one hospital official recounted. "He didn't know what to say. The men could see that." Some of the wounded were amiable during their brief conversations with the president. Others were sullen and hostile.

Afterward, the White House did not release any photographs from the president's visit to Walter Reed. Anonymous government officials told Patrick J. Sloyan of *Newsday* that "withholding the pictures is part of a damage-limitation strategy devised by David Gergen." A public relations specialist, Gergen at that time held the position of counselor to the president.

One senior Pentagon official recommended that President Clinton hold a public ceremony on the White House Lawn in which he would meet the wounded and present them with decorations. Earlier in the year, Clinton had done as much for Marines returning from Somalia. But the White House issued no invitations to the veterans of Gothic Serpent. The Pentagon official lamented that White House strategists "hope people will forget about Somalia."

FOR JSOC AND most other American special operators, Gothic Serpent would be the last combat engagement of the 1990s. That fact proved beneficial to the survivors of the operation in certain respects. The military's promotion system habitually favors combat veterans, so individuals with an exclusive claim to recent combat experience were destined to receive a disproportionate share of promotions. Participation in the Battle of Mogadishu also gave these veterans enhanced credibility with others in the military, most of whom regretted that they had missed out on the action.

JSOC spent a large fraction of the decade's remaining years preparing for the "next Mogadishu," an event that never materialized—in no small part because Mogadishu had convinced the Clinton administration to keep US troops away from similar hot spots. The organization also devoted much attention to weapons of mass destruction, laying plans to sabotage enemy production sites and interdict terrorists seeking to infiltrate nuclear, chemical, and biological weapons into the United States. JSOC's most celebrated successes of the 1990s came in an advisory capacity, in Colombia, where it helped build elite military forces to defeat drug cartels that had overwhelmed Colombia's police through assassination and bribery. Assistance to Colombian special operations forces culminated in the shooting of cartel impresario Pablo Escobar during his final scamper across the rooftops of Medellín.

Beginning in 1995, American special operators deployed to the former Yugoslavia to assist North Atlantic Treaty Organization (NATO) peacekeeping forces. JSOC units helped locate and apprehend fugitives who had been indicted for war crimes. Special Forces teams established outposts in Bosnian and Kosovar towns, where they met with local leaders to obtain information on war criminals and potential breakers of the international peace agreements. For men who heretofore had been focused on hostage rescue, airfield seizure, reconnaissance, or training of partner forces, these experiences developed skills in working with local populations and ferreting out villains, skills that they could pull out of their pockets in wars still to come.

Other special operators filled out the decade training and advising the security forces of a host of nations beset by internal conflict. With the demise of the Soviet Union in 1991 having apparently rendered conventional warfare among major powers obsolete, the Special Forces and their smaller Navy and Air Force siblings increasingly staked claims to counterinsurgency and other forms of internal defense. The largest and most effective of their internal defense efforts took place in Colombia.

Following the death of Pablo Escobar, the Colombian government failed to consolidate political and military control over the country, permitting the rise of the Fuerzas Armadas Revolucionarias de Colombia (FARC) insurgency. So menacing did the FARC become that 800,000 well-to-do Colombians fled the country by the end of the decade. At the behest of the Colombian government, American special operators poured into the country in the late 1990s to train military and police officers. In contrast to the ad hoc foraging for willing partners that had characterized

American SOF efforts in other countries, this effort was designed systematically, with long-term objectives taking precedence over short-term expediencies. Targeted at leadership development, the training program possessed enough American special operators to train large numbers of Colombians long enough to effect real improvements in skills and motivation. The Colombian trainees were to assume leadership roles of escalating seniority during the Colombian government's war against the FARC, which took a decided turn for the better during the presidency of Álvaro Uribe from 2002 to 2010.

SOF training programs, it should be noted, were not the decisive element in the defeat of the FARC. That distinction belonged to improvements in Colombia's top political and military leadership, driven by belated recognition that the country's sclerotic government and armed forces could not hold back the revolutionary tide much longer. The transformation of Colombia's senior military leadership, though, was influenced by the involvement of America's special operations forces in training and education programs dating back to the 1960s. Through decades of helping the Colombians form schools at centralized locations, develop curricula, and teach students, the American special operators inculcated positive cultural values into the junior leadership, which eventually became the senior leadership. "The most important thing that Colombia gained from US military assistance was the transfer of culture," said General Carlos Alberto Ospina Ovalle, the head of Colombia's armed forces from 2004 to 2007. "The Americans served as our role models. We watched their behavior, their discipline, their humility, and their commitment to their country, and tried to emulate them."

At the dawn of the twenty-first century, proponents of American special operations forces trumpeted Colombia as a role model for all the countries where special operators were helping partners contend with insurgency, criminality, and other scourges. Through broadened and prolonged training of allies, SOF could help contain localized threats at a low cost and with little fanfare. For those who had joined the military profession to kick down doors and blow things up, the world seemed to have become rather boring.

JUST TWO MONTHS before President Clinton's trip to Walter Reed Medical Center, special operations forces had been the new toy that no one wanted to put down. Clinton and his advisers, few of whom knew anything about military affairs, had hoped that JSOC could quickly and easily put a silver bullet through the heart of America's Somalian nemesis. After events in Somalia disabused Clinton of that notion, he shoved the special operators back into the toy box, pushing them down near the bottom lest their appearance give cause for rueful remembrance. Veterans of Gothic Serpent would long remember how the political leadership had sent them into battle and bragged about it, then abandoned them when the political winds shifted. Nor would they forget that their political masters had refused requests for resources that could have averted tactical and strategic catastrophes.

The Joint Special Operations Command had been created in 1980 to execute raids in hostile territory, but prior to Gothic Serpent it had seldom carried out any missions, and it had never attempted to defeat an insurgency. In Aidid's militias, it faced a large enemy that enjoyed support from the people and intermingled with them for self-protection, a combination that afforded the militias strong defenses against sporadic raids, the principal weapon in JSOC's arsenal. Only large-scale counterinsurgency operations, requiring far more troops than the JSOC possessed, stood a chance of defeating this sort of popular insurgency.

Other special operations forces might have been able to accomplish more in Somalia by training Somalis in counterinsurgency. The Colombian experience would soon show that the US Army Special Forces could make a real difference in that capacity. Counterinsurgency training, however, was not a quick fix, either, for a country lacking a professional officer corps requires a decade or more of foreign assistance to build effective security forces. Colombia, moreover, had a population that was more highly educated than that of Somalia, and it had political leaders who were more committed to the nation's well-being—both of which were key ingredients in Colombia's remarkable turnaround.

In the short term, therefore, a large foreign military presence was the only viable way to prevent the insurgents from taking over Somalia. The withdrawal of US forces in the spring of 1994 enabled the insurgents to regain their strength, and the departure of the last UN forces in 1995 allowed the militias to overrun the whole country. Not until large Ethiopian forces entered Mogadishu in 2006 to drive out a recently installed extremist group would Somalia have a central government that was favorably disposed to the West.

Special operators and their political backers had billed the deployment of Task Force Ranger to Somalia as an opportunity to show that SOF were a strategic force, capable of winning a war on their own. Some JSOC veterans would maintain that the task force could have achieved strategic success had it been permitted to continue operations, pointing to the physical and psychological damage sustained by Aidid's militias. For most observers, however, the events of October 3–4, 1993, and the ensuing US withdrawal discredited the idea that special operations forces could decide strategic outcomes. That idea would lie in hibernation for nearly two decades, until Gothic Serpent had faded from the consciousness of political and military leaders.

To the conventional military, Gothic Serpent demonstrated conclusively the absurdity of SOF pretensions to strategic might and tactical invincibility. With the White House disowning Gothic Serpent, and the operation's participants unable or unwilling to explain what had happened, critics found it easy to assemble a montage of SOF incompetence, featuring the mistaken arrests of UN and Somali officials, the crashing of American helicopters, the hauling of dead Americans through the streets, and the termination of the hunt for Aidid. Conventional military officers who had resented the diversion of resources to special units and the self-importance of special operators viewed the debacle as a self-inflicted comeuppance. "Special ops people are hard to deal with," one former military official commented. "They are arrogant, they overestimate their own capability, and they're very secretive. This all came back to bite them in Somalia."

CHAPTER 8

REGIME CHANGE

Ascending a mound of charred and smoldering rubble, George W. Bush grasped a bullhorn in one hand while putting his other arm around Bob Beckwith, an elderly fireman in an oversized blue fire helmet. As Bush brought the bullhorn to his mouth, conversation ceased and notebooks flipped open among the pool reporters who had been pursuing the president through the debris of the World Trade Center. Few among the press had supported Bush during his election the preceding year, but at this dire moment in history, they appeared as eager as any Americans to see him rise to the occasion and, like Pericles before the Athenians, deliver an oration with the passion and majesty to buoy a traumatized nation.

"I want you all to know," Bush began, then paused as people swarming toward the scene urged him to turn up the volume on the bullhorn. "It can't go any louder," he said with a wry grin.

"I want you all to know," the president intoned, "that America today is on bended knee, in prayer for the people whose lives were lost here, for the workers who work here, for the families who mourn. The nation stands with the good people of New York City and New Jersey and Connecticut as we mourn the loss of thousands of our citizens."

Rescue workers and firemen toward the rear of the throng bellowed in salty New York accents, "We can't hear you!"

"I can hear you!" Bush exclaimed. "I can hear you! The rest of the world hears you! And the people who knocked these buildings down will hear all of us soon!"

Chants of "USA! USA! USA!" erupted across Ground Zero, and at offices, schools, construction sites, and watering holes across the country. Americans of all persuasions, even Manhattanites who looked down their noses at Bush as a Texas boor who had stolen the 2000 election from Al Gore, would hail Bush's impromptu Ground Zero speech as a model of presidential leadership. The event, eight months into Bush's first term, may have been the zenith of his eight-year presidency.

In Washington, Congress was on this same day, September 14, 2001, voting on a bill authorizing the president to "use all necessary and appropriate force against those nations, organizations, or persons he determines planned, authorized, committed, or aided the terrorist attacks that occurred on September 11, 2001, or harbored such organizations or persons." The bill passed the House 420–1 and the Senate 98–0. At no other time in the nation's history had the American people been so unified in their outrage, so unequivocal in their resolve for retribution.

Before taking the nation to war, Bush would offer some of the accomplices a chance to be spared from America's terrible swift sword. On September 15, his CIA station chief in Pakistan, Robert L. Grenier, met secretly with a high emissary of the Taliban government of Afghanistan, the government harboring Osama bin Laden and other Al Qaeda militants behind the 9/11 attacks. The United States, said the station chief, wanted the Taliban to hand over Bin Laden and his associates to the United States, or to kill them in the trying. The message was relayed to Mullah Mohammed Omar, supreme commander of the Taliban regime and the founding father of the Taliban movement. The one-eyed Mullah Omar concluded that the Americans were bluffing, telling a senior subordinate that there was "less than a ten percent chance that America would resort to anything beyond threats." Calling the supposed bluff, Mullah Omar refused to evict his guests. War it would be.

The 9/11 attacks touched most Americans in some way, but few were to be as affected as America's special operators. The cataclysm was to draw the United States into wars that outlasted a pair of two-term presidents, in which America's special operations forces went into harm's way more frequently than any other military force. The demands of these unending wars would transform special operations, special operations forces, and the special operators themselves. Relations between special operations forces and the White House, Congress, conventional military forces, and the American public would be forever altered.

CAPTAIN JASON AMERINE had just been seated at a restaurant in Kazakhstan when his senior communications sergeant phoned him to report that two planes had flown into the World Trade Center. Jumping up from the table, Amerine rushed back to the military installation where his Special Forces team was based. There, the Americans watched the Pentagon burn and the Twin Towers collapse.

"This means war," Amerine intoned to his team sergeant. Their lives were about to change, Amerine believed, though the only change he could foresee with any confidence was the premature termination of the team's mission of training Kazakh paratroopers. Where would they go next, he wondered, and what trials awaited them there? The same questions whirled through the heads of special operators in the jungles of Latin America, the deserts of Africa, and the rice paddies of Asia.

Within days, Amerine's team and many of the others would be pulled out of their assignments and ordered to prepare for deployment to Afghanistan.

In Afghanistan's northern provinces, a collection of 22,000 Afghan militiamen known as the Northern Alliance had been waging war against the Taliban for the past five years. Outnumbered four to one by the Taliban's armed forces, the motley Northern Alliance militias clung to isolated enclaves, from which they occasionally launched fruitless attacks on the Taliban-held cities. For President Bush and his national security team, lending support to the Northern Alliance was the obvious first step in a military campaign against the Taliban. Landlocked and ringed in by countries hostile or standoffish toward the United States, Afghanistan was too far removed from US air and naval bases to be invaded in the near term, so supporting the resistance groups would have to be America's main effort until American expeditionary forces could be marshaled. Bush quickly authorized the insertion of small CIA teams into Afghanistan and gave them $1 billion in cash for buying the assistance of the Northern Alliance and other rebel groups.

Hank Crumpton, head of special operations at the CIA's Counterterrorism Center, handpicked the teams from the CIA's paramilitary corps. A shadow of its Vietnam-era self, the paramilitary corps consisted of only a few dozen personnel, ensuring that the number of CIA personnel entering Afghanistan would remain low. The first of the CIA teams, code-named Jawbreaker, arrived in the Panjshir Valley on September 26. Leading the seven-man team was Gary Schroen, a sixty-year-old veteran with deep Afghanistan experience and a rank that was the CIA's equivalent of a three-star general.

CIA Director George Tenet asked the Defense Department to send special operations units to Afghanistan to work alongside Crumpton's teams. These special operators would provide a layer of protection for the CIA's lightly armed officers, train Afghan forces, and direct air strikes onto enemy positions. Tenet offered to place his CIA teams under the authority of General Tommy Franks, who as head of Central Command was the chief US military commander for Afghanistan. It was an exceptional act of bureaucratic altruism in the turf-conscious world of Washington, DC, of the sort that rarely occurs except in time of national crisis.

For several weeks, Tenet's request for special operators went unfulfilled. Franks and Major General Dell Dailey, the JSOC commander, worried that sending troops into an area beyond the range of US rescue helicopters posed inordinate risks. Some senior military commanders saw little need to hurry, because they expected that US assistance to the Northern Alliance would have minimal impact. One American officer recounted that leaders at Central Command "thought they'd let the Special Forces go in and play around for a few months, and then the real fight would occur when the 101st and the 82nd Airborne arrived." Further delaying matters were squabbles within the special operations community over who would get to deploy first and who would work for whom.

The insertion of Jawbreaker, combined with a British news story showing that mere reporters had been able to visit the front lines with Northern

Alliance commanders, finally persuaded Franks to put special operations forces with the Northern Alliance. Several more weeks were to pass before any special operators set foot in Afghanistan, however, as the Defense Department was still in the process of securing permission from Afghanistan's next-door neighbors to use bases from which it could provide the necessary logistical and air support for a few hundred troops.

Afghanistan fell within the area of operations of the 5th Special Forces Group. Prior to 9/11, the 5th Group had given little attention to Afghanistan, its exertions focused instead on other places in its operational area where it believed conflict more likely to occur, principally Egypt, Jordan, and the countries fronting the Persian Gulf. Most of the Green Berets in the 5th Group had taken lessons in Arabic or French. None had received training in the languages of Afghanistan.

In the wake of the 9/11 catastrophe, the 5th Group commander, Colonel John Mulholland, put his Special Forces teams into an isolation facility at Fort Campbell, Kentucky. The first job, Mulholland stated, was to acquaint themselves with Afghanistan's geography, people, and government. Team members searched public and classified databases for information on the Northern Alliance, but the best they could find were a few books on the Soviet-Afghan War of the 1980s. The amount of information they obtained on the Northern Alliance commanders with whom they were hoping to work could fit onto a single index card.

As reports came in from Crumpton's teams, though, it became clear that the Special Forces were not needed for their ability to bridge linguistic or cultural divides. The CIA personnel with whom they would work in Afghanistan included enough individuals with country expertise that the CIA could deal with Afghan political issues. The resistance forces of the Northern Alliance had already been organized and trained, moreover, so the unconventional warfare skills of the Special Forces were not in high demand. What the Afghans did need from the Special Forces was their ability to guide American bombs.

In preparation for deployment to Afghanistan, Mulholland's Special Forces teams were assigned Air Force tactical air controllers who had trained and deployed with the Special Forces in the past and were versed in the employment of the laser acquisition marker. Resembling a pair of oversized, tripod-mounted binoculars, the laser acquisition marker used an infrared laser beam to pinpoint targets several kilometers away for destruction by "smart bombs"—computerized bombs that steered themselves to the laser point. The air controllers also knew how to aim Joint Direct Attack Munitions, which were guided to map coordinates by means of GPS technology.

Just before departing the isolation facility for Afghanistan, members of the 5th Group wrote letters that would be forwarded to their families in the event of death. Mike McElhiney wrote to his eight-year-old son, "I hope Mommy has explained where I am and what I had to do. This war and what has happened to me is for you and all children of your age. I have gone and suffered this fate so you don't have to. You are now the man of the house and I know this is a big responsibility but when you grow up you will understand. Take care of your mother and sister and I will be watching over you from heaven. I love you always. Your Daddy."

On October 10, Mulholland and his headquarters arrived at K2 Air Base in Uzbekistan, to which the US government had just acquired basing rights. Mulholland assumed command of Joint Special Operations Task Force–North, also known as Task Force Dagger, which would direct the special operations forces heading into northern Afghanistan. The first two Special Forces teams entered Afghanistan on October 19 aboard Chinook helicopters piloted by Nightstalkers of the 160th Special Operations Aviation Regiment.

The twelve Green Berets of Special Forces Operational Detachment Alpha (ODA) 595 arrived at the Dari-a-Souf Valley, about fifty miles south of Mazar-i-Sharif, at 2 a.m. A sandstorm was sweeping northern Afghanistan that night, giving the landing an ominous resemblance to Desert One. The Nightstalker pilots, however, delivered the Green Berets safely and departed the scene without incident.

Out of the swirling sand, the Special Forces saw the approach of Afghans whose robes and strange dialect reminded at least one of the Americans of the Sand People in *Star Wars*. The mysterious Afghans guided ODA 595 to a camp held by General Abdul Rashid Dostum, one of the top Northern Alliance commanders. What little information the Special Forces had been able to find on Dostum was not especially encouraging.

Said to be a ruthless Uzbek warlord in his mid-fifties, Dostum was reputed to have fought for the Soviets against Afghanistan's Islamic rebels in the 1980s and led an independent militia in the civil warfare of the 1990s. Word had it that he was in ill health. The ODA commander, Captain Mark Nutsch, was worried that Dostum might try to kill the Americans at their first meeting.

At sunrise, the Green Berets watched thirty rough-hewn soldiers arrive on horseback, AK-47s and machine guns poking through their robes and long checkered scarves. A second wave of twenty horsemen followed. One of these men, riding a white stallion with a red pom-pom embroidered into the coarse hair of its forehead, jumped from his saddle. Shaking hands with each American, the regal figure introduced himself as General Dostum.

To the surprise of the Americans, Dostum was a healthy and vigorous bear of a man. Standing over six feet tall and weighing at least 240 pounds, he had a barrel chest and a short beard flecked in black and gray. Affable and outgoing, he did not seem capable of the cruelty that he was rumored to have perpetrated in years past.

Dostum escorted the Green Berets inside a walled compound. Seated on carpets, the Americans sipped tea while the general explained the current situation and his battle plans on a map. Dostum's "army," the Americans learned, consisted of fewer than one hundred hardcore fighters. When he needed a larger force, he drew on a pool of 2,000 part-time militiamen.

At the end of the meeting, Dostum said that half of the American team should join him for a trip westward to his command post, several hours away on horseback. They would be leaving in fifteen minutes. An invitation to a forward command post, no matter how short the notice, was something a Green Beret could not pass up.

For Captain Nutsch and the five other Americans selected for the journey, Dostum's lieutenants led forth six horses. Descendants of the steeds of Genghis Khan, the horses had short, thick legs, perfectly matched to Afghanistan's mountainous terrain. The saddles were tiny by American standards, having been designed for Afghan men, who on average weighed about 140 pounds, whereas no one on Nutsch's team tipped the scales at less than 200 pounds. The stirrups were so short that the taller Americans rode with their knees sticking up near their ears.

ODA 595's excursion to the front would be the first of many horseback rides for the Green Berets sent to assist the Northern Alliance. The horses plodded up and down mountain trails that narrowed to two feet in places, with 1,000-foot drops awaiting the rider whose horse put a hoof in the wrong place. Prolonged riding on the stout beasts chafed the legs of the Americans, in some cases drawing blood, and left them struggling to walk after they dismounted. When they reached a well-situated observation point, the Americans fetched their rucksacks from the pack mules and unloaded their laser acquisition markers, laptops, and other high-tech gear. "It's as if the Jetsons had met the Flintstones," one of the Special Forces soldiers quipped.

The first six smart bombs directed by ODA 595 missed their intended targets, most of them by a mile or more. For troops who had been inserted for the express purpose of guiding precision munitions, nothing could have been more humiliating or discouraging. As the team members stewed in dejection, an English-speaking Afghan approached them to convey General Dostum's reaction. Expecting to receive word of the warlord's grave disappointment, the Americans were stunned to hear the Afghan report Dostum to be in a state of elation. "You made an aircraft appear and drop bombs," the man said. "General Dostum is very happy."

Captain Nutsch believed that the main cause of the initial debacle was the team's distance from the front lines. Dostum had forbidden the Americans from getting close to the fighting, for fear that an American would get killed and the US government would then pull everyone out, as it had done in Somalia after Operation Gothic Serpent. Captain Nutsch, endeavoring to drown out the whispers of Gothic Serpent's ghosts with persistent cajoling about the value of accurate air strikes, eventually secured Dostum's permission to move the team closer to the Taliban.

As soon as the Special Forces came near the front lines, their bombs started hitting their intended targets with pinpoint precision. Tuning in to Taliban radio frequencies, Dostum followed Taliban discussions of the bombardments with the eagerness of a boy listening to a broadcast of his favorite sports team. The voices of the hitherto arrogant Taliban wavered with fear as huge explosions vaporized installations and fighting positions nearby. Dostum, astonishing the Americans once again, dialed up the opposing Taliban commanders on the phone to taunt them. "I have the

Americans with me, and they have their death ray," Dostum notified his adversaries. "Surrender or die!"

On the same day that Nutsch's ODA landed south of Mazar-i-Sharif, ODA 555 set down in the Panjshir Valley, home to the Northern Alliance warlord Fahim Khan, with whom Gary Schroen's Jawbreaker team had been working for nearly a month. One of the Jawbreaker officers promptly briefed ODA 555 on the CIA's plans for working with the Northern Alliance. Within twenty-four hours, the Special Forces team was at the dividing line between the Northern Alliance and the Taliban, at Bagram, twenty-five miles north of Kabul.

A Northern Alliance commander took ODA 555 up a dilapidated Soviet-era control tower at the Bagram air base, giving them a panoramic vista of the Shomali Plain. The Americans could see the Taliban trenches and bunkers that for years had served as the Taliban's main defensive barrier against a Northern Alliance thrust across the plain to Kabul. Having ascended the tower on the assumption that they were receiving an introductory tour of the battlefield, the Americans were taken by surprise when the Afghan commander started pointing out specific Taliban artillery positions, assembly points, and command centers within plain sight. Grabbing their laser guiding equipment, the Americans began marking targets.

Locating enemy positions, the Special Forces quickly learned, would be much easier than getting aircraft to bomb them. At this point in time, only sixty-five American aircraft were dropping bombs in all of Afghanistan, and they were spread thinly across a country the size of Texas. On the first day and for many thereafter, most of the pleas of ODA 555 for air strikes went unmet. A master sergeant on the team lamented that they had "more targets than a hound dog has fleas," but they would "be lucky to get two or three aircraft to respond to our requests for strikes." Fahim Khan and his militiamen began to lose confidence in the Americans for the lack of bombs. Radio intercepts revealed that Taliban commanders on the Shomali Plain were laughing about how weak and ineffective the Americans were.

On November 1, the American bombing intensified in northern Afghanistan, but it was concentrated near Mazar-i-Sharif, in support of Dostum's forces. Fahim Khan's remonstrations to the Americans that they were showing favoritism to Dostum produced no change in the geographic distribution of bombs. On November 9, Dostum's forces advanced the final forty kilometers on Mazar-i-Sharif at a gallop, striving to enter the city ahead of the forces of rival warlord Atta Mohammed Noor, some of whom were speeding toward Mazar-i-Sharif in Taliban vehicles that they had bought, stolen, or captured. Taliban leaders surrendered the city that day.

The bombing of the Shomali Plain finally swung into gear on November 11. Precision bombs plastered Taliban buildings, tanks, artillery, and command bunkers, killing unsuspecting troops by piercing their vital organs or crushing them with overpressure. Within a matter of hours, American airpower had blown gaping holes in a defensive line that the Northern Alliance had been unable to penetrate for years. Fahim Khan's forces surged into the holes right behind the strikes, with the bulk of the men and vehicles advancing on or near the highway leading to Kabul. Taliban commanders switched sides in droves under the combined weight of punishing air strikes, Northern Alliance assaults, and wads of $100 bills offered by the CIA.

Most of the Taliban units that defected were under the command of native Afghans, for whom opportunistic shifting of allegiances was a storied cultural tradition. Units led by Arabs, Pakistanis, and Chechens, meanwhile, continued to do battle. Making a fighting retreat toward Kabul, the diehards intended to form a defensive ring around the capital city. But they had barely begun digging foxholes on the city's outskirts when the onrushing Northern Alliance crashed through their positions as easily as the original front lines. On November 13, the Taliban leadership scurried out of a chaotic Kabul just before the arrival of cargo trucks crammed with Northern Alliance troops.

ONE DAY AFTER the fall of Kabul, four Black Hawk helicopters flew Jason Amerine's Special Forces team, ODA 574, to the town of Tarin Kowt in southern Afghanistan. Communications Sergeant Wes McGirr, who at twenty-five years of age was the youngest member of ODA 574, looked down from his Black Hawk in wonderment as it soared over lofty mountain peaks, thinking that he must be experiencing the same mixture of fear and exhilaration that the Jedburghs had felt when they flew across the English Channel into occupied France. *"It's dark, and I've got more gear than I can possibly run with,"* McGirr thought. *"Once we get dropped off, we're on our own. God, this is awesome. This is a war and we're live and we've got ammo and anything can happen from here on out."*

Amerine's mission was to support an Afghan opposition leader who had just returned from exile, Hamid Karzai. The CIA had infiltrated Karzai from Pakistan by air in the hope that he could take charge of a new national government, one capable of securing the country and preventing another outbreak of civil war once the Taliban were gone. Upon arrival at Tarin Kowt, Amerine's team met a CIA contingent led by "Greg," who reported to the CIA station chief in Pakistan, Robert L. Grenier.

In contrast to the CIA officers working with SOF in northern Afghanistan, Greg did not let the special operators in on his broad strategic plans, leaving the special operators with the impression that no such plans existed and hence they themselves were calling the shots. Higher military headquarters had led the Green Berets to believe that the CIA agents were "tourists and cashiers," present only to observe and hand out money while the Special Forces directed the destruction of the enemy. To special operators who liked to plan everything in exacting detail, the freewheeling ways of Greg's team appeared amateurish; some members of ODA 574 joked that CIA stood for "Children in Action." The special operators eventually learned that their CIA counterparts were much more than tourists and cashiers, and were making decisions on crucial political and military matters without informing them. Greg even had the clout to overturn tactical military decisions he found disagreeable—for instance, pulling Amerine's troops away from terrain that he did not deem ideally suited to defense.

Amerine and Greg competed for influence with the primary object of their mutual interest, Hamid Karzai. Born into a leading family of Afghanistan's most prominent tribal confederation, Karzai had lived abroad for years, first as a university student in India and later as a political organizer of Afghan exiles in Pakistan. Unlike the warlords of the Northern Alliance, Karzai did not possess his own militia, and he did not have the military experience to form one from the local Afghans who were prepared to take up arms against the Taliban. The Special Forces, therefore, expected that they would need to help him recruit, organize, train, and lead a force. Amerine thought it would take at least six months to build this force and capture its first objective.

The onrush of events nullified Amerine's plan almost immediately. The unraveling of the Taliban in the north and the sudden appearance of Karzai incited an anti-Taliban uprising in Tarin Kowt, delivering the provincial capital into Karzai's lap just a few days after the Special Forces arrived. In Kandahar, the Taliban's central hub of power in southern Afghanistan, alarmed Taliban authorities resolved to snuff out Karzai and his local allies before they could move beyond Tarin Kowt. On November 17, a convoy of eighty Taliban vehicles departed Kandahar for Tarin Kowt, advancing in three columns. The Americans estimated that 1,000 Taliban fighters were packed into the vehicles.

Amerine devised a plan to smash the vehicles and their passengers with American airpower before they could reach Tarin Kowt. The team set up an observation post on a ridge overlooking a valley through which the Taliban vehicles would have to pass. From this position, the Special Forces enjoyed unrestricted observation of a huge, open kill zone, seven miles across and four miles deep. The Air Force sent three F-18s to Tarin Kowt and put them on standby at an altitude of 30,000 feet.

When the long convoy slithered into view, the Special Forces marked the vehicles at the front, and then Amerine asked the F-18s to commence firing. The first bomb landed a few hundred yards in front of the lead Taliban vehicle. The second hit the lead vehicle squarely, obliterating it. A cheer went up among the Americans. Then they noticed that they could no longer hear the voices of the Afghans who had driven them to the site. As soon as the first bomb had missed its target, the Afghans had run back to their trucks, convinced that the Americans had failed and the Taliban would imminently slay all in their path.

Most of the drivers had started their engines and thrown the trucks in gear before the Americans could reach them. Amerine did not want to abandon the fantastic mountain aerie, but most of the American gear and ammunition was in those vehicles, so the Americans leapt into the beds of the departing pickups for the return ride to Tarin Kowt. Between bumps, the Americans attempted to coax the drivers into reversing course, but to no avail.

By the time they were back at Tarin Kowt, Amerine's patience and cultural sensitivity had been exhausted. Locating Karzai, he heatedly explained that the Afghan drivers had panicked and fled. While Karzai berated the Afghans, the Americans took the keys and drove the vehicles back toward the high ground. The Taliban had by now occupied the original observation post, so the Americans found another spot.

In the end, the delay and repositioning were not enough to spare the Taliban convoy from destruction. Guided by Amerine's team, US aircraft pulverized 45 vehicles over the course of the day. The remainder of the Taliban drivers turned back. After the battle, search parties found the corpses of 300 Taliban fighters in the kill zone.

After the annihilation of the Taliban attack force outside Tarin Kowt, Karzai told Amerine that they should move quickly toward Kandahar. Amerine replied that they did not have enough troops to take a major city like Kandahar, which the Taliban still held in a vise-like grip.

"I believe Kandahar will be surrendered to us," Karzai replied. "We just need to get our army to the outskirts of the city so we can talk to the Taliban leadership face-to-face."

Amerine begged permission to administer two weeks of basic military training to Karzai's newly created armed forces before they headed to Kandahar. Karzai reluctantly agreed. The Special Forces spent the remainder of the month training an "army" that one American officer described as "25 to 30 well-meaning friends, farmers, and shopkeepers."

At this juncture in the campaign, with additional ODAs entering Afghanistan in various places to work with the anti-Taliban forces, General Franks decided to send higher-ranking SOF officers to Afghanistan to manage the burgeoning enterprise and serve as liaisons with Northern Alliance leaders. Field-grade Special Forces officers arrived in theater to command the equivalents of battalion headquarters. According to Special Forces doctrine, these officers did not have authority over an ODA team's operations. When the colonel overseeing ODA 574 showed up, he assured Amerine that he and his staff were there to "give you top cover" and "facilitate." They would provide military advice to Karzai, not get into the team's tactical affairs.

On November 30, ODA 574 and its Afghan protégés drove slowly toward Kandahar in a small convoy. Toyota and Subaru trucks, overstuffed with well-wishers, cruised alongside to wave at Karzai and his entourage. One observer called it "a cross between the Baja, California, off-road races and scenes from the movie, 'Mad Max.'" Large numbers of Pashtuns volunteered to join Karzai's "army," but their unruliness worried Karzai, who refused to induct most of them into his ranks.

As the column neared Kandahar, the American Special Forces colonel who had previously promised to stay out of the ODA's tactical business started to micromanage. He and his staff told Amerine which hills to take, and demanded to see Amerine's plans before he took them. On December 5, the newcomers issued bombing orders to an Air Force tactical controller who was supposed to be taking his orders from Amerine and his subordinates. Watching the proceedings through binoculars, Amerine fumed as he saw the bombs fall on targets he did not think needed to be hit.

The colonel's air campaign lasted only a few minutes before catastrophe struck. Just after the tactical controller entered the coordinates for one of the colonel's targets into the laser acquisition system, the batteries died. The controller replaced the batteries and turned the system back on, assuming that the coordinates entered previously would still be in the system. But on this particular piece of hardware, unlike some of the other models, a loss of power reset the targeting coordinates to the device's location.

The coordinates were transmitted to a B-52 bomber, which disgorged a 2,000-pound bomb, second in size only to the BLU-82 "Daisy Cutter" in the US Air Force's bomb inventory. The munition landed precisely where it had been directed, the hilltop where the laser acquisition marker and all of ODA 574 were located.

The blast killed three members of Amerine's team and fifty-six Afghans. It wounded ODA 574's other nine Green Berets, along with sixty-five Afghans and sixteen other Americans who had recently arrived in support. The Americans who had not been injured, whose number included the colonel, provided first aid to Amerine and the other surviving Green Berets, most of whom were soon evacuated to the US military hospital in Landstuhl, Germany. Karzai, who had been inside a building looking at maps with Greg, was tossed in the air by a massive gush of hot air that tore through the structure's rear wall, yet aside from a few cuts on his face he escaped injury.

Although the errant bomb all but ruined Karzai's army, the drive on Kandahar would continue, thanks to Gul Agha Sherzai, a warlord whose eight-hundred-man militia was receiving support from another Special Forces team. In the succeeding days, waves of air strikes swept the roads leading into Kandahar, clearing paths for Sherzai's hundred-vehicle armada of Toyota pickups, Jinga transport trucks, and farm tractors. The going was tougher for Sherzai's forces than for the militias of the north, for by early December the Taliban and Al Qaeda fighters had devised tactics that reduced their vulnerability to American airpower. Hiding in bunkers or enclosed irrigation canals, they held their fire until hostile forces approached within one hundred meters or less, putting them too close for the use of US air support. Sherzai's fighters had to root out the more stubborn enemy soldiers with grenades and knives.

Sherzai's militiamen reached Kandahar on December 7. As Karzai had foretold, Taliban leaders did not defend the city to the death, but instead met the advancing forces on the city's outskirts and entered into surrender negotiations. Dragging out the surrender talks for several days, the Taliban negotiators bought time for Taliban and Al Qaeda leaders to flee the city.

WITH THE FALL of Kandahar, the Taliban and Al Qaeda leaders abandoned all hope of holding Afghanistan's cities and sought refuge in remote regions of Afghanistan and neighboring Pakistan. The fugitive of greatest concern to the Americans, Osama bin Laden, was reported to be retreating toward Tora Bora, one of the most imposing natural landmarks in a land renowned for the beauty of its rugged terrain. Abutting Afghanistan's eastern border with Pakistan, Tora Bora was dominated by craggy mountains that soared to altitudes of 12,000 to 15,000 feet. In the late 1990s, Al Qaeda had built up Tora Bora as a training ground and hiding place, carving caves into its mountainsides from which to shoot approaching enemies. When the Taliban regime had begun to crumble, Al Qaeda fighters had started falling back on Tora Bora, stocking its caves with food, weapons, and ammunition. By early December 2001, between 500 and 3,000 enemy fighters were believed to be holed up in the region.

For JSOC, Tora Bora presented a chance for redemption after several frustrating months. A few days after the 9/11 attack, Secretary of Defense Donald Rumsfeld had asked JSOC's parent organization, SOCOM, to lay plans for striking Al Qaeda leaders, based upon the mistaken impression that the SOCOM commander wielded authority over all special operations forces. When Rumsfeld learned that SOCOM did not have such authority, he set out to bestow it.

Serving his second tour as secretary of defense—his first had been in the Ford Administration, twenty-five years earlier—Rumsfeld enjoyed wide latitude in imprinting his stamp on the Defense Department. George W. Bush was the type of chief executive who did not meddle in the day-to-day business of subordinates, and Rumsfeld's age and experience accorded him additional leeway. Rumsfeld, moreover, had the energy, impatience, bluntness, and callous indifference to criticism required to pull an enormous bureaucratic sled. Yet even he found that weeks of pawing in the dirt often would not move the sled an inch, on account of the department's bureaucratic sclerosis and the affinity of some of its generals for the status quo.

Rumsfeld asked the SOCOM commander, General Charles R. Holland, to come up with a global counterterrorism campaign and request transfer of authority over deployed special operations forces from regional combatant commanders to SOCOM. Such an undertaking called for a general who was ready and willing to joust with the four-star generals who headed the regional commands and the armed services, as well as with Cabinet officials and ambassadors. Holland, a soft-spoken pilot with a preference for compromise over confrontation, had neither the temperamental predisposition nor the desire to wage a bureaucratic war. He did not directly refuse Rumsfeld's offer of sweeping new powers over special operations forces, but instead continued to manage SOCOM as before while discreetly torpedoing a number of planning efforts aimed at giving new authorities to his command. "Holland was given the keys to the kingdom and he didn't want to pick them up," observed Stephen Cambone, an aide to Rumsfeld.

Holland's demurral led Rumsfeld to go directly to JSOC in pursuit of his global war on Al Qaeda. The JSOC commander at the time, Major General Dell Dailey, was more willing than Holland to take the keys to the kingdom, and his two-star rank gave him the advantage of raising fewer hackles with the rest of the military than the SOCOM commander. His personality and skills, however, clashed with those of the JSOC ground operators who made up most of JSOC's blade edge. An Army aviator by trade, Dailey exercised caution and operated by the book, whereas the ground operators liked to take risks and adapt on the fly. When Delta operators advocated thinking outside the box, Dailey countered that those who had ventured outside the box of standard aviation procedures had caused aircraft to crash and people to die.

During the planning for one of the first JSOC operations in Afghanistan, an assault on a fertilizer factory, a Delta planner had proposed parachuting in a small number of Delta operators to hit the target with maximum stealth and speed. Dailey preferred a less risky raiding model, in which hundreds of troops and dozens of helicopters took part in the operation. "What in the hell kind of bullshit is that?" Dailey yelled at the planner when he briefed the proposal to a group of officers.

At Dailey's behest, JSOC's first operations in Afghanistan consisted of raids on an abandoned airstrip and an empty compound in Kandahar belonging to Taliban leader Mullah Omar. Dailey invited CNN and other media outlets to record the operations on video and broadcast them to the world, in the belief that the raids would unnerve the enemy by demonstrating America's ability to enter Taliban territory with impunity. The airstrip, moreover, was needed to facilitate future operations inside Afghanistan, and intelligence indicated that Omar might be paying a short visit to his compound.

The allocation of much of JSOC's time and manpower to these two operations appalled Robert Grenier, the CIA station chief in Pakistan, as well as much of Delta Force. A senior Delta officer scoffed: "Would the type of person who volunteers to sacrifice his own life in a suicide mission, just to get to a place where he can have his way with seventy-two virgins, really back down due to 'moral distress' inflicted by a CNN video clip of bombings on targets he knows are empty?" But a paucity of intelligence, from both the CIA and military intelligence organizations, left JSOC with few other targets onto which it could clamp its jaws.

As the 5th Special Forces Group gained international acclaim for its support of the Northern Alliance, Dailey fretted that JSOC's ground forces—Delta Force and SEAL Team Six—were being left by the wayside. He thus became more receptive to suggestions from his unit commanders to send small detachments into places where enemy personnel were still believed to be located. When Delta officers requested permission to advance on Tora Bora, Dailey gave the green light.

Delta Force and the CIA began by sending four of their best men into Tora Bora to find and kill as many members of Al Qaeda as possible. In little time, the four men discovered large concentrations of Al Qaeda running around the mountains and the valley. Hiding in a rock crevice with sweeping views, they directed torrents of bombs onto enemy positions over a period of three days.

One of the four men sent into Tora Bora, a CIA officer who had previously served in Delta Force, recommended inserting a Ranger battalion into Tora Bora to block escape routes. Gary Berntsen, the senior CIA officer in Afghanistan, concurred, submitting a request for eight hundred Rangers to CIA headquarters. "We need Rangers now!" Berntsen pleaded. "The opportunity to get bin Laden and his men is slipping away!!"

When the request reached Hank Crumpton at the CIA's Counterterrorism Center, he forwarded it to General Franks. The commanding general turned it down on the grounds that the combination of Afghans and small numbers of American personnel had worked so far and hence the formula needed no modification.

On December 8, a fifty-man Delta Force unit led by Major Thomas Greer arrived in Tora Bora with orders to push into the enemy's lair. Greer had the added responsibility of managing the "Eastern Alliance," a loose-knit conglomeration of local Afghan militias with approximately 2,500 fighters. In the absence of a large US ground presence, these militias would bear most of the responsibility for searching and clearing territory in Tora Bora.

The preponderance of men in the Eastern Alliance belonged to either Mohammed Zaman Ghun Shareef or Hazrat Ali. Neither man made for an especially appealing partner. Ali wanted the Americans to bomb the enemy into oblivion while his men waited in the surrounding area. As the bombs turned Tora Bora into a moonscape, Ali explained, his militia troops would kill the few Al Qaeda survivors who trickled out. "The Arabs will fight to the death," Ali told Greer in justifying his caution. "I don't want to sacrifice all my men to get them. Ten thousand fighters won't be enough to get them out of the trenches."

After prolonged subjection to American badgering and enticements, Ali agreed to send some of his troops into Tora Bora. The Americans were dismayed, although not especially surprised, when they learned that Ali was proceeding in a manner quite different from what had been asked of him. Moving forward in the daylight hours, Ali's men fasted in observance of Ramadan, so that when night came, they were ravenous and could only focus on two things, eating and drinking. Because they did not carry military rations or other provisions into the combat zone, they left the ground taken during the day to move back to areas where they could obtain food and drink. The next morning, it was back to square one.

Greer's D-boys, meanwhile, pushed forward into the valley on foot by themselves. Manning concealed observation posts, they used thermal imaging devices to spot Al Qaeda positions for destruction by strike aircraft. Without large and capable ground forces, however, it was impossible to close off escape routes, scour cave complexes, or capture enough prisoners to triangulate Bin Laden's whereabouts.

Delta Force remained at Tora Bora to rain down destruction until the day when the enemy was no longer to be seen, which turned out to be December 19. According to US estimates, Al Qaeda suffered 1,100 casualties at Tora Bora, while 1,500 of the militants escaped with their lives. Although the Americans would not know it until much later, Bin Laden was among those who slipped out unhurt.

At the end of January 2002, just as the Americans thought the war was coming to an end, US intelligence detected a concentration of Taliban and Al Qaeda personnel in the vicinity of the Shahikot Valley, another longtime extremist redoubt near the Pakistani border. According to intelligence analysts, an estimated 1,000 fighters had gathered in an area ten by ten kilometers. Inside this square lay the valley floor—at an elevation of 8,000 feet—and a hodgepodge of mountain peaks and ridges poking several thousand feet higher.

The planning for an operation into the valley, code-named Anaconda, commenced at the headquarters of Major General Franklin Hagenbeck. In December 2001, Hagenbeck had entered Afghanistan as commander of both the 10th Mountain Division and Combined Joint Task Force Mountain, the latter constituting the new command element for all US ground forces in Afghanistan. Planners from the 5th Special Forces Group and JSOC joined Hagenbeck's staff in organizing Operation Anaconda.

For both General Franks and the special operators, Anaconda offered a welcome opportunity to make up for the Tora Bora disappointment and to disprove the claim, running rampant among US military officers in Afghanistan, that the United States would have caught Bin Laden at Tora Bora had it sent in conventional US ground forces. Rather than rely primarily on big American units to clear out the Shahikot Valley, Franks chose to double down on the combination of Afghan militias and American special operators. The valley floor was dotted with Afghan villages, which the Americans believed to be occupied by both civilians and members of Al Qaeda and the Taliban, and hence, Franks reasoned, the militiamen would be needed to distinguish the enemy combatants from the other Afghans. Six ODAs from the 5th Special Forces Group would run the Afghan militia units through a three-week training course and provide them with combat advisers for the operation. Franks did not have enough Afghan militiamen at his disposal to seal off potential escape routes, so, as something of a sop to the conventional forces, he gave the job of blocking the valley exits to a few thousand American regulars from the recently deployed 10th Mountain Division and 187th Infantry Regiment.

Planning for Operation Anaconda took more than one month, the result of having too many participants in the planning room. Fortunately for the planners, the intended victims of the operation did not learn that they were in the crosshairs and remained in the valley. According to the final plan, the Afghan militiamen would serve as the operation's "hammer," driving through the villages on the valley floor from the west into an "anvil" of American soldiers occupying blocking positions on the trails through which the Taliban and Al Qaeda were expected to flee.

Ahead of the hammer-and-anvil action, Delta Force and SEAL Team Six operators were to conduct reconnaissance of the valley under the guidance of a senior Delta officer, Lieutenant Colonel Pete Blaber. Like many special operators of his generation, Blaber had been drawn to special operations two decades earlier by the Eagle Claw catastrophe. He had first heard of the failed Iran hostage rescue when it flashed on a television screen at the student center of Southern Illinois University, where he was enrolled at the time. Glued to the news for the next several days, Blaber learned of the secret desert base, the aircraft crashes, and the participation of Delta Force. The bravery and sacrifices of the special operations task force caused Blaber to think about his own purpose in life, and in the process sparked an interest in military service. When Blaber told the local Army recruiter he wanted to become an officer in the US Army, he explained that he wanted to make sure that the United States never again bungled a critical mission, and that good men would never again die as the result of bad command decisions. Was he interested in the Army Medical Corps, the recruiter inquired? No, said Blaber, Delta Force.

The operators under Blaber's command in the Shahikot Valley belonged to what were called "Advance Force Operations" teams. Conceived before 9/11 as part of an expansion of Delta's intelligence apparatus, Advance Force Operations encompassed small, covert operations in hostile countries in preparation for the next Panama or Somalia. After the fall of Kabul, General Franks had asked Delta to assign forty-five men to Advance Force Operations teams in Afghanistan for the purpose of locating the scattering Taliban and Al Qaeda leaders.

Blaber had eagerly sold Combined Joint Task Force Mountain on the value of his teams, explaining how the conventional forces assigned to Operation Anaconda stood to benefit from JSOC's world-class reconnaissance capabilities. Entering the valley on the ground in very small detachments, they would establish hidden observation posts from which to locate enemy fighters before and during the battle. Blaber did not keep General Dailey apprised of his plans, as he suspected that Dailey would find them objectionable, representing as they did a repudiation of the large set-piece raids that had become the hallmark of Dailey's tenure at JSOC. Blaber's suspicions were well founded. When Dailey belatedly learned of Blaber's participation in Anaconda, he tried to remove Blaber's teams from the operation. Blaber stonewalled long enough to keep his men in the game.

On February 27, three days before the hammer was scheduled to strike the anvil, Blaber's Advance Force Operations teams infiltrated into the valley. Juliet team, consisting of five Delta operators, entered the Shahikot from the north on ATVs with ultra-quiet mufflers. Mako 31, a team of five SEALs, followed behind Juliet to occupy a ridgeline with a commanding view of the valley. From the southwest, moving on foot, came the three men of India team—two Delta operators and a signals intelligence specialist from the secretive Defense Department intelligence agency known variously as Gray Fox, the Intelligence Support Activity, and the Army of Northern Virginia.

Ascending the high ground undetected, the reconnaissance teams scanned the Shahikot with Schmidt-Cassegrain spotting scopes, instruments with lenses so potent that the viewer could discern whether an individual was carrying a Kalashnikov at a distance of seven kilometers. Observation of "the Whale," a humpbacked ridgeline six kilometers wide by two kilometers across that bisected the valley, revealed a staggering array of enemy observation posts and concealed fighting positions. "The enemy is everywhere," Juliet reported to Blaber by satellite radio. The reconnaissance teams transmitted the coordinates of the positions they saw for future air strikes.

Most of these enemy positions had not been identified by the high-tech surveillance and communications intelligence assets with which the Americans had swept the valley in recent days. The Taliban and Al Qaeda fighters had taken care to make their foxholes, bunkers, and weapons invisible from the air, and had refrained from using electronic communications devices. Had it not been for the Advance Force Operations teams, US and Afghan forces would have had no idea that the enemy possessed significant combat power on the Whale or other high ground.

In the predawn hours of March 2, the hammer force of four hundred Afghan militiamen drove into the valley in two columns, riding in a miscellany of thirty-seven trucks that included Jingas, Toyotas, Mitsubishis, and a handful of Mercedes. Their Special Forces advisers had organized them into squads, platoons, and companies and assigned them accordingly into the procession of vehicles. Just as the convoy entered the valley, an AC-130 gunship, call sign Grim 31, spotted what appeared to be a hostile truck convoy heading toward them from the opposite direction.

Chief Warrant Officer Stanley L. Harriman, a Special Forces adviser riding with the Afghans, was listening to the gunship's reporting through his headset. The more he heard, the more the reported enemy vehicles sounded like those in his own convoy. Harriman hurriedly broadcast his coordinates to make sure that the aircraft had not mistaken friendly vehicles for the enemy.

Grim 31 issued a set of coordinates for the vehicles it was watching. A check by headquarters staff determined those coordinates to be more than six kilometers from Harriman's position. To be extra certain, the crew of Grim 31 shone a special light, invisible to the human eye, to illuminate the "glint" tape affixed to US vehicles for identification purposes. The beam detected no glint tape on the vehicles. Nor did Grim 31 see any of the orange and purple VS-17 panels that Americans were supposed to put on friendly vehicles as another means of identification from the air.

The AC-130 was cleared to fire. Its stabilized 105mm howitzer spewed an artillery shell every six seconds, while the 25mm and 40mm cannons began a steady rat-a-tat of automatic fire. The gunners stayed with the vehicles as they drove off the road in their desperation to escape the deluge.

"I'm taking incoming! I'm taking incoming!" Harriman hollered into his radio, while the driver of his truck swerved at forty miles per hour to evade large shellbursts that were chasing the vehicle. The explosions soon caught up with the truck. An artillery shell landed right next to the vehicle, spraying its side with shrapnel, including a racquetball-sized chunk that punctured the passenger side door and went through Harriman's lower back. Other bits of metal penetrated Harriman's legs, severed fingers, tore off an ear, and cut up his face. The truck's driver was hit in the hand, stripping the flesh from his fingers down to the bone.

The convoy's other vehicles zigzagged away from the road, chased by rounds of all sorts of calibers. Blaber, following the radio traffic and reports from his reconnaissance teams, soon realized that the shells striking the American convoy might be coming from the AC-130. "Cease fire! Cease fire! Cease fire!" Blaber yelled into the hand mike on his satellite radio. Fortunately for the Americans on the ground, the AC-130 was low on fuel and had to discontinue fire after two minutes and thirteen seconds, just before Blaber uttered the words.

Blood seeped from Harriman's numerous injuries, external and internal, turning his face a ghostly white. One of the other Americans got on the radio to inform headquarters that Harriman had suffered grievous injuries. "Chief is dying! Chief is dying!" he blurted out. A medical helicopter rushed to the scene and picked up Harriman, but a few minutes later he went into cardiac arrest and the medical personnel were unable to revive him.

Long afterward, the Americans would struggle to understand how a plethora of high-tech safeguards and the concerted efforts of seasoned operators had failed to prevent the friendly-fire tragedy that took Harriman's life. An investigation attributed the mistake to a faulty inertial navigation system on the aircraft. It was unable, however, to solve several mysteries surrounding the incident, including the inability of the aircraft's beam to detect the glint tape.

Once the deadly projectiles stopped falling from the sky, all of the trucks came to a halt to assess and address the damage. During this pause, at 6:15 a.m., militia commander Zia Lodin and his subordinates turned their heads expectantly toward the Whale. According to the Special Forces advisers, the United States was about to subject the large terrain feature to a fifty-five-minute barrage of air strikes, the likes of which might be expected to extinguish all life on the ridge.

A lone B-1B bomber came into view, soared over the Whale, and dropped six bombs during the space of one minute. Zia Lodin jumped up with his hands in the air and exclaimed, "All the Afghans are screaming 'Yay!'"

The waves of aircraft that Zia and the Americans expected to follow, however, did not materialize. American air planners had wanted to carpet bomb the Whale, but they had been overruled by ground planners who believed that heavy bombing would kill civilians and induce the enemy to flee before the ground forces could close in. As a consequence, the preparatory bombardment was limited to precision strikes on thirteen targets identified by Blaber's operators. Three more aircraft were supposed to strike the seven additional targets, but one was waylaid when a bomb got stuck in its bomb bay, and the other two aborted their runs after hearing a report that the first bombs had landed too close to the US reconnaissance teams.

As the remaining fifty-four minutes passed without sight of another aircraft, euphoria turned to despair. Zia, speaking through an interpreter to his Special Forces counterpart, Lieutenant Colonel Chris Haas, asked plaintively, "Where are the bombs you promised us? Where are the planes?"

With the rising of the sun, Al Qaeda spotters received unimpeded views of the inert militia convoy. From positions on the Whale that had survived the mini-bombardment, mortar tubes fired rounds onto the jumbled collection of trucks and militiamen. Zia's militia commanders, many of whom had lost contact with their troops when the trucks split up to escape the AC-130, ran away in panic. Other militiamen followed suit, casting off helmets and body armor to facilitate a rapid escape. The majority of militiamen departed the valley on foot, the remainder riding out on trucks whose drivers had been calm enough to recognize that running away was not the swiftest or easiest method of escape. The hammer was no more.

For the anvil, the morning was only marginally better. Aided by information provided by Blaber's teams, the helicopters managed to insert the American infantrymen into the valley without getting shot down, but soon after the insertion a company of American paratroopers came under heavy mortar fire from Takur Ghar, the highest of the valley's mountains. Three groups of enemy fighters, between fifty and one hundred men each, attacked the American company from three directions. Pinned down until sunset, the unit suffered twenty-six casualties before it was evacuated by air.

Over the course of the battle's first day, enemy fighters clambered out of caves and bunkers to attack the Afghan militiamen and US soldiers on the valley floor, while others moved from neighboring valleys toward the Shahikot for their chance to participate in the kill. The Taliban and Al Qaeda forays continued into the second day as the American infantry moved out of blocking positions to do the hunting that the Afghan militiamen were supposed to have done. Blaber's three reconnaissance teams kept vectoring precision munitions onto newly appearing fighters, inflicting most of the casualties that the enemy was to suffer during the battle.

Late on March 3, Blaber received a call from Air Force Brigadier General Gregory L. Trebon, Dailey's deputy. Trebon told Blaber to withdraw his three teams from the valley and turn the reconnaissance mission over to a couple of units from SEAL Team Six. Trebon wanted one of those SEAL units to go to Takur Ghar to eliminate the enemy mortars that were continuing to bombard the valley floor.

In the opinion of Blaber and other Delta operators, Trebon was a nice guy who knew plenty about flying aircraft but very little about operations on the ground. The ground operators were willing to tolerate aviators like Dailey and Trebon who, in the interest of comity among the services, held leadership positions in a joint command. But they had little patience for those who thought their authority entitled them to override the views of men with ground expertise and firsthand awareness of the situation, as appeared to be happening now. They also suspected that Trebon was pushing for insertion of the SEALs as a means of giving another service its turn.

Blaber attempted to dissuade Trebon from the proposed course of action. "Sir, my teams are fine for at least another forty-eight hours," Blaber explained. Any new teams that came into the area, Blaber added, would need to go through the same preparations as the teams already there, which included spending time at the forward base at Gardez to get acclimated to the altitude and talk with Americans familiar with the area.

Blaber's objections failed to sway Trebon. Having become acquainted with Blaber's skirting of orders from above, Trebon knew better than to get into a lengthy debate. He proceeded, instead, to force the issue by sending in two SEAL teams without notifying Blaber. The teams, Mako 21 and Mako 30, arrived at Blaber's headquarters with their own commanding officer, Lieutenant Commander Vic Hyder, whom Trebon had not placed under Blaber's authority.

Trebon directed Hyder to put the SEALs into the Shahikot that night, which meant flying them into the valley by helicopter. To limit the risks to helicopters and passengers alike, the SEALs would fly to offset locations and move on foot under cover of darkness to their observation posts. Mako 21 was to land on the valley floor and march toward the Upper Shahikot. Mako 30 would land at a site 1,300 meters northeast of Takur Ghar and climb for several hours to the top of the mountain.

The performance of Mako 21 was one of several episodes in the battle that would become subjects of complaints from Delta participants about the capabilities of SEAL Team Six. According to the account of journalist Sean Naylor, the members of Mako 21 neglected to take along all of the required equipment when they boarded the helicopters for insertion. Once they were on the ground, therefore, they had to request an immediate re-supply, thereby putting more aircraft at risk and divulging their location. After the team had established an observation post, the team leader reported that the SEALs could not see any enemy and requested extraction. But analysis at higher headquarters determined that Mako 21 was six hundred meters away from where they were supposed to be, and hence could not see the section of the Upper Shahikot Valley that they were supposed to be watching. After rebuffing several exhortations from Blaber to move the observation post, Mako 21 eventually shifted location, but at the new location they still could not see the upper valley. It later came to light that they were telling their SEAL headquarters that they were cold and tired and wanted to be withdrawn from the battlefield.

Mako 30 was scheduled to insert before midnight in order to give its SEALs enough time to climb to the top of Takur Ghar before dawn. The helicopter slated to deliver the team, however, developed engine trouble, necessitating the dispatch of a replacement helicopter from Bagram. By the time the new helicopter was ready, the insertion time had been moved back to 2:30 a.m. If the team departed at that hour, the march from the landing zone to the top of Takur Ghar would not be completed before the rising of the sun exposed them to enemy eyes.

SEAL Petty Officer Britt Slabinski, the leader of Mako 30, recommended delaying the insertion by twenty-four hours. Task Force 11, the JSOC headquarters element overseeing the battle, rejected the recommendation, notifying Slabinski, "We really need you to get in there tonight." To get in before sunrise, they would have to land on top of Takur Ghar. A cardinal rule of reconnaissance was that a team did not insert by helicopter onto its observation post, since it would give away its position and could draw overwhelming enemy forces to the location. But now they had no choice.

American surveillance aircraft had spotted no enemy combatants on the summit of Takur Ghar. To make doubly sure, an AC-130 flew over the peak and scanned it with an array of sophisticated infrared sensors, optical devices, and radars. It detected nothing. "Nobody is there," the AC-130 reported to the Chinook that was carrying Slabinski and the rest of Mako 30. "You are cleared in."

On the Chinook's approach to the landing zone, the sixty-foot blades of its twin rotors swirled up funnels of snow. Squinting through night-vision goggles, the crewmen and the SEALs began to glimpse disturbing signs of human activity.

"Footprints in the LZ," reported pilot Al Mack, using the acronym for landing zone.

"Got a donkey at three o'clock in the tree line," related the helicopter crew chief, Sergeant Dan Madden, through the aircraft's internal communications system. Another man attested that he saw decapitated goat carcasses hanging from trees.

Crew chief Jeremy Curran was the first to see a live person on the landing zone. "Guy just popped his head up," Curran said into his microphone.

"What's he doing?" Mack asked.

"He put his head back down."

Mack was concerned that there might be Afghan civilians on the mountain. Perhaps the butchered goats had belonged to innocent goatherds. Mack directed his men to fire only if fired upon.

Moments later, Mack saw a man stand up from behind a snowy berm twenty-five yards away, the grenade launcher on his shoulder pointed straight at the helicopter. The rocket-propelled grenade rushed at the helicopter with a glare that blinded Mack and others who were looking through night-vision devices. A bevy of RPGs followed in rapid succession, several of them penetrating the Chinook's fuselage and exploding inside. The helicopter lost electrical power, disabling the potent miniguns. Hydraulic fluid and oil spilled across the floor. From three directions, automatic weapons fire screeched through the frigid night air and banged into the Chinook in a metallic cacophony.

"Fire in the cabin," Sergeant Madden shouted over the intercom. "Go! Go! Go!"

That command was meant for the pilot, directing him to leave the landing zone before more munitions slammed into the lumbering beast. But one of the SEALs, Petty Officer First Class Neil Roberts, thought that Madden was telling the passengers to get out of the helicopter, which at the moment was just a few feet off the ground. Heading toward the ramp at the aircraft's rear, Roberts slipped on the syrupy mixture of hydraulic fluid and oil. Madden and Sergeant Alexander Pedrossa, the left door gunner, saw Roberts sliding down the ramp and reached out to stop him, Madden catching hold of a boot, Pedrossa grabbing the SEAL's ruck belt. Roberts himself, discerning that something was amiss, attempted to reverse course, but the soles of his boots could gain no traction. Carrying an eighty-pound pack and a twenty-seven-pound machine gun, Roberts altogether weighed more than three hundred pounds, giving him a momentum that pulled Madden and Pedrossa along with him across the helicopter's slick steel floor.

Mack, having correctly interpreted Madden's directive as aimed at him, had begun to lift the helicopter skyward. As Roberts neared the back of the aircraft, Madden's safety harness went taut, which halted the SEAL's progress momentarily. The crew chief clung desperately to Roberts's foot, straining every muscle to keep him on board. Three seconds later, the injured helicopter jerked violently. Madden lost his grip, and Roberts and Pedrossa went out the back.

Pedrossa's immersion in the frosty mountain air was followed immediately by the hard jerk of his safety harness as the line reached full extension. No such tether restrained Roberts, either because he had disconnected his harness moments earlier, or because he had never connected it in the first place, a common SEAL practice that helicopter crewmen bemoaned as reckless bravado. As Roberts hurtled past, his belt was ripped from Pedrossa's hand, severing the SEAL's last tie to the aircraft. Roberts fell into the snow ten feet below.

The helicopter had pulled away from Takur Ghar by the time Madden was able to key his mike. "We lost one," he informed the cockpit. "We got a man on the ground. Break right! We got to go back in!"

Mack attempted to steer the Chinook back to the mountain. Within seconds, however, the hemorrhaging of the hydraulic fluid caused the controls to lock up. The helicopter was "shaking and shimmying like a washing machine out of balance," as Mack later described it. Madden poured cans of hydraulic fluid into an emergency port and cranked a small handle that fed the fluid into the lines. The infusion bought enough time to land the helicopter, but not enough to go back to the mountaintop. Mack landed at the nearest clearing he could find. The rescue plan was off.

The SEALs and the Chinook's crew set up a perimeter in the snow and awaited their own rescue. A helicopter soon showed up to take them to the airfield at Gardez, twenty miles to the north. Intent on saving Roberts, Petty Officer Slabinski searched the base for a helicopter and a pilot that would carry his SEAL team back to Takur Ghar. One of the Nightstalker pilots agreed to take them to the mountain in his Chinook, Razor 04.

Slabinski requested that gunships saturate Takur Ghar with lead before his team paid its second visit. From overhead, airmen could see the heat signatures of twenty-five men walking around on the summit. But the gunship crews refused to open fire, on the grounds that they might hit Roberts. Haunted by the friendly-fire disaster that had taken the life of Harriman, the airmen were taking no chances.

Upon reaching the mountaintop, the Nightstalker pilot steered Razor 04 into a swale that shielded the helicopter from most of the enemy fire. Slabinski, four other SEALs, and Air Force radioman John T. Chapman jumped out of the helicopter, which then flitted away, unscathed, into the darkness. Alerted by the rumble of the Chinook, an enemy force roughly four times the size of Mako 30 locked horns with the Americans. The SEALs espied several well-protected machine-gun positions, which they attempted to flank and destroy with close-range fire and grenades. An enemy gunner knocked Chapman down. A SEAL was hit in the leg.

Taking fire from three sides, with two of his men incapacitated, Slabinski decided to pull back. The SEALs had to leave behind Chapman, who appeared to have stopped breathing. To cover the withdrawal, Slabinski threw a smoke grenade and the SEALs took turns providing suppressive fire. Another SEAL took a bullet to the lower leg during the retreat, but the five SEALs were able to get away. None of them had seen any sign of Neil Roberts. It would later be learned that Roberts had been killed by enemy fighters before the rest of his team returned to Takur Ghar to save him.

General Trebon now decided to send a force to rescue the unsuccessful rescue force. Two Chinooks took off from Bagram with a Ranger platoon that served as a quick-reaction force for JSOC. The headquarters of the

160th Special Operations Aviation Regiment wanted the two Chinooks to take the Rangers to an offset landing zone, below the top of Takur Ghar, from which they would fight their way up the mountain. Because of communications mishaps, however, the Chinooks received instructions to land on the summit.

The Chinook that was carrying the Ranger platoon commander, Captain Nate Self, reached the top of Takur Ghar at 6:10 a.m. Flaring fifty feet above the peak, it was suddenly assailed with swarms of projectiles, as if it were a knight just coming within range of a castle's archers. Bullets penetrated the chin bubble and smacked into pilot Greg Calvert, who would likely have been killed had it not been for the protection of his Kevlar body armor. A Nightstalker noted for his daring, Calvert decided that the intensity and accuracy of the enemy fire warranted aborting the landing.

Before Calvert could steer the helicopter clear of danger, enemy fire shredded the turbine blades of the right engine, leaving him no choice but to set the helicopter down on the mountaintop as best he could. Like a bird with an injured wing, the helicopter fluttered down without full control of its speed or direction. Drawing upon an array of skills mastered through thousands of hours in the cockpit, Calvert kept the helicopter upright until it thudded on the ground, sparing the passengers from anything worse than bumps, bruises, and scrapes. The aircraft came to rest in the middle of a bowl, the rim of which was dotted with prepared defensive positions. The men inside those positions fired excitedly into the fifty-foot hull of the motionless helicopter.

Rangers Brad Crose and Matt Commons decided that they were better off trying to attack the enemy than sitting in the helicopter, waiting to be killed by grenades or bullets. The moment the ramp of the helicopter went down, Crose and Commons charged out. Both were shot dead at the bottom of the ramp. Two more Americans fell dead while still inside the cabin. The helicopter had been on the ground for only fifteen seconds.

Captain Self was still in a daze when the first four men lost their lives. During the landing, he had been thrown onto the helicopter deck, hitting his head on the floor and knocking his night-vision goggles off their mount. His nose felt numb, as if he had been punched in the face, and his eyes watered. When he looked up, he saw tracer rounds and rocket-propelled grenades flying through the aircraft. Calvert came toward him from the cockpit, an injured hand dangling from tendons and bone, arterial blood squirting between the fingers of his good hand as he tried to stanch the flow.

Like Crose and Commons, Captain Self deduced that to stay in the helicopter was to court death. Crawling on all fours over men who had been immobilized by injury or fear, Self enjoined them to follow him out of the death trap. Escaping into the freezing air, Self saw that three Rangers were already prone in the snow, trading fire with enemy fighters who would stick up their heads to shoot, disappear for a moment, and then pop up in a new location. Finding no other able-bodied men aside from these three Rangers, Self could do little except add his rifle to make their trio a quartet.

The four Rangers were surrounded, outnumbered, fighting in daylight, bereft of air support, and facing a skilled force that had just repulsed a SEAL team. They would have to hold the enemy at bay with only their rifles until help could arrive, whenever that would be. Snapping off rounds at the heads of enemy combatants as they popped into view, the Rangers scored several early hits, which instilled greater caution in the remaining militants. Kept in a hyperalert state by the fear of death, the Rangers scanned the terrain in every direction for enemy movement, pinching their triggers at any sign of an imminent thrust. Their well-placed shots frustrated every enemy initiative during the first hour of the battle. Few episodes in the history of special operations forces ever did as much to vindicate what to some minds were the excessive hours that Rangers spent on the rifle range.

At the one-hour mark, the first American air support materialized, in the form of two F-15E Strike Eagles. A twin-engined fighter, the Strike Eagle excelled at dueling other aircraft, but not at supporting ground forces. Captain Self asked the pilots to conduct strafing runs with their 20mm cannon, for the enemy was too close to the American perimeter to use bombs without a high risk of friendly casualties. Streaking past Takur Ghar at speeds that rendered them invulnerable to machine guns and rocket-propelled grenades, the Strike Eagles sprayed thousands of heavy rounds onto the enemy positions. The Rangers celebrated the destruction with cheers and cries of "F-you Al Qaeda." The enemy's fortifications, however, insulated the militants from the ammunition's wrath. As soon as the strafing ceased, they were back to the game of shooting, ducking, and moving.

Enemy mortar rounds started crashing into the middle of the bowl a short time later. Fearing complete annihilation, Self promptly dropped his reservations about the use of bombs. To minimize the risk of harm to Americans, he directed the pilots to drop their munitions on the reverse slopes of the mountain.

The Chinook carrying the other half of Self's Ranger platoon, which had canceled its planned landing on Takur Ghar after seeing what had happened to the first helicopter, deposited its passengers on a nearby plateau, 2,000 vertical feet below the mountaintop. Heading toward the sound of the guns, ten Rangers ascended snow-covered slopes that ranged in grade from forty to seventy degrees. Although they did not know it, they were in a race against enemy fighters who were at this same time heading up another side of the mountain to reinforce their own comrades.

At this altitude, even the fittest of men struggled to carry their heavy packs up the inclines. Many of the Rangers became dizzy and lightheaded, and several vomited. As their difficulties mounted, Rangers started casting off heavy pieces of gear. Most of them ditched their rear Kevlar plate, though two men held onto theirs for fear that the Army would later bill them for the item, which had a price tag of $2,000.

According to the initial projection of the Ranger commander, the relief force would reach Self's position in forty-five minutes. The climb took two and a half hours. Upon cresting the mountain, the Rangers found Self and four other men guarding a small perimeter while medics tended to a large number of wounded.

With ten additional Rangers, Self could now shift from the role of rifleman to that of platoon leader. He explained to the newcomers that they needed to drive the enemy off the summit as quickly as possible, so that helicopters could evacuate the wounded. After cursory preparations, the Rangers assaulted the peak with the ease and precision of men who have rehearsed assaults for years. They encountered only one live fighter on their way to the crest, whom one of the Rangers shot instantaneously.

The able-bodied began carrying the seriously wounded to the top on Skedco plastic litters. The caravan's progress was interrupted by raking gunfire from approximately twenty-five enemy shooters on a ridgeline one hundred yards away. One of the injured Americans, Staff Sergeant Dave Dube, was left in the open when the two men carrying him jumped for cover. Another man, Staff Sergeant Eric W. Stebner, ran out and began pulling Dube's Skedco toward the peak, forty feet above. Staff Sergeant Harper Wilmoth, astounded by Stebner's daring, warned him that he had better get out of the open or he would get shot. Stebner paid him no heed. Wilmoth thought to himself, "OK, I'll just sit here and watch Stebner get killed."

The enemy marksmen did not hit Stebner. They did, however, strike several other Americans, of whom the most severely injured was Jason Cunningham, an Air Force pararescue jumper, whose liver was pierced by a bullet. Preserving the life of a man with such an injury lay beyond the capabilities of a combat medic and his small array of tools and salves. Cunningham needed to get to a hospital, and fast.

Once US airpower had squelched the enemy counterattack, Self notified Task Force 11 headquarters that Cunningham and another wounded man were in need of urgent medical evacuation. General Trebon wanted to dispatch a helicopter to retrieve the wounded, but he had reason to fear that the enemy would shoot down the next helicopter too. Reports were coming in of more enemy personnel heading toward the landing zone, including a camera crew that intended to film the annihilation of the Americans. The less risky option would be to send a helicopter after dark.

The preliminary reply from the headquarters was, "We're working to get the package ready for you." Minutes without word of an inbound helicopter turned into hours. A distraught Self started sending Trebon's headquarters assurances that the enemy had been so thoroughly thrashed that an American medical evacuation helicopter would have nothing to fear. On several occasions, however, he was still on the radio when the gunfire of newly resurfaced adversaries perforated the mountain air.

As the afternoon wore on, the warnings from the medics took on tones of pleading and despair. Self notified headquarters that if the casualties did not get out soon, three of them might die. Eventually, a voice on the other end said, "It's not nighttime. It's a hot LZ. We don't feel safe." No helicopter would be coming before nightfall.

Cunningham's condition took a sharp downward turn in the waning hours of daylight. Medic Matt LaFrenz kept telling Cunningham, "They're going to come get us. We're going to be out of here soon." Cunningham, who himself knew combat medicine and could sense that his end was near, whispered to LaFrenz a message that he wished to be passed on to his wife. When the last drops of his life force appeared to be draining out, the medics inserted a breathing tube and administered CPR.

At 6 p.m., Jason Cunningham died under a twilight sky. Self looked across the snowcapped peak to see LaFrenz and several others weeping.

The first rescue helicopter arrived ninety minutes later. Trebon had put a group of SEALs aboard to help secure the landing zone and load the Ranger casualties. When the aircraft landed, however, the SEALs ran off to set up defensive positions without offering any assistance in the loading of the wounded. The job of hauling the casualties aboard the helicopters was left to the Rangers who had escaped injury, whose exhaustion was now blended with anger at the SEALs. The loading took twenty minutes, much longer than anticipated, although not long enough to cost any more men their lives.

For several more days, American infantry continued to battle the extremists in the Shahikot. The enemy gradually withdrew fighters from the valley, using routes that the US ground forces, having abandoned their blocking positions in order to take the place of the hammer, were unable to seal off. When Zia Lodin's forces finally got up the nerve to sweep through the valley, on March 6, most of the enemy were either dead or gone.

After the battle, the count of enemy who perished and the count of those who escaped became matters of high controversy. Combined Joint Task Force Mountain estimated the enemy death toll at 800. The small number of enemy corpses and body parts found on the battlefield, however, led others to conclude that the number was in the vicinity of 150 to 300. Whatever the number of enemy actually killed, the majority of enemy combatants most likely escaped, considering that the enemy had an estimated 1,000 fighters at the battle's beginning and sent additional combatants into the valley during the fracas.

The escape of large numbers of enemy fighters, and whatever senior leaders were with them, ensured that Anaconda would not be seen as a redemption of the Tora Bora operation. The collapse of the Afghan militias put the advising of US Special Forces further into disrepute, bolstering the argument of conventionally minded officers that if Americans wanted to get a job done, they had to do it themselves. Anaconda's numerous calamities exposed serious flaws in the organizational and operational relationships between Army and Navy SOF, between air and ground units, and between tactical units and higher headquarters. They showed, too, that the most advanced optical devices, precision weapons, and communications systems of the information age had not eliminated the "fog and friction" of war that the Prussian military theorist Carl von Clausewitz had identified two centuries earlier—the misperceptions, confusion, and chance mishaps that made the easiest of tasks difficult.

Anaconda marked the end of major combat operations in Afghanistan. With the departure of most Taliban remnants into Pakistan and the installation of Hamid Karzai as head of a new Afghan government, Anaconda seemed to have been merely an unpleasant afterthought to what had been the surprisingly easy and rapid overthrow of the Taliban. The US military checked Afghanistan off its to-do list and moved on to the next item, a new addition that was becoming the talk of Washington.

PRESIDENT BUSH WAS at this moment rattling America's saber at Iraq, demanding that dictator Saddam Hussein come clean on his inventory of chemical, biological, and nuclear weapons. US intelligence agencies suspected that Saddam would furnish weapons of mass destruction to anti-American terrorists, who would employ them in attacks that might eclipse even the destruction of the Twin Towers. American suspicions grew as Saddam refused to give a full accounting of his weapons programs.

In early 2003, with war plans coming together at the Pentagon, Secretary of Defense Rumsfeld decided to commit 10,000 SOF to the invasion force, the largest SOF contribution to any war in US history. Although JSOC was still struggling to become a global counterterrorism powerhouse, Rumsfeld's admiration for special operations forces as a whole was continuing to rise, fueled by the perception that their leaders had the intellectual flexibility and creativity required to reshape the military for the new millennium—qualities that Rumsfeld had found wanting in the conventional forces, especially the regular Army. Rumsfeld was at this time preparing to install a Special Forces officer, General Peter Schoomaker, as Army chief of staff, making him the first special operator ever to head an armed service.

Schoomaker was to take the place of General Eric Shinseki, an infantry officer who had upset Rumsfeld with, among other things, his resistance to radical change and his hostility toward special operations forces. Shinseki, who had once scoffed to Rumsfeld that "no Special Forces soldier ever pulled me off the battlefield," had attempted to snub the special operators by authorizing every Army soldier to wear the black beret, which had hitherto been reserved exclusively for the Rangers. The Ranger community howled that the policy would make a mockery of the black beret, while the Special Forces denounced it as an assault on their own beret-wearing tradition. Rumsfeld, concluding that Shinseki had been led astray by his dislike for SOF, had intervened personally in the matter, forcing a compromise in which the Rangers adopted the tan beret as their own while regular soldiers were allowed to don the black one.

Rumsfeld at first contemplated invading Iraq with a small force, such that SOF teams would constitute a large percentage of the ground troops. Military planners, however, persuaded him that defeating the Iraqi armed forces—which were far larger than those of Afghanistan and did not have a hostile army like the Northern Alliance near their capital—would require an invasion force of 145,000 ground troops. In the final war plan, some of the special operations units were assigned to supporting tasks for conventional units, such as reconnoitering bridges in advance of conventional columns, or infiltrating the enemy rear to help rain bombs on supply depots and radar installations. Others were charged with unconventional warfare, raiding, and other missions in which conventional forces would support them.

General Tommy Franks, who still headed Central Command and thus was in charge of this invasion as well, divided authority for special operations forces among several multinational commands. The Naval Task

Force would command the US Navy SEALs and Polish naval commandos, who would be transported within the theater by regular Army and Navy units. At the start of the invasion, on March 20, its forces seized oil and gas platforms and the tanker terminal at Al Faw to keep Saddam from sabotaging them.

The western desert of Iraq belonged to Task Force Dagger, consisting of the 5th Special Forces Group, a company of National Guardsmen from the 19th Special Forces Group, and several foreign special operations units. The 5th Group spent the early days of the war looking for Scud missiles, based on intelligence reports that Saddam had several dozen Scuds in the desert, but not a single Scud was found. Two ODAs from Task Force Dagger attempted to mobilize resistance forces in the southern Iraqi city of Najaf, whose predominantly Shiite residents were believed to be simmering with hatred for the Sunni-dominated Iraqi government. When the Special Forces sent two Iraqi dissident officers into Najaf to link up with resistance groups, however, the men were captured and put on Iraqi state television. Abandoning the resistance support mission, the Special Forces teams turned to collecting intelligence for conventional forces. A company of the 5th Special Forces Group that attempted to back resistance elements in the city of Basra likewise failed to make any headway and ended up supporting conventional units.

Task Force Viking, which had three hundred soldiers of the 10th Special Forces Group as its core and was subsequently reinforced by the 3rd Special Forces Group and several conventional units, had responsibility for supporting 50,000 Kurdish rebels in northern Iraq. The main objective in the north was to tie down the 150,000 Iraqi troops in the region so that they could not reinforce the Iraqi units defending Baghdad. Through the direction of air strikes, American special operators enabled the Kurds to wipe out much of the Iraqi fighting strength in the north and keep most of the remainder from heading south prior to the fall of Baghdad, all without a single American casualty.

JSOC and a supplemental quick reaction force from the 82nd Airborne Division fell under Task Force 20. Two days before the invasion, the Delta Force commander, Colonel Ron Russell, suffered a brain aneurysm while jogging around the Saudi airfield where the unit was staging. Russell was not one of the 40 percent of victims for whom a brain aneurysm is fatal, but that was only modest consolation for a man who had trained and sacrificed for decades to lead troops into a war such as this. To take the place of the incapacitated Russell, JSOC commander Dell Dailey had several options. He decided on Pete Blaber, an act of considerable respect and magnanimity considering Blaber's prior clashes with Dailey.

Operation Iraqi Freedom, the invasion of Iraq, began on March 20, 2003. While the massive convoys of a US Army Corps and a combined task force of US Marines and British armor rolled from Kuwait into southern Iraq, helicopters ferried Delta operators and Rangers to sites suspected of holding the chemical and biological weapons that had provided America's *causus belli*. The special operators did not find any such weaponry.

Dailey lobbied for the use of the Rangers in taking down the Baghdad International Airport, but the task ended up going to the US Army's 3rd Infantry Division, which could bring much greater firepower to bear. The Rangers did get to capture three airfields in western Iraq, the garrisons of which offered little resistance before capitulating. At Haditha, Rangers seized the city's five-mile-long dam to prevent the Iraqis from unleashing a flood against oncoming US forces. The dam's civilian staff did not even know that the Rangers and their supporting aircraft had overpowered the installation's defensive force until a group of Rangers barged into their sixth-floor office.

As in the case of Afghanistan, Dailey dedicated some of his JSOC units to assaults on locations known to be empty, for the purpose of generating footage that could be aired publicly to demonstrate American impunity. As in Afghanistan, too, Pete Blaber tried to find innovative ways to involve Delta in the bigger war, and ran afoul of Dailey in so doing. Blaber wanted to insert seventy-five Delta operators into Iraq one day before the opening of hostilities, using fifteen Swiss-made Pinzgauer vehicles and two civilian sport utility vehicles. To help them interact with locals, they would bring along a psychologist, an Iraqi American veterinarian from Philadelphia, and a former Iraqi Army private who had fled Iraq by hiking through the desert on foot before becoming a successful real estate agent in San Francisco. Blaber contended that this approach would attract less attention from the Iraqis and yield more information than if the men were inserted by air, which was what Dailey advocated. When Dailey attempted to scuttle Blaber's plan, General Franks intervened personally to preserve it, owing to his high regard for Blaber, whom he had come to know in Afghanistan.

Blaber combined other Delta operators with an armored unit to form what he called Team Tank. Borrowing from the playbook of General Erwin Rommel, Nazi Germany's crafty Desert Fox, Team Tank shuffled its ten Abrams tanks from place to place in such a way as to fool unwary observers into believing that it had a much larger number of vehicles. If the Iraqis came to believe that hundreds of American tanks were stampeding into Iraq's western desert from Jordan, they would maintain forces in the west that could otherwise be used to defend Baghdad. Keeping up the charade became harder by the day as the number of tanks declined, owing to maintenance problems and a thirty-five-foot ditch that swallowed up one of the tanks.

Team Tank ultimately succeeded in convincing Saddam Hussein to guard the western desert with an army division, one previously earmarked for reinforcement of the Karbala Gap. That gap, a twenty-mile band between the Razzaza Lake and the Euphrates swamp flats in south-central Iraq, constituted one of the last obstacles between US forces and Baghdad. The gap's diluted defenses soon broke under the pressure of US infantry and armor, collapsing so quickly as to unhinge the final defense of the Iraqi capital.

Baghdad fell on April 9. Two days later, Team Tank reached Tikrit, Saddam Hussein's hometown, which was still under the control of regime loyalists. The tanks, by this time numbering just five, navigated through the outskirts of Tikrit in yet another effort to conjure an illusion of overwhelming strength. An unexpectedly potent enemy force showed up, approximately five hundred men in all, brandishing vehicle-mounted anti-tank weapons.

On Blaber's command, the American tanks opened fire. While one of the tanks was maneuvering, its treads became entangled in telephone wire, which was akin to binding a man's legs with rope. The other tanks moved toward their debilitated comrade to provide protection while two Delta operators dismounted and tried to remove the wire. The senior tank

REGIME CHANGE | 261

officer recommended withdrawing once they had freed the stranded tank, and Blaber concurred.

Dailey, who had been monitoring the radio communications from another country, interrupted the discussion. "Negative, negative, negative!" he roared at Blaber. "You are not to pull out of that city. I want you to keep moving forward into the city and destroy the enemy."

Blaber suspected that Dailey wanted Team Tank to replicate the glory of the "thunder runs," in which long US armored columns had torn through Baghdad one day earlier. Blaber objected that the US armored divisions in Baghdad had possessed more than three hundred tanks each, and twice that number of support vehicles, whereas Team Tank had only five tanks left, one of which was barely functional, and no support vehicles. With few infantrymen accompanying them, they would be unlikely to remain alive for long inside a city crawling with antitank weapons. Dailey, for his part, believed that Team Tank needed to continue in order to facilitate a snatch operation that was taking place nearby. Neither man would budge.

Rather than confront Blaber directly, Dailey had his deputy contact Blaber via satellite phone. The deputy, whom Blaber considered "a genuinely nice guy," was plainly not cut out for issuing threats he knew in his heart to be wrongheaded.

"Hey, uh, Pete, listen," the deputy muttered. "I think you should, uh, send your guys into the city. If you don't, uh, move through that city, your, uh, future as a commander could be affected."

Blaber ignored the threat. Back on the radio, he instructed his tank crews to pull back from the city.

Dailey, continuing to monitor the radio net, butted into the conversation. "What did you say?" he barked at Blaber. "You listen to me, I told you to—" The line went dead. Evidently someone on Dailey's staff had decided to disconnect the radio before more acid could cross the airwaves.

WHEN GEORGE W. Bush came into office, special operations forces did not rank high on his agenda. Nor were they a priority for his secretary of defense, Donald Rumsfeld, to whom the hands-off Bush had delegated broad powers over the defense establishment. But the 9/11 cataclysm and the peculiar circumstances in Afghanistan turned the special operators into indispensable instruments of regime change. In 2003, Rumsfeld sent special operations forces to Iraq in numbers exceeding those of any previous conflict to help take down Saddam Hussein's regime.

Although the 5th Group's 2001 campaign in Afghanistan bore some resemblance to unconventional warfare, and would routinely be described as such by proponents of unconventional warfare, it differed in major respects from the unconventional warfare of the past. The Northern Alliance did not require extensive organizing or training, and it fought a war that was more conventional than guerrilla in character. The principal contribution of SOF to the Taliban's overthrow was technical—the guidance of precision munitions by the Special Forces and their Air Force tactical air controllers in support of rebel military attacks. At Tora Bora and, especially, the Shahikot Valley, JSOC reconnaissance teams distinguished themselves by locating and targeting well-concealed enemy fighters. In Iraq, the absence of insurgents comparable to the Northern Alliance and the large size of the Iraqi armed forces demanded the use of America's conventional forces, leaving SOF to play supporting roles.

The overthrow of the Taliban regime was the greatest strategic victory ever achieved by American SOF operating in isolation from conventional forces. Three hundred US special operators and 110 CIA officers precipitated the collapse of the Taliban government and its 90,000 armed forces without the loss of a single American to hostile fire. The Americans and their Afghan allies were not, however, able to catch most of the fleeing Al Qaeda and Taliban leaders. During the Iraq War, SOF diversionary activities in northern Iraq and the western desert achieved strategic effects by tying down Iraqi forces that could have bolstered the defenses around Baghdad. Raids on suspected Iraqi Scud missiles and weapons of mass destruction sites could have been strategically significant had they actually found what they were seeking.

The defeat of the Taliban regime in Afghanistan resuscitated the idea, dormant since the Somalian imbroglio, that special operations forces could win wars without conventional forces. But Bin Laden's escape from Tora Bora, under the noses of local militias supported by American special operators, elicited counterarguments that conventional forces were critical to the pursuit of terrorists. The poor showing by the Afghan militiamen in Operation Anaconda further stoked criticism of local forces advised by American SOF. The Iraq War subsequently demonstrated that some populations were devoid of willing participants in armed resistance against their own government, in which case divisions of US ground forces were required to take and hold ground. As the spring of 2003 drew to a close, both special and conventional operators had cause to view their capabilities as superior and essential, ensuring that new contestation between the two groups would not be far off.

CHAPTER 9

COUNTERINSURGENCY AND COUNTERTERRORISM

In the spring, summer, and fall of 2003, JSOC cast an ever-widening net for individuals linked to Saddam Hussein. JSOC's intelligence specialists interrogated anyone and everyone who might know something about Saddam's whereabouts, or who might know someone who might know something about his whereabouts—from close confidants and relatives to mistresses and tailors. A long string of apprehensions and interrogations brought them progressively closer until finally, on December 12, 2003, a JSOC raid in Baghdad nabbed Muhammed Ibrahim Omar al-Muslit.

A member of Saddam's inner circle, Muslit was one of only four people who knew where the ousted Iraqi leader had taken refuge. He initially refused to cooperate, but buckled when an interrogator told him that he and the forty other members of his family in US custody would go free if he divulged Saddam's location. Muslit revealed that the erstwhile dictator was hiding in the town of Dawr, across the Tigris River from his hometown of Tikrit. When pressed for more specific information, Muslit identified two small farms on the east bank of the Tigris.

The next day, a JSOC task force headed to Dawr with a droopy-eyed Muslit in tow. Suspecting that Saddam would have twenty or thirty armed guards wielding automatic weapons and rocket-propelled grenades, the Americans decided to send along six hundred troops from the US Army's 4th Infantry Division in armored vehicles. The skies above Dawr resembled a Memorial Day airshow, with a panoply of America's finest military aircraft buzzing hither and thither. Planners named the operation Red Dawn, after the 1984 movie in which American teenagers outfought invading Soviet paratroopers in Colorado. In honor of the intrepid teen warriors, who had named their improvisational army the Wolverines after their high school's mascot, the two farms were designated Wolverine 1 and Wolverine 2.

At 8 p.m., the infantry established a cordon around the farms to prevent anyone from escaping, and then the search parties moved in. Stepping quietly, peering through night-vision goggles, Delta operators combed through sheep pens, wheat fields, fruit orchards, palm groves, and farmhouses. They did not encounter any armed guards. They did, however, see two men bolting through an orchard, whom they chased down and took into custody. One of them was later identified as Saddam's personal cook, the other as the cook's brother. The Americans interrogated the two men in the presence of a sniffer dog, since Iraqis were often intimidated by these animals, but the two were far from cooperative, most of the information from their mouths turning out to be false.

The Americans again probed Muslit for more information, and again he spilled some beans, guiding them to a mud farmhouse. Inside the structure was a bedroom with two beds, above which a pair of gray trousers and a dirty towel hung from a clothesline. The furnishings included a Noah's Ark–themed calendar and a trunk, the latter topped with a stack of books and a can of Raid to ward off insects. The house also had a small kitchen, whose keeper had apparently hurried out, by the look of the broken eggshells and dirty dishes on the counter. Inside the kitchen's small refrigerator, the searchers found Bounty candy bars, hot dogs, and a can of Seven-Up.

After further cajoling from the special operators, Muslit directed their attention to a floor mat just outside the house. Pulled to the side, it unveiled a trapdoor made of thick Styrofoam block. Several Delta operators slowly lifted the door, firearms at the ready, while another prepared to throw a flash-bang grenade to stun whoever was inside.

The trapdoor opened to a dark hole, four feet by six feet. Aiming lights and weapons into the opening, the Americans caught site of a scruffy bearded man who looked to be in his sixties. By his shabby appearance, they adjudged that he did not pose an imminent threat and thus held their fire. Through an interpreter, the D-boys asked the prisoner to identify himself.

"I am Saddam Hussein, the president of Iraq," the man said, "and I am willing to negotiate."

One of the Americans replied, "President Bush sends his regards." Then the American said to the interpreter, "Tell him to put his hands up and come out."

Two empty hands emerged from the hole in the universal gesture of surrender. Delta operators grabbed at the disheveled figure from every direction, pulling him by the neck, beard, hair, and clothes, as if they were hoisting a wayward dog.

The Americans checked their catch for Saddam's signature tattoos, which included a sunburst on the right hand and three dots on the left hand representing "God, Country, Leader." When the captive tried to shove the soldiers away, they struck back, cutting him above the eye and in the mouth. The inspection continued without further incident. The body art was a match.

Zip-tying Saddam's hands and putting a sandbag over his head, the Americans loaded him aboard a Little Bird helicopter that whisked him away to a nearby US base. For public relations purposes, the US government filmed a compliant Saddam receiving an examination from an American physician. Clad in rubber gloves, the doctor checked the captive's hair for lice, then used a tongue depressor and penlight to peer inside his mouth, a spectacle that at once proved Saddam's capture to skeptical Iraqis and demonstrated the powerlessness of the formerly omnipotent man. US officials and America's Iraqi friends exulted at the capture of Saddam Hussein and expressed hope that it would dissolve the unremitting gloom that had hung over Iraq for months.

The fall of Baghdad, eight months earlier, had been full of promise, seeming to portend a bright new dawn for Iraq. On April 9, foreign news crews had filmed jubilant Iraqis cheering the arrival of American tanks and infantry in Baghdad. At Firdos Square, Marines helped Iraqis tear down a giant statue of Saddam Hussein while the world watched on live television. After unsuccessful attempts by the Iraqis to topple the monument with a sledgehammer and rope supplied by the Marines, the crew of a Marine M-88 tank recovery vehicle attached one of their cables around the neck of Saddam's likeness and pulled it down.

Minutes after the statue fell, Secretary of Defense Rumsfeld told reporters at the Pentagon, "The scenes of free Iraqis celebrating in the streets, riding American tanks, tearing down the statues of Saddam Hussein in the center of Baghdad are breathtaking. Watching them, one cannot help but think of the fall of the Berlin Wall and the collapse of the Iron Curtain." Rumsfeld asserted that "the Iraqi people are well on their way to freedom." Others drew parallels to the liberation of Paris from the Nazis. "Like newly freed Parisians tossing flowers at Allied tanks," columnist William Safire wrote in the *New York Times*, "the newly freed Iraqis toppled the figure of their tyrant and ground their shoes into the face of Saddam Hussein."

The Americans had done little planning for the post-Saddam period, having presumed that Iraqis would be able to take care of themselves like the Parisians in 1944 and the East Germans in 1989. General Tommy Franks, commander of the US occupation forces, predicted that a new Iraqi government would be up and running within sixty days, and he laid plans to withdraw most of America's 145,000 troops in six months' time. In the haste to go home, the United States allowed Iraq to degenerate into a state of insurgency, one of such virulence as the United States had not encountered since the Viet Cong. Special operations forces were destined to be pulled back into the fray, and as in Vietnam, they would be pushed into it by the president. This time, however, they would concentrate on the narrow mission set of counterterrorism rather than the broader enterprise of counterinsurgency. The constricted focus of special operations forces would constrain their strategic impact and give rise to new conflicts with the conventional military.

The American leadership learned all too soon that Iraqis did not think or behave like Frenchmen or Germans. Having lived under brutal dictatorship their entire lives, Iraqis had little conception of the virtues and responsibilities required of citizens in a free society. In the days and weeks after the fall of Saddam Hussein, mobs of Iraqis looted shops, stole vehicles, and stripped the fixtures and wiring from public buildings. Brandishing AK-47s with a newfound abandon, they murdered old enemies, officials of Saddam's regime being favorite targets. Members of the Shiite majority who had languished beneath the lashes of the regime's whip now angled for power at the expense of the Sunni minority.

Most of the US troops on the ground had not been prepared for such an outcome, and they were not ordered to intervene. The abstention of the only forces capable of restoring order permitted antisocial behavior to propagate while also eroding Iraqi respect for American power. The US official responsible for governance in post-Saddam Iraq, L. Paul Bremer, banned members of Saddam's Baath Party from serving in the new Iraqi government, depriving that government and its newly created security forces of experienced leaders and at the same time driving the most capable Iraqis into the insurgency that erupted in the summer of 2003.

Devastating attacks on the new Iraqi security forces and the impotence of Bremer's Coalition Provisional Authority soon convinced the Bush administration to reverse the outflow of US forces from Iraq. General John Abizaid, successor to Franks as commander of Central Command, worried that putting US forces into the forefront of counterinsurgency operations would alienate Iraqis and inhibit the growth of a self-sufficient Iraqi government, so he insisted that his commanders in Iraq use their forces primarily to improve and empower Iraqi forces. Supporting foreign forces in counterinsurgency operations was right up the alley of the Army Special Forces and Navy SEALs. But special operations forces were too few in number to handle the task on their own. The conventional units of the US Army and Marine Corps would be needed to train hundreds of thousands of new Iraqi soldiers and policemen and provide enough security to prevent the insurgents from devouring the fledgling Iraqi government in its nest.

Some SOF officers wanted to carve out niches in which their units could assist Iraqi forces in counterinsurgency operations, as special operators had done with South Vietnamese forces. By leveraging their knowledge of counterinsurgency and foreign cultures, they could empower the

Iraqi government to regain control over the population. Civil Affairs and Psychological Operations soldiers were indeed assigned to such niches, since their skill sets closely aligned with critical nonmilitary tasks that no other Americans were performing. In conjunction with Iraqi and American administrators and US conventional forces, they organized town councils, dug wells, funded construction of schools and health clinics, and disseminated information that reflected favorably on the American occupation and its Iraqi allies. They were often paired with conventional American units, whose commanders generally made good use of their services, although there were exceptions, like the officer who asked a psychological operations team to drive up and down a road with loudspeakers blaring, simply to draw fire that would reveal enemy positions for his troops to attack.

For most of the special operations forces, however, the main activity in Iraq would not be assistance of Iraqis in counterinsurgency, but rather surgical strikes against insurgent leaders, an activity that in official parlance was labeled "counterterrorism," or CT for short. The "black" special operations forces—the term that had come into use for JSOC's units, including Delta Force and SEAL Team Six—had been preparing for this type of mission for years. Much less traveled in surgical strikes were the "white" special operations forces—the forces assigned to theater special operations commands, which included the Army Special Forces and all the Navy SEAL teams except for Team Six. But now black SOF and white SOF alike would focus on eliminating insurgent leaders.

Rumsfeld's emphasis on manhunting was one of several factors that led the white special operations forces to take on the counterterrorism mission at the expense of the counterinsurgency and advisory missions that were nearer to their skills and traditions. The white forces could see the money and resources for surgical strikes flowing from Defense Department spigots and found the allure of those riches difficult to ignore. The widespread perception that the United States could get out of Iraq as soon as it decapitated Saddam's Baath Party, moreover, led Americans to believe that developing Iraqi capabilities was unimportant and that participating in combat was a fleeting opportunity. Most of the white SOF operators had accumulated years of experience in assisting others, but few had stared the demons of combat directly in the eye, and they were, for all their talk of helping others, the type of men who wanted their shot at kicking down doors and gunning down terrorists.

The white SOF did spend time working with Iraqi security personnel from the outset, mainly because they needed people who could provide information on Iraqi culture and serve as intermediaries with Iraqis during raids. A secondary objective was the administration of training to these Iraqis, most of it of the "on-the-job" variant. In 2004, as it became clear that the war would be long, the weight of the training effort shifted to a newly formalized organization, the Iraqi Special Operations Forces. In time, the Iraqi SOF were to reach a strength of 4,100 troops, enough for two Iraqi SOF brigades and an elite Emergency Response Brigade.

Among the US Special Forces, worries mounted that the Pentagon was interested solely in counterterrorism operations and the units that conducted them. Demands for participation in surgical strikes, it was argued, were frittering the Green Berets away on activities that were less special and less valuable than traditional Special Forces activities. Mark Haselton, a retired Special Forces lieutenant colonel, told reporter Sean Naylor, "If we spend the rest of our lives 'capturing and killing' terrorists at the expense of those SF missions that are more important—gaining access to the local population, training indigenous forces, providing expertise and expanding capacity—we're doomed to failure."

The black SOF of JSOC were even more focused on surgical strikes during the early years of the Iraq War. In 2002, Rumsfeld had tasked JSOC with taking out Al Qaeda's leadership in Afghanistan and the other countries to which it had dispersed after 9/11, in the belief that decapitation was the most efficient way to destroy Al Qaeda. The secretary of defense enlarged JSOC and infused it with a wealth of resources. Bob Andrews, the acting assistant secretary of defense for special operations and low-intensity conflict, said of Rumsfeld, "Once he fastened on the manhunt thing, he looked at that as the silver bullet against terrorism and he built a unit [JSOC] that can do manhunts."

To give JSOC better access to information for the manhunts, Rumsfeld granted the JSOC commander operational control over the Gray Fox intelligence organization, which had hitherto been a strategic asset available to the regional combatant commanders. Rumsfeld compelled conventional forces to provide greater support to JSOC by altering the relationship between its higher headquarters—SOCOM—and the regional commanders. Whereas SOCOM had been a "supporting command" since its creation, meaning that it existed solely to support the regional commands, Rumsfeld declared that SOCOM would now "function as both a supported and a supporting command." Thus, regional commanders would at times be required to use their forces to support SOCOM's operations. In other words, the special operators would now get to play the lead role some of the time, and the conventional forces would have to take their turn in bit roles.

After the fall of the Iraqi regime, JSOC Commander Dell Dailey wanted to remove his organization from Iraq and take it back to Fort Bragg, where it would practice for the next war and prepare to deploy small manhunting teams to dozens of countries where Al Qaeda was incubating. Rumsfeld, however, insisted that Dailey keep forces in Iraq to hunt down Saddam Hussein, who had fled in a white Oldsmobile when US forces entered Baghdad on April 9, and other top figures from the regime. Delta Force set up a headquarters at a former Baath Party compound in the Green Zone, a section of central Baghdad along the Tigris River that the Americans had cordoned off as the nerve center of the new political order. Luxurious by military standards, the headquarters facility had a pool, gym, and large bedrooms. The D-boys, though, would have little time for lounging poolside or shooting hoops, for the hunt started at one hundred miles per hour and never slowed down.

The surgical strikes that were carried out beneath the marquee of counterterrorism were often construed as entirely separate from counterinsurgency, particularly by critics who alleged that counterterrorism was "enemy-centric," and hence incongruent with counterinsurgency, which was said to be "population-centric." Some even alleged that the counterterrorism operations actually undermined counterinsurgency, asserting that killing members of the local population would invariably turn their relatives into insurgents.

This distinction between counterterrorism and counterinsurgency, which was to feature prominently in strategic discussions in Washington, was both inaccurate and misleading. Effective counterinsurgency had always consisted of a mixture of "enemy-centric" and "population-centric" operations, and it remained so in Iraq. Operations to capture or kill enemy personnel—whether they were surgical strikes or regular military operations—were essential to the protection of counterinsurgent personnel and the population. It was true, though, that if those operations were not coordinated with operations aimed at securing and governing the population, they could cause more resentment among the population than they were worth.

That type of coordination was often absent in the early stages of the Iraq War. Special operations forces did not always feel obliged to provide advance notice to the regular Army and Marine Corps commanders in whose operational areas they conducted raids. Appearing out of thin air in the middle of the night, they shot uncooperative Iraqis inside houses or hauled preeminent citizens away in handcuffs before vanishing as quickly as they had come, leaving behind physical and political messes for the regular commanders to clean up. Aggrieved conventional commanders complained that these unannounced raids interfered with their own counterinsurgency activities, not to mention violating the principle of unity of command and evidencing the prima-donna character of special operations forces. The conventional forces, moreover, resented that the special operators had gained control over a large fraction of the Predator drones and other overhead reconnaissance platforms, scarce assets that battlefield commanders had come to prize as "unblinking eyes" keeping watch over the battlefield.

To assist the forces that were chasing down the remnants of the ancien régime, occupation authorities issued decks of playing cards containing the faces of high Baath Party figures. The higher the card, the more important the individual was considered to be. Saddam Hussein was the ace of spades, and his sons Uday and Qusay were the aces of clubs and hearts. Some coalition leaders believed that eliminating the high cards, especially Saddam and his sons, would suffocate the insurgency.

On July 22, Task Force 20 and soldiers from the 101st Airborne Division surrounded a house in Mosul where Uday and Qusay were reported to be located. The brothers and their bodyguards fired AK-47s at the special operators, so the Americans stepped back and discharged seventeen

TOW antitank missiles into the building, killing both brothers. Bremer announced that the deaths of Saddam's sons demonstrated that "these Baathists have no future" and thus would "help reduce the security threat to our forces."

The apprehension of Saddam Hussein in December sparked predictions that the fever of insurgency had at last been broken. Lieutenant General Ricardo Sanchez, who was now the top US military commander in Iraq, told the press that while he did not expect Saddam's detention to end all hostile activity immediately, "I believe that we are now much closer to a safe and secure environment here." Jalal Talabani, Iraq's foremost Kurdish politician, went further, asserting that Saddam's arrest "will put an end to terrorist acts in Iraq."

Yet neither the elimination of Saddam and his sons, nor that of the other Baath Party leaders in the deck of cards, nor that of religious extremists, slackened the pace of insurgent depredations. Drawing upon hundreds of thousands of former soldiers as well as foreign volunteers, the insurgents were able to replace the leaders whom the Americans removed from the scene. Insurgent fighters terrorized the Iraqi government and Iraqi civilians who abetted it, and they used ambushes and improvised explosive devices (IEDs) to disrupt US forces that tried to fill the security gaps left by the ineffectual Iraqi army and police. American casualties climbed in 2004 while American public support for the war slid.

The strategic ineffectiveness of the decapitation strikes gnawed at the man who replaced Dailey as JSOC commander at the end of 2003, Major General Stanley McChrystal. A tall and exceptionally fit man of forty-nine years, McChrystal hailed from a family that was as military as they came. His father, Herbert J. McChrystal Jr., had fought in Korea and Vietnam, attaining the rank of major general. All four of Herbert's sons had joined the Army, and his daughter had married an Army officer. As a boy and young man, Stanley idolized his father, intent on being just like his old man when he grew up.

Stanley McChrystal arrived at West Point in 1972. During his first two years, he struggled academically, particularly in math and science, which he found far less interesting than his military history classes and the biographies of great military leaders that he read in his spare time.

He racked up demerits for drinking alcohol in his room and for general rowdiness. The one area in which he consistently scored highly was peer ranking—a prime indicator of leadership aptitude.

At the end of his second year, McChrystal applied for one of the few positions reserved for West Point cadets at the summer session of the Ranger School. He was turned down on account of his poor academic and disciplinary scores. Sobered by the rejection, he became a much more serious student during his remaining two years, bringing up his grades and putting an end to his demerits. He did well enough that when the day of branch selection came, with all of the cadets seated together to pick their branch in order of class ranking, he was not among the bottom tier of cadets who got stuck in the infantry after all other jobs had been taken. When McChrystal's turn came, nevertheless, he chose infantry for his branch.

From West Point, McChrystal went to the 82nd Airborne Division. Two years later, he entered the 7th Special Forces Group. Serving a tour in Thailand, he taught Thai Army officers how to shoot the Dragon antitank missile system, which the Thais thought they might need in the event that the Vietnamese Communists followed their conquest of South Vietnam with an invasion of Thailand. McChrystal learned that the demoralization and indiscipline that had infected the regular Army in the 1970s was present in the Special Forces as well. He saw one sergeant yanked off a stage for lecturing while intoxicated. McChrystal's company commander was fired for mooning someone at an officers' club, and McChrystal had to relieve his own team sergeant for laziness.

Returning to the regular Army in 1980, McChrystal served in a mechanized infantry division until joining the newly formed 3rd Ranger Battalion in 1985. He spent four years in the Rangers and then moved over to the JSOC staff, where he delighted in his liberation from the shoe shining and rule books that encumbered the Rangers and the rest of the Army. Graeme Lamb, a British officer who later attained the exalted position of commander of the Field Army, met McChrystal during his first year at JSOC and was amazed by his flourishing intellect. "McChrystal was the sharpest, fastest staff officer I had ever come across," Lamb remembered.

In 1991, McChrystal shared the disappointment of most JSOC officers at the meager involvement of JSOC in Desert Storm. The episode convinced him that JSOC needed to improve its organizational and personal linkages to the conventional forces. As he later explained, he came to the conclusion that to better those ties, "we'd have to open up more, educate conventional leaders about what we did, and importantly, we had to avoid even the appearance of elitist attitudes or arrogance."

Later in the 1990s, McChrystal commanded the 2nd Ranger Battalion, and then the entire 75th Ranger Regiment. He also held fellowships at Harvard's Kennedy School of Government and the Council on Foreign Relations. "I'd expected Harvard to be full of antimilitary sentiment," McChrystal recalled, "but instead we received compelling questions and thoughtful looks, as if we were rare animals they'd never seen up close."

In the summer of 2002, McChrystal received an assignment to the Joint Staff, his first job at the Pentagon. For his preceding twenty-six years in uniform, he had worked hard to avoid a posting at the Pentagon or anywhere else in Washington, leery of the rice-bowl politics and slow-footed bureaucracy of the nation's capital. The Pentagon lived up to his low expectations. Decisions that could have been made after a short conversation were instead put through the bureaucratic wringer, subjected to inflexible processes and senselessly long meetings. McChrystal yearned for command of the 82nd Airborne Division as his next position, but in the end he was plucked from Washington by an offer to command JSOC.

From his post in Washington and then from the forward JSOC headquarters near Baghdad, McChrystal watched Iraq's insurgents withstand one decapitation strike after another. The enemy's staying power drove him to the conclusion that the middle and lower levels of insurgent leadership had to be destroyed if the insurgents were to be defeated. Decimating those leaders through surgical strikes would require an exponential increase in the number of fruitful operations. McChrystal believed that JSOC could and should achieve such an increase. Some of his subordinates were skeptical about the mass production of surgical strikes, however, noting that no one in history had been able to do anything like it. Others objected that employing JSOC against the lowest ranks of the insurgency was as wasteful as using a world-class neurosurgeon to treat skinned knees. McChrystal, finding the objections less than compelling, pressed ahead.

The most difficult part of a surgical strike was locating the enemy. It was the reason why no one had been able to mass-produce surgical strikes in the past. What made industrial-scale production of surgical strikes possible now was the arrival of the information revolution in Iraq. The American occupation facilitated explosive growth in the numbers of cellphones, computers, and other personal electronic devices, many of which came into the possession of insurgents who had little understanding of how to encrypt or otherwise conceal their information. The resultant opportunities for collecting intelligence knew no precedent in human history.

Task Force 714, which had succeeded Task Force 20 as JSOC's manhunting command in Iraq, was in a relatively primitive technological state when McChrystal took charge. Operators raiding a site dumped cellphones, computers, and papers into empty sandbags, burlap sacks, or trash bags and sent them to a warehouse in Baghdad. Seldom did anyone have time to process the contents of the bags and transmit information back to the operators while the information was still useful.

By happenstance, Congress had doubled the SOCOM budget for equipment just before McChrystal's arrival. As a result of the successes achieved by special operators in Afghanistan and Iraq, Congress had been tripping over itself to give additional money to SOCOM and its components. A report from the House Armed Services Committee in the middle of 2003 asserted that SOCOM "is clearly a treasured national asset in the war on terrorism and our best asset in disrupting the enemy in foreign lands."

Flush with congressional cash, McChrystal raked in new gadgets that could comb the call logs and computer files of detainees in a matter of minutes. He and his intelligence chief, Colonel Mike Flynn, hired hundreds of Arab linguists and intelligence analysts to translate captured documents and interrogate prisoners. The information from one raid could now be used for a raid the following night, or even the same night if the stars aligned. McChrystal pushed the JSOC task force in each of Iraq's regions to conduct at least one raid every night, in order to ratchet up pressure on the enemy and generate further targeting information.

Overcoming the rice-bowl predilections of the government's bureaucracies, McChrystal gained access to the raw intelligence information of

278 | OPPOSE ANY FOE

the National Security Agency, the Central Intelligence Agency, and the National Geospatial Intelligence Agency. He convinced the agencies to send representatives to the massive clamshell-shaped hangar at Balad Airbase, north of Baghdad, where he had set up JSOC's global headquarters. "McChrystal had a remarkable ability to bring everybody inside the tent and make them feel like a team player," said a Special Forces colonel. "He'd co-opt them so in some respects when they went back to [their] agency they became his ambassadors and advocates."

The Balad operations center had two cavernous rooms, each the size of a basketball court, separated from one another by a plywood wall. Staff from a multitude of agencies and functional areas sat at desks with computer workstations, facing a wall of large plasma televisions that displayed surveillance feeds, intelligence information, and lists of the day's missions. Some denizens of the facility referred to it as "Battlestar Galactica." Others called it "The Death Star," because, in the words of one onlooker, it conveyed the impression that "you could just reach out with a finger, as it were, and eliminate somebody."

In contrast to Dailey, McChrystal decentralized decision-making and encouraged risk-taking and innovation. Junior officers received extraordinary freedom to make decisions without obtaining prior permission from higher headquarters. "As long as it is not immoral or illegal, we'll do it," McChrystal told his officers. "Don't wait for me. Do it." JSOC was at last released into the wild.

Instrumental though McChrystal was, these changes were facilitated by a shift in mood within the Department of Defense and the White House. Ever since Gothic Serpent, Washington had been loath to send JSOC units abroad for extended periods, and when it had deployed them, it had demonstrated a marked tendency for risk aversion and micromanagement. As is often the case in war, only a sense of desperation, resulting from unremitting bad news out of Iraq, led the national leadership to open the cage doors and desist from long-distance second-guessing.

By tapping new intelligence sources and shifting to small operations with decentralized command, McChrystal increased the number of Task Force 714 operations from ten per month in 2004 to three hundred per month in 2006. The influx of information from US intelligence agencies ensured that the preponderance of operations hit pay dirt. To maintain this extraordinary tempo, McChrystal drove his JSOC subordinates hard. The general, who ran seven miles a day, ate only one meal, and slept only four hours a night, wanted everyone in JSOC to share his monk-like devotion to work. When one commander attempted to get some time at home for his men, McChrystal retorted, "I need them to realize that they don't have a life—this is their life."

McChrystal's expectations exceeded the capacity of some of his charges, particularly those who had been worn down by the physical and psychological stress of four or five or more combat tours. To some observers, pushing subordinates to the breaking point was as natural a part of wartime leadership as studying terrain and moving supplies. Many of history's finest generals, from Alexander the Great to Viscount Slim to Chesty Puller, had prevailed by marching their troops farther and higher than their opponents. To other observers, including some within the command, McChrystal pushed too hard. One of his own task force commanders remarked, "That dude's hard as fucking nails and probably the best war-fighting general we've had . . . since Patton. But his shortcoming there was he expected that out of everybody, and he didn't realize that not everyone . . . [had] the drive to perform at that level."

The upsurge in JSOC operations led to an upsurge in JSOC casualties. In May 2004, Delta Force suffered its first killed in action in more than two years, and then lost two more men in June and three in August. Insurgents had learned to fortify hideouts and pre-position automatic weapons for maximum effect. During one Delta squadron's three-month tour, close to 50 percent of its men were wounded. The mounting casualties sapped JSOC's enthusiasm for capturing targets, leading them instead to pound enemy positions with heavy weaponry from a distance before searching the rubble for the body parts of the targets.

American and coalition special operations forces took out a staggering number of insurgents from 2004 to 2006. To the surprise of many who knew the full extent of these secret operations, the insurgent groups remained on their feet. Retaining control over much of the Iraqi population, the Sunni and Shiite insurgents continued to obtain new recruits to offset their losses. The war's outcome, it turned out, would ultimately depend on the counterinsurgency operations of conventional forces, for only those operations could establish permanent control over the populous territory and prevent the insurgents from siphoning the population's resources.

By 2006, most of the special operators had come to recognize that their counterterrorism operations were not enough to defeat the enemy, and that everyone on the American side stood to gain by integrating the surgical strikes of special operations forces with the population-security and area-security operations of conventional forces. SOF officers worked more closely with the conventional commanders, keeping them informed of upcoming operations or working directly under their authority. They conducted raids in areas where the conventional forces were coming under heavy attack, and put snipers in hidden observation posts to pick off insurgents who sought to ambush conventional forces on patrol. Conventional commanders reciprocated by turning over information obtained during their routine interactions with locals. At times, conventional units deliberately acted as "safari beaters," traipsing noisily into neighborhoods to stir up enemy communications and movements that would allow SOF to target the insurgent leaders.

ONE MIGHT HAVE expected all the high marks on the special operations report card to imbue the father of manhunting, Donald Rumsfeld, with the deep and calming satisfaction of a parent whose child has been named valedictorian. Rumsfeld, however, evidenced more concern with what had not been accomplished. While special operations forces were concentrated in great numbers in Iraq and Afghanistan, their presence ranged from minimal to nonexistent in most of the other fifty-eight countries where Al Qaeda cells were believed to exist. Only in the Philippines were large numbers of special operators active against Al Qaeda affiliates, and the task force in that country consisted of Special Forces soldiers who were helping improve Philippine counterinsurgency capabilities, rather than launching raids themselves.

General Bryan D. Brown, who had succeeded Charles Holland as SOCOM commander in late 2003, had accepted the previously declined invitation from Rumsfeld to give SOCOM the power to execute counterterrorism operations, establishing a Center for Special Operations in Tampa for that purpose. That center, though, had not been able to ramp up operations beyond Iraq and Afghanistan. "Essentially what we have is a two-country solution to a 60-country problem," concluded Mike Vickers, a leading special operations thinker, after performing an official review for Rumsfeld in 2005.

During an October 2005 meeting with Vice Admiral Eric Olson, the SOCOM deputy commander, Rumsfeld bemoaned the lack of small man-hunting teams in the fifty-eight countries. "What have you guys been do-ing for the past few years?" the secretary of defense demanded. SOCOM leaders explained that deploying forces beyond the active conflict zones of Iraq and Afghanistan depended upon cooperation from the regional mili-tary commanders, ambassadors, and civilian agencies, who in many cases were choosing not to cooperate. The demands of two wars, moreover, had stretched special operations forces thin.

Rumsfeld was able to do more about the second problem than the first. To free up additional special operations manpower, he expanded the existing forces and redoubled a push for the Marines to create SOF units. Several years earlier, Rumsfeld had begun calling for Marine special op-erations forces, to which the Marine leadership had responded with a de-cided lack of enthusiasm. As in decades past, Marine generals believed that Marines were inherently special in terms of aptitude and activities, and that trying to make part of the Corps extra special would drain too much talent away from the core of the Corps. Further undermining the push had been the fact that Rumsfeld himself did not have a clear vision of what Marine special operations forces would do, but simply wanted some of the Marines to become special operations forces because he fore-saw a greater need for special operations forces down the road. "Exactly how they fit in, I assumed would evolve," Rumsfeld said later. "I wasn't in a position to look at that from a micro standpoint."

The 9/11 attacks had created some momentum within the Marine Corps for the creation of new units along the lines Rumsfeld wanted. Shortly after 9/11, Marine Corps Commandant General James Jones of-fered SOCOM a Marine Force Reconnaissance platoon. But, as often hap-pens with the bright ideas of generals, the concept hit snags when it came time for the colonels to implement it. The Navy's Special Warfare Command resisted the addition of Marine SOF, because Marine capabilities overlapped with the those of the Navy SEALs and their supporting units. Naval special operators, moreover, still resented the Marines for refusing to sign up for SOCOM in the 1980s, and for claiming to possess units that were "special operations capable."

At the end of 2002, after a year of bureaucratic wrangling, the Marines set up a pilot special operations unit, Detachment One, composed of thirty reconnaissance specialists. Activated in June 2003, the unit went through nine months of training before deploying to Iraq the following April. Like the white SOF of the Special Forces and SEALs, Detachment One was assigned to the mission of eliminating enemy leaders, and it received enough intelligence to keep its men busy around the clock on surgical strike operations, albeit oftentimes against youthful gunslingers or bomb makers who did not amount to "leaders" by most definitions.

In May, after the inconclusive First Battle of Fallujah, elements of Detachment One were reassigned to Fallujah to advise an Iraqi militia unit in that city. Labeled the Fallujah Brigade, the unit was supposed to secure the city without help from US combat units. The special operations Marines spent months advising and assisting the militiamen as they attempted to subdue the thousands of insurgents who were prowling Fallujah's streets.

Their time and effort would come to naught. The Fallujah Brigade had to be disbanded in September after it failed to respond to attacks on Marines and was implicated in the murder of a pro-American Iraqi leader. Pacifying Fallujah would end up requiring the services of six American combat battalions, replete with armor and air support, in a high-intensity battle that lasted six weeks and claimed six hundred American casualties.

Detachment One returned to the United States after a six-month tour. Its commanding officer, Colonel Robert J. Coates, briefed General Brown of SOCOM and the Marine Corps commandant, General Michael Hagee, on the unit's experiences. Mustering every fiber of salesmanship in his body, Coates informed the generals that the prototype was worthy of mass production, because the unit had thoroughly distinguished itself in Iraq and possessed capabilities found nowhere else in SOCOM. At the end of the briefing, General Brown pronounced that SOCOM did not need Detachment One or any other Marine special operations unit. General Hagee concurred.

Just when Marine special operations forces seemed to have been killed off, Donald Rumsfeld reappeared, stepping in with new directions that the generals had no choice but to obey. The secretary of defense ordered Brown and Hagee to study the concept of a Marine Special Operations Command and get back to him with concrete proposals for creating one. During the ensuing deliberations, Colonel Coates lobbied for the use of Detachment One as the model for the new command, but officers of greater clout squeezed him out of the planning and arranged for the deactivation of Detachment One. In its place, the Marine Corps proposed the formation of the 1st and 2nd Marine Special Operations Battalions under a new Marine Special Operations Command (MARSOC). Rumsfeld signed off on the proposal straightaway.

The Marine Corps filled the new battalions with Marines from its Force Recon Battalions, which it then dissolved and replaced with smaller reconnaissance units. MARSOC did not receive a separate career track, so it had to rely on the temporary rotation of Marines from other career tracks, as had been the case with the Army's Special Forces in their infancy. Because Marine promotions were heavily influenced by time spent in an individual's occupational specialty, Marines of high ambition were unlikely to sign up for a stint in the new units.

The Marines assigned only 2,600 troops to MARSOC, leaving it a runt in a Marine Corps barnyard of 180,000 troops. Army Special Operations, by contrast, had reached a strength of 28,500 personnel in an Army of 500,000, and unlike their Marine counterparts, most of these troops were permanently segregated from the rest of the Army. The growth of Army Special Operations since 9/11, stimulated by Rumsfeld's interest in manhunting, was eliciting complaints that they were too large to be considered "elite" any longer.

In Iraq, as perhaps never before, the adverse consequences of concentrating top talent in the Army's special operations forces reared their heads. Counterinsurgency demands leaders who are risk-tolerant and capable of improvising in uncertain and changing conditions. The Special

Forces attracted these types of individuals in large numbers, by virtue of an organizational culture that rewarded those who took risks and thought outside the box. Yet, in Iraq, Special Forces ended up focusing on surgical counterterrorism strikes rather than the broader mission of counterinsurgency. Because of the gravitation of maverick officers to the Special Forces, the leadership of the rest of the Army—which bore most of the responsibility for counterinsurgency—was heavily skewed toward the other type of officer, the one who strives to avoid risk, adheres strictly to rules, and relies on standard operating procedures to get the job done. A 2009 survey of Army and Marine Corps counterinsurgency veterans found that only 28 percent of Army respondents believed their service encouraged risk taking. By comparison, 58 percent of Marine respondents said the same. For the Army, the consequences of risk-averse and conformist leadership included ineffectiveness in the field and needless American casualties.

The Iraq War turned in favor of the counterinsurgents in 2007, with the arrival of a US troop surge and a new commander, General David Petraeus. Repudiating the earlier policy of seeking maximum Iraqi participation, Petraeus increased participation by US conventional forces. Petraeus and US ambassador Ryan Crocker used their diplomatic clout to induce the purging of incompetent and rapacious leaders from the Iraqi security forces. The insurgent groups lost control of territory and population, facilitating the rise of the "Sons of Iraq," counterinsurgent militia units that Sunni tribes had begun forming the previous year. By the middle of 2008, the Iraqi government had suppressed the main insurgent groups, Sunni and Shiite alike.

The government's newfound strength tempted the Shiite prime minister, Nouri al-Maliki, to squash the Sunni politicians who had joined with the government in fighting the insurgents, using Iraqi Special Operations Forces as his instrument. In August 2008, he directed those forces to arrest Sunni leaders on trumped-up charges of supporting terrorism. The United States caught wind of Maliki's machinations and used the threat of suspending aid to forestall the arrests.

Barack Obama, who came to office in January 2009 promising to get the United States out of Iraq, was less willing to blow the whistle on Maliki for such infractions, and less willing to use America's remaining military assets to rein in Shiite militias that were persecuting Sunnis. In the spring of 2009, the Obama administration acquiesced to a demand from Maliki that American special operations forces no longer target Shiites without first clearing the operations through him. Two years later, by which time the Obama administration was on a path to withdrawing all US forces from Iraq, Maliki purged the leaders of the three Iraqi special operations brigades and discontinued all operations against Shiites. In another of his self-aggrandizing schemes, Maliki imposed stringent new restrictions on US special operations forces. This measure, however, had the unintended side effect of alleviating pressure on the Sunni insurgents. Maliki's oppression of Sunnis, his coddling of Shiite militias, and his shackling of American special operators were to facilitate the resurgence of Sunni extremism in Iraq.

ALTHOUGH AFGHANISTAN'S TALIBAN government fell more than a year before Saddam Hussein's Baathist regime, American counterinsurgency in Afghanistan would peak several years after the high-water mark of counterinsurgency in Iraq. In the first years following the Taliban's overthrow, Afghanistan had largely been at peace. The Bush administration maintained 7,000 troops in Afghanistan, most of them conventional, and assigned the conventional forces responsibility for training the Afghan National Army. A small special operations task force built outposts near the Pakistani border, which served as bases for combined operations with Afghan militias. The Americans and their Afghan allies chased small groups of extremists around the border region and attempted to intercept those transiting from Pakistan into Afghanistan.

Events were to reveal that the quietude had been the result of enemy calculation rather than incapacity. After licking their wounds in Pakistan for a few years, the Taliban and Al Qaeda returned in force in 2005 to wage an insurgency. Employing the Maoist model of insurgency, the Taliban and Al Qaeda intermingled with the rural population and mobilized them for progressively more intensive forms of warfare. By recruiting impressionable youth from Pashtun tribes with long-standing ties to the Taliban, the insurgents built up guerrilla forces that could count on local populations for support. The American special operators attacked the insurgents repeatedly and often successfully, but could not prevent them from gaining control over large sections of southern and eastern Afghanistan. Neither European forces, which arrived in 2005 for what they had expected to be a peacekeeping mission, nor the nascent Afghan national security forces were able to turn the insurgents back.

Colonel Edward Reeder, the commander of America's joint special operations task force in Afghanistan during 2006 and 2007, started wondering whether the concentration of special operations forces on finding and killing extremist fighters made sense. "How many times had Special Forces done this?" he asked himself after one smashing of Taliban forces in 2007. "To what end?" Reeder, who had served several previous stints in Afghanistan, lamented, "It seems like every time I come back here, the security situation is worse."

In 2009, newly elected President Barack Obama was preoccupied with an ambitious domestic agenda, but he did have to devote significant time and attention to the Afghan War. Although he had run for president on a platform of withdrawal from Iraq, he had at the same time vowed to escalate the war in Afghanistan. He had staked out a tough position on the Afghan War—which he called "the good war"—to reassure centrist voters that his opposition to the "dumb war" in Iraq did not signify a knee-jerk aversion to the use of force.

On the advice of top defense officials, Obama made General Stanley McChrystal the commander of all US forces in Afghanistan. McChrystal was the first US special operator ever entrusted with command of an entire war, but his success at JSOC had been so spectacular that few raised the questions about a special operator's suitability that would otherwise have proliferated. In August 2009, the newly installed McChrystal submitted a proposal for an enlarged counterinsurgency campaign. He recommended deploying an additional 40,000 US troops to Afghanistan for counterinsurgency operations, a measure backed by Secretary of Defense Robert Gates, Secretary of State Hillary Clinton, and the Joint Chiefs.

Vice President Joe Biden argued that sending more troops to Afghanistan for counterinsurgency was unnecessary. Counterinsurgency, Biden asserted, was focused on the Taliban, when the real enemy was Al Qaeda.

As an alternative, the vice president proposed a strategy of "light-footprint counterterrorism," in which US special operations forces and drones surgically removed the terrorists.

Gates, McChrystal, and General David Petraeus, who was now the commander of CENTCOM, countered that the United States could not get enough information to target the terrorists without a large and protracted counterinsurgency campaign in which US troops provided security and trained Afghan forces until they could take over. The counterinsurgency operations of conventional forces in Iraq, they noted, had been critical to the success of surgical-strike counterterrorism. The United States had already tried Biden's strategy in Afghanistan between 2002 and 2008, and during that time the Taliban had increased sixfold in strength and taken control of much of the country.

Biden's strategy appealed to Obama because surgical strikes were easy to tout as evidence of presidential toughness and did not require entanglement in messy local affairs. The president, however, was reluctant to disregard a recommendation that had been made by the commanding general and endorsed by nearly all of the administration's top national security officials. In the end, Obama decided to send 30,000 of the 40,000 US troops McChrystal had sought. But surgical strikes by special operations forces would play a big part in this troop surge, and they would play an even bigger part after the surge, which would come much sooner than the proponents of counterinsurgency had advocated. To limit the financial and political costs, Obama chose to maintain the surge for only eighteen months, far shorter than the five years desired by McChrystal and other military leaders.

At first, it appeared that the division of labor between special and conventional units in Afghanistan would mirror that in Iraq. McChrystal directed conventional commanders to focus their troops on protecting and assisting the population, while enlarged SOF attacked the enemy's leadership. The low profile of the special operators, McChrystal reasoned, would tamp down Afghan complaints about civilian casualties committed by coalition forces.

The areas occupied by the US Marines diverged from this model from the beginning. Confident that Marines were capable of whatever raiding needed to be done, some Marine commanders refused to allow special operators into their "battle spaces," as the Americans called the areas that conventional units were responsible for controlling. Ongoing mistrust between Marines and special operators played its part in at least some of these decisions.

The second divergence came from within SOF. Edward Reeder, returning to Afghanistan as commander of the white special operations forces in 2009, sought ways to shift his forces from manhunting to counterinsurgency. He experimented with the insertion of Army Special Forces into Afghan villages, where they lived alongside the Afghans and helped them secure and govern their villages. Some Afghans proved highly receptive to the idea of American oversight of local security, for the Americans did not beat them or steal their sheep as the Taliban and Afghan government forces were wont to do.

Gaining momentum from early successes in organizing villages to defend themselves, the program continued to grow under Reeder's successor, Brigadier General Scott Miller. A crossover from the world of black SOF, Miller had led the Delta ground element in Somalia during Operation Gothic Serpent and had later commanded all of Delta Force, giving him influence with the JSOC element in Afghanistan that a career white SOF officer could never have acquired. He thus was able to obtain JSOC's help in eliminating hostile forces from Afghan villages where his white SOF were working with the locals. That assistance proved critical in breaking the Taliban opposition in a number of villages.

Lieutenant Colonel Brian Petit, a Special Forces battalion commander who oversaw some of the early efforts in southern Afghanistan, observed that convincing villages to participate in the new American program required demonstrations of military superiority and the establishment of a permanent military presence. "Villages and villagers principally aim to survive and prosper," Petit stated. "To do so, they will visibly align or subjugate themselves to the dominant, lasting presence." Once the village had been secured, Petit noted, governmental control could be solidified by rehabilitating local governance and bolstering economic activity.

General McChrystal was sufficiently impressed that he decided to allocate a large fraction of white SOF to the program, which became known as Village Stability Operations. To the delight of those who thought that special operations forces had been too preoccupied with surgical counterterrorism since 2003, Village Stability Operations became the top global priority for white SOF, making it the largest US special operations program since Vietnam. The white units responsible for all of the other regions of the world were required to rotate their troops into Afghanistan for their turn.

Village Stability Operations helped McChrystal correct what he had identified as a severe deficiency of the war effort—the tendency of US and other NATO forces to barricade themselves in large forward operating bases. The thick concrete blast walls surrounding these bases afforded the occupants some protection from attack, but they also encouraged risk-averse commanders to keep their troops on their bases, when they needed to be outside the wire, interacting with the Afghan population and mobilizing it against the insurgents. Under the Village Stability Operations program, the Americans rented compounds within their assigned villages, forgoing the concrete cocoons of the forward operating bases, not to mention the running water and air conditioning. Their vulnerability to attack gave them no choice but to seek the assistance of the local community. Sitting for long hours in Afghan homes, drinking tea and eating dishes that stood a good chance of wrenching their bowels, they obtained information and recruited young men into the Afghan Local Police, as the village security forces came to be called. The Americans organized community councils, funded small infrastructure projects, and mediated disputes over territorial boundaries and livestock. In company with any members of the Afghan Local Police they could muster, the Americans patrolled villages and their environs day and night.

For someone accustomed to the comforts of twenty-first-century America, the hardship, boredom, and danger of living and fighting in an Afghan village seemed a recipe for unadulterated misery. Most of the special operators, however, quickly became inured to the disagreeable aspects and were able to find an abiding satisfaction in the experience. Isolated from pesky authorities—both American and Afghan—they relished a contest in which wits, charisma, fighting skills, and endurance determined who won and lost. In a hostile wilderness on the edge of the Earth, dependence upon a small group of comrades for survival fostered the brotherly love that has bound warriors together since the dawn of time.

General McChrystal's involvement with the Village Stability Operations program was cut short by his unexpected firing in June 2010. As someone who had spent most of his career in the shadows, McChrystal lacked practice in the public side of the national security world, where journalists and politicians scrutinized every word emitted by a top military commander. In the fall of 2009, McChrystal had made several public endorsements of counterinsurgency, which a hypersensitive White House interpreted as attempts to force the administration's hand on strategy. President Obama's dissatisfaction with McChrystal reached its apogee with the publication of a *Rolling Stone* article in which journalist Michael Hastings reported that McChrystal and his staff had made derogatory remarks about Obama and other senior civilian officials. It later came to light that most of the incendiary statements had originated with a single junior staff officer while in an advanced state of inebriation, and much else in the article was misleading, but McChrystal was summoned back to Washington with such rapidity that he lacked the information to rebut the allegations. Even had he possessed such information, he would have been reluctant to do so, imbued as he was with the principles of a military that discouraged vigorous self-defense. Obama fired McChrystal during a brief White House tête-à-tête.

To take McChrystal's place in Afghanistan, Obama appointed General David Petraeus, the man who had salvaged American equities in an Iraq War that many observers had thought to be a lost cause. In the view of Petraeus, Village Stability Operations had the potential to mobilize 100,000 Afghans against the insurgents and turn the tide in much the same manner as the Sons of Iraq. Petraeus spent his first weeks in the new job lobbying Afghan president Hamid Karzai to authorize a huge increase in the Afghan Local Police. His enthusiasm was not shared by Karzai, to whom these forces seemed dangerously similar to Afghan militias that had run amok during the civil warfare of the 1990s. Although the Americans might be able to keep matters in hand at the beginning, the Local Police could be very difficult for the central government to control once the Americans pulled back. Karzai eventually consented to a modest figure of

10,000 Afghan Local Policemen, and only on the stipulation that they be subordinated to his Ministry of Interior. That condition marked a critical departure from the Sons of Iraq program, which had been directly under American authority.

Building the Afghan Local Police turned out to be a much more difficult task than building the far larger Sons of Iraq. Iraq's insurgents had been concentrated in towns and cities clustered along the Tigris and Euphrates rivers, where 70 percent of Iraq's population resided. Afghanistan's insurgents were ensconced in widely dispersed villages in a country whose population was 70 percent rural. Afghanistan's society was more heterogeneous than Iraq's, divided into a bewildering array of ethnic groups, tribes, and clans. Communist persecution of rural elites in the 1970s, Soviet intervention in the 1980s, civil warfare and Taliban rule in the 1990s, and rekindled war since 2005 had torn deep gashes in Afghanistan's traditional communities, many of which had never healed. The councils of elders that had governed villages for millennia had been supplanted in much of the country by violent warlords, men of charisma or military prowess who thumbed their noses at traditional deference to elders. In these circumstances, empowering a group of Afghan villagers ran a high risk of alienating rival groups to such a degree that they would side with the insurgents.

In recognition of this peril, General Miller brought in anthropologists, historians, Afghan expatriates, and local civilians to help the staff at his special operations headquarters comprehend the intricate social webs of rural Afghanistan. He required his intelligence staffs to spend several months analyzing an Afghan village before the special operators could select any of its members for the Afghan Local Police. If analysts identified an intractable social cleavage or a vacuum of local leadership, Miller refused to authorize Local Police for the village.

Despite the high priority accorded to Village Stability Operations, the number of special operations forces available for the program was modest in comparison with the magnitude of the task. Some special operations forces were still deemed necessary in a plethora of other countries in Africa, Latin America, Asia, and the Middle East, and special operators had to be rotated back to the United States for lengthy spells so that they would not burn out. Within Afghanistan, some of the white SOF were assigned to the training and advising of elite Afghan units.

A Special Forces Operational Detachment Alpha, SEAL platoon, or Marine Special Operations Team could at best hope to cover ten Afghan villages, with a total of about three hundred Local Policemen. Early experiences showed that a prolonged American presence, up to two years in duration, was required to impart the skills and attitudes that would ensure that the Afghan Local Police continued to function properly after the American mentors left. Consequently, the white SOF did not have enough manpower even to support the first 10,000 Local Policemen. Several conventional battalions had to be brought into the Village Stability Operations program, with widely varying levels of effectiveness.

Village Stability Operations and the Afghan Local Police were to achieve some noteworthy tactical successes, bringing security to districts that had been Taliban hotbeds since the war began. Afghans generally proved more willing and able to fight when assigned to their native villages, as they were under the Afghan Local Police, than when sent to distant villages, as they were under the Afghan National Police and Afghan National Army. The presence of US special operations forces on a continuous basis resulted in training, supervision, and guidance of quality and consistency much superior to what the Afghan government could offer.

The results could be stunning in their rapidity. Villages that years of counterinsurgency had been unable to free from the Taliban's leash were suddenly rid of insurgents. In the village of Siah Choy, west of Kandahar, the Taliban had kept control of the citizens by banning cellphones, restricting travel, and putting booby-trapped bombs outside the doors of people's homes at night to keep them from going out. When US or Afghan forces had traveled to the village, they had inevitably come under attack from the Taliban, with innocent civilians caught in the crossfire. Taliban improvised explosive devices dotted the roads into the village, blowing the legs off of counterinsurgents unlucky enough to trip the wires or pressure plates connected to the detonators.

The recruitment of a small number of resolute local men into the Afghan Local Police broke the Taliban's grip on Siah Choy almost overnight. The Local Policemen drove the handful of hardcore Taliban from the village with ease, then helped nearby security forces identify and remove the IEDs. "There used to be fighting here every day before the ALP came," farmer Ali Mohammed recounted. "Now, we have more security and can go out without fear."

For every victory, however, there was a draw or a defeat. The Taliban, quick to discern the program's potential, sent some of its best fighters to attack the Americans and the Afghan Local Police, inflicting casualties and in some instances stunting the recruitment of policemen. As time went along, changes in American and Afghan oversight together with pressure from higher authorities to expand the program curtailed the careful scrutiny of villages prior to organization of Local Police units. Partisans of ethnic groups, tribes, or families hence found it easier to gain influence over the units and use them as instruments with which to club their rivals. That sort of oppression in turn enabled the Taliban to win over the aggrieved group with offers of armed partnership against the government and the Americans.

Abuses of power were most prevalent in northern Afghanistan, where the Local Police were expanded in response to pressure from Afghan politicians desirous of resources for their districts and US officials fixated on expanding the program's size. Rival power brokers, divided by ethnic and personal hatreds, converted their militias into Afghan Local Police Forces and wielded them in feuds over water rights, women, and "chai boys"— the euphemism for prepubescent boys sodomized by powerful Afghan men. The Village Stability Operations personnel in the districts had the unenviable task of trying to disentangle the Afghan Local Police from petty squabbles and focus them instead on promoting stability and countering extremism. "Everybody in some way or form is a bad guy here," said one of the Americans in Baghlan Province. "So you just have to pick the people who are less bad than others to work with you."

In the early days of the Afghan Local Police, the Afghan police chiefs and governors who had legal authority over the program let the American special operators command the units. As the Afghan Local Police matured and the United States laid plans for withdrawal, these Afghan leaders increasingly asserted authority over the local police, shifting control over the fate of the units from Americans to Afghans. Where Afghan leaders bungled or preyed on the weak, the Afghan Local Police alienated the population and heightened its receptivity to insurgents. In areas with strong Afghan leadership, the Local Police became formidable instruments in triumphant counterinsurgency campaigns. Human rights organizations denounced the Afghan leaders in some of those areas for torturing and executing Taliban prisoners—a practice Afghans justified by citing the sieve-like conditions of Afghanistan's corrupt judicial system—while also reporting security improvements in many areas where the Local Police had taken root.

Constraints on the size of the Afghan Local Police would ultimately ensure that they could not exert a decisive strategic impact. Despite the aggressive efforts of some Afghans and Americans to enlarge the program, it never approached the 100,000 men envisioned by Petraeus. During the period of US involvement, its authorized strength peaked at 30,000. The Afghan National Army and Afghan National Police, with close to 350,000 troops, would, by virtue of their size, be the main tools with which the Afghan government would win or lose the war.

Whereas white SOF concentrated on counterinsurgency in Afghanistan from 2010 onward, JSOC remained focused on surgical strikes. During McChrystal's year in Afghanistan, the number of special operations raids tripled. From the middle of 2010 to the end of that year, it tripled again. By mid-2011, special operations forces reached an operational rate comparable to that in Iraq, averaging ten raids per night.

Although the drones, linguists, signals interceptors, and technology wizards of JSOC's behemoth intelligence apparatus all made the move from Iraq to Afghanistan, information on the enemy was much scarcer in Afghanistan than in Iraq. Afghans had fewer cellphones and computers, and insurgents intimidated cellphone companies into switching off their towers at night. Launching raids at the same rate but with smaller stockpiles of intelligence, the operators more often acted on the basis of flawed information. Half of Ranger raids failed to net any enemy suspects.

The frequent missing of the mark compelled raiding parties to carry large sums of cash to compensate homeowners for demolished walls or trampled crops. Shots were not fired during most of the raids, and when they were, the Americans usually hit insurgent suspects and no one else, but reports and rumors of harm to innocent Afghans fueled widespread criticisms. President Karzai repeatedly deplored errant American raids in public to score points with his Afghan supporters and deflect American criticisms of his regime for corruption and other flaws.

Maintaining the same pace as in Iraq without comparable amounts of intelligence also compelled JSOC to aim a large share of its operations at the lowliest of enemy combatants and to go after enemy units rather than just individuals. In 2010, the 75th Ranger Regiment assigned some of its elements to Team Darby, named after Ranger founder William Darby, later renamed Team Merrill after Frank Merrill of Merrill's Marauders. The team was to be employed against sizable hostile forces in areas where the enemy was strong in order to deprive the insurgents of sanctuaries and inflict casualties on diehard elements. One favored tactic was to enter a private compound in the middle of an insurgent stronghold and goad the enemy into attacking. Barging into civilian residences, the Rangers paid the owners cash for the damages that were certain to ensue and told them to get out with their families while they still could. To turn the compounds into what they affectionately called their Alamos, the Rangers knocked holes in the walls for firing ports and positioned claymore mines around the exterior.

The Rangers encountered no shortage of hostile men willing to do battle. "For a Ranger, it's good and bad," said a Team Merrill veteran. "This is the highlight of what a Ranger wants to do. He wants to get in these massive fights, kill as many people as he can kill, destroy as much as he can destroy, but at the same time, we start to take casualties." Team Merrill was shut down in late 2011 because of the high number of Ranger casualties and doubts about the outfit's strategic utility.

On several occasions in 2010, JSOC inadvertently killed innocent civilians during raids, provoking a stream of protests from President Karzai. JSOC acquiesced to new rules of engagement, according to which the strike forces had to announce their presence whenever they arrived at a compound and had to offer those inside the opportunity to surrender. JSOC operators complained that this procedure allowed the enemy time to destroy phones, computers, and other incriminating evidence.

Building upon collaborative relationships developed in Iraq, American special operations forces and conventional forces generally worked well together in Afghanistan. Special operations forces bequeathed intelligence, targeting data, and psychological warfare assets to the conventional forces, and in return received access to aircraft and surveillance platforms as well as information about the local population and government. Colonel William B. Ostlund, one of the few officers to command both special operations and conventional forces in Afghanistan, observed that bilateral operations involving both types of forces were consistently superior to unilateral operations by one or the other.

WHILE NEITHER GEORGE W. Bush nor Barack Obama wanted counterinsurgency to feature prominently in his presidency, both found themselves investing large amounts of national treasure in counterinsurgency, and hence both of their administrations would have to grapple with the question of how best to use the burgeoning special operations forces in this type of warfare. Bush developed a strong interest in his counterinsurgency wars, but left most of the details to subordinates. From the perspective of special operations, the critical subordinate was Donald Rumsfeld, whose preoccupation with surgical strikes guided the trajectory of special operations forces for most of Bush's presidency. Obama had an interest in neither the generalities nor the particulars, but the use of special operations forces in surgical counterterrorism appealed to him as a means of showing the American people he could get tough with terrorists, and could do so at a relatively low cost.

Special operators entered the wars of the early twenty-first century viewing themselves as the nation's premier counterinsurgency practitioners. The large scale of these wars, however, led the conventional forces to take on most of the counterinsurgency work, with the major exception of the Village Stability Operations program in Afghanistan. Animated by Rumsfeld's belief that surgical counterterrorism could cripple insurgencies, SOF focused so heavily on precision strikes that they had to expand beyond high-level leaders to low-level leaders and eventually to insurgents of any kind. General Stanley McChrystal's organizational genius and his exploitation of advances in information technology allowed SOF to locate and eliminate individual insurgents with a hitherto unfathomable frequency, first in Iraq, and then in Afghanistan. Whereas manhunting had been a core competency for JSOC, it represented a major departure for the Special Forces and other white SOF, of such proportions as to provoke concern about the diversion of these forces from their original core competencies.

The exponential growth of precision counterterrorism operations yielded an extraordinary number of tactical successes in Iraq and Afghanistan, some of which contributed to strategic successes. But when the surgical strikes were the sole performer in the counterinsurgent show, they proved incapable of influencing strategic outcomes. Only when they were part of an ensemble, with members who could hold ground, was strategic victory attainable. Village Stability Operations and the Afghan Local Police could hold ground, and they did so in some important areas, but their forces were too small to hold ground on a strategic scale. Collaboration with holders of ground, therefore, usually meant collaboration with conventional NATO forces and the Afghan national security forces. The effectiveness of such partnerships was subject to the capabilities of the partners, which in the case of the Afghan forces were often underwhelming.

The counterinsurgencies of the early twenty-first century began with a souring of relations between special operations and conventional forces, as the special operators attempted to pursue surgical strikes without so much as notifying the conventional commanders into whose neighborhoods they were intruding. Rumsfeld's announcement that SOCOM was no longer the perpetual handmaiden to the military's regional commanders encouraged special operators to view themselves as more valuable than conventional forces, compounding suspicions among conventional force personnel that SOF exaggerated their own importance. Within a few years, the special and conventional operators came to see that surgical strikes and population-security operations could be mutually reinforcing, and hence collaboration surged. The practical necessity of relying on conventional forces in large counterinsurgency campaigns again called into question the concentration of talent in the Army Special Forces, and gave the Marines further reason to constrain the new special operations organization that they had been forced, at bureaucratic gunpoint, to create.

For all its difficulties, the first decade of the post-9/11 era was a period of spectacular growth for special operations forces, in terms of resources, authorities, and prestige. Only the Kennedy era rivaled it in any respect, and no period matched it in terms of the magnitude of new responsibilities assumed. The special operators entered the next decade on an upward trajectory that seemed to know no bounds. But, as in the case of the Kennedy boom, the steep ascent had set the conditions for a painful fall.

CHAPTER 10

OVERREACH

To residents of the eastern Afghan province of Nangarhar, the two helicopters that departed Jalalabad airfield at 11 p.m. the night of May 1, 2011, appeared no different from the thousands of others that had come and gone for the past decade. A careful investigation of the passenger rosters for these two Black Hawks would have been required to discern that the twenty-three US Navy SEALs did not all belong to one of the units that were launching raids every night, but instead came from a multitude of units, some of which were not currently deployed to Afghanistan. What was most unusual about the two helicopters were the special stealth technologies that had been applied to them, which included a coating that deflected radar as well as engine modifications that reduced emissions of heat and noise.

Bearing east on a course paralleling the ancient Silk Road, the pilots flew the Black Hawks just a few feet above the treetops. Within fifteen minutes, they were inside Pakistani air space, climbing above the Spin Ghar mountains. US intelligence picked up no indication that the Pakistani military had detected the initial intrusion. No other signs of heightened alertness within Pakistan's air defense systems emerged during the remaining seventy-five minutes of the flight.

The first Black Hawk to reach the mysterious compound in Abbottabad attempted to set down in the largest courtyard. During its descent, the air from its blades cascaded into the compound walls and produced an unexpected rebound of air current, tilting the helicopter sideways. The tail rotor clipped a wall and shattered into pieces, an unrecoverable injury that sent the helicopter keeling over on its side and tumbling into the dust.

In the White House Situation Room, where President Obama and other top officials were watching a live video feed, the crash triggered a flurry of gasps. For those old enough to remember Operation Eagle Claw, the parallels seemed inescapable. America had sent its best to rescue the hostages from Iran in April 1980, and yet a helicopter had crashed before the ground operation could even get started.

What could not be seen from the overhead video camera was the Nightstalker pilot's handling of the helicopter as it plunged into the dust cloud. In contrast to the pilots who had been assigned to unfamiliar aircraft for Eagle Claw, the pilots chosen for this mission were career special operations airmen who knew their aircraft as well as they knew their wives, if not better. The pilot was able to keep the Black Hawk from flipping over as it fell to the earth and, most importantly, to catch the tail boom on a twelve-foot privacy wall, which prevented the rotors from slamming into the ground. This exceptional piece of flying spared the passengers from injury, and thus permitted the mission to continue as planned.

Neptune Spear, as the Abbottabad raid was code named, had buried one of the ghosts of Eagle Claw by getting its aircraft to their intended destination, and buried another by keeping all of its men alive. It was to inter more along the way. But if Eagle Claw's failures would provide the impetus for future successes, the immediate triumph of Neptune Spear was to be the wellspring of later woes. Mesmerized by the ephemeral thrills of victory, politicians and special operators were to draw all the wrong lessons from the operation, precipitating a series of decisions that damaged America's geopolitical standing and undermined its special operations forces.

THE TALL CONCRETE compound in Abbottabad had come to the attention of the CIA the previous summer, becoming the first solid lead on the terrorist mastermind in the nearly ten years that had passed since Tora Bora. The CIA's post-2001 search for Osama bin Laden, colossal in its size and expense, had been fixated on villages and cave complexes in Pakistan's remote tribal regions, when in actuality Bin Laden had moved into Pakistan's urban areas after fleeing Afghanistan, switching locations repeatedly to keep his enemies off his scent. In the middle of 2005 he had settled down in the newly built Abbottabad compound, and he had lived there for more than five years before the Americans caught a whiff of him. The CIA ultimately found the Abbottabad hideout by pursuing Bin Laden's primary courier, known as Abu Ahmed al-Kuwaiti, whose identity had been disclosed by an Al Qaeda captive when the CIA subjected him to the "enhanced interrogation techniques" of the Bush administration.

The compound stood just a few hundred yards from Pakistan's military academy, fueling suspicions that Pakistan's government had known of Bin Laden's presence all along. Pakistani police and intelligence agencies kept close tabs on houses near military installations because, among other things, those installations had frequently been attacked by opponents of the government. According to extensive research by *New York Times* reporter Carlotta Gall, the Pakistani government's Inter-Services Intelligence agency had a special desk responsible solely for protecting Bin Laden, the existence of which was known to a small number of senior Pakistani officials.

Residents of the neighborhood only occasionally saw the two tall brothers who ran Bin Laden's compound, Arshad and Tariq Khan. None of the compound's residents attended wedding celebrations or other community events. When some local boys hit a cricket ball over the compound's wall, the brothers refused to let them inside to retrieve it. Arshad and Tariq burned all trash within the compound rather than leaving it outside for collection, lest it give snoopers any clues to the identities of the inhabitants.

Bin Laden's counterintelligence measures were sufficiently strong that even after the CIA started focusing its best human and technical intelligence collection resources on the compound, it was unable to obtain definitive proof that he was inside. Most CIA analysts, indeed, believed it quite possible that the chief perpetrator of the 9/11 attacks was not there. Within the CIA, the evidence of Bin Laden's presence in Abbottabad was considered less compelling than the evidence available in 2003 showing that Saddam Hussein possessed weapons of mass destruction, which, as it turned out, he did not possess.

In August 2010, word of the Abbottabad discovery reached Admiral William McRaven, the JSOC commander. A towering SEAL from San Antonio, Texas, McRaven had a consummate military bearing and spoke in a powerful baritone, reminiscent of that of television news anchor Tom Brokaw. McRaven was one of the few special operations officers who could be considered a scholar, and he was as much of a public scholar as a special operator could be. In 1995, he had published a well-received book on special operations, in which he derived theories from eight of the twentieth century's most momentous raids. A leading proponent of the view that special operations forces were decisive strategic actors, McRaven published an article in 2004 arguing that special operations should be considered both "a unique form of warfare" and "a perfect grand strategy."

McRaven recommended that his special operations forces sneak into Pakistan by helicopter for a raid on the Abbottabad compound. The raiding force would apprehend the occupants and determine whether Bin Laden was among them. If any of the occupants put up resistance and had to be killed, the Americans could find out whether they had bagged Bin Laden by collecting tissue samples and testing them against DNA culled from Bin Laden's relatives. The other option that was floated, an air strike on the compound, would require thirty-two 2,000-pound bombs to destroy the compound and any tunnels and bunkers below it, killing large numbers of civilians in the surrounding neighborhood and precluding a definitive determination of Bin Laden's presence.

McRaven assured the White House that JSOC could take down the compound with little difficulty. "This is a relatively straightforward raid from JSOC's perspective," McRaven said. "We do these ten, twelve, fourteen times a night. The thing that makes this complicated is it's one hundred and fifty miles inside Pakistan, and logistically getting there; and then the politics of explaining the raid, is the complicating factor."

McRaven's arguments found favor with most of the senior national security leadership, including President Obama. The main skeptics, Secretary of Defense Robert Gates and Vice President Joe Biden, warned that US ground forces could get caught in a fight with Pakistani forces, and that the Pakistani government was more likely to terminate cooperation with the US government on key activities in Afghanistan and Pakistan if the United States put troops on Pakistani soil than if it struck from the air.

Gates and Biden were unable to sway Obama. The White House gave the green light for a raid on the suspected hideout at the beginning of May.

AFTER THE FIRST Black Hawk crashed in Bin Laden's courtyard, the pilot of the second helicopter opted to set down outside the compound's walls. The SEALs filed out the doors of both aircraft, broke into small groups, and headed toward the buildings, as specified in a plan they had rehearsed interminably on a full-scale replica at Harvey Point, North Carolina. A few adult males opened fire on the SEALs, achieving nothing save for the exposure of their own locations. The return fire of the SEALs, exceptional in its accuracy, killed all of the hostile shooters in seconds.

In one of the buildings from which the SEALs had taken fire, they came upon the grizzled figure of Osama bin Laden. The fifty-four-year-old terrorist was unarmed, two of his wives by his side. The SEALs shot him without hesitation, on the theory that all adult males in the building were to be considered hostile. A stray bullet wounded one of the wives, a twenty-nine-year old Yemeni who was Bin Laden's fifth betrothed, and she shrieked at the SEALs in Arabic like a wounded banshee. Within twenty minutes, the compound and its occupants were under the complete control of the SEALs.

In the twenty remaining minutes, the SEALs filled sacks with computers, flash drives, compact discs, and documents. A medic inserted a needle into Bin Laden's corpse to extract bone marrow for DNA testing. On board the downed Black Hawk, the pilot smashed the instrument panel with a hammer, while demolition experts placed C-4 charges on the avionics system, communications gear, engine, and rotor head. To shield the compound's women and children from the blast, SEALs handcuffed them and herded them, kicking and screaming, to the opposite side of the compound. The Americans then rolled thermite grenades underneath the helicopter, igniting it like a matchhead, its fiery orange glow illuminating the erstwhile terrorist hideout for the citizens of Abbottabad to see. The SEALs loaded Osama bin Laden's body and possessions onto helicopters and took off into the night, leaving behind the shackled wives and children to wail at their losses and await the arrival of Pakistani authorities.

Forensic experts at CIA and Defense Department laboratories promptly analyzed the bone marrow sample. The DNA signature matched that of one of Bin Laden's sisters, whose body had been subpoenaed by the FBI a few years earlier after her death from brain cancer in a Boston hospital. The Americans took Bin Laden's body to a ship and dumped it into the sea to prevent his remains from becoming holy relics for other radicals.

President Obama, who normally shunned public mention of armed conflict, was eager to speak to the world about Operation Neptune Spear. A few hours after receiving confirmation of the raid's success, he went on television to deliver an address that achieved instant notoriety for its profusion of first-person references. "Shortly after taking office, I directed Leon Panetta, the director of the CIA, to make the killing or capture of Bin Laden the top priority of our war against Al Qaeda," the president announced. "Last August, after years of painstaking work by our intelligence community, I was briefed on a possible lead to Bin Laden. . . . I met repeatedly with my national security team as we developed more information about the possibility that we had located Bin Laden hiding within a compound deep inside of Pakistan. And finally, last week, I determined that we had enough intelligence to take action, and authorized an operation to get Osama bin Laden and bring him to justice. Today, at my direction, the United States launched a targeted operation against that compound in Abbottabad, Pakistan."

One day before Operation Neptune Spear, Obama's national security team had taken a solemn vow to keep the raid's details secret in order to safeguard the tactics, techniques, and procedures of US special operations forces. Within hours of Bin Laden's demise, however, some of Obama's lieutenants were spilling information to the press, mainly, it seemed, to bolster the popularity of the raid and the commander-in-chief who had authorized it. Gates was infuriated to see the leakers divulge sensitive operational methods, as he believed it would compel JSOC to shelve those methods in planning future operations. What was more, the leaks were giving away clues about the identities of the raid's participants, causing those individuals to fear for the safety of their families.

Gates went to National Security Adviser Tom Donilon to register his displeasure with the leaks. "I have a new strategic communications approach to recommend," Gates told Donilon.

What was it, Donilon asked?

"Shut the fuck up," the secretary of defense said.

The killing of Osama bin Laden did improve Obama's popularity among an American public hungry for the punishment of the lead architect of 9/11. It also added to public admiration, even veneration, of the SEALs. Motion picture studios scrambled to produce new feature films on the SEALs and their exploits. Disney attempted—although futilely in the end—to obtain a trademark for "SEAL Team Six" that would have given the corporation exclusive rights to slap the team's name on action figures, games, snow globes, and the like. SEAL veterans wrote books, starred in workout shows, consulted on military videogames, and hawked paintball games offering participants the opportunity to kill Al Qaeda.

Some SEAL leaders fretted that narcissism and greed were overpowering the SEAL ethos, which held, "We do not advertise the nature of our work, nor do we seek recognition of our actions." In September 2012, Rear Admiral Sean Pybus, head of the Naval Special Warfare Command, told the 2,500 SEALs and 5,500 support troops under his authority, "We must immediately reconsider how we properly influence our people in and out of uniform NOT to seek inappropriate monetary, political, or celebrity profit from their service." The message may have had some effect on the 2,500 active-duty SEALs, but it did little to impede former SEALs.

Within Pakistan, the unauthorized incursion of American special operations forces sparked anti-Americanism of an intensity that few in the Obama administration had foreseen. A slew of retaliatory measures ensued. The Pakistani government evicted US special operations forces who had been sent the previous year to help Pakistan's military conduct counterinsurgency operations. As a consequence of the eviction, Pakistani counterinsurgency capabilities declined noticeably, to the benefit of several extremist groups deemed high threats to the United States.

Pakistan's government also demanded that the United States remove all its armed drones from Pakistani skies. Those drones had been America's main instrument for surgical strikes against extremists in the country; Pakistani officials had readily authorized American drones to fire missiles into certain regions, whereas they had steadfastly refused permission for raids by American ground forces. When the Obama administration insisted that the drones would keep operating, the Pakistanis booted the CIA out of the Shamsi Airfield in the Balochistan desert, necessitating reductions in the number of American drone strikes. Pakistani intelligence operatives harassed CIA personnel and denied the visa applications of individuals whom the CIA wished to send to Pakistan, diminishing the CIA's ability to obtain information on Al Qaeda and other extremist groups and thereby facilitating the resurgence of those groups in Pakistani cities.

In public, the Obama administration downplayed the harmful side-effects of Operation Neptune Spear, while playing up its immediate result in support of an impending overhaul of America's national security strategy. According to administration officials, the Bin Laden raid had shown that small, elite teams of special operations forces could take the place of conventional military units in solving the nation's security problems. In the official national security strategy promulgated at the end of 2011, the Obama administration stated that the United States would use surgical counterterrorism by special operations forces and drones to suppress what terrorist threats remained, obviating the need for large-scale counterinsurgency campaigns. The end of the counterinsurgency era was in turn invoked as justification for cutting America's conventional ground forces by 100,000 troops.

In accordance with this new strategy, President Obama withdrew the last US troops from Iraq at the end of 2011. The CIA and American contractors, Obama vowed, could maintain pressure on remaining terrorists in Iraq in the absence of a US military footprint. He shrank the American presence in Afghanistan at such a pace as to force the cancellation of the US military's plans for a large counterinsurgency campaign in eastern Afghanistan, where the Taliban and other miscreants were still skulking in large numbers. According to senior White House officials, the high tallies of enemies neutralized by special operations raids in Afghanistan had proven that surgical strikes were a viable substitute for a broad counterinsurgency campaign. American military leaders in Afghanistan, both those of special operations forces and those of conventional forces, disagreed with that interpretation, convinced that the counterterrorism raids in question could have lasting effects only if they were conducted in conjunction with counterinsurgency. Where surgical strikes took place without counterinsurgency operations to control territory and people, the enemy continued to recruit local men to offset their losses.

The ability of Afghan insurgents to replace low-level fighters in areas that had not been secured through counterinsurgency, in fact, was having a detrimental impact on JSOC morale. By 2011, one Ranger officer said, "I have to convince NCOs to go out. I have to yell at them to go on a mission. They're like, 'Sir, fuck this. It doesn't matter. I don't want to do this. This raid, for this low-level guy is not going to change anything.'"

Adding to JSOC's troubles were improvements in the enemy's capabilities for evading and counterattacking the raiders. On August 6, 2011, a Ranger platoon was searching a compound in Wardak Province when overhead surveillance detected several individuals fleeing the scene, triggering the dispatch of a SEAL quick-reaction force to intercept them. Seventeen SEALs, along with five Naval Special Operations support personnel, three US Air Force Special Tactics airmen, and seven Afghan soldiers, were rushed to the scene in a Chinook. The aircraft flew "blacked out," without any visible lighting or external beacons that would give its location away. The Chinook approached the landing zone at an altitude of 150 feet, the pilot slowing to 50 knots in preparation for landing.

From a two-story mud-brick compound approximately 220 meters away, a previously unnoticed person fired two rocket-propelled grenades at the helicopter. The first missed. The second hit the aft rotor and detonated. The aircraft spun violently for a few seconds and then the blades separated from the rotors. Plummeting into a dry creek bed, the helicopter burst into flames, which licked higher as fuel and munitions ignited. None of the thirty-eight people aboard the helicopter survived.

On October 7, 2013, a line of Rangers inched forward along the outside wall of a compound in Kandahar Province, where US intelligence had pinpointed a Taliban leader. What awaited them had apparently been arranged ahead of time by a smart enemy who was expecting them and had studied their operational methods. A suicide bomber darted from a hiding place into the middle of the American line and blew himself up. Before the Rangers could regroup, someone else detonated a dozen IEDs that had been planted in locations where the Americans were expected to move after the suicide blast. When it was all over, four American special operators lay dead and thirty were injured.

The number of such setbacks was quite small, considering the number of raids launched night after night. Nevertheless, a decade of unstinting combat deployments was wearing down the special operators as a whole, physically and mentally. Overseas deployments, combat stress, and casualties far outpaced those of any other period in SOF history. In the decade after 9/11, total SOF strength increased by 66 percent, from 38,000 to 63,000, while the number of deployed SOF personnel increased by 335 percent, from 2,886 to 12,560. The Ranger Regiment alone sustained 64 killed and 672 wounded in action between 9/11 and the middle of 2014.

In America's earlier wars, such heavy burdens rested on the shoulders of millions of young American men, a large fraction of them draftees. Most of those men were able to endure the physical and psychological strains of one or two combat tours. But in the all-volunteer force of the twenty-first century, America's armed forces did not receive a large influx of new draftees each year, necessitating that a much smaller group of men bear the burdens, and in a period of war longer than any other in US history. The weight fell especially heavily on special operators, since they accounted for a disproportionate share of combat troops in the wars in Afghanistan and Iraq, and were also the principal operators and combat advisers in other countries like the Philippines, Yemen, Syria, and Mali.

Special operators, their political leaders, and the nation became inured to a world in which an individual with five combat deployments was unexceptional and someone with ten was increasingly common. Sergeant First Class Kristoffer Domeij, of the 2nd Battalion, 75th Ranger Regiment, was on his fourteenth deployment when a booby-trapped bomb took his life in October 2011. The condolence letter from President Obama to the Ranger's mother, Scoti Domeij, illustrated the extent to which the sacrifices of America's special warriors had become matters of dreary routine to the nation's political leadership. The envelope arrived in Mrs. Domeij's mailbox long after her son had died—many days later than the handwritten letter sent to her by former president George W. Bush—and the letter appeared, in the mother's estimation, to have been "signed by an automatic pen."

Under stress so protracted, the superior mental toughness of special operators could not prevent rates of mental illness, alcoholism, suicide, and divorce from climbing to levels that deeply troubled the senior SOF leadership. But, despite living in a society where people could be found complaining about trivialities on twenty cable television channels at any one time, most of the special operators kept quiet about their woes, out of fealty to a warrior culture that extolled stoicism. The public therefore remained largely unaware of the price of sending the same men into war over and over.

For several years, the occasional operational setbacks and the quiet suffering of troops did little to dim the glamor that special operations forces had acquired as a result of Neptune Spear. By late 2011, the public acclaim showered on SOCOM for killing Bin Laden, together with the shift in national strategy toward light-footprint counterterrorism, had put special operations forces at the pinnacle of US national security for the first time in the nation's history. Admiral McRaven, who became SOCOM commander in August 2011, capitalized on these developments and the popularity accruing from his role in Neptune Spear to mount a campaign aimed at expanding the authority and influence of special operations forces.

Soon after his assumption of command, McRaven formed several operational planning teams in Tampa to orchestrate this campaign. He enjoined these teams to consult with the regular SOCOM staff, but the principal reason he had created them was to bypass that staff, for the Tampa headquarters was populated mainly by military personnel with no SOF experience and by civil servants with a reputation for inertia. Most prominent among the new planning teams was the Global SOF Network team, led by one of McRaven's favorite officers, Colonel Stu Bradin. A JSOC veteran, Bradin had impressed McRaven in prior tours by interweaving the multinational strands of NATO special operations forces in Afghanistan and at the NATO special operations headquarters in Mons, Belgium.

One objective of Bradin's team was to increase SOCOM's authority over forces deployed overseas. With the US military drawing down in Iraq and Afghanistan, opportunities to move special operations forces into new countries would abound, and McRaven was keen to be the ringmaster who decided where all the special operators would go and what they would do. Gaining control of deployed forces was a tall order; McRaven's immediate predecessor, Admiral Eric T. Olson, as well as General Charles Holland at the beginning of the century, had not sought it because they did not want to become enmeshed in a bureaucratic brawl with the regional military commanders.

Another objective of Bradin's team was to justify greater resources for special operations forces. By enlarging and enriching the SOF presence overseas, McRaven sought to make SOF the "force of choice" for regional commanders who had a variety of forces at their beck and call. It, too, was a tall order, for steep budget cuts were forcing the military as a whole to make do with less, and the rest of the military was certain to cry foul if SOF were taking additional marbles instead of giving up marbles like everyone else.

In Washington, Bradin set up a large SOCOM office to coordinate SOF activities with the rest of the US government and foreign allies and to oversee SOF personnel stationed in the national capital region. As the office grew in size, it was moved under the authority of the SOCOM vice commander, who served as McRaven's senior representative in the nation's capital. The office became a new power center in Washington, taking on resourcing functions that had previously belonged to the assistant secretary of defense for special operations and low-intensity conflict.

McRaven was able to find supporters for his new vision among the Joint Chiefs and the regional combatant commanders. At lower bureaucratic levels, however, sparks were soon flying as his fast-moving initiatives banged into the plodding hull of the national security establishment. The hard-charging JSOC veterans who spearheaded McRaven's programs in Washington were accustomed to getting their way, and to getting it without having to answer a lot of questions or caress other people's egos. Veterans of the wars in Iraq and Afghanistan, they had risen through the ranks in a wartime environment in which rules could be bent or broken in the name of expediency without adverse consequences, and they presumed that the continuation of war in Afghanistan meant that the same lenience would prevail in Washington. When confronted with congressional staffers, Pentagon officials, conventional military officers, or State Department diplomats who asked for information or raised objections, McRaven's emissaries in Washington had a tendency to ignore them, or to brush them off with a reminder that special operations forces had killed Bin Laden.

This behavior, of course, did not go over well with those on the receiving end, who in many cases did not share the same sense of wartime urgency and already resented SOCOM for seeking additional resources while the rest of the military was hemorrhaging. At first, McRaven appeared to enjoy so much support from the White House and so much prestige from the Bin Laden raid that no one dared fight back. During his first two years in command, McRaven made significant headway in obtaining the funding and authorities he desired. Special operations forces were set on a path to increase from 64,000 to 70,000 troops, at a time when the Army and Marine Corps were being cut by a combined 100,000 troops. He gained combatant commander status with respect to the theater special operations commands, which enabled him to achieve efficiencies by reconfiguring those organizations. Secretary of Defense Leon Panetta authorized Colonel Stu Bradin's team to craft a Global SOF Network Campaign Plan that would increase the global reach of special operations forces and the authority of SOCOM.

As McRaven's three-year tenure progressed, however, the opposition forces coalesced, emboldened by the knowledge that the sand in his hourglass was running down, and by the perception that his presidential top cover was fading because of declining White House interest in special operations. McRaven's efforts to increase his control over deployed units ran into resistance from other four-star generals, of the sort that had dissuaded General Holland and Admiral Olson from seeking a more powerful SOCOM. Generals and ambassadors foiled many of McRaven's attempts to expand his command's overseas presence and authorities.

The most formidable opposition came from Congress. The institution that had given birth to SOCOM in 1986 had been a doting parent throughout the organization's childhood and early adulthood, warding off bullies when they tried to steal the youth's lunch money. Now, however, Congress had reason to believe that its offspring had strayed so far off course that the time had come for tough love. Members of the House Appropriations Committee were miffed when they learned that SOCOM had decided to form the new office in Washington without notifying them. Moving additional military personnel inside the Beltway required legal authorities that belonged to Congress, not SOCOM or any other component of the Defense Department. When congressional staff members requested information and explanations from SOCOM, their emails and phone calls received incomplete or contradictory answers, or no answers at all.

Congressional displeasure with the lack of communication from SOCOM led Jennifer Miller, a staff member at the House Appropriations Committee, to probe further into the SOCOM Washington office, the Global SOF Network Campaign Plan, and McRaven's other new initiatives. Miller, who was known to have a low tolerance for obstructionism, began to scrutinize the SOCOM budget for anything that did not fit within the parameters of Major Force Program 11, the designated special operations funding line. Budgetary documents revealed that SOCOM was shelling out large sums for graduate education as well as for the Human Performance Program, which hired physical therapists, dieticians, and conditioning coaches to help troops deal with the mental and physical wear and tear of unending deployments. Miller and others on Capitol Hill believed that these expenses were the responsibilities of the armed services, not SOCOM. Pentagon officials who were frustrated with SOCOM's lack of transparency, and who knew that budgetary authority left Congress as one of the few remaining entities with any power over SOCOM, complained to their congressional contacts that SOCOM was paying for these items as part of a power play to become a fifth armed service.

The anti-SOCOM coalition leapt into action in the spring of 2013. Members of the House Appropriations and Armed Services Committees decided to axe several SOCOM budget items, including the Washington office, and to put a $1 million cap on expenses for graduate education. The committees inserted unusually harsh language into the 2014 Defense Appropriations Act, chiding SOCOM for failing to make clear the purpose and capabilities of the Washington office.

These rebukes, however, failed to convince the SOCOM leadership of the need to show deference toward Congress. In the spirit of wartime expediency, McRaven proceeded to spend money on graduate education beyond the $1 million. When Representative Rodney Frelinghuysen, the chairman of the House Appropriations Subcommittee on Defense, eventually figured out what was going on, he called McRaven onto the carpet in a closed hearing. In the ensuing Defense Appropriations Act, Congress blasted SOCOM for initiating "significant new programs, contracts, and activities that were not previously identified or explicitly justified in budget justification materials," and for waiving funding restrictions "in a manner inconsistent with existing Department of Defense directives and regulations."

Congressional exasperation with the SOCOM leadership led to additional slashing of budget items that appeared to fall outside of SOCOM's purview. Through the withholding of money, the House forced SOCOM to abort plans for multinational coordination centers that were integral to the Global SOF Network Campaign Plan. Congress also denied SOCOM the authorities and funds it had been seeking to transform its Joint Special Operations University from a training center into a world-class research institution. It was a stunning reversal of fortune for an organization that for so long had received everything it wanted from Congress and more.

During McRaven's final months in command, Pentagon leaders who had seethed with rage at SOCOM's intrusions into strategic planning slow-rolled the Global SOF Network Campaign Plan, in anticipation of scrapping it once McRaven left office. The Global SOF Network team would be disbanded shortly before McRaven's retirement at the end of August 2014, its formerly privileged members tossed to the wolves of the previously marginalized SOCOM headquarters staff. McRaven's successor, General Joseph Votel, would be so engrossed in repairing relations with Congress and the Pentagon that he would back away from the Global SOF Network Campaign Plan and other controversial initiatives.

Votel's retrenchment, along with his low-key demeanor, restored a degree of trust within the legislative and executive branches. But Congress continued to poke its nose into the business of SOCOM in ways that some elements of the special operations community found deeply vexing. At the beginning of 2016, members of Congress pressured Navy Secretary Ray

Mabus to rescind the promotion of Rear Admiral Brian L. Losey, head of the Naval Special Warfare Command. The congressional opposition derived from an inspector general's determination that Losey had retaliated against several subordinates on suspicion of submitting anonymous whistleblower complaints against him. The case, however, was less than clear-cut, for many of Losey's actions against his accusers appeared to have been the result of their poor performance or misconduct. Secretary Mabus had decided that Losey deserved the promotion because the inspector general had provided insufficient evidence to support the accusations. But when Congress learned of the Navy's decision to promote Losey, a number of congressmen interpreted it as evidence that the military was unwilling to discipline its own leaders or protect whistleblowers. Ultimately, the congressional complaints convinced Mabus to overturn the promotion, bringing Losey's career to an abrupt end.

From his retirement perch at the University of Texas, William McRaven penned an op-ed in defense of Losey. The individuals who had leveled accusations against Losey, stated McRaven, were simply "a few guys fighting to maintain their comfortable life at a time when others were at war and needed their support." As SOCOM commander, McRaven continued, he had initiated a separate investigation that ultimately cleared Losey of wrongdoing. McRaven characterized the rescinding of the promotion as yet another example of Congress wrongly punishing the military for political purposes. "Over the past decade I have seen a disturbing trend in how politicians abuse and denigrate military leadership, particularly the officer corps, to advance their political agendas," the retired admiral wrote. In words that could not have been fully appreciated by a public unaware of his brush with Representative Frelinghuysen, McRaven asserted, "During my past several years in uniform, I watched in disbelief how lawmakers treated the chairman, the service chiefs, the combatant commanders and other senior officers during Congressional testimony. These officers were men of incredible integrity, and yet some lawmakers showed no respect for their decades of service."

When Votel assumed command of SOCOM in the summer of 2014, special operations forces were phasing out their participation in Village Stability Operations and most other activities in Afghanistan, as part of the contraction of the US military presence in the country to 10,000 troops. Concomitant with this change, Army Special Forces leaders were fighting to downgrade what was now commonly termed the "direct approach" of surgical strikes—conducted directly by US forces—in favor of the "indirect approach" of working "by, with, and through" foreign partners. It was an effort to divest the Special Forces from a shrinking business and return them to traditional missions such as counterinsurgency and the development of partner forces. "We have, in my view, exquisite capabilities to kill people," asserted Lieutenant General Charles T. Cleveland, commander of US Army Special Operations Command. "We need exquisite capabilities to manipulate them." Cleveland emphasized the value of the indirect approach in preventing conflicts from heating up to the point that large-scale American intervention became necessary.

Even Naval Special Operations, which had always been more inclined than the Special Forces toward the direct approach, called for emphasis on indirect missions. A new edition of its core doctrinal publication, NWP 3-05, issued in May 2013, paid homage to Admiral Eric Olson's remark that "direct action is important, not decisive; indirect action is decisive." The shift signified recognition that the SEALs, like the rest of SOF, would soon be spending most of their time outside of active war zones, in countries where they could not raid homes on a nightly basis.

New opportunities to test the indirect approach soon appeared. In the middle of 2014, special operations forces were summoned back to Iraq in response to the capture of Mosul, Iraq's second-largest city, by the Islamic State of Iraq and Syria (ISIS). Following the withdrawal of all US military forces from Iraq at the end of 2011, Prime Minister Nouri al-Maliki had accelerated the persecution of Sunni politicians and the purging of Sunni officers from the security forces, which rekindled the Sunni population's interest in supporting Islamic extremists. At the same time, Maliki had sidelined the American civilians whom the Obama administration had hoped would carry out counterterrorism operations in lieu of US military forces. With Baghdad now in danger of falling, Obama rushed several thousand US troops to Iraq, a large percentage of them special operators.

The White House tasked the newly returned troops with advising and assisting Iraqi forces, but forbade them to leave the bases where they were stationed. During the heat of battle, Iraqi forces had to direct American air strikes on their own, a process for which they were ill prepared. Obtaining American concurrence to an Iraqi request for a strike often took an hour, by which time ISIS fighters had usually moved someplace else. For the next year, ISIS continued to seize territory in Iraq's Sunni areas, including the critical city of Ramadi in May 2015.

The accumulation of ISIS victories ultimately led Obama to loosen restrictions on American participation in operations. He made the change without notifying the public, but it came to light in October 2015, when an ISIS gunman killed a Delta operator, Master Sergeant Joshua L. Wheeler, one of thirty Americans from Delta Force who had joined Iraqi Kurdish forces in raiding an ISIS facility near Kirkuk. News of Wheeler's death, the first American fatality from hostile fire in Iraq since the return of US forces, infuriated liberals as well as conservatives, doves as well as hawks, who pointed out that it contradicted repeated White House assertions that US forces in Iraq had no combat role. The Obama administration, it appeared, was exploiting the secrecy surrounding special operations forces to involve the United States more deeply in Iraq than it was saying publicly, much as Lyndon Johnson had done in Vietnam fifty years earlier.

The allegations provoked a series of convoluted and contradictory verbal contortions from Obama administration spokespersons, which only exacerbated the doubts about the government's candor and policies. Pentagon press secretary Peter Cook initially attempted to explain away the raid by describing it as a onetime event, a "unique circumstance" driven by urgent battlefield necessity. Secretary of Defense Ashton Carter then backed away from that argument, conceding, "We'll do more raids." Carter proceeded to explain that US involvement in the raid "doesn't represent us assuming a combat role. It represents a continuation of our advise and assist mission." When pressed on the administration's parsing of words, Carter admitted that "this is combat."

The White House also gave special operations forces the task of training 5,000 rebels to fight ISIS inside Syria, where a vicious civil war dating back to 2011 had facilitated the growth of Sunni extremist movements. To fund the program, Obama asked Congress for $500 million, or $100,000 per Syrian rebel, which seemed a steep price at the time. According to the administration, the force was intended merely to secure select areas and facilitate a diplomatic resolution of the civil war, not to wipe out ISIS, as that task would have required much larger forces.

Congress approved funding for the training program in September 2014, and the search for recruits began soon thereafter. The barriers to organizing Syrian rebel forces proved immense. Past American reluctance to support rebel factions had allowed Syria's government and Syrian extremist groups to destroy or co-opt the moderate nationalist elements of the opposition, leaving few people on the Syrian dance floor whom the Americans did not find repulsive. Because most of the remaining oppositionists inside Syria were extremists or closely tied to extremists, the White House restricted recruitment of the new force to Syrians in exile, but even many of the exiles turned out to carry the taint of extremism. Furthermore, a narrow White House focus on the ISIS threat resulted in a stipulation that the rebels should combat only ISIS, not the Syrian regime of Bashar al-Assad, which turned off many resistance elements, for whom the Assad regime was the most loathsome enemy.

One year into the program, CENTCOM commander Lloyd Austin reported that just fifty-four rebel fighters had been trained. The total number operating in Syria, he disclosed, was "four or five." Derisive press reports noted that the program's costs, which in total had risen to $580 million, came out to nearly $10 million per trained fighter. The White House terminated the program in October 2015.

Backsliding also occurred in Afghanistan. In the hurry to extricate the United States from a war that was more difficult and less popular than originally anticipated, the Obama administration had taken the training wheels off the Afghan forces too soon. As US troops had pulled out of Afghanistan in 2013 and 2014, the insurgents had inflicted staggering casualties on Afghan security forces, to include the Afghan Local Police. The task of preventing the Afghans from landing face-first on the pavement went to the dwindling number of special operations forces remaining in the country. Those forces, which were supposed to have turned everything over to their Afghan counterparts by the beginning of 2015, were still going on six to ten missions with the Afghans per week in the middle of that year. Forty times per week, Americans were providing the Afghan special operations forces with intelligence, logistical support, air cover, or other assistance. Some American special operators continued to launch unilateral raids against Al Qaeda and other high-priority targets.

This residual American support for the Afghan government failed to prevent the insurgents from regaining control of much of the countryside during 2015. Several dozen districts came entirely under Taliban sway. Insurgents overran the city of Kunduz in September 2015 and held it for several days before elite Afghan forces, supported by US troops, arrived to drive them out. The situation so alarmed Obama that he decided on October 15, 2015, to cancel his plans to remove all US troops from Afghanistan by the end of his second term.

In January 2016, American special operators deployed to Helmand Province to prevent the Taliban from overrunning the besieged provincial capital and help Afghan forces retake territory lost in 2015. Insurgent control of the population put the Afghan government forces and the American special operators at serious disadvantage, as the citizens were likely to tip off the insurgents of approaching adversaries, and unlikely to divulge the location of insurgents or their IEDs. On January 5, hostile forces killed Sergeant Matthew McClintock of the 19th Special Forces Group and wounded two other American special operators.

News of an American special operator killed in combat again raised complaints that US troops were more heavily engaged than the president was admitting publicly. According to the official White House line, America's "combat mission" in Afghanistan had come to a "responsible conclusion" at the end of 2014. In October 2015, Obama had said that US forces in Afghanistan "remain engaged in two narrow but critical missions, training Afghan forces and supporting a counterterrorism mission against the remnants of al-Qaida." Most of the enemy combatants in the area where Sergeant McClintock died, however, belonged not to Al Qaeda, but to the Taliban.

"Light-footprint" counterterrorism fared even worse in the other countries where it was applied, for in those countries a number of conditions that had aided in the success of surgical strikes in Afghanistan and Iraq were absent. The possession of 100,000 conventional US troops, and the diplomatic clout that goes with such a presence, had prevented the governments of Afghanistan and Iraq from imposing severe constraints on American strike teams. In most other countries, the government refused to give foreign special operators carte blanche to break into houses and handcuff suspects. Threats from the Pakistani government deterred American SOF operations into Pakistan after the Bin Laden raid. The Libyan government forbade American raids after an operation in October 2013 in which American special operators had abducted a terrorism suspect on Libyan soil. In Yemen, where Al Qaeda in the Arabian Peninsula plotted sophisticated bombing attacks that nearly downed several international airliners, the government of Ali Abdullah Saleh rejected the Obama administration's requests to let American special operators target extremists in the nation's hinterlands.

Such governments were generally more receptive to American offers to train their forces in counterinsurgency operations, for expansion of their control over national territory held greater appeal than sporadic raids against individuals whom the Americans deemed threatening. American special operators assisted the Pakistanis in counterinsurgency—until they were kicked out in the aftermath of the Bin Laden raid. Libyan authorities reached agreements with the United States and other countries to train security forces that would reclaim ground from fractious militia groups, though the United States was slow to follow through on its training promises, owing to security concerns and the theft of equipment from a base where Americans had begun training a small counterterrorism force.

In Iraq and Afghanistan, the enormity of the US military presence had given the Defense Department a privileged position in internecine bureaucratic swordfights, a reality that led many in uniform to believe that the military could do as it pleased in any foreign country. In most other nations, however, the Defense Department had to gain concurrence from the State Department before taking actions, and the State Department often refused to concur. Special operators who showed up in third-world countries expecting to employ skills honed on the battlefields of Iraq or Afghanistan found themselves put on indefinite hold by diplomats who viewed the proposed actions as unnecessary and reckless. Civilian officials obstructed SOF interaction with foreign military personnel through the use of the Leahy Amendment, which prohibited training of units alleged to have committed human rights violations. When State Department diplomats became sufficiently fed up, they employed their authority over the entrance of US government personnel into foreign nations to deny special operators permission to set foot in a country.

One of the most serious clashes between special operators and the State Department took place in the West African country of Mali. During early 2012, special operations forces warned of a growing Al Qaeda presence in northern Mali and recommended more robust military support to the Malian government. The US ambassador to Mali dismissed the warnings as unwarranted alarmism and rejected the recommendations. Subsequent Al Qaeda advances against poorly supplied Malian Army forces sparked accusations among Malian military officers that a corrupt civilian government had let the army down, leading to a military coup d'état on March 21.

American special operators wanted, at minimum, to maintain existing levels of support to Mali's armed forces after the coup. They were overridden by US civilian officials, who terminated all military aid as a means of punishing the Malian military for ousting a democratically elected government. The loss of US support and the turmoil resulting from post-coup purges crippled Mali's armed forces, thereby throwing open the door to Al Qaeda, which gained control of all northern Mali within a few weeks. When Al Qaeda attempted to conquer Mali's capital in January 2013, American special operators recommended that they be given permission to help the Malian armed forces, but permission was denied by the State Department. Only the intervention of French air and ground units prevented the Al Qaeda curtain from falling over all of Mali.

The discord between US special operations forces and the State Department over Mali eventually leaked into the press. Under fire for ignoring warnings about rising extremism, State Department officials attempted to shift blame to the special operators. "Years of training by United States Special Forces did not stop the Malian military from fleeing when the Islamist insurgency started last January," sniped Vicki Huddleston, the former US ambassador to Mali. "In fact, the military exacerbated the chaos by overthrowing Mali's democratically elected government last March."

US military officers countered that the weaknesses of Mali's military stemmed from corruption and inefficiency at the upper levels of Mali's civil government—problems that fell within the State Department's port-folio. Malian bureaucrats had reshuffled soldiers after they received a round of American training, denying those soldiers the prolonged expo-sure to American training that was required for major improvements in skills and organizational culture. Special operators did, however, admit to one serious mistake, the sporadic scheduling of their training cycle. Amer-ican trainers had often shown up for thirty days or six weeks at a time, which was too short, even if the Malian soldiers were not undergoing fre-quent reshuffling. Recognition of this deficiency in the Malian training programs ultimately led SOF to shift from episodic training to continuous training in a multitude of nations.

Further resistance to special operations beyond Iraq and Afghanistan came from the White House, whose principal occupant was especially in-clined to worry that aggressive military actions on the ground would en-tangle the United States in protracted wars. Captain Robert A. Newson, the commander of the US special operations headquarters in Yemen from 2010 to 2012, advocated assistance to Yemeni forces in counterinsurgency so that those forces could eject Al Qaeda, Iranian-backed Houthi rebels, and other insurgent groups. Surgical strikes alone could not keep the en-emy at bay, argued Newson, because "you cannot hold the jungle back with a weed whacker." The White House rejected Newson's recommen-dation out of concern that it would draw the United States into conflicts with rebel groups that did not already have plans to attack the United States. For several years, the Obama administration would rely on preci-sion drone strikes as the main counterterrorist weapon in Yemen.

The unwillingness of the United States to help the Yemeni government assert control over its population impeded the collection of intelligence for the surgical strikes, a fact that contributed to the high number of drone missiles that mistakenly hit civilian targets, including a passenger bus and a wedding party. The killing of innocent civilians by drones so enraged Yemeni tribes that they sent young men in droves to serve in Al Qaeda. During the peak period of the drone campaign, the strength of Al Qaeda's Yemen branch increased from 300 to more than 1,000. Widespread con-demnation of the drone program in Yemen, on practical as well as moral grounds, eventually convinced the Obama administration to curtail the number of strikes.

The lack of counterinsurgency operations in Yemen ultimately allowed the insurgent jungle to swallow up the national government. At the beginning of 2015, Houthi rebels seized the capital city of Sanaa and dismembered the central administration, resulting in the collapse of the national armed forces and intelligence services. The Houthis and Al Qaeda looted $500 million worth of US military equipment from military arsenals. Flinging open the doors to the regime's jails, they set free extremists who had taken years, and in some cases large amounts of US assistance, to incarcerate. The Obama administration evacuated all US government personnel, including the CIA and special operations personnel who had directed the surgical strikes.

The few ground raids that special operations forces actually conducted outside of Iraq and Afghanistan in Obama's second term showed raiding to be enormously difficult in places where the absence of counterinsurgency operations left insurgents fully in charge. In Somalia, occasional raids by US and European special operations forces against extremists were often cut short by the need to escape before a hostile armed population surrounded and overpowered them. On the night of October 5, 2013, for instance, a team of Navy SEALs that went ashore in the coastal city of Baraawe to target an extremist commander had to turn back after a sentry's opening shots drew much of the local community to the scene, assault rifles in hand.

While the overwhelming majority of raids in the Obama era were aimed at capturing or killing the enemy, a small number sought to liberate Americans or other westerners held hostage by extremists. The rescue of Jessica Buchanan and Poul Hagen Thisted in January 2012 stood out as a notable victory, as did the liberation of five British and American aid workers in Afghanistan in May and December of that year.

Several other rescue missions did not end as happily. In the early summer of 2014, two dozen Delta operators raided an oil refinery in northern Syria where they thought ISIS was holding journalist James Foley and other American hostages. The raiding force discovered that the hostages were gone, having been relocated on a prior date. A few months later, ISIS beheaded Foley and posted a video of the act online.

On December 6, 2014, forty Navy SEALs raided an Al Qaeda prison camp in Yemen, where they hoped to find American Luke Somers and

South African Pierre Korkie. As the rescue team advanced on the ground, a guard dog barked, putting an end to any sleepiness or complacency that might have encumbered the Al Qaeda guards. One guard, discerning that American forces were attempting a hostage rescue, shot Somers and Korkie. The special operators quickly vanquished the guards, and when they found Somers and Korkie discovered that the two men were still alive, but just barely. Medics rushed the bleeding men out on a V-22 Osprey. Korkie died on the aircraft, and Somers died on an operating table aboard the USS *Makin Island*.

The renewed need for special operations forces in Iraq and Afghanistan and the multitude of tasks that the White House kept assigning the special operations forces dashed hopes that the frequent deployments of the post-9/11 era would come to an end. While the special operators were not deploying as frequently as at the peak of the wars in Iraq and Afghanistan, an average of 7,200 were deployed at one time in 2015, far above the 2,900 of 2001. Unfavorable rates of divorce, mental illness, and other maladies continued.

Late in Obama's second term, special operations forces were swept up in the White House push for integrating women into combat units. During Defense Department reviews of the matter in 2015, a Rand Corporation survey of 7,600 special operations troops found that 85 percent of those in combat specialties opposed allowing women into combat positions. The opposition was based not only on personal views about gender differences and roles, but also on actual experiences in the latest wars, where women had been placed alongside special operations combat units as members of Cultural Support Teams and other programs to interact with female civilians in countries that abhorred contact between their women and American military men.

The special operators who opposed the change, of whom a substantial number were women, predicted a host of adverse consequences. Among those most commonly cited were declines in unit cohesion, reductions in entrance standards in the name of gender diversity, illicit sexual liaisons, and interpersonal conflicts. Such problems had already emerged in the Cultural Support Team program. In addition, more than 80 percent of the survey respondents said that women did not have the physical strength required for combat jobs. "I weigh 225 pounds, and 280 pounds in full kit, as did most of the members of my ODA," one respondent said. "I expect every person on my team to be able to drag any member of my team out of a firefight. A 130 pound female could not do it, I don't care how much time she spends in the gym. Do we expect a wounded man to bleed out because a female soldier could not drag him to cover?"

In December 2015, Obama decreed that women would be allowed into all combat positions in the military, special operations forces included. For the special operators, of whom so much was still asked, the indifference to their opinions was another indication that the White House's love affair with special operations forces was over.

FOLLOWING OPERATION NEPTUNE Spear, President Barack Obama designated the surgical strike America's principal counterterrorism weapon, asserting that it could attain strategic objectives independently of other scalpels and hammers. Obama cited the replacement of counterinsurgency with light-footprint counterterrorism in justifying the withdrawal of US military forces from Iraq and Afghanistan. Taking advantage of the secrecy inherent in America's special operations forces, he involved the United States in military operations without informing the public, presumably because keeping military forces hidden from view would prevent the American people from questioning the reopening of wars that he had previously declared over. When special operations forces began to suffer fatalities, discontent arose in an American public that wished to remain apprised of its nation's participation in combat.

Surgical strikes remained JSOC's top priority throughout Obama's presidency, but the number of strikes declined as America's presence in Afghanistan shrank and JSOC ran into high obstacles erected by foreign governments, the State Department, and the White House. As Village Stability Operations came to an end in Afghanistan, the special operations units that had been assigned to that program looked for new places where they could work by, with, and through partners. The rise of ISIS appeared to portend opportunities in Iraq, Syria, and beyond, but those opportunities were slow to develop because of White House reluctance to deploy large numbers of troops into danger zones.

The Bin Laden raid was a tactical success that may have had some strategic benefit in weakening Al Qaeda, but its negative strategic consequences likely outweighed its benefits. By antagonizing the Pakistani government, it gravely undermined US counterterrorism and counterinsurgency efforts in Pakistan, ensuring that Al Qaeda could stay in business under new management. In Afghanistan, SOF strike forces took huge bites out of the enemy, yet they could not have decisive strategic effects because of the premature withdrawal of US forces from counterinsurgency. In Yemen, reliance on precision counterterrorism in the absence of counterinsurgency resulted in total failure, as insurgents tore down the whole government and sent the Americans packing.

Because of President Obama's emphasis on surgical strikes, conventional forces served increasingly often in supporting roles to special operations forces. The lavishing of praise, funding, and power on special operations forces after the Bin Laden raid led Admiral McRaven to seek new resources and authorities, and to trample over the rest of the military in the process. SOCOM alienated not only the Pentagon but also Congress, which used its constitutional prerogatives to stifle much of McRaven's agenda. After a brief period in which special operations forces appeared to be the kings of the mountain, they were thrown from the crest, compelled to go back to working in cooperation with the rest of their military brethren.

CHAPTER 11

CONCLUSION

H istorical facts, and generalizations derived from those facts, do not provide ready-made formulas for future action. Indeed, those who have endeavored to generate such formulas have a lengthy record of committing strategic errors, the result of assuming similarities between situations that are dissimilar in part or in whole. Acquisition of historical understanding, nevertheless, is the most important step in developing the familiarization that is essential to making sound decisions in a complex environment. Individuals who have examined a variety of historical situations can draw on a broader range of tools and gauge the effectiveness of the tools more accurately than individuals who have not. Their awareness of past failures reduces the likelihood that they will repeat the errors of the past.

PRESIDENTIAL LEADERSHIP

From the beginning, American presidents and their top appointees have guided the development of special operations forces, devoting to them amounts of attention well out of proportion to the size of those forces. President Franklin Roosevelt and his top military adviser, General George Marshall, sired a large family of special operations forces in World War II, mainly for reasons of alliance politics, in the case of the Rangers, Force-men, and Marauders, or amateurish fascination, in the case of the Raiders and the OSS special operations forces. Among the special operations units of World War II, only the Navy's Frogmen were formed as the result of dispassionate assessment of their military usefulness. It was not coincidental that the Frogmen were the most effective and strategically valuable special operations forces of the war.

Of all US presidents, only John F. Kennedy arrived in office with a strong interest in special operations forces, and for that reason he would do more than any other president to further their cause. Multiplying the Army Special Forces and forming new units in the Navy and Air Force, he built special operations forces up to sizes that would safeguard them from the disbandment that had stricken some of their forerunners. Kennedy broadened the geographic reach of the special operations forces and shifted their operational focus to a new mission, counterinsurgency, for which their services were much needed in light of the Communist world's support for third-world insurgencies.

Although none of Kennedy's successors entered the presidency with much knowledge of or affection for special operations forces, the onset of war or other national emergencies drove many of them to take an interest. The inability of diplomacy to resolve the Iran hostage crisis led Jimmy Carter to turn to special operations forces for a last-ditch rescue mission. When airpower could not defeat Saddam Hussein's Scud missiles, President George H. W. Bush called upon JSOC. Bill Clinton summoned Delta Force to get rid of the warlord who was interfering with the administration's nation-building project in Somalia. George W. Bush sent the Special Forces into Afghanistan after the 9/11 attacks because they were the military force capable of striking back most quickly at the Taliban and Al Qaeda. The need to hit Al Qaeda around the world led Bush's secretary of defense, Donald Rumsfeld, to transform JSOC into a global manhunting force.

Special operations forces became instruments of partisan politics for a few presidents. In the case of Lyndon Johnson, the secrecy surrounding special operations forces made them an attractive weapon for jabbing

North Vietnam during the presidential campaign of 1964, when he wanted Vietnam to stay out of the newspapers. Barack Obama was drawn to the use of surgical strikes because, among other things, they enabled him to show the American public that he was combating terrorism forcefully and efficiently. When conditions deteriorated in Afghanistan, Iraq, and Syria late in his presidency, Obama sent special operations forces into combat surreptitiously—and in contravention of public promises that US troops would not participate in combat—for what appeared to be reasons of political self-interest. Revelations of these activities, via the deaths of special operators, damaged confidence in the government and its commander-in-chief among Americans who expected their government to be transparent on the use of American troops in combat.

Special operators have learned the hard way that large reservoirs of presidential support for special operations forces can evaporate at a moment's notice. The early enthusiasm of the Roosevelt, Clinton, and Obama administrations gave way to indifference, the result of disappointing performances or changes in White House priorities. In a few instances, the special operators even became scapegoats for failed policies. With the loss of presidential backing, special operations forces lost resources and prestige, and were exposed to the kicks and punches of bureaucratic adversaries. The special operations forces of the future will have to make the case for their importance to each new president and strive to maintain presidential favor by proving their importance to national security, while keeping in mind the possibility that a president can lose interest or turn against them despite their best efforts.

History suggests that future presidents will be prone to making decisions on the sizes and activities of special operations forces based on superficial and romanticized views of those forces. To avert that outcome, presidents and their staffs will need to receive sober assessments of SOF capabilities and strategic utility, which they must then incorporate into the decision-making process. Presidents, being highly political animals, will continue to face temptations to use special operations forces to serve partisan political agendas. For the good of the republic and the special operations forces, they would be well advised to resist those temptations.

ROLES AND MISSIONS

From their founding, special operations forces have struggled to find roles and missions that matched both their capabilities and the nation's strategic needs. Special operations doctrine writers, Pentagon hairsplitters, and guardians of bureaucratic turf have repeatedly tried to solidify roles and missions by promulgating definitions of special operations. Congress and the Department of Defense have also attempted to delineate special operations by specifying a set of SOF missions.

These efforts have been undercut by the overlap between the purported SOF roles and missions and the actual activities of conventional forces. Further weakening the viability of definitions and mission sets has been their irrelevance to real-world decisions on the assignment of roles and missions. Throughout the history of special operations forces, the evolution of roles and missions has been guided not by conformance to a particular definition or list, but rather by the determination of political or military leaders that the military needed new capabilities to keep pace with evolving tactical or strategic requirements. Eager to participate in the nation's wars, special operations forces have tailored their roles and missions to make themselves attractive to the holders of executive and budgetary authority.

The roles and missions for which the special operators trained often ended up bearing little resemblance to what the nation ultimately demanded of them. During World War II, the training of most special operations forces concentrated on raiding behind enemy lines, but few opportunities for such raids presented themselves, so the units ended up fighting as line infantry, a task for which they were not sufficiently equipped. The Rangers went through the same experience in Korea, where the war shifted from one of fluid front lines to one of fixed defensive positions before most of the Rangers were ready to commence raiding.

The preparation of OSS special operations forces for supporting resistance forces proved a better match to the operational requirements prevailing at the time when the forces came off the assembly line. The effective utilization of OSS special operators in World War II inspired the creation of the US Army Special Forces in 1952 and the designation of unconventional warfare as their main mission. For their first decade, the Special Forces were trained to support resistance forces in Eastern Europe during a world war that was never to be.

President Kennedy's insistence that SOF take a leading role in counterinsurgency and expand beyond Europe put an end to nearly a decade of peace for the special operators. The largest special operations program in Vietnam, the Civilian Irregular Defense Groups, began as a counterinsurgency initiative, though it morphed into an unconventional warfare program as time wore on. In Vietnam, the Special Forces also entered the business of covert reconnaissance in enemy territory, and the SEALs began their tradition of unilateral surgical strikes.

For several decades after Vietnam, changes in the global security environment steered the evolution of SOF roles and missions. The rise in hostage taking in the 1970s led to the revival of the Rangers and the creation of Delta Force, SEAL Team Six, and JSOC. Opportunities to rescue hostages were scarce, inducing the special operators and their civilian overseers to search for other tasks. The Rangers delved into air assault, while the Special Forces worked further on reconnaissance, enabling both to participate in the invasions of Grenada and Panama. JSOC developed surgical strike capabilities that it put to use in Colombia and Somalia.

Technological advancement spurred changes in SOF roles and missions at the beginning of the twenty-first century. The advent of precision bombs afforded new opportunities to direct firepower in support of conventional forces, a task the special operators performed so well in Afghanistan in 2001 that the Northern Alliance vanquished the much larger Taliban in nine weeks. The information revolution enabled SOF to collect and exploit information on insurgent personnel to a degree never before seen. These developments, it should be noted, did not simply fall into the lap of special operations forces, but were instead driven by proactive and creative leadership, and also by high funding levels and acquisition authorities that put the new technologies in the hands of operators much more quickly than the plodding military acquisition bureaucracy normally permitted.

The new opportunities for surgical strikes fueled demand for special operations forces in Iraq and Afghanistan, ending a three-decade period in which the supply of special operations forces exceeded demand. This turn of events relieved SOF of the task of conjuring up new missions to justify their existence, and instead necessitated choices as to which roles and missions they would perform and which they would not. In Iraq, the emphasis on surgical strikes kept the "white SOF"—all those besides JSOC—out of the population-security operations of counterinsurgency, which had traditionally been one of their strengths. White SOF moved back into that mission in Afghanistan with the Village Stability Operations program, rotating personnel in from all regions of the world to work with the Afghan Local Police. They sought to continue in that direction as they pulled out of Afghanistan, but their attempts to support foreign governments in counterinsurgency, in places like Yemen and Guatemala, encountered stiff resistance from the White House and the State Department, which were leery of deepening US involvement in armed conflicts. White SOF, moreover, were needed to shore up security forces in the countries that the US government had intended to leave—Iraq and Afghanistan.

The downsizing of America's presence in Iraq and Afghanistan brought an end to the era of ten raids per night, which forced JSOC to look elsewhere for opportunities. But outside of Iraq and Afghanistan, foreign governments and the US State Department restricted their activities. Escalating strife and turmoil in the Middle East and Eastern Europe during Obama's second term, however, ensured that JSOC would still have extremists to hunt, hostages to rescue, and partners to train.

Today's SOF should expect that changing administrations and changing circumstances will require SOF to take on new roles and missions. Although the future is in many respects unpredictable, SOF will be better prepared if they devote some attention now to potential trouble spots. Once the 911 call comes in from the White House, they will likely have little or no time for further study of places, people, or tasks.

The White House's 2012 Defense Strategic Guidance ruled out preparedness for large-scale counterinsurgency campaigns in the belief that the United States would not need to fight such wars in the future. But in neither Afghanistan nor Iraq did the United States expect or want to get involved in prolonged counterinsurgency. It is not difficult to imagine the United States getting sucked into another large counterinsurgency in a country from which a devastating terrorist attack has been launched on the United States, such as Syria, Libya, Yemen, Pakistan, or Somalia. There is also reason to believe that the United States could get drawn into prolonged operations in a host of other unstable countries, such as North Korea, Iran, Turkey, Saudi Arabia, Tunisia, Egypt, Panama, Ukraine, or the Baltic States. Special operations forces therefore ought to resist the urge to put their counterinsurgency capabilities in the attic.

Counterinsurgency skills are worth keeping not just for the sake of counterinsurgency, but also for the sake of insurgency, since the two require most of the same skills. The United States is already supporting insurgents in Syria, Libya, and Yemen. Next could be Iran, Pakistan, or the Baltic States.

Because linguistic and cultural proficiencies are highly valuable assets in counterinsurgency and insurgency, SOF would be well advised to maintain those proficiencies. Individuals and units will need to be prepared for a broad range of languages and cultures, considering the unpredictability of future conflict. In the period leading up to 9/11, it should be remembered, the Special Forces had learned the languages of a lengthy list of countries where they expected to operate, and yet the list had not included Afghanistan.

Although nuclear deterrence has greatly reduced the likelihood of war between large powers, recent events have given reason to believe that a war could still break out between the United States and either China or Russia. The United States could also find itself in a conventional war against a smaller power, such as Iran or North Korea. In the event of a conventional conflict, large numbers of special operations forces could be needed to help organize resistance movements, conduct strategic reconnaissance, guide bombs, serve as combat advisers to allied forces, or raid targets in the enemy's rear. The odds of a conventional war remain sufficiently low, though, that training in specialized skills for such wars should be reserved for a relatively small subset of SOF.

There already exists a strong need for SOF to advise partner forces in small-scale conventional warfare, as a result of deteriorating security in Afghanistan and Iraq and the rise of hostile armies in failing or failed states such as Syria, Somalia, Libya, and Yemen. These are the latest of many unforeseen cases in which SOF have ended up training conventional forces in combined arms warfare. In the past, special operations forces have not always been sufficiently prepared for this type of work, and given their many other roles and missions, they probably will not be able to keep enough troops versed in this capability to meet the demand. It is one of several activities for which conventional forces can and should take over some of the burden.

Whatever else happens, SOF are certain to remain heavily engaged in training and educating a multitude of foreign partners, in everything from surgical strikes to guerrilla warfare to combat policing to forensics. Having allies do the heavy lifting is almost always less expensive, politically as well as economically, than having Americans do it. But training and educating allies is easier said than done. SOF must obtain State Department and White House concurrence for most of these activities, and difficult decisions must be made on which countries and which organizations within those countries are the optimal partners.

EFFECTIVENESS

Because decisions on SOF resources, roles, and missions have been based heavily on perceptions of SOF tactical and strategic effectiveness, special operators have worked hard to make the case that they are highly effective, and their detractors have likewise labored to paint them as ineffectual. Assessing tactical success is relatively straightforward, and SOF, by virtue of superior talent and special training, have usually excelled tactically, albeit with some significant exceptions. In strategic terms, however, SOF contributions have usually been disputed, for strategic consequences are often opaque or ambiguous. The strategic impact of special operations has usually been constrained by the parameters of the strategic environment, the small size of SOF, or flaws in the overall strategy.

The Rangers and Forcemen, like the British Commandos that inspired them, were originally conceived as strategic raiding forces whose raids against Nazi Germany would obviate a massive invasion of Western Europe. When the United States and Britain changed their minds and decided to invade Europe with 2 million men, raiding forces became bit players in a contest between titanic conventional armies. Frequently fighting as regular infantry, the Rangers and Forcemen lacked adequate heavy weaponry, which largely offset the tactical advantages accruing from the superiority of their personnel. In the Pacific, the tactical effectiveness of Marine Raiders and Merrill's Marauders was likewise undermined by insufficiencies of heavy equipment. In both theaters, opportunities for raiding and other specialized missions suited to their capabilities were so scarce that the units were disbanded before war's end.

The successes of OSS special operations forces in supporting resistance movements in France and Burma were momentous enough to influence military events at the strategic level, though they were always secondary in importance to the labors of heavy divisions and heavy bombers. OSS special operators attempted to exert strategic influence in the war's latter days by managing resistance groups that aspired to run their countries after the war, at times without consulting senior US military or civilian officials. This influence was mainly by accident rather than by design, a by-product of the fact that the OSS operators were the only Americans working directly with the resistance leaders. Untutored in local politics, they dabbled in political affairs so amateurishly that their actions often undermined American interests, as in the cases of Yugoslavia and Indochina.

In the European and Asian theaters of World War II, and also in later conflicts where special operations forces attempted to support resistance movements, the effectiveness of resistance organizations depended more on the insurgents, counterinsurgents, and civilian populations already on the ground than on the foreign special operators who showed up to assist. The armed strength of Axis security forces varied widely from place to place, in some areas being so potent as to deter or destroy any would-be resistance. The willingness of local civilians to abet resistance movements figured heavily in the results achieved by those movements.

In Korea, the Rangers made significant tactical contributions by executing especially difficult infantry missions. The strategic gains of those operations were modest, however, and they came at the expense of the quality of US front-line units that had lost personnel to the Rangers. American special operators who organized resistance forces in North

Korea met with unequivocal tactical success, necessitating the diversion of enemy forces from the front lines, although not in quantities sufficient to affect the strategic outcome.

The geographic expansion of SOF beyond Europe, which began under Kennedy, had far-reaching effects for the training and educating of foreign military personnel, providing initial investments in countries where the United States would need friends decades down the road. The results of these efforts have varied enormously. The most effective took several decades to reach fruition, because that amount of time was needed to influence the culture of a generation of officers in its formative years and develop that generation as it rose into senior leadership positions. Short-term training, of which SOF have done a large amount, has generally been insufficient because it does not change cultural attitudes.

The relatively small size of special operations forces has put major limitations on their training of foreign forces. Lacking the manpower to train a nation's entire armed forces in a short period of time, the special operators have often focused on training elite forces, which are small and typically have missions similar to those of their American counterparts. But the meager size of those elite forces usually prevents them from working strategic changes in a country. A few elite companies cannot keep insurgents out of any country larger than Liechtenstein. American special operations forces have made the most of small numbers when concentrating their personnel at a government's central institutions of training and education, because it has enabled them to influence much of that government's leadership.

Ever since President Kennedy's immersion of special operations forces in counterinsurgency, the strategic value of their participation in counterinsurgency has been constrained by scale. The mobilization of South Vietnam's tribal minorities through the Civilian Irregular Defense Group program helped America's allies in South Vietnam gain control over territory and combat infiltrators from North Vietnam, but it was limited to one part of the country. Counterinsurgency, moreover, became secondary in strategic importance when Hanoi upped the ante by introducing North Vietnamese Army divisions, which could be stopped only through conventional warfare.

In Afghanistan, the commitment of a large share of SOF global manpower to Village Stability Operations yielded patches of tactical success. It was not enough, however, to make the program into a decisive strategic player, because the Afghan Local Police never constituted more than a small percentage of the Afghan government's security forces. Had the Afghan government authorized much larger numbers of Local Policemen, US conventional forces would have been obliged to provide most of the manpower for Village Stability Operations, since they had far more troops than SOF did, and hence the program would have become a conventional one, with conventional officers calling most of the shots.

America's special operations forces could attempt to overcome the limitations of size by growing further. But they have already increased from 38,000 to 70,000 since 9/11, while the rest of the military is in the midst of a protracted downsizing, a state of affairs that has necessarily lowered SOF selectivity. Another expansion of special operations forces would dilute the quality of those forces still further while depriving conventional forces of much-needed talent. Given the dependence of special operations forces on recruitment from the regular forces and the persistence of threats requiring conventional remedies, the best solution at the present time would be to expand conventional forces rather than special operations forces.

In the period after the Nunn-Cohen Amendment, the independent special operations funding line permitted quantitative and qualitative improvements in ground special operations forces as well as the creation of air forces dedicated to special operations. It also led to growth in the number of people who believed that SOF were a strategic instrument in their own right, rather than merely a supporting arm to conventional forces. This belief inspired the use of Delta Force in Operation Gothic Serpent. The failure of that operation resulted in the withdrawal of the entire US military from Somalia and the shelving of the idea of SOF as an independent strategic actor for the remainder of the decade. The idea returned early the next decade on account of the SOF role in the defeat of the Taliban. That brief war demonstrated the high strategic potential of combat advising in an era of precision munitions. It also showed, however, that the effectiveness of combat advising was still contingent upon the quality of the leaders who were being advised. The advising of the Northern Alliance succeeded

338 | OPPOSE ANY FOE

in large measure because Northern Alliance commanders were adept at organizing and leading large ground operations, whereas the advising of Afghan militias at Tora Bora was unproductive because those militias had inept leaders.

Donald Rumsfeld further advanced the concept of strategically decisive SOF with his manhunting campaigns. The "light-footprint counterterrorism" of the Obama administration took it further still, moving surgical strikes to the top of the nation's list of counterterrorism tools. Surgical strikes inflicted far more damage on insurgents in Iraq and Afghanistan than in any prior war, yet they did not win the war in either place. They could and did play a large part in defeating insurgents when undertaken in tandem with counterinsurgency operations that permanently secured the population. When they were not undertaken in such a manner, as in the early years of the Iraq War and the latter years of the Afghan War, the insurgents continued to prosper. The Obama administration's strategy of suppressing Yemen's terrorists with only surgical counterterrorism failed spectacularly, as insurgents were able to overrun the government and eliminate Yemeni and American counterterrorism capabilities. The raid that killed Osama bin Laden alienated Pakistan to such a degree that the Pakistani government ceased cooperation with the United States on numerous fronts, including counterterrorism operations against Al Qaeda.

Fate could hand SOF another opportunity to serve as a strategic weapon, as occurred in Afghanistan in 2001. But the scarcity of such opportunities in the historical record suggests that these opportunities will be few. Consequently, SOF will need to be integrated into the broader strategic enterprise under the direction of a unified theater military commander, as is generally true under the current system—preferably a unified commander who understands the strengths and limitations of special operations and does not harbor strong prejudices against those who execute them.

RELATIONSHIP WITH THE CONVENTIONAL MILITARY

Special operations forces were destined to clash with conventional forces from the moment they lured conventional troops with promises of service in an elite unit, which is to say from the very beginning. Selective recruitment, specialized training, and self-designation as elite forces encouraged special operators to view themselves as superior beings, which inevitably antagonized the conventional forces. The segregation of talented individuals in special operations forces aroused concerns about the detrimental effects on the conventional forces, concerns that multiplied as special operations forces grew in size. The conventional forces clearly suffered a loss in quality when some of their best people were transferred to special operations forces, but it was seldom as clear that the special operations forces accomplished enough to justify weakening the rest of the forces.

The emergence of research showing that a small, aggressive minority of combat troops did most of the fighting in World War II sparked complaints that SOF reliance on volunteers robbed the rest of the combat forces of the aggressive men who served as the spines of regular units. The end of the draft in 1973 and the advent of the all-volunteer force alleviated this problem, as young men who were devoid of aggressive spirit generally stayed out of the military. In terms of general aptitude and creativity, however, the special operations forces have remained a breed apart from most of their conventional colleagues.

The growth of special operations forces has resulted in the organizational separation of the two main types of military leaders, especially within the Army. Most individuals who attain leadership positions in large organizations fit into one of two personality categories, which the widely used Myers-Briggs typology calls "intuitive-thinking" and "sensing-judging." The special operations forces have attracted into their ranks large numbers of individuals from the "intuitive-thinking" category. People in this personality group rely heavily on intuition in comprehending the world, and they have a strong interest in the big picture and its changing dynamics. Willing to take large risks, they seek new solutions to strategic problems and eschew rigid adherence to standard operating procedures, which they view as unimaginative and unduly constraining. They appreciate the value of history but are selective in employing its lessons, weighing context heavily before drawing conclusions. They excel at sifting the flakes of gold from a mass of facts, and at using those flakes to reach decisions quickly. In the business world, these leaders predominate in fast-changing fields like investment banking and information technology, where their capabilities for understanding and adapting to complex environments are vital to profitability.

The concentration of "intuitive-thinking" officers in special operations forces has left the rest of the military's leadership with a high proportion of "sensing-judging" individuals. Relying mainly on the five senses to comprehend the world, the "sensing-judgers" are preoccupied with facts and tactics. They prefer to assemble massive PowerPoint decks, replete with statistics and charts, before making decisions. Averse to risks, they are inclined to do what has been done in the past and what is stipulated by rulebooks or doctrines. In the private sector, such leaders overflow in the leadership ranks of corporations whose activities change little over time and hence are well suited to standardization, such as facilities management and transportation.

The predominance of these "sensing-judging" leaders in conventional forces has put those forces at a disadvantage in tackling complex problems, a shortcoming that was manifested in combating insurgents in Iraq and Afghanistan. It could also affect US forces in a future conventional war, for conventional warfare also privileges leaders who can think outside the box, in the manner of Hannibal, Napoleon, and Nimitz.

One noteworthy exception to the personality trends of special operations forces is to be found in aviation. Officers in special operations aviation units have often demonstrated sensing-judging behaviors, presumably because the hell-raising pilots are too small in number to overrule the numerous officers in logistics, maintenance, engineering, and other mundane specialties that prize standardization and minimization of risk. Because of "jointness" requirements stemming from the Goldwater-Nichols Act of 1986, special operations ground units have often come under the command of special operations aviators whose sensing-judging tendencies clashed with the risk-taking and unconventional thinking of ground operators.

The most obvious remedy to this problem is to let the ground commanders deal with the ground operations and the aviation commanders with the air operations. But the two can seldom be separated so neatly, for air and ground operations routinely take place in concert, each one affecting the other, both requiring a single conductor to keep the orchestra playing in unison. Ground operators who wish to insert by helicopter in enemy territory must impose on aviators to take large risks, such as flying through bad weather or past enemy weaponry. Aviators intent on minimizing casualties must impose on ground operators to follow safety procedures that impede their effectiveness, like snapping in safety tethers or keeping aircraft doors shut. Ultimately it is up to the joint commander to balance the tradeoffs and decide which side must yield. Given that aviation almost always plays a supporting role to the ground forces and that its leadership's risk aversion can easily stifle action in an industry that demands risk taking, it makes more sense for that joint commander to be a ground operator.

The ongoing popularity of special operations forces among America's political leaders leaves little chance that they will be reduced in size for the purpose of improving the quality or creativity of the rest of the military. But other measures are available that could increase the percentage of unconventional thinkers in the conventional forces. The military could administer personality tests and employ personality profiles as a major criterion in recruiting and promotion, as the private sector does habitually. Officers who demonstrate creativity and insight could be given priority for the positions where those qualities are most in demand, such as combat arms leadership and strategic planning, while officers inclined toward standardization and risk mitigation could be steered to specializations best suited to those attributes, such as logistics, engineering, and financial management.

In the early decades of SOF, special operators had ample reason to complain that the conventional commanders were misusing them and depriving them of resources. With the growth of SOCOM, however, the pendulum began to swing, so that by the early twenty-first century, the conventional units were often used to support special operations forces that had equal or greater resources. The Bin Laden raid led SOCOM to push for a still more eminent position, which would come at the expense of the conventional forces. But, like Icarus, SOCOM tried to fly higher than its wings could carry it and ended up crashing back to earth.

For those in the military who sought to obstruct Admiral William McRaven's quest for a more powerful SOCOM, a chief point of contention was authority over the special operations forces deployed overseas. Whereas McRaven contended that the ability of adversaries to operate in multiple regions called for a US command that could operate across regional boundaries, the four-star regional commanders argued that they should be the masters of all military forces in their regions in the interest of unity of command. Both arguments have some merit. The resistance that McRaven encountered is likely to dissuade future SOCOM commanders from aspiring to the global authority that Donald Rumsfeld once envisioned for that organization. But such a change is possible if another president or secretary of defense champions the cause, or if the US government scraps the system of regional commanders and replaces it with a centralized command structure, as some reformers now advocate.

The evolving relationship between special and conventional forces has not consisted solely of envy and strife. After the first few years in Iraq, special operations forces and conventional forces learned that each could accomplish more by working together than separately, and therefore they often joined together in defeating insurgents in Iraq and Afghanistan. Such collaboration offers reason for hope that the two sides can work alongside one another fruitfully in the future. But collaboration of this sort is never inevitable; rather, it requires leaders who recognize the value of collaboration and are not obsessed with getting credit for their own actions. It also requires continuous effort by special operators to allay the resentments that flow naturally from the existence of elite forces. They should steadfastly heed General Stanley McChrystal's admonition after Desert Storm that special operators ought to "open up more, educate conventional leaders," and "avoid even the appearance of elitist attitudes or arrogance."

OPENNESS

Secrecy enables special operations forces to catch enemies unaware, and to undertake actions that might generate hostility toward the perpetrating nation were the identity of the perpetrating forces known. For these reasons, certain activities and methods of special operations forces deserve to remain enshrouded in secrecy. Some elements of the special operations bureaucracy, including a number of senior leaders, are inclined to hide not merely such secrets, but also a far broader range of information, much of which cannot in reality be kept hidden from enterprising journalists or members of Congress. Such an approach runs contrary to the long-term interests of America's special operations forces and the American nation as a whole.

External oversight and criticism are seldom pleasurable for those who are overseen or criticized, and they are sometimes misguided, but they are nonetheless as critical for special operations forces as for the rest of the military. Organizations that refuse to listen to recommendations for change, be they from outsiders or their own members, are likely to atrophy, if not become obsolete. No matter whether a military organization operates in the shadows or in broad daylight, it must share some information with the American public, Congress, other executive branch agencies, the media, and watchdog organizations, for the American people and their representative institutions are the fundamental sources of SOF personnel, funding, and authority. America's other military organizations, which in general have as much need as special operations forces to conceal certain methods and technologies from adversaries, have been able to keep secrets without perpetually cloistering themselves in high-security buildings.

One of the most damaging effects of excessive secretiveness is a lack of accountability for what in military parlance are called "toxic leaders"— individuals who put their interests above all else and thereby undermine subordinates, the institution, and the mission. Owing to the dearth of external monitoring, special operations forces are often left to police themselves, and they have sometimes been reluctant to remove toxic leaders because of personal connections, fear of attracting outside attention, or bureaucratic red tape. The elite status of SOF, the public adulation heaped onto the special operators, and the existence of the word "special" have contributed to the problem of toxic leadership by nurturing arrogance. They are not the root cause, though, for toxic leadership and arrogance can be found anywhere and they are often absent from SOF leaders. As Navy SEAL veteran Bob Schoultz has noted, the struggle between virtue and vanity in the leadership of militaries is timeless. "We can go back nearly 3,000 years and look at Homer's *Iliad*," Schoultz observes. Whereas Hector was "a great citizen, husband, father, and son," Achilles was "a selfish and ego-driven prima-donna who fought primarily for personal glory."

In recognition of the problems caused by toxic leaders within their ranks, the Navy SEALs recently modified their personnel selection processes to put more emphasis on personal integrity. Acing "Hell Week" and other SEAL selection rituals dating back to the Underwater Demolition Teams no longer guarantees admission into the club. Exceptional physical and mental fortitude remain prerequisites for SEALs, but the SEAL community has learned from hard experience that individuals of great strength and toughness can still suffer from severe flaws of character, which can manifest themselves when SEALs interact with each other, or, as is increasingly often the case, with people outside of their tight-knit organization.

If special operations forces are to have a bright future, the deciding factors will lie not in the realm of gadgets, money, or selection ordeals. Rather, they will be found in the talents and character of the people to whom the privilege of command is given. The decisions of these commanders, along with those of the civilian commander-in-chief, will determine whether the skills, valor, and devotion of special operations forces are channeled into activities of commensurate value to the national interest.

More broadly, undue secretiveness impedes the understanding, dialogue, and reflection that promote excellence in a profession, and especially a profession of arms. Published books, articles, and speeches encourage individuals to join an organization, and give them mental and emotional inspiration during their careers. Countless young Americans have sought entry into the special operations forces as a result of reading detailed and sober accounts of Eagle Claw or Gothic Serpent. Senior SOF officers seeking solutions to contemporary problems routinely turn to published histories of special operations forces in Vietnam, Colombia, or Iraq. Classified histories, by contrast, are too few in number, too inconsistent in quality, and too limited in dissemination to hold the attention of the special operations world.

To keep special operations forces under a broad blanket of secrecy is to aid those who would promote extreme and unrealistic views on the effectiveness of those forces. If little is known about their activities, SOF can easily be depicted as ineffectual, nefarious, or both. Conversely, lack of knowledge facilitates exaggeration of the capabilities and achievements of special operations forces. On repeated occasions, unscrupulous political and military leaders and media outlets have oversold special operations forces to American leaders and citizens who did not possess enough information to assess the sales pitches. Among those influenced by such salesmen have been commanders-in-chief and other high officials, such as John F. Kennedy, Donald Rumsfeld, and Barack Obama. Those leaders consequently relied too heavily on special operations forces, to the detriment of US foreign policy and the well-being of special operators. As a group of senior special operations veterans attested in October 2016, the makers of American foreign policy need to "educate themselves" on "the relative strengths and weaknesses of SOF, and when they should and should not be used."

History is the primary reference manual for humans confronting difficult challenges. It can be used well or poorly, but in general people make better decisions when they consult the manual than when they ignore it. How well history is used depends upon the capabilities and motives of the user, and also upon the quality of the history. If secretiveness renders history shallow or inaccurate, then even the most astute citizens, soldiers, and statesmen are liable to make bad decisions. For the sake of the special operations forces, their history must be published, the good as well as the bad, and it must be read.

ACKNOWLEDGMENTS

This book came to be as the result of a special operations history course I taught at the Joint Special Operations University in 2014 and 2015. I had the privilege of teaching the class with Will Irwin, a retired Special Forces lieutenant colonel and distinguished historian, who taught me a great deal about the history of the Jedburghs, of which he is a preeminent expert, and other special operations forces. Will helped me realize the need for a comprehensive history that pulled together the nuggets of truth scattered across thousands of special operations books and articles. Several additional colleagues at the Joint Special Operations University—Colonel Bill Knarr, Colonel Pete McCabe, Rob Nalepa, Jason Quirine, Rich Rubright, Colonel Greg Salomon, Anna Wyant, and Fred Zimmerman—further enriched my understanding of special operations.

Colonel Jeff Goble, the Joint Special Operations University vice president at the time, was also instrumental in convincing me of the need to write a book on this subject. Once the first draft of the manuscript was finished, he provided comments that were extremely helpful in the process of revision. A number of others in the special operations community, who cannot be named, also gave invaluable feedback on preliminary drafts.

A large number of current and former special operations personnel permitted me to interview them for this book. The interviewees whom I can mention by name are Lieutenant Colonel Wil R. Griego, Brigadier

General Hector E. Pagan, Brigadier General Richard W. Potter, Colonel Mark Rosengard, and Lieutenant General William P. Tangney.

I am indebted to those special operators who have blazed the way for historians through their analyses of special operations history, including Lieutenant Colonel Irwin as well as Colonel Bernd Horn, Admiral William McRaven, Colonel Alfred H. Paddock Jr., Major John L. Plaster, and Colonel Charles Simpson. Also deserving of gratitude are the veterans of special operations forces who have deepened the historical record by writing about their own experiences. Among them are James J. Altieri, Frank Antenori, Colonel Charlie Beckwith, Colonel Pete Blaber, Colonel Robert W. Black, Lieutenant General Jerry Boykin, Colonel Carl Eifler, Colonel John Gargus, Colonel Henry G. Gole, Major Thomas Greer, Eric L. Haney, Colonel Francis J. Kelly, Colonel R. Alan King, Colonel James H. Kyle, General Stanley McChrystal, Colonel Brian S. Petit, Nate Self, Major General John K. Singlaub, Marty Skovlund Jr., General Carl Stiner, Jeff Struecker, and Keni Thomas.

At Basic Books, Lara Heimert and Alex Littlefield saw promise in this subject matter and encouraged me to write a book about it. Lara and Roger Labrie offered highly incisive editorial advice, much to the benefit of the final product. In addition, Lara demonstrated exceptional patience when the government's security review of the book took far longer than scheduled. The extraordinary attention to detail of Katherine Streckfus and Melissa Veronesi in the latter stages of production removed errors and infelicities that had escaped my attention.

Deep thanks are due to Nadia Schadlow and the Smith Richardson Foundation, which supplied a grant that made this project possible. Chris Griffin gave me a home in Washington, DC, at the Foreign Policy Initiative while I completed the manuscript. Steve Sherman supplied documents on US Special Forces and connected me with Special Forces veterans.

My family provided the most vital support. My loving wife, Kelli, and our dutiful children, Greta, Trent, and Luke, bravely weathered the dislocations of a two-year odyssey to Tampa. They put up with a husband and father who at times became so absorbed in thoughts about special operations forces that he needed to be told repeatedly about dance performances, soccer games, and dinner dates.

NOTES

PROLOGUE

x   *shift to an alternate location:* Sean Naylor, *Relentless Strike: The Secret History of the Joint Special Operations Command* (New York: St. Martin's Press, 2015), 425–426.

x   *without a sound:* Jessica Buchanan and Erik Landemalm, *Impossible Odds: The Kidnapping of Jessica Buchanan and Her Dramatic Rescue by SEAL Team Six* (New York: Atria, 2013), 235–238.

x   *a desert hideout:* "In Somalia, Surviving a Kidnapping Against 'Impossible Odds,'" National Public Radio, May 14, 2013.

x   *their bargaining position:* Rachel Quigley, "American Aid Worker Describes Her 93 Days of Hell at the Hands of Somali Bandits Who Kidnapped Her and the Dramatic Navy SEAL Rescue Mission That Freed Her," *Daily Mail,* May 12, 2013.

xi   *big downer in the evening:* "Navy Seals Who Killed Osama bin Laden Rescue of 2 Hostages in Somalia," Associated Press, January 25, 2012.

xi   *lay back down:* "In Somalia, Surviving a Kidnapping Against 'Impossible Odds.'"

xii *". . . come to take you home":* Buchanan and Landemalm, *Impossible Odds,* 251.

xiii *". . . happy to be an American":* Quigley, "American Aid Worker Describes Her 93 Days of Hell."

xiii *". . . Good job tonight":* Abdi Sheikh, "U.S. Commandos Free Two Hostages in Daring Somalia Raid," Reuters, January 25, 2012.

xiv *". . . large-scale military deployments":* Karen DeYoung and Greg Jaffe, "Two Aid Workers Freed in Somalia," *Washington Post,* January 26, 2012.

xiv *". . . treasure over the past decade":* Kimberly Dozier and Robert Burns, "Navy SEAL Raid in Somalia Shows Campaign Ahead," Associated Press, January 26, 2012.

xiv "... *less problematic for the country involved*": Mark Bowden, *The Finish: The Killing of Osama Bin Laden* (New York: Atlantic Monthly Press, 2012), 262.

xix *lagged behind other fields of military history:* The situation has not changed very much since Colin Gray described it nearly twenty years ago. Colin Gray, "Handfuls of Heroes on Desperate Ventures: When Do Special Operations Succeed?" *Parameters* 29, no. 1 (Spring 1999): 2–24. For a recent discussion of the field, see Christopher Marsh, James Kiras, and Patricia Blocksome, "Special Operations Research: Out of the Shadows," *Special Operations Journal* 1, no. 1 (2015): 1–6.

xx *mathematical computation:* This problem is at least as severe as it was three decades ago when Richard E. Neustadt and Ernest R. May observed that the US government was filled with "lawyers who may know only the history they learn through the constricting prisms of court opinions; economists who may learn neither economic history nor much if any economic thought except their own; scientists who may know next to nothing of the history of science; engineers who may be innocent of history entirely, even that of their professions; graduates of business schools with but a smattering of theirs; and generalist B.A.s who may, with ingenuity, have managed to escape all history of every sort." Richard E. Neustadt and Ernest R. May, *Thinking in Time* (New York: Free Press, 1986), 245.

CHAPTER 1: RANGERS AND FORCEMEN

2 "... *viciously, and without rest*": William O. Darby and William H. Baumer, *We Led the Way: Darby's Rangers* (San Rafael, CA: Presidio, 1980), 85.

3 "... *will not fail in your duty*": James J. Altieri, *The Spearheaders: A Personal History of Darby's Rangers* (Indianapolis, IN: Bobbs-Merrill, 1960), 252.

3 *sergeant from Pocahontas, Iowa:* Patrick K. O'Donnell, *Beyond Valor: World War II's Ranger and Airborne Veterans Reveal the Heart of Combat* (New York: Free Press, 2001), 41.

3 *"personal medicinal alcohol":* Rex A. Knight, "Fighting Engineers on Sicily," *World War II* 14, no. 3 (September 1999): 42.

4 *convulsed in its final pumps:* O'Donnell, *Beyond Valor,* 42.

4 *intestines were spilling out:* Robert W. Black, *The Ranger Force: Darby's Rangers in World War II* (Mechanicsburg, PA: Stackpole, 2009), 142–143.

5 "... *shaking with patriotism*": Paul Jeffers, *Onward We Charge: The Heroic Story of Darby's Rangers in World War II* (New York: NAL Caliber, 2007), 134.

5 *knock out a Renault:* Michael J. King, *William Orlando Darby: A Military Biography* (Hamden, CT: Archon Books, 1981), 85–86.

6 *surviving German forces withdrew northward:* Rick Atkinson, *The Day of Battle: The War in Sicily and Italy, 1943–1944* (New York: Henry Holt, 2007), 103–104.

6 *found in the restaurant's cellar:* Darby and Baumer, *We Led the Way,* 90.

7 *raiding weapon in Churchill's arsenal:* Andrew L. Hargreaves, *Special Operations in World War II: British and American Irregular Warfare* (Norman: University of Oklahoma Press, 2013), 17–20; Christopher M. Bell, *Churchill and Sea Power* (Oxford: Oxford University Press, 2013), 207–286.

7 *Commando training and operations:* David W. Hogan Jr., *U.S. Army Special Operations in World War II* (Washington, DC: US Army Center of Military History, 1992), 12.

8 *victory against all odds:* Kenneth Finlayson and Robert W. Jones Jr., "Rangers in World War II: Part I, The Formation and Early Days," *Veritas* 2, no. 3 (2006): 64.

8 *encyclopedia called the* Book of Knowledge: King, *William Orlando Darby*, 5–11.

8 "... *complexion you've ever seen":* Jeffers, *Onward We Charge*, 13.

8 "... *jump in and do a job":* Darby and Baumer, *We Led the Way*, 1–2.

8 *"like it had been poured on":* King, *William Orlando Darby*, 16.

9 "... *filled with enthusiasm":* L. K. Truscott Jr., *Command Missions* (New York: E. P. Dutton, 1954), 39.

9 *depended upon complete silence:* King, *William Orlando Darby*, 33–34.

9 "... *initiative and common sense":* Darby and Baumer, *We Led the Way*, 24.

9 "... *daring in battle":* Ibid., 26.

10 *regimentation of Army life:* David W. Hogan Jr., *Raiders or Elite Infantry? The Changing Role of the U.S. Army Rangers from Dieppe to Grenada* (Westport, CT: Greenwood, 1992), 18.

11 *Rangers 11 of 50:* Jim Defelice, *Rangers at Dieppe: The First Combat Action of U.S. Army Rangers in World War II* (New York: Berkley Caliber, 2008).

12 *wares to the invaders:* Black, *Ranger Force*, 83.

13 *as needs arose:* Hogan, *Raiders or Elite Infantry*, 37.

13 *signed up as Rangers:* Altieri, *Spearheaders*, 247.

14 "... *rugged looking":* Darby and Baumer, *We Led the Way*, 83.

14 *radioed to the Fifth Army headquarters:* Atkinson, *Day of Battle*, 210–211.

15 *plug holes on the front:* King, *William Orlando Darby*, 135–137.

15 *mental convalescence:* Black, *Ranger Force*, 222.

16 "... *man who thinks":* John Nadler, *A Perfect Hell: The Forgotten Story of the Canadian Commandos of the Second World War* (Toronto: Doubleday Canada, 2005), 25.

16 "... *snow as we have of the sea":* Robert D. Burhans, *The First Special Service Force: A War History of the North Americans, 1942–1944* (Washington, DC: Infantry Journal Press, 1947), 3.

16 *oil fields of Texas:* Robert H. Adleman and George H. Walton, *The Devil's Brigade* (Philadelphia: Chilton Books, 1966), 124.

20 *recalled Captain Dermot O'Neill:* Adleman and Walton, *Devil's Brigade*, 133.

20 *description of the regimental commander:* Kenneth H. Joyce, *Snow Plough and the Jupiter Deception: The Story of the 1st Special Service Force and the 1st Canadian Special Service Battalion, 1942–1945* (St. Catharines, Ontario: Vanwell, 2006), 165.

20 "... *huge machine":* Ernie Pyle, *Brave Men* (New York: Henry Holt, 1944), 205.

21 "... *pitching arm":* Adleman and Walton, *Devil's Brigade*, 137.

21 *within two to three weeks:* Nadler, *Perfect Hell*, 141, 283.

21 "... *better hills to climb":* Herb Peppard, *The Light Hearted Soldier: A Canadian's Exploits with the Black Devils in WWII* (Halifax, Nova Scotia: Nimbus, 1994), 93.

21   *sixty-five North American casualties:* Scott R. McMichael, *A Historical Perspective on Light Infantry* (Fort Leavenworth, KS: Combat Studies Institute, 1987), 186–187; Nadler, *Perfect Hell*, 140–144.

22   *remainder could escape:* Lloyd Clark, *Anzio: Italy and the Battle for Rome—1944* (New York: Grove, 2006), 94–95.

23   *". . . stranded whale":* Winston S. Churchill, *The Second World War*, vol. 5, *Closing the Ring* (New York: Houghton Mifflin, 1951), 432.

23   *concentrations near Cisterna:* Michael J. King, *Rangers: Selected Combat Operations in World War II* (Fort Leavenworth, KS: Combat Studies Institute, 1985), 34; John Bowditch III, *Anzio Beachhead, 22 January–25 May 1944* (Washington, DC: US Army Center of Military History, 1990), 27.

24   *"ever heard of":* King, *Rangers*, 35.

26   *". . . coming into the building now":* Darby and Baumer, *We Led the Way*, 164.

27   *". . . God bless you":* Collie Small, "The Third: Tops in Honors," *Saturday Evening Post*, August 11, 1945.

27   *". . . Good luck . . . Colonel":* Altieri, *Spearheaders*, 312.

27   *to no avail:* King, *Rangers*, 38–39.

27   *"put his head down on his arm and cried":* Darby and Baumer, *We Led the Way*, 170.

28   *". . . drive to keep control":* Black, *Ranger Force*, 272.

28   *four-month period:* Bernd Horn and Michel Wyczynski, *Of Courage and Determination: The First Special Service Force, "The Devil's Brigade," 1942–1944* (Toronto: Dundurn, 2013), 224.

28   *received specialized training:* Joyce, *Snow Plough and the Jupiter Deception*, 201.

29   *". . . major part in an operation":* Horn and Wyczynski, *Of Courage and Determination*, 218.

29   *missing or wounded:* Joseph A. Springer, *The Black Devil Brigade* (New York: iBooks, 2001), 206–232.

30   *dozens of fourteen-inch shells:* Stephen E. Ambrose, *The Victors: Eisenhower and His Boys. The Men of World War II* (New York: Simon and Schuster, 1998), 143.

31   *had to be retracted:* Ronald J. Drez, *Voices of D-Day: The Story of the Allied Invasion Told by Those Who Were There* (Baton Rouge: Louisiana State University Press, 1994), 262–264.

32   *". . . shoot him on the spot":* Marcia Moen and Margo Heinen, *Reflections of Courage on D-Day and the Days That Followed: A Personal Account of Ranger "Ace" Parker* (Elk River, MN: DeForest Press, 1999), 118.

32   *". . . enough to go back out":* G. K. Hodenfield, "I Climbed the Cliffs with the Rangers," *Saturday Evening Post*, August 19, 1944.

32   *homing in on the command post:* Ronald L. Lane, *Rudder's Rangers: The True Story of the 2nd Ranger Battalion D-Day Combat Action*, 2nd ed. (Altamonte Springs, FL: Ranger Associates, 1994), 157.

33   *". . . yourself, damn it!":* Patrick K. O'Donnell, *Dog Company: The Boys of Pointe du Hoc—The Rangers Who Accomplished D-Day's Toughest Mission and Led the Way Across Europe* (Boston: Da Capo, 2012), 110–111.

33   *". . . all I had coming to me":* Ibid., 122.

33   *killed, wounded, or captured:* Douglas Brinkley, *The Boys of Pointe du Hoc: Ronald Reagan, D-Day, and the U.S. Army 2nd Ranger Battalion* (New York: William Morrow, 2005), 93.

34   *medieval warfare:* Rick Atkinson, *The Guns at Last Light: The War in Western Europe, 1944–1945* (New York: Henry Holt, 2013), 152.

34   "... *nobody will attempt to rescue you*": Roger B. Neighborgall, "The 5th Ranger Battalion and the Battle of Irsch-Zerf," *On Point* 15, no. 2 (Fall 2009): 8.

35   "... *nothing like the Germans*": O'Donnell, *Beyond Valor*, 313.

35   *328 prisoners:* King, *Rangers*, 53.

35   *several Japanese-held islands:* William H. McRaven, *Spec Ops: Case Studies in Special Operations Warfare: Theory and Practice* (Novato, CA: Presidio, 1995), 250–252.

38   *Japanese reinforcements could arrive:* Forrest Bryant Johnson, *Hour of Redemption: The Heroic WWII Saga of America's Most Daring POW Rescue* (New York: Warner Books, 2002); Hampton Sides, *Ghost Soldiers: The Forgotten Epic Story of World War II's Most Dramatic Mission* (New York: Doubleday, 2001); King, *Rangers*, 55–71; McRaven, *Spec Ops*, 261–283.

39   "... *prima donnas and hooligans*": Hogan, *Raiders or Elite Infantry*, 45.

CHAPTER 2: RAIDERS AND FROGMEN

43   "... *undesirable and superfluous*": Joseph H. Alexander, *Edson's Raiders: The 1st Marine Raider Battalion in World War II* (Annapolis, MD: Naval Institute Press, 2001), 27.

43   *antagonize the rest:* Allan R. Millett, *Semper Fidelis: The History of the United States Marine Corps* (New York: Free Press, 1991), 346–347; David W. Hogan Jr., *Raiders or Elite Infantry? The Changing Role of the U.S. Army Rangers from Dieppe to Grenada* (Westport, CT: Greenwood, 1992), 21.

43   *referred to themselves as "Supermarines":* W. S. Le Francois, "We Mopped Up Makin Island," *Saturday Evening Post*, December 4–11, 1943.

44   "... *complete annihilation*": Ibid.

45   *until he himself was killed:* Ibid.

45   "... *toughest thing I'd ever done*": John Wukovits, *American Commando: Evans Carlson, His WWII Marine Raiders, and America's First Special Forces Mission* (New York: NAL Caliber, 2009), 130.

46   "... *paddling like automatons*": Oscar Peatross, *Bless 'Em All: The Raider Marines of World War II* (Irvine, CA: Raider Publishing, 1995), 61.

46   *intention of surrendering:* Jon T. Hoffman, *From Makin to Bougainville: Marine Raiders in the Pacific War* (Washington, DC: Marine Corps Historical Center, 1995), 8–9; Wukovits, *American Commando*, 134–141.

46   "... *frayed their spirits*": Le Francois, "We Mopped Up Makin Island."

46   "... *son on the island*": Wukovits, *American Commando*, 170.

48   "... *at least ten years*": Peatross, *Bless 'Em All*, 84.

48   "... *they never smiled*": Richard Tregaskis, *Guadalcanal Diary* (New York: Random House, 1943), 72.

48   *"Mad Merritt the Morgue Master":* Jon T. Hoffman, *Once a Legend: "Red Mike" Edson of the Marine Raiders* (Novato, CA: Presidio, 1994), 213.

49   "... *before we went by*": Dick Camp, *Shadow Warriors: The Untold Stories of American Special Operations During WWII* (Minneapolis: Zenith, 2013), 100.

49   "... *enemy was thrown back*": Tregaskis, *Guadalcanal Diary*, 73.

50 *17 flasks of sake:* Samuel B. Griffith II, *The Battle for Guadalcanal* (Philadelphia: Lippincott, 1963), 109.

51 *". . . their Samurai swords":* Alexander, *Edson's Raiders*, 153.

51 *". . . dark jungle as a corpse":* George W. Smith, *The Do-or-Die Men: The 1st Marine Raider Battalion at Guadalcanal* (New York: Pocket Books, 2003), 279.

52 *"Death to Roosevelt!":* Alexander, *Edson's Raiders*, 179.

52 *"Get back!":* Richard Frank, *Guadalcanal: The Definitive Account of the Landmark Battle* (New York: Random House, 1990), 240.

52 *better man for the job:* Hoffman, *Once a Legend*, 204.

52 *". . . Come up on this hill and fight!":* Merrill B. Twining, *No Bended Knee: The Memoir of Merrill B. Twining USMC (Ret.)* (Novato, CA: Presidio, 1996), 100.

52 *advance on Henderson Field:* Ibid.

52 *total may have been much higher:* Frank, *Guadalcanal*, 245.

53 *all thoughts of taking prisoners:* Edwin P. Hoyt, *The Marine Raiders* (New York: Pocket Books, 1989), 110–132; Wukovits, *American Commando*, 204.

54 *" . . . same underwear on for thirty days":* Wukovits, *American Commando*, 236–237.

54 *Marines at Henderson Field:* Blankfort, *The Big Yankee: The Life of Carlson of the Raiders* (Boston: Little, Brown, 1947), 305.

54 *". . . half-sock of rice a day":* Wukovits, *American Commando*, 257–258.

55 *could conduct raids:* Alexander, *Edson's Raiders*, 235–236.

55 *". . . like a bull captain in the old navy":* Twining, *No Bended Knee*, 43, 139, 145.

56 *250 casualties:* Charles L. Updegraph Jr., *U.S. Marine Corps Special Units of World War II* (Washington, DC: US Marine Corps History and Museums Division, 1972), 30.

56 *". . . good Marine battalion couldn't do":* Alexander, *Edson's Raiders*, 307.

56 *fully capable of conducting raids:* John W. Gordon, "The U.S. Marine Corps and an Experiment in Military Elitism: A Reassessment of the Special Warfare Impetus, 1937–1943," in William Love Jr., ed., *Changing Interpretations and New Sources in Naval History: Papers from the Third United States Naval Academy History Symposium* (New York: Garland, 1980), 367–368.

56 *wreaking havoc on the Japanese:* Gavin Mortimer, *Merrill's Marauders: The Untold Story of Unit Galahad and the Toughest Special Forces Mission of World War II* (Minneapolis: Zenith, 2013), 3–5.

56 *officer in the new unit lamented:* Charles Ogburn, *The Marauders* (New York: Harper, 1959), 34.

57 *less than big weapons:* Frank McLynn, *The Burma Campaign: Disaster into Triumph, 1942–45* (New Haven, CT: Yale University Press, 2011), 328–337; Scott R. McMichael, *A Historical Perspective on Light Infantry* (Fort Leavenworth, KS: Combat Studies Institute, 1987), 36–43.

57 *"stuffed baboons," and worse:* Ian Fellowes-Gordon, *The Magic War: The Battle for North Burma* (New York: Scribner, 1971), 37; Geoffrey Perret, *There's a War to Be Won: The United States Army in World War II* (New York: Random House, 1991), 294–295.

58 *Chinese and British to continue fighting:* Charles F. Romanus and Riley Sutherland, *Stilwell's Command Problems* (Washington, DC: US Army Center of Military History, 1987), 188–191.

58   *injury, illness, capture, or death:* Mary Ellen Condon-Rall and Albert E. Cowdrey, *The Medical Department: Medical Service in the War Against Japan* (Washington, DC: US Army Center of Military History, 1998), 309–310.

58   *set flares for naval gunfire:* John B. Dwyer, *Scouts and Raiders: The Navy's First Special Warfare Commandos* (Westport, CT: Praeger, 1993).

58   *thirty-foot waves and enemy machine-gun fire:* Michael Lee Lanning, *Blood Warriors: America's Military Elites* (New York: Ballantine, 2002), 14–15.

58   *program by week's end:* Elizabeth Kauffman Bush, *America's First Frogman: The Draper Kauffman Story* (Annapolis, MD: Naval Institute Press, 2004), 82–83.

59   *queuing up for D-Day:* Chet Cunningham, *The Frogmen of World War II: An Oral History of the U.S. Navy's Underwater Demolition Teams* (Waterville, ME: Thorndike Press, 2005), 58–70.

60   *channels on Omaha Beach were fully cleared:* Francis Douglas Fane, *The Naked Warriors: The Story of the U.S. Navy's Frogmen* (Annapolis, MD: US Naval Institute Press, 1995), 57.

60   *thirty-one were killed and sixty wounded:* Orr Kelly, *Brave Men—Dark Waters: The Untold Story of the Navy SEALS* (Novato, CA: Presidio, 1992), 27.

61   *across the beaches:* John B. Dwyer, *Commandos from the Sea: The History of Amphibious Special Warfare in World War II and the Korean War* (Boulder: Paladin Press, 1998), 188–191.

61   *". . . train and equip the Teams":* Fane, *Naked Warriors*, 122.

61   *" . . . courageous work of the Underwater Demolition Teams":* Andrew L. Hargreaves, *Special Operations in World War II: British and American Irregular Warfare* (Norman: University of Oklahoma Press, 2013), 217.

CHAPTER 3: OSS

64   *". . . adaptable to any problem":* Richard Dunlop, *Donovan: America's Master Spy* (Chicago: Rand McNally, 1982), 25.

65   *poor Irish Catholics:* Anthony Cave Brown, *The Last Hero: Wild Bill Donovan* (New York: Times Books, 1982), 19–21.

65   *". . . fixed on some other object":* Dunlop, *Donovan*, 25.

65   *"a youngster at Halloween":* Douglas Waller, *Wild Bill Donovan: The Spymaster Who Created the OSS and Modern American Espionage* (New York: Free Press, 2011), 22.

65   *"delusions of grandeur":* Ibid., 44.

66   *". . . he never knew me":* Dunlop, *Donovan*, 44.

66   *". . . cannot afford to be a sissy":* Thomas F. Troy, *Donovan and the CIA: A History of the Establishment of the Central Intelligence Agency* (Frederick, MD: University Publications of America, 1981), 29.

66   *favorable impression on the American:* Joseph E. Persico, *Roosevelt's Centurions: FDR and the Commanders He Led to Victory in World War II* (New York: Random House, 2013), 380–381.

66   *telescopic bombsights:* Michael Fullilove, *Rendezvous with Destiny: How Franklin D. Roosevelt and Five Extraordinary Men Took America into the War and into the World* (New York: Penguin, 2013), 93–94.

67   *". . . paralyzing Washington":* Dunlop, *Donovan*, 222.

67   *revolver to and from work:* Christopher Andrew, *For the President's Eyes Only: Secret Intelligence and the American Presidency from Washington to Bush* (New York: HarperCollins, 1995), 77–78.

67   *bored him terribly:* Bradley F. Smith, *The Shadow Warriors: O.S.S. and the Origins of the C.I.A.* (New York: Basic Books, 1983), 89–90.

68   *". . . liable to sudden changes":* Brown, *Last Hero*, 191.

68   *". . . men and women who wanted to help":* Ray S. Cline, *Secrets, Spies and Scholars: Blueprint of the Essential CIA* (Washington, DC: Acropolis, 1976), 39–40.

68   *and William Casey:* Joseph E. Persico, *Piercing the Reich: The Penetration of Nazi Germany by American Secret Agents During World War II* (New York: Viking, 1979), 6.

69   *soprano pitch:* Stanley P. Lovell, *Of Spies & Stratagems* (New York: Pocket Books, 1963), 84–85.

69   *". . . mad with longing":* Waller, *Wild Bill Donovan*, 108.

69   *froze to death:* Andrew, *For the President's Eyes Only*, 126.

69   *Spanish embassy at the same time:* Curt Gentry, *J. Edgar Hoover: The Man and the Secrets* (New York: Norton, 1991), 294–295.

69   *". . . responsibility for a war activity":* Breckinridge Long, *The War Diary of Breckinridge Long: Selections from the Years 1939–1944* (Lincoln: University of Nebraska Press, 1966), 234.

70   *create guerrilla and commando forces using US military personnel:* Troy, *Donovan and the CIA*, 190; Smith, *Shadow Warriors*, 203.

71   *". . . maximum volume":* Richard Dunlop, *Behind Japanese Lines: With the OSS in Burma* (Chicago: Rand McNally, 1979), 245.

71   *". . . talented and unusual men":* Thomas N. Moon and Carl F. Eifler, *Deadliest Colonel* (New York: Vantage, 1975), 42.

71   *inches into his desk:* Ibid., 44–45.

72   *able to fend them off:* Troy J. Sacquety, *The OSS in Burma: Jungle War Against the Japanese* (Lawrence: University Press of Kansas, 2013), 20.

72   *Stilwell informed Eifler:* Ibid., 2.

72   *". . . less than three months to do it in":* Dunlop, *Behind Japanese Lines*, 121.

72   *". . . verification of his belief":* Richard Harris Smith, *OSS: The Secret History of America's First Central Intelligence Agency* (Berkeley: University of California Press, 1972), 248.

72   *Anglo-Burmese descent:* James R. Ward, "The Activities of Detachment 101 of the OSS," *Special Warfare* 6, no. 4 (October 1993): 14–21.

73   *never heard from again:* Sacquety, *The OSS in Burma*, 39–43.

74   *pull Eifler onto the deck:* Dunlop, *Behind Japanese Lines*, 208–210.

74   *until none were left:* Sacquety, *The OSS in Burma*, 41–42.

74   *had not fallen to the Japanese:* Edward Hymoff, *The OSS in World War II* (New York: Richardson and Steirman, 1986), 146–147; Sacquety, *The OSS in Burma*, 35–36; Roger Hilsman, *American Guerrilla: My War Behind Japanese Lines* (Washington, DC: Brassey's, 1990), 122.

75   *bow to Japan's will:* Dunlop, *Behind Japanese Lines*, 33–34.

75   *as invisibly as they had come:* Thomas N. Moon, *This Grim and Savage Game: OSS and the Beginning of U.S. Covert Operations in World War II* (Cambridge, MA: Da Capo, 2000), 109–110.

77   *volunteers were flown:* Dunlop, *Behind Japanese Lines*, 214–220.

77   *architect planning a building:* William R. Peers and Dean Brelis, *Behind the Burma Road: The Story of America's Most Successful Guerrilla Force* (Boston: Little, Brown, 1963), 144.

78   *cleaving it in two:* Dunlop, *Behind Japanese Lines*, 248–249.

78   *somehow had to be aborted:* Moon and Eifler, *The Deadliest Colonel*, 168–173, 193, 214, 233.

78   *". . . get a Bull Dozer and level it":* Sacquety, *The OSS in Burma*, 71.

79   *". . . buoy their spirits":* Dunlop, *Behind Japanese Lines*, 425–426.

80   *". . . before we even got started":* Sacquety, *The OSS in Burma*, 133.

80   *15 Americans killed:* Kermit Roosevelt, *The Overseas Targets: War Report of the OSS*, vol. 2 (New York: Walker and Company, 1976), 391–392.

80   *"set Europe ablaze":* William Manchester and Paul Reid, *The Last Lion: Winston Spencer Churchill, Defender of the Realm, 1940–1965* (Boston: Little, Brown, 2012), 273.

81   *one fell swoop:* Jean Overton Fuller, *The German Penetration of SOE: France 1941–1944* (London: Kimber, 1975), 30–35.

81   *loyal to the Germans:* David A. Walker, "OSS and Operation Torch," *Journal of Contemporary History* 22, no. 4 (October 1987): 668–675; Dunlop, *Donovan*, 370–375.

82   *"They haven't burned the White House yet":* Waller, *Wild Bill Donovan*, 140.

82   *parachuting, sabotage, and guerrilla warfare:* Albert Lulushi, *Donovan's Devils: OSS Commandos Behind Enemy Lines—Europe, World War II* (New York: Arcade, 2016), 61–74; *War Report of the OSS* (New York: Walker and Company, 1976), 223–225.

82   *". . . when we got back":* Dunlop, *Donovan*, 399.

82   *dinners in black tie:* Waller, *Wild Bill Donovan*, 180.

82   *". . . prerequisite for success":* Max Corvo, *The O.S.S. in Italy, 1942–1945: A Personal Memoir* (New York: Praeger, 1990), 131.

82   *away from the Winter Line:* Brown, *Last Hero*, 474; Lulushi, *Donovan's Devils*, 190–202.

83   *the sixtieth day:* Will Irwin, *The Jedburghs: The Secret History of the Allied Special Forces, France 1944* (New York: PublicAffairs, 2005), 67–70.

84   *". . . unpleasant assignment":* Aaron Bank, *From OSS to Green Berets* (Novato, CA: Presidio, 1986), 1–3.

84   *meats and starches:* Dick Camp, *Shadow Warriors: The Untold Stories of American Special Operations During WWII* (Minneapolis: Zenith, 2013), 64; Irwin, *The Jedburghs*, 43–44.

84   *punched out five-mile runs:* Douglas Waller, *Disciples: The World War II Missions of the CIA Directors Who Fought for Wild Bill Donovan* (New York: Simon and Schuster, 2015), 98–100; Bank, *From OSS to Green Berets*, 5–6.

85   *piercing of vital organs:* Serge Obolensky, *One Man in His Time: The Memoirs of Serge Obolensky* (New York: McDowell, Obolensky, 1958), 347–348; Irwin, *The Jedburghs*, 47–48; Lulushi, *Donovan's Devils*, 73–74.

85   *French military and police forces:* Corey Ford and Alastair MacBain, *Cloak and Dagger: The Secret Story of the OSS* (New York: Grosset and Dunlap, 1945), 64; Waller, *Disciples*, 171–172; William B. Dreux, *No Bridges Blown* (Notre Dame, IN: University of Notre Dame Press, 1971), 49–52.

86   " . . . our mutual war effort": Colin Beavan, *Operation Jedburgh, D-Day and America's First Shadow War* (New York: Viking, 2006), 93.

86   *good cheer:* Waller, *Disciples*, 173–175; Beavan, *Operation Jedburgh*, 92–104.

88   " . . . I am your commanding officer": Smith, *OSS*, 184–185.

89   *intended for his forces:* Roger Ford, *Steel from the Sky: Behind Enemy Lines in German-Occupied France* (London: Weidenfeld and Nicolson, 2004), 155.

89   "Vive les Américains!": Bank, *From OSS to Green Berets*, 34–37.

89   " . . . needling the enemy": Ibid., 41.

90   " . . . consider necessary": Ibid., 48.

90   *and other Allied officers:* David W. Hogan Jr., *U.S. Army Special Operations in World War II* (Washington, DC: US Army Center of Military History, 1992), 53–54.

90   *11th Panzer Division:* Benjamin F. Jones, *Eisenhower's Guerrillas: The Jedburghs, the Maquis, and the Liberation of France* (New York: Oxford University Press, 2016), 224–225.

90   *harassing the withdrawing Germans:* Ford, *Steel from the Sky*, 156.

90   *personnel, aircraft, and supplies for the mission:* Harry C. Butcher, *My Three Years with Eisenhower: The Personal Diary of Captain Harry C. Butcher, USNR, Naval Aide to General Eisenhower, 1942 to 1945* (New York: Simon and Schuster, 1946), 654; Smith, *Shadow Warriors*, 291–292.

91   *laid down their weapons:* Robert E. Mattingly, "Herringbone Cloak–GI Dagger: Marines of the OSS," US Marine Corps History and Museums Division, 1989, 120; Phil Mehringer, "Operation Union II: Marines Land in France 60 Years Ago," Leatherneck.com, August 23, 2004.

91   *1,574 personnel into occupied France:* Smith, *Shadow Warriors*, 293; Beavan, *Operation Jedburgh*, 164–165; Jay Jakub, *Spies and Saboteurs: Anglo-American Collaboration and Rivalry in Human Intelligence Collection and Special Operations, 1940–1945* (Houndmills, UK: Macmillan, 1999), 180–181.

92   *212 urban centers:* Waller, *Wild Bill Donovan*, 247; Waller, *Disciples*, 196–197, 257–259; Jones, *Eisenhower's Guerrillas*, 274–276.

92   " . . . cowboys and red Indians": Andrew L. Hargreaves, *Special Operations in World War II: British and American Irregular Warfare* (Norman: University of Oklahoma Press, 2013), 120.

92   " . . . elements in his community": Louis Huot, *Guns for Tito* (New York: L. B. Fischer, 1945), 229.

92   *rivals against the Germans:* William L. White, "Some Affairs of Honor," *Reader's Digest* 47 (December 1945), 138.

93   *ensuing war between the United States and North Vietnam:* Dixee R. Bartholomew-Feis, *The OSS and Ho Chi Minh: Unexpected Allies in the War Against Japan* (Lawrence: University Press of Kansas, 2006), 188–264.

93   " . . . no thought of its elimination": Smith, *Shadow Warriors*, 307.

94   " . . . agencies of this government": Maochun Yu, *OSS in China: Prelude to Cold War* (New Haven, CT: Yale University Press, 1996), 250.

CHAPTER 4: THE FORGOTTEN WAR

97   " . . . become an infantry leader": Chuck Williams, "Sunday Interview with Retired Col. Ralph Puckett," *Columbus Ledger-Enquirer*, August 2, 2014.

99   "... *take me into that Ranger company*": Ibid.
99   *culled seventy-three enlisted men*: Robert W. Black, *Rangers in Korea* (New York: Ivy Books, 1989), 13–14.
100 "... *a lot of Mexicans live in Texas*": T. R. Fehrenbach, *This Kind of War* (New York: Macmillan, 1963), 190.
101 *frozen tundra*: S. L. A. Marshall, *The River and the Gauntlet: Defeat of the Eighth Army by the Chinese Communist Forces, November 1950, in the Battle of the Chongchon River, Korea* (New York: William Morrow, 1953), 195–196; Roy E. Appleman, *Disaster in Korea: The Chinese Confront MacArthur* (College Station: Texas A&M University Press, 2008), 106–107.
102 *"We're depending on you"*: Williams, "Sunday Interview."
103 *were being overrun*: Neil Sheehan, *A Bright Shining Lie: John Paul Vann and America in Vietnam* (New York: Random House, 1988), 464.
104 "... *key communications centers or facilities*": Richard L. Kiper, *Spare Not the Brave: The Special Activities Group in Korea* (Kent, OH: Kent State University Press, 2014), 232.
105 *performed acts of sabotage*: David W. Hogan Jr., *Raiders or Elite Infantry? The Changing Role of the U.S. Army Rangers from Dieppe to Grenada* (Westport, CT: Greenwood, 1992), 109–110; Black, *Rangers in Korea*, 19–20; "Rangers 'Reborn,' Filter Red Lines," *New York Times*, March 11, 1951.
105 "... *hitting the ground*": William B. Breuer, *Shadow Warriors: The Covert War in Korea* (New York: John Wiley and Sons, 1996), 160.
106 *moped about in dejection*: Black, *Rangers in Korea*, 35–36.
106 *eighty-four Rangers were injured*: Billy C. Mossman, *United States Army in the Korean War: Ebb and Flow, November 1950–July 1951* (Washington, DC: US Army Center of Military History, 1988), 339–340.
107 *short of its objective*: Martin Blumenson, "The Rangers at Hwachon Dam," *Army* 17 (December 1967): 36–53.
107 *vulnerable point*: See, for example, Bob Channon, ed., *The Cold Steel Third: 3rd Airborne Ranger Company, Korean War (1950–1951)* (Franklin, NC: Genealogy Publishing Service, 1993), 147–171; "Rangers Fight Toe to Toe on Bloody Nose Ridge," *Army Times*, June 2, 1951; Clay Blair, *The Forgotten War: America in Korea, 1950–1953* (New York: Times Books, 1987), 438.
107 *special capabilities squandered*: Hogan, *Raiders or Elite Infantry*, 119; Hanson Baldwin, "Rangers Broken Up as Misfits in Korea," *New York Times*, August 26, 1951.
107 *matters that were decided by generals*: Robert W. Black, *A Ranger Born: A Memoir of Combat and Valor from Korea to Vietnam* (New York: Ballantine Books, 2002), 122.
108 *back to regular units*: Kiper, *Spare Not the Brave*, 234–235; Black, *Rangers in Korea*, 196; Eighth US Army Korea, "Special Problems in the Korean Conflict," http://cgsc.cdmhost.com/cdm/ref/collection/p4013coll11/id/1695, 84–88.
108 "... *inspiration to fight*": "The Rangers Lose," *Time*, September 3, 1951.
108 *deactivation of all Ranger units in Korea*: Hogan, *Raiders or Elite Infantry*, 128; Kiper, *Spare Not the Brave*, 235.
109 *flee northward*: Allan R. Millett, *The War for Korea, 1950–1951: They Came from the North* (Lawrence: University Press of Kansas, 2010), 286.

109 *"... mad as hell":* Michael E. Haas, *In the Devil's Shadow: UN Special Operations During the Korean War* (Annapolis, MD: Naval Institute Press, 2000), 33.

109 *not yet dead:* Ed Evanhoe, *Darkmoon: Eighth Army Special Operations in the Korean War* (Annapolis, MD: Naval Institute Press, 1995), 66.

109 *2,000 to 30,000:* Ibid., 70.

110 *inside collapsible walls:* Rod Paschall, "Special Operations in Korea," *Conflict* 7, no. 2 (1987): 162.

110 *"... 'pass' at a Korean woman":* Haas, *In the Devil's Shadow*, 64.

110 *retained control of its main island bases:* Evanhoe, *Darkmoon*, 125–126, 150–151; Paschall, "Special Operations in Korea," 165–166.

111 *None of its men ever returned:* Operations Research Office, Johns Hopkins University, "UN Partisan Warfare in Korea, 1951–1954," June 1956, 91; Evanhoe, *Darkmoon*, 158–159.

111 *only a handful came back:* Haas, *In the Devil's Shadow*, 60; Richard L. Kiper, "Unconventional Warfare in Korea: Forgotten Aspect of the 'Forgotten War,'" *Special Warfare* 16, no. 2 (August 2003): 30–31.

111 *resistance experience to the CIA:* Haas, *In the Devil's Shadow*, 62.

111 *ashore on coastal raids:* Joseph C. Goulden, *Korea: The Untold Story of the War* (New York: Times Books, 1982), 467; Haas, *In the Devil's Shadow*, 150–151.

112 *appointed hour:* Haas, *In the Devil's Shadow*, 99.

112 *"... wounded were civilians":* Operations Research Office, Johns Hopkins University, "UN Partisan Warfare in Korea," 5.

112 *western coast at any one time:* Ibid., 13, 17.

113 *"We will withdraw":* Glenn Muggelberg, Oral History Interview, 1985, US Army Military History Institute.

113 *locating enemy weapons:* Kenneth Finlayson, "From a Standing Start: U.S. Army Psychological Warfare and Civil Affairs in the Korean War," *Veritas* 7, no. 1 (2011): 1–3.

114 *resembling OSS forebears:* Alfred H. Paddock Jr., *U.S. Army Special Warfare: Its Origins*, rev. ed. (Lawrence: University Press of Kansas, 2002), 123; Aaron Bank, *From OSS to Green Berets* (Novato, CA: Presidio, 1986), 154.

114 *less costly and time-consuming:* Mike Guardia, *American Guerrilla: The Forgotten Heroics of Russell W. Volckmann* (Havertown, PA: Casemate, 2010), 171.

115 *1,500 men:* Bank, *From OSS to Green Berets*, 156–158.

115 *"rub off on Special Forces":* Charles Simpson, *Inside the Green Berets: The First Thirty Years* (Novato, CA: Presidio, 1983), 21.

115 *"... that'll be peanuts":* Bank, *From OSS to Green Berets*, 164.

116 *"... 'country cousin' to the Psychological Warfare Center":* Paddock, *U.S. Army Special Warfare*, 142.

116 *"... essential qualities":* Bank, *From OSS to Green Berets*, 177.

117 *reduce their chances for promotion:* Simpson, *Inside the Green Berets*, 22; Bank, *From OSS to Green Berets*, 176–177.

117 *signed up for Special Forces:* Paddock, *U.S. Army Special Warfare*, 146.

117 *no one else in the Army wanted them:* Simpson, *Inside the Green Berets*, 22.

118 *"... understanding of another culture":* Operations Research Office, Johns Hopkins University, "UN Partisan Warfare in Korea," 115.

119 *grounds for the practice of guerrilla war:* Simpson, *Inside the Green Berets*, 39; Bank, *From OSS to Green Berets*, 190.

120 *". . . solely responsible":* Paddock, *U.S. Army Special Warfare*, 131.

120 *but to no avail:* Ibid., 101, 133.

120 *". . . hadn't thought the thing through very well":* Orr Kelly, *From a Dark Sky: The Story of U.S. Air Force Special Operations* (Novato, CA: Presidio, 1997), 113.

120 *air transport at the request of the Army and CIA:* Ibid., 118.

CHAPTER 5: VIETNAM

125 *defeating insurgency in underdeveloped countries:* Roger Hilsman, *To Move a Nation: The Politics of Foreign Policy in the Administration of John F. Kennedy* (Garden City, NY: Doubleday, 1967), 413; Lloyd Norman and John B. Spore, "Big Push on Guerrilla Warfare," *Army*, March 1962, 33; Douglas S. Blaufarb, *The Counterinsurgency Era: U.S. Doctrine and Performance, 1950 to the Present* (New York: Free Press, 1977), 68–72.

125 *"Boy Scouts with guns":* Richard Reeves, *President Kennedy: Profile of Power* (New York: Simon and Schuster, 1993), 284.

125 *could pass for soap:* Norman and Spore, "Big Push on Guerrilla Warfare."

126 *skin snakes:* Charles Simpson, *Inside the Green Berets: The First Thirty Years* (Novato, CA: Presidio, 1983), 67.

126 *Robert Kennedy once inquired:* Andrew F. Krepinevich Jr., *The Army and Vietnam* (Baltimore, MD: Johns Hopkins University Press, 1986), 35.

126 *form the 5th Special Forces Group:* Ibid., 103–105.

126 *from 90 percent to 30 percent:* David W. Hogan Jr., *Raiders or Elite Infantry? The Changing Role of the U.S. Army Rangers from Dieppe to Grenada* (Westport, CT: Greenwood, 1992), 160–161.

126 *dangerous camps:* Francis J. Kelly, *U.S. Army Special Forces: 1961–1971* (Washington, DC: Department of the Army, 1973), 168.

127 *". . . often doubtful":* Simpson, *Inside the Green Berets*, 70.

127 *passenger seats:* Michael O'Brien, *John F. Kennedy: A Biography* (New York: Thomas Dunne, 2005), 625; Philip D. Chinnery, *Any Time, Any Place: Fifty Years of the USAF Air Commando and Special Operations Forces, 1944–1994* (Annapolis, MD: Naval Institute Press, 1994), 67–72.

127 *twenty miles inland:* T. L. Bosiljevac, *SEALs: UDT/SEAL Operations in Vietnam* (Boulder: Paladin Press, 1990), 16–17.

127 *returned to their original units:* Joel Nadel and J. R. Wright, *Special Men and Special Missions: Inside American Special Operations Forces, 1945 to the Present* (Mechanicsburg, PA: Stackpole, 1994), 61.

128 *". . . fight under the sea":* Kevin Dockery, *Navy SEALs: A Complete History from World War II to the Present* (New York: Berkley, 2004), 237.

128 *other supporting assets:* Nadel and Wright, *Special Men and Special Missions*, 64.

128 *multitude of counterinsurgency tasks:* US Army John F. Kennedy Center, "Multipurpose Force Study: The US Army Special Forces—A Review of their Indochina Commitment and a Projection of Future Tasks," October 28, 1976, www.governmentattic.org/12docs/ArmySFreviewIndochina_1976.pdf, II-4.

128 *Buon Enao for training:* Christopher K. Ives, *US Special Forces and Counterinsurgency in Vietnam: Military Innovation and Institutional Failure, 1961–63* (New York: Routledge, 2007), 16–21.

129 *repairing roads and bridges:* Kelly, *U.S. Army Special Forces*, 60.

129 *". . . nice bonus":* Henry G. Gole, *Soldiering: Observations from Korea, Vietnam, and Safe Places* (Dulles, VA: Potomac Books, 2005), 154.

129 *62,000 Montagnards:* Ives, *US Special Forces and Counterinsurgency in Vietnam*, 101, 104.

130 *sobriquet "Raider" Johnson:* Robert A. Caro, *The Years of Lyndon Johnson: Means of Ascent* (New York: Alfred A. Knopf, 1990), 41–50.

130 *North Vietnamese in the near term:* Mark Moyar, *Triumph Forsaken: The Vietnam War, 1954–1965* (New York: Cambridge University Press, 2006), 305, 342.

131 *". . . believed this myth":* Richard H. Shultz Jr., *The Secret War Against Hanoi: Kennedy's and Johnson's Use of Spies, Saboteurs, and Covert Warriors in North Vietnam* (New York: HarperCollins, 1999), 293.

131 *principal motive was monetary:* MACSOG Documentation Study, Annex N to Appendix B, "Comments by These Interviewees on MACSOG's Operations and Intelligence," July 10, 1970, Texas Tech University Virtual Vietnam Archive, Item 2861211001, B-n-57; Shultz, *Secret War*, 37–38, 94–107.

131 *November 1963 coup:* Moyar, *Triumph Forsaken*, 304.

132 *missions could not be performed:* John K. Singlaub, with Malcolm McConnell, *Hazardous Duty: An American Soldier in the Twentieth Century* (New York: Summit Books, 1991), 303.

132 *blow a leg off a footbridge:* Shultz, *Secret War*, 58, 83–88.

132 *internal security apparatus:* MACSOG Documentation Study, "Comments by These Interviewees"; Kenneth Conboy and Dale Andradé, *Spies and Commandos: How America Lost the Secret War in North Vietnam* (Lawrence: University Press of Kansas, 2000), 200.

133 *". . . no chance of success":* Conboy and Andradé, *Spies and Commandos*, 208.

133 *against large North Vietnamese assaults:* Kelly, *U.S. Army Special Forces*, 40.

133 *unexpected frequency:* Shelby L. Stanton, *Green Berets at War: U.S. Army Special Forces in Southeast Asia, 1956–1975* (Novato, CA: Presidio, 1985), 232–252.

134 *100 rounds per second:* Nadel and Wright, *Special Men and Special Missions*, 78–80; Chinnery, *Any Time, Any Place*, 98–103.

134 *beyond the reach of enemy machine guns:* Orr Kelly, *From a Dark Sky: The Story of U.S. Air Force Special Operations* (Novato, CA: Presidio, 1997), 150–155.

135 *". . . bury themselves with concrete":* Jeffrey J. Clarke, *Advice and Support: The Final Years, 1965–1973* (Washington, DC: US Army Center of Military History, 1987), 198.

135 *advising the South Vietnamese:* Army Concept Team in Vietnam, "Employment of a Special Forces Group," April 20, 1966, National Archives II, RG 472, 5th Special Forces Group, Entry P131, box 137.

135 *surreptitious movement:* Kelly, *U.S. Army Special Forces*, 52.

136 *award for actions in Vietnam:* Moyar, *Triumph Forsaken*, 301–303.

137 *recalcitrant mutineer:* Anne Blair, *There to the Bitter End: Ted Serong in Vietnam* (Crows Nest, Australia: Allen and Unwin, 2001), 99–100; William C. Westmoreland, *A Soldier Reports* (Garden City, NY: Doubleday, 1976), 79–81.

137 *conventionally equipped North Vietnamese battalions:* Hogan, *Raiders or Elite Infantry,* 178–182; Kelly, *U.S. Army Special Forces,* 141; US Army John F. Kennedy Center, "Multipurpose Force Study," II-11.

137 *137 in 1966:* Mike Guardia, *Shadow Commander: The Epic Story of Donald D. Blackburn* (Havertown, PA: Casemate, 2011), 166–177; Shultz, *Secret War,* 68.

138 *big enough to take Cuba:* Singlaub, *Hazardous Duty,* 297; Benjamin F. Schemmer, *The Raid* (New York: Harper and Row, 1976), 60.

138 *". . . a shit and a dove":* Shultz, *Secret War,* 303.

138 *secret factory in Japan:* John L. Plaster, *SOG: The Secret Wars of America's Commandos in Vietnam* (New York: Simon and Schuster, 1997), 34.

139 *thirty to forty minutes:* William Rosenau, *Special Operations Forces and Elusive Enemy Ground Targets: Lessons from Vietnam and the Persian Gulf War* (Santa Monica, CA: Rand, 2001), 20–21.

139 *splice into the line:* Robert M. Gillespie, *Black Ops, Vietnam: The Operational History of MACVSOG* (Annapolis, MD: Naval Institute Press, 2011), 233; Singlaub, *Hazardous Duty,* 298–299.

139 *". . . can't handle it":* Plaster, *SOG,* 137.

140 *man who always succeeded:* Alan Hoe, *The Quiet Professional: Major Richard J. Meadows of the U.S. Army Special Forces* (Lexington: University Press of Kentucky, 2011), 23, 42–43, 84–85.

141 *recovered all of the men:* George J. Veith, *Code-Name Bright Light: The Untold Story of U.S. POW Rescue Efforts During the Vietnam War* (New York: Free Press, 1998), 124–125; Gillespie, *Black Ops, Vietnam,* 75; Conboy and Andradé, *Spies and Commandos,* 165–166; Hoe, *Quiet Professional,* 92–95.

141 *served anti-Communist fare:* Alfred H. Paddock Jr., *U.S. Army Special Warfare: Its Origins,* rev. ed. (Lawrence: University Press of Kansas, 2002), 160–161.

142 *grenade under the hat:* John Mecklin, *Mission in Torment: An Intimate Account of the U.S. Role in Vietnam* (Garden City, NY: Doubleday, 1965), 55.

142 *potent American weaponry:* Mark Moyar, *Phoenix and the Birds of Prey: The CIA's Secret Campaign to Destroy the Viet Cong* (Annapolis, MD: Naval Institute Press, 1997), 110–111.

142 *". . . broadcasts made":* Kelly, *U.S. Army Special Forces,* 171.

143 *remarkably few casualties:* Moyar, *Phoenix and the Birds of Prey,* 164–173.

144 *rude welcome for American rescue aircraft:* Gillespie, *Black Ops, Vietnam,* 172–174; Plaster, *SOG,* 80–82.

144 *". . . severe on Prairie Fire":* William C. Gibbons, *The U.S. Government and the Vietnam War: Executive and Legislative Roles and Relationships,* vol. 4 (Princeton, NJ: Princeton University Press, 1995), 927.

145 *twenty kilometers past the border:* Graham A. Cosmas, *MACV: The Joint Command in the Years of Escalation, 1962–1967* (Washington, DC: US Army Center of Military History, 2006), 381.

145 *during 1967:* Plaster, *SOG,* 131.

146 *". . . hole to hide":* MACVSOG, Command History, 1968, Texas Tech University Virtual Vietnam Archive, Item 2861205001, F-III-4-2; Conboy and Andradé, *Spies and Commandos,* 172, 230; Shultz, *Secret War,* 120–121.

146 *several thousand Vietnamese, Cambodians, Thais, and Laotians:* Shultz, *Secret War,* 54, 68.

146 *destroyed by American air power:* Warren A. Trest, *Air Commando One: Heini Aderholt and America's Secret Wars* (Washington, DC: Smithsonian Institution Press, 2000), 220–223.

147 *and 9 disappeared:* MACSOG Documentation Study, Appendix D, "Cross-Border Operations in Laos," July 10, 1970, Texas Tech University Virtual Vietnam Archive, Item 2860715001, D-57a; Shultz, *Secret War*, 250.

147 *". . . short-term loan":* George Hoffman, "In Memory of David Ives Mixter," Special Forces List, www.sflistteamhouse.com/Memorial/mix.htm.

149 *eastward toward safety:* John L. Plaster, *Secret Commandos: Behind Enemy Lines with the Elite Warriors of SOG* (New York: Simon and Schuster, 2004), 283–285; Plaster, *SOG*, 317; Headquarters, Department of the Army, Silver Star citation for David I. Mixter, March 30, 1972; Gene McCarthy, ed., *Special Operations Association* (Paducah, KY: Turner, 2005), 83–84.

150 *drive to the camp:* Schemmer, *The Raid*, 57–59.

150 *outskirts of their own capital:* Lucien S. Vandenbroucke, *Perilous Options: Special Operations as an Instrument of U.S. Foreign Policy* (New York: Oxford University Press, 1993), 63–64.

150 *". . . just what they'd do":* Melvin Small, *The Presidency of Richard Nixon* (Lawrence: University Press of Kansas, 1999), 83.

150 *hiccups and opportunities:* William H. McRaven, *Spec Ops: Case Studies in Special Operations Warfare: Theory and Practice* (Novato, CA: Presidio, 1995), 326–327.

151 *whole rehearsal again:* Schemmer, *The Raid*, 91.

151 *". . . 'They're still there'":* Ibid., 147.

151 *intruded from the west:* John Gargus, *The Son Tay Raid: American POWs in Vietnam Were Not Forgotten* (College Station: Texas A&M University Press, 2007), 120–132, 277–279; Vandenbroucke, *Perilous Options*, 55–57.

152 *". . . cells in a minute":* Schemmer, *The Raid*, 168.

152 *meaning no prisoners:* Gargus, *Son Tay Raid*, 202–203.

152 *nearby Black River:* Earl H. Tilford Jr., *Search and Rescue in Southeast Asia, 1961–1975* (Washington, DC: Center for Air Force History, 1992), 104; Jerry L. Thigpen, *The Praetorian STARShip: The Untold Story of the Combat Talon* (Maxwell Air Force Base, AL: Air University Press, 2001), 157.

152 *other a gunshot wound:* Chinnery, *Any Time, Any Place*, 203–206.

152 *brief history of the Green Berets:* US Army John F. Kennedy Center, "Multipurpose Force Study," II-5.

153 *as much North Vietnamese traffic as ever:* Kelly, *U.S. Army Special Forces*, 158.

153 *more than one hundred times the friendly casualties:* Charles F. Reske, ed., *MAC-V-SOG Command History, Annex B, 1971–1972*, vol. 1 (Sharon Center, OH: Alpha Press, 1990), 10–11; Plaster, *SOG*, 340.

153 *Admiral Elmo Zumwalt:* Andrew J. Birtle, *U.S. Army Counterinsurgency and Contingency Operations Doctrine, 1942–1976* (Washington, DC: US Army Center of Military History, 2006), 479; Susan Marquis, *Unconventional Warfare: Rebuilding U.S. Special Operations Forces* (Washington, DC: Brookings Institution Press, 1997), 38–39.

CHAPTER 6: JSOC AND SOCOM

158 *parachute, helicopter, and boat:* David W. Hogan Jr., *Raiders or Elite Infantry? The Changing Role of the U.S. Army Rangers from Dieppe to Grenada* (Westport, CT: Greenwood, 1992), 198–201.

159 *his past sins:* Eric L. Haney, *Inside Delta Force: The Story of America's Elite Counterterrorist Unit* (New York: Delacorte, 2002), 79, 207–209.

159 *locksmiths, electricians, and climbers:* Charlie Beckwith and Donald Knox, *Delta Force: The Army's Elite Counterterrorist Unit* (San Diego: Harcourt Brace Jovanovich, 1983), 112–117; Michael Lee Lanning, *Blood Warriors: American Military Elites* (New York: Ballantine, 2002), 129–130.

159 *at year's end:* Rod Lenahan, *Crippled Eagle: A Historical Perspective of U.S. Special Operations, 1976–1996* (Charleston, SC: Narwhal, 1998), 8–9; Beckwith and Knox, *Delta Force*, 108–110.

160 *exacting standards:* Beckwith and Knox, *Delta Force*, 139–140.

162 *contact Meyer's office:* Ibid., 153–156.

162 *wearing fatigues and boots:* Haney, *Inside Delta Force*, 13.

162 *eliminated from contention:* Ibid., 35–36; Beckwith and Knox, *Delta Force*, 136.

163 *shooter had hit:* Beckwith and Knox, *Delta Force*, 158–159.

164 *contempt for the white American male:* Mark Bowden, *Guests of the Ayatollah: The First Battle in America's War with Militant Islam* (New York: Atlantic Monthly Press, 2006), 224–225; Lenahan, *Crippled Eagle*, 25–30.

164 *overland phase of the operation:* Alan Hoe, *The Quiet Professional: Major Richard J. Meadows of the U.S. Army Special Forces* (Lexington: University Press of Kentucky, 2011), 147–160; Lucien S. Vandenbroucke, *Perilous Options: Special Operations as an Instrument of U.S. Foreign Policy* (New York: Oxford University Press, 1993), 126–128; Daniel P. Bolger, *Americans at War, 1975–1986: An Era of Violent Peace* (Novato, CA: Presidio, 1988), 114–115.

165 *calm and at ease:* Beckwith and Knox, *Delta Force*, 4.

165 *". . . step-by-step rundown":* Hamilton Jordan, *Crisis: The Last Year of the Carter Presidency* (New York: G. P. Putnam's Sons, 1982), 256.

166 *"We certainly are":* Vandenbroucke, *Perilous Options*, 139; Beckwith and Knox, *Delta Force*, 8.

166 *". . . my many questions":* Jimmy Carter, *Keeping Faith: Memoirs of a President* (Fayetteville: University of Arkansas Press, 2013), 517.

167 *bags of blood:* Bowden, *Guests of the Ayatollah*, 433; Jerry L. Thigpen, *The Praetorian STARShip: The Untold Story of the Combat Talon* (Maxwell Air Force Base, AL: Air University Press, 2001), 213–214.

167 *continued to fly:* David C. Martin and John Wolcott, *Best Laid Plans: The Inside Story of America's War Against Terrorism* (New York: Harper and Row, 1988), 18, 34; Vandenbroucke, *Perilous Options*, 132.

168 *storms had been lost:* John E. Valliere, "Disaster at Desert One: Catalyst for Change," *Parameters* 22, no. 3 (Autumn 1992): 76; Special Operations Review Group, "Rescue Mission Report," National Security Archive, George Washington University, http://nsarchive.gwu.edu/NSAEBB/NSAEBB63/doc8.pdf, 38–39.

168 *". . . bowl of milk":* Paul B. Ryan, *The Iranian Rescue Mission: Why It Failed* (Annapolis, MD: Naval Institute Press, 1985), 71.

168 *suck it up:* Bowden, *Guests of the Ayatollah,* 450–451.

169 *nerve among the pilots:* James H. Kyle and John R. Eidson, *The Guts to Try: The Untold Story of the Iran Hostage Rescue Mission by the On-Scene Desert Commander* (New York: Orion, 1990), 287–288.

169 *vulnerability to enemy fire:* Vandenbroucke, *Perilous Options,* 129–130; Special Operations Review Group, "Rescue Mission Report," 33–34.

170 *". . . with his recommendation":* John T. Carney and Benjamin F. Schemmer, *No Room for Error: The Covert Operations of America's Special Tactics Units from Iran to Afghanistan* (New York: Ballantine Books, 2002), 93; Kyle and Eidson, *Guts to Try,* 289–293; Gary Sick, *All Fall Down: America's Tragic Encounter with Iran* (New York: Random House, 1985), 351.

171 *issue an apology:* Beckwith and Knox, *Delta Force,* 312–314.

171 *". . . we let you down":* Carter, *Keeping Faith,* 529.

171 *". . . never to return":* Haney, *Inside Delta Force,* 207.

171 *assigned staff and forces:* Special Operations Review Group, "Rescue Mission Report," 61.

171 *halfway through the briefing:* Sean Naylor, *Relentless Strike: The Secret History of the Joint Special Operations Command* (New York: St. Martin's Press, 2015), 6.

173 *". . . say 'fuck' to":* Richard Marcinko with John Weisman, *Rogue Warrior* (New York: Pocket Books, 1992), 190–191.

173 *". . . take the troops drinking":* Robert A. Gormley, *Combat Swimmer: Memoirs of a Navy SEAL* (New York: Dutton, 1998), 176.

173 *bars along the boardwalk:* Orr Kelly, *Brave Men—Dark Waters: The Untold Story of the Navy SEALS* (Novato, CA: Presidio, 1992), 189.

173 *". . . too good to fail":* Chuck Pfarrer, *SEAL Target Geronimo: The Inside Story of the Mission to Kill Osama* (New York: St. Martin's, 2011), 38.

174 *reprimand for the escapade:* Naylor, *Relentless Strike,* 17.

174 *sent to work at the Pentagon:* Gormley, *Combat Swimmer,* 177–179; Kelly, *Brave Men—Dark Waters,* 191.

175 *had been scrimshawed:* Kelly, *Brave Men—Dark Waters,* 191–203.

175 *fined him $10,000:* John M. Broder, "Ex-SEAL Unit Head Convicted of Fraud," *Los Angeles Times,* January 26, 1990; Marcinko with Weisman, *Rogue Warrior,* 312.

175 *trials of beer swilling:* Chuck Pfarrer, *Warrior Soul: The Memoir of a Navy SEAL* (New York: Random House, 2004), 268–270.

175 *". . . Marcinko stink on us":* Naylor, *Relentless Strike,* 48.

175 *". . . takes over the presidency of the United States":* William M. LeoGrande, *Our Own Backyard: The United States in Central America, 1977–1992* (Chapel Hill: University of North Carolina Press, 1998), 69.

176 *from military rule to liberal democracy:* Robert D. Ramsey, *Advising Indigenous Forces: American Advisors in Korea, Vietnam, and El Salvador* (Fort Leavenworth, KS: Combat Studies Institute Press, 2006), 85–97; Kalev I. Sepp, *The Evolution of United States Military Strategy in Central America, 1979–1991,* PhD diss., Harvard University, 2002; Hugh Byrne, *El Salvador's Civil War: A Study of Revolution* (Boulder: Lynne Rienner, 1996); Mark Moyar, *A Question of Command:*

Counterinsurgency from the Civil War to Iraq (New Haven, CT: Yale University Press, 2009), 173–189.

178 *guarding it:* Tom Clancy, Carl Stiner, and Tony Koltz, *Shadow Warriors: Inside the Special Forces* (New York: G. P. Putnam, 2002), 11.

178 *flew into the country:* Library of Congress, Federal Research Division, "A History of the 160th Special Operations Aviation Regiment (Airborne)," October 2001, 8.

178 "... *Air Force delays*": Ibid., 9.

178 *abortive raid:* Daniel P. Bolger, "Special Operations and the Grenada Campaign," *Parameters* 18, no. 4 (December 1988): 58; Carney and Schemmer, *No Room for Error*, 146–147.

179 *campus buildings near the airstrip:* Mark Adkin, *Urgent Fury: The Battle for Grenada* (Lexington, MA: Lexington Books, 1989), 204–212; Ronald H. Cole, *Operation Urgent Fury* (Washington, DC: Joint History Office, 1997), 41–42.

179 *two dozen wounded:* H. Norman Schwarzkopf, *It Doesn't Take a Hero* (New York: Bantam, 1992), 256; Cole, *Operation Urgent Fury*, 53–54; Carney and Schemmer, *No Room for Error*, 152; Adkin, *Urgent Fury*, 278–285.

180 *closed-door session:* Kelly, *Brave Men—Dark Waters*, 213.

180 *separate SOF funding line:* James R. Locher III, "Congress to the Rescue: Statutory Creation of USSOCOM," *Air Commando Journal* 1, no. 3 (Spring 2012): 33–39; Lenahan, *Crippled Eagle*, 205–213; Susan Marquis, *Unconventional Warfare: Rebuilding U.S. Special Operations Forces* (Washington, DC: Brookings Institution Press, 1997), 107–144.

181 *theater search and rescue:* Public Law 99-61, November 14, 1986, US Code, US House of Representatives, http://uscode.house.gov/statutes/pl/99/661.pdf.

181 *remainder of the century:* John P. Piedmont, *Det One: U.S. Marine Corps U.S. Special Operations Command Detachment* (Washington, DC: US Marine Corps History Division, 2010), 1–8.

181 "... *build higher*": Lanning, *Blood Warriors*, 196.

182 "... *setting sail out to sea*": Marquis, *Unconventional Warfare*, 171.

182 "... *things inside it*": Clancy et al., *Shadow Warriors*, 221–223.

183 *standard-bearers of the reform movement:* Richard W. Potter, interview with author, 2016.

183 *Noriega propaganda:* Thomas Donnelly, Margaret Roth, and Caleb Baker, *Operation Just Cause: The Storming of Panama* (New York: Lexington Books, 1991), 122–130.

183 *as a result of these conversations:* United States Special Operations Command History, 1987–2007 (MacDill Air Force Base, FL: USSOCOM, 2007), 41–43.

184 *huddled in his cell's bathroom:* Library of Congress, Federal Research Division, "A History of the 160th Special Operations Aviation Regiment (Airborne)," 26–27; Kurt Muse and John Gilstrap, *Six Minutes to Freedom: How a Band of Heroes Defied a Dictator and Helped Free a Nation* (New York: Citadel Press, 2006), 278–285.

184 *pulled a gun on them:* Donnelly et al., *Operation Just Cause*, 208; *United States Special Operations Command History*, 34–35.

185 *Panamanians capitulated:* United States Special Operations Command History, 35.

185 *jars of human organs:* Ronald H. Cole, *Operation Just Cause: The Planning and Execution of Joint Operations in Panama, February 1988–January 1990* (Washington, DC: Joint History Office, 1995), 38; William G. Boykin with Lynn Vincent, *Never Surrender: A Soldier's Journey to the Crossroads of Faith and Freedom* (New York: FaithWords, 2008), 211–212.

185 *effort to unsettle him:* Per Liljas, "These Five Songs Have All Been Used to Torture People," *Time*, October 29, 2013.

185 *interacted effectively with conventional forces:* Interviews with veterans of Operation Just Cause, 2015–2016.

186 *deep interest in global politics:* Douglas C. Waller, *The Commandos: The Inside Story of America's Secret Soldiers* (New York: Simon and Schuster, 1994), 229–230.

186 *participate in combat operations:* Thomas K. Adams, *US Special Operations Forces in Action* (London: Frank Cass, 1998), 232–237.

186 *trouble and embarrassment:* Clancy et al., *Shadow Warriors*, 408–411; Marquis, *Unconventional Warfare*, 231.

188 "*. . . four-star in the theater*": Rick Atkinson, *Crusade: The Untold Story of the Persian Gulf War* (Boston: Houghton Mifflin, 1993), 142; Waller, *Commandos*, 247–250.

188 *foreign conventional forces needed:* US Department of Defense, "Conduct of the Persian Gulf War: Final Report to Congress," April 1992, Appendix J, 8–9, 28.

188 *operate behind Iraqi lines against the Scuds:* Michael R. Gordon and Bernard E. Trainor, *The Generals' War: The Inside Story of the Conflict in the Gulf* (Boston: Little, Brown, 1995), 241–242; Atkinson, *Crusade*, 142–144.

189 "*. . . They're going*": Clancy et al., *Shadow Warriors*, 435–436.

189 *uncaging of JSOC in the desert:* Waller, *Commandos*, 341–350; Naylor, *Relentless Strike*, 52.

CHAPTER 7: GOTHIC SERPENT

193 "*. . . might lose the war*": Rick Atkinson, "The Raid That Went Wrong: How an Elite U.S. Force Failed in Somalia," *Washington Post*, January 30, 1994.

195 "*Screw you!*": Keni Thomas, *Get It On! What It Means to Lead the Way* (Nashville: B&H, 2011), 54–61; Mark Bowden, *Black Hawk Down: A Story of Modern War* (New York: Atlantic Monthly Press, 1999), 15.

196 *chance of survival:* Matt Eversmann, "Operation Gothic Serpent," in Matt Eversmann and Dan Schilling, eds., *The Battle of Mogadishu: First Hand Accounts from the Men of Task Force Ranger* (New York: Presidio, 2004), 15–17.

197 *every day for war wounds:* Keith B. Richburg, *Out of America: A Black Man Confronts Africa* (New York: Basic Books, 1997), 51.

197 *500,000 Somalis:* Robert B. Oakley, "An Envoy's Perspective," *Joint Force Quarterly*, Autumn 1993, 45.

197 "*. . . chaotic clan war*": "Do It Right in Somalia," *New York Times*, December 1, 1992.

197 "*. . . relieve suffering*": Richburg, *Out of America*, 59.

197 *from the ports to the country's interior:* John L. Hirsch and Robert B. Oakley, *Somalia and Operation Restore Hope: Reflections on Peacemaking and Peacekeeping* (Washington, DC: US Institute of Peace, 1995), 103–104.

198 *". . . community of nations":* Jane Boulden, *Peace Enforcement: The United Nations Experience in Congo, Somalia, and Bosnia* (Westport, CT: Praeger, 2001), 60.

198 *participation of conventional forces:* Daniel P. Bolger, *Savage Peace: Americans at War in the 1990s* (Novato, CA: Presidio, 1995), 306.

199 *little support in the US military or Congress:* Patrick J. Sloyan, "Mission in Somalia," *Newsday*, December 5–9, 1993; David Tucker and Christopher J. Lamb, *United States Special Operations Forces* (New York: Columbia University Press, 2007), 120–121.

199 *precautions against capture:* Bolger, *Savage Peace*, 308.

199 *set up its headquarters:* Vernon Loeb, "The CIA in Somalia," *Washington Post*, February 27, 2000.

200 *". . . gonna make general":* Bowden, *Black Hawk Down*, 24.

200 *Russian roulette:* Loeb, "CIA in Somalia."

200 *mysteriously disappeared:* Sloyan, "Mission in Somalia"; Loeb, "CIA in Somalia."

200 *". . . Aidid has been reported":* Atkinson, "The Raid That Went Wrong."

201 *work for the UN:* John Lancaster, "U.S. Raid Was Based on a Tip," *Washington Post*, August 31, 1993.

201 *". . . can't shoot straight!":* Sloyan, "Mission in Somalia."

201 *Aidid's top men:* Loeb, "CIA in Somalia."

204 *to kill Americans:* Thomas, *Get It On*, 63–73.

204 *lifeless bodies into the dirt:* Bowden, *Black Hawk Down*, 42–43.

205 *barreled across:* Thomas, *Get It On*, 91–93.

207 *". . . can't find us":* Ibid., 106–110.

207 *". . . birds to land":* Mike Kurth, "Through My Eyes," in Matt Eversmann and Dan Schilling, eds., *The Battle of Mogadishu: First Hand Accounts from the Men of Task Force Ranger* (New York: Presidio, 2004), 73.

207 *several men would likely die:* Kent DeLong and Steven Tuckey, *Mogadishu! Heroism and Tragedy* (Westport, CT: Praeger, 1994), 29.

208 *different route:* Jeff Struecker with Dean Merrill, *The Road to Unafraid: How the Army's Top Ranger Faced Fear and Found Courage Through "Black Hawk Down" and Beyond* (Nashville: W Publishing Group, 2006), 101.

209 *vehicles back to their base:* Lawrence E. Casper, "Quick Reaction Force, Falcon Brigade, 10th Mountain Division, Summary of Combat Operations on 3 October 1993"; Lawrence E. Casper, *Falcon Brigade: Combat and Command in Somalia and Haiti* (Boulder: Lynne Rienner, 2001), 44–48; Bolger, *Savage Peace*, 320–323; Rick Atkinson, "Deliverance from Warlord's Fury: Rangers Pinned Down in Mogadishu Recall Harrowing Rescue," *Washington Post*, October 7, 1993.

209 *Durant's crash site:* Lee A. Rysewyk, "Experiences of Executive Officer from Bravo Company, 3d Battalion, 75th Ranger Regiment and Task Force Ranger During the Battle of the Black Sea on 3–4 October 1993 in Mogadishu, Somalia," US Army Maneuver Center of Excellence Libraries, May 1994, www.benning.army.mil/library/content/Virtual/Donovanpapers/other/STUP5/RysewykLee%20A.%20CPT.pdf.

209 *reliance on diplomacy:* John W. Warner and Carl Levin, "Review of the Circumstances Surrounding the Ranger Raid on October 3–4, 1993 in Mogadishu,

Somalia," United States Senate, Committee on Armed Services, September 29, 1995, 32–36; United States Forces Somalia, *After Action Report*, vol. 1 (Washington, DC: Center of Military History, 2003), 35–36.

210 *contact with hostile forces:* Bowden, *Black Hawk Down*, 165.

210 *". . . ostrich egg":* Michael J. Durant with Steven Hartov, *In the Company of Heroes* (New York: Putnam, 2003), 29.

211 *". . . ever had to make":* William Boykin, *Never Surrender: A Soldier's Journey to the Crossroads of Faith and Freedom* (New York: FaithWords, 2008), 271.

211 *Mogadishu at nightfall:* Frank Hoffman, "One Decade Later—Debacle in Somalia," *Proceedings* 130, no. 1 (January 2004): 69.

211 *started to cry:* Kurth, "Through My Eyes," 104.

212 *". . . whipped ass":* Bowden, *Black Hawk Down*, 299.

212 *stop killing people:* Ibid., 311.

212 *2 dead and 22 wounded:* Richard W. Stewart, *The United States Army in Somalia, 1992–1994* (Washington, DC: Center of Military History, 2003), 13.

213 *". . . open season on Americans":* William J. Clinton, "Message to the Congress Transmitting a Report on Somalia," October 13, 1993, US Government Publishing Office, Federal Digital System, www.gpo.gov/fdsys/pkg/PPP-1993 -book2/pdf/PPP-1993-book2-doc-pg1739.pdf.

213 *value of killing Americans:* Benjamin Runkle, *Wanted Dead or Alive: Manhunts from Geronimo to Bin Laden* (New York: St. Martin's Press, 2011), 154–155.

213 *". . . day after the fight":* Bowden, *Black Hawk Down*, 329.

213 *". . . pounded their fists":* Struecker, *The Road to Unafraid*, 137.

213 *to carry out:* In early October, some senior administration officials were recommending a shift from hunting for Aidid to a diplomatic solution, but Clinton had never rescinded Task Force Ranger's orders to hunt down Aidid. He had still been hoping to bag the warlord. Michael R. Gordon and John H. Cushman Jr., "Mission in Somalia: After Supporting Hunt for Aidid, U.S. Is Blaming U.N. for Losses," *New York Times*, October 18, 1993; Hirsch and Oakley, *Somalia and Operation Restore Hope*, 128.

214 *". . . not sufficiently attentive":* Gordon and Cushman, "Mission in Somalia."

214 *micromanage the military:* Tucker and Lamb, *United States Special Operations Forces*, 127.

214 *Aspin fired, too:* Sloyan, "Mission in Somalia."

214 *". . . thin-skinned vehicles":* Barton Gellman, "The Words Behind a Deadly Decision," *Washington Post*, October 31, 1993.

214 *". . . political cowards":* Dan Schilling, "On Friendship and Firefights," in Matt Eversmann and Dan Schilling, eds., *The Battle of Mogadishu: First Hand Accounts from the Men of Task Force Ranger* (New York: Presidio, 2004), 165–166.

215 *". . . forget about Somalia":* Sloyan, "Mission in Somalia."

215 *share of promotions:* Sean Naylor, *Relentless Strike: The Secret History of the Joint Special Operations Command* (New York: St. Martin's Press, 2015), 60.

216 *similar hot spots:* Rowan Scarborough, *Rumsfeld's War: The Untold Story of America's Anti-Terrorist Commander* (Washington, DC: Regnery, 2004), 229.

216 *rooftops of Medellín:* Mark Bowden, *Killing Pablo: The Hunt for the World's Greatest Outlaw* (New York: Atlantic Monthly Press, 2001).

216 *wars still to come:* Charles T. Cleveland, "Command and Control of the Joint Commission Observer Program, U.S. Army Special Forces in Bosnia," US Army War College Strategy Research Project, April 2001.

216 *end of the decade:* Peter DeShazo, Johanna Mendelson Forman, and Phillip Mc-Lean, "Countering Threats to Security and Stability in a Failing State: Lessons from Colombia," Center for Strategic and International Studies, September 2009, http://csis.org/files/publication/090930_DeShazo_CounteringThreats _Web.pdf, 8–9.

217 *became the senior leadership:* Mark Moyar, Hector Pagan, and Wil R. Griego, *Persistent Engagement in Colombia* (Tampa, FL: Joint Special Operations University Press, 2014).

217 *". . . emulate them":* Ibid., 54.

219 *". . . bite them in Somalia":* Elizabeth Drew, *On the Edge: The Clinton Presidency* (New York: Simon and Schuster, 1994), 322.

CHAPTER 8: REGIME CHANGE

222 *". . . anything beyond threats":* Abdul Salam Zaeef, *My Life with the Taliban* (London: Hurst, 2010), 149–150.

223 *training Kazakh paratroopers:* Allan Zullo, *Battle Heroes: Voices from Afghanistan* (New York: Scholastic, 2010), 5–6.

224 *and other rebel groups:* Michael Smith, *Killer Elite: The Inside Story of America's Most Secret Special Operations Team* (New York : St. Martin's Press, 2007), 211.

224 *would remain low:* Henry A. Crumpton, *The Art of Intelligence: Lessons from a Life in the CIA's Clandestine Service* (New York: Penguin, 2012), 178–193.

224 *in time of national crisis:* Bob Woodward, *Bush at War* (New York: Simon and Schuster, 2002), 193–194.

224 *". . . when the 101st and the 82nd Airborne arrived":* Max Boot, *War Made New: Technology, Warfare, and the Course of History: 1500 to Today* (New York: Gotham, 2006), 355.

224 *who would work for whom:* Gary C. Schroen, *First In: An Insider's Account of How the CIA Spearheaded the War on Terror in Afghanistan* (Novato, CA: Presidio, 2005), 159–160.

225 *few hundred operators:* Yaniv Barzilai, *102 Days of War: How Osama bin Laden, Al Qaeda and the Taliban Survived 2001* (Dulles, VA: Potomac Books, 2013), 34–37.

225 *languages of Afghanistan:* Charles H. Briscoe, Richard L. Kiper, Kalev I. Sepp, and James A Schroder, *Weapon of Choice: ARSOF in Afghanistan* (Fort Leavenworth, KS: Combat Studies Institute, 2003), 52, 125–126.

225 *single index card:* Doug Stanton, *Horse Soldiers: The Extraordinary Story of a Band of U.S. Soldiers Who Rode to Victory in Afghanistan* (New York: Scribner, 2009), 195–196.

226 *GPS technology:* Steve Call, *Danger Close: Tactical Air Controllers in Afghanistan and Iraq* (College Station: Texas A&M University Press, 2007), 15–16; Gary Berntsen and Ralph Pezzullo, *Jawbreaker: The Attack on Bin Laden and Al Qaeda: A Personal Account by the CIA's Key Field Commander* (New York: Crown, 2005), 134–135.

226 *" . . . Your Daddy":* Eric Blehm, *The Only Thing Worth Dying For: How Eleven Green Berets Forged a New Afghanistan* (New York: Harper, 2010), 53.

226 *Sand People in* Star Wars: Stanton, *Horse Soldiers*, 100–101.

227 *kill the Americans at their first meeting:* Briscoe et al., *Weapon of Choice*, 122.

227 *perpetrated in years past:* Berntsen and Pezzullo, *Jawbreaker*, 133–134; Stanton, *Horse Soldiers*, 109–122.

227 *knees sticking up near their ears:* Stanton, *Horse Soldiers*, 121–125; Boot, *War Made New*, 354.

228 *after they dismounted:* Robin Moore, *The Hunt for Bin Laden: Task Force Dagger* (New York: Random House, 2003), 71–72; Stanton, *Horse Soldiers*, 134–136.

228 *soldiers quipped:* Stanton, *Horse Soldiers*, 346.

228 *" . . . very happy":* Briscoe et al., *Weapon of Choice*, 127.

229 *"Surrender or die!":* Schroen, *First In*, 138.

229 *working with the Northern Alliance:* Dana Priest, "'Team 555' Shaped a New Way of War: Special Forces and Smart Bombs Turned Tide and Routed Taliban," *Washington Post*, April 3, 2002.

229 *began marking targets:* Donald P. Wright, with the Contemporary Operations Study Team, *A Different Kind of War: The United States Army in Operation Enduring Freedom, October 2001–September 2005* (Fort Leavenworth, KS: Combat Studies Institute, 2005), 97.

229 *" . . . requests for strikes":* Schroen, *First In*, 290–292.

231 *"from here on out":* Blehm, *The Only Thing Worth Dying For*, 13.

231 *"Children in Action":* Ibid., 18, 77, 249–250.

233 *found another spot:* John Hendren and Richard T. Cooper, "Fragile Alliances in a Hostile Land," *Los Angeles Times*, May 5, 2002.

233 *fighters in the kill zone:* Robert L. Grenier, *88 Days to Kandahar: A CIA Diary* (New York: Simon and Schuster, 2015), 226–227; Briscoe et al., *Weapon of Choice*, 157.

233 *" . . . leadership face-to-face":* Blehm, *The Only Thing Worth Dying For*, 159.

233 *" . . . friends, farmers, and shopkeepers":* Briscoe et al., *Weapon of Choice*, 173.

233 *liaisons with Northern Alliance leaders:* Tommy Franks, with Malcolm McConnell, *American Soldier* (New York: Regan Books, 2004), 309.

234 *team's tactical affairs:* Blehm, *The Only Thing Worth Dying For*, 177.

234 *" . . . the movie, 'Mad Max'":* Briscoe et al., *Weapon of Choice*, 173.

234 *most of them into his ranks:* Wright et al., *A Different Kind of War*, 108.

234 *needed to be hit:* Blehm, *The Only Thing Worth Dying For*, 264–274.

234 *device's location:* Wright et al., *A Different Kind of War*, 110.

235 *grenades and knives:* Stephen Biddle, *Afghanistan and the Future of Warfare: Implications for Army and Defense Policy* (Carlisle, PA: Strategic Studies Institute, 2002), 26–28; Briscoe et al., *Weapon of Choice*, 107–108, 167; Grenier, *88 Days to Kandahar*, 275–283.

236 *holed up in the region:* Wright et al., *A Different Kind of War*, 114–116.

236 *Cambone, an aide to Rumsfeld:* Rowan Scarborough, *Rumsfeld's War: The Untold Story of America's Anti-Terrorist Commander* (Washington, DC: Regnery, 2004), 3–4, 20–21.

237 *proposal to a group of officers:* Sean Naylor, *Relentless Strike: The Secret History of the Joint Special Operations Command* (New York: St. Martin's Press, 2015), 92.

237 *much of Delta Force:* Grenier, *88 Days to Kandahar*, 169.

237 "*. . . targets he knows are empty*": Pete Blaber, *The Mission, the Men, and Me: Lessons from a Former Delta Force Commander* (New York: Berkley Caliber, 2008), 152.

238 "*. . . slipping away!!*": Berntsen and Pazzullo, *Jawbreaker*, 277, 290.

238 *needed no modification:* Crumpton, *Art of Intelligence*, 258–259.

238 *enemy's lair: United States Special Operations Command History, 1987–2007* (MacDill Air Force Base, FL: USSOCOM, 2007), 95.

239 "*. . . out of the trenches*": Dalton Fury, *Kill Bin Laden: A Delta Force Commander's Account of the Hunt for the World's Most Wanted Man* (New York: St. Martin's Press, 2008), 113.

239 *obtain food and drink:* Wright et al., *A Different Kind of War*, 117–118.

239 *destruction by strike aircraft: United States Special Operations Command History*, 96–97.

239 *slipped out unhurt:* Wright et al., *A Different Kind of War*, 118–119.

240 *recently deployed 10th Mountain Division and 187th Infantry Regiment:* Lester W. Grau and Dodge Billingsley, *Operation Anaconda: America's First Major Battle in Afghanistan* (Lawrence: University Press of Kansas, 2011), 106; Sean Naylor, *Not a Good Day to Die: The Untold Story of Operation Anaconda* (New York: Berkley Books, 2005), 45–48; Wright et al., *A Different Kind of War*, 137.

241 *No, said Blaber, Delta Force:* Blaber, *The Mission, the Men, and Me*, 19–30.

242 *keep his men in the game:* Naylor, *Not a Good Day to Die*, 80–81, 141–142; Blaber, *The Mission, the Men, and Me*, 227.

242 *satellite radio:* Blaber, *The Mission, the Men, and Me*, 254.

244 *detect the glint tape:* Ellen Crean, "Friendly Fire," CBS News, March 12, 2003; Naylor, *Not a Good Day to Die*, 200–206; Call, *Danger Close*, 63–64.

245 "*. . . Where are the planes?*": Briscoe et al., *Weapon of Choice*, 286; Grau and Billingsley, *Operation Anaconda*, 138; Naylor, *Not a Good Day to Die*, 207–208.

245 *easiest method of escape:* Grau and Billingsley, *Operation Anaconda*, 191–193; Naylor, *Not a Good Day to Die*, 214–215.

245 *evacuated by air:* Headquarters United States Air Force, *Operation Anaconda: An Air Power Perspective*, February 7, 2005, 62–66; Wright et al., *A Different Kind of War*, 143–154.

246 *familiar with the area:* Blaber, *The Mission, the Men, and Me*, 273.

247 *withdrawn from the battlefield:* Naylor, *Not A Good Day to Die*, 371–372.

247 "*. . . get in there tonight*": Blaber, *The Mission, the Men, and Me*, 277.

248 *detected nothing:* Andrew N. Milani, "Pitfalls of Technology: A Case Study of the Battle on Takur Ghar Mountain," US Army War College, 2003, 8.

248 *"Go! Go! Go!":* Malcolm MacPherson, *Roberts Ridge: A Story of Courage and Sacrifice on Takur Ghar Mountain, Afghanistan* (New York: Delacorte Press, 2005), 16–24.

249 *ten feet below:* Milani, "Pitfalls of Technology," 11–12; MacPherson, *Roberts Ridge*, 29–30.

249 "*. . . go back in!*": MacPherson, *Roberts Ridge*, 30.

249 *Mack later described it:* Naylor, *Not a Good Day to Die*, 314.

250 *taking no chances:* MacPherson, *Roberts Ridge*, 89–93.

250 *stopped breathing:* Post-battle investigations found considerable evidence suggesting that Chapman was still alive when the SEAL team left him, and that he

was killed in an ensuing firefight with hostile fighters. In August 2016, the Air Force concluded that newly refined analysis of grainy overhead drone footage showed that Chapman had indeed been alive and had continued to fight on alone until he was shot dead by an enemy machine gun. Sean D. Naylor and Christopher Drew, "SEAL Team 6 and a Man Left for Dead: A Grainy Picture of Valor," *New York Times*, August 27, 2016.

251 *aborting the landing:* Grau and Billingsley, *Operation Anaconda*, 247–248; MacPherson, *Roberts Ridge*, 144–145, 156–157.

253 *slopes of the mountain:* Headquarters United States Air Force, *Operation Anaconda*, 75–76; Nate Self, *Two Wars: One Hero's Fight on Two Fronts—Abroad and Within* (Carol Stream, IL: Tyndale House, 2008), 176–179; MacPherson, *Roberts Ridge*, 184–189.

254 *". . . watch Stebner get killed":* MacPherson, *Roberts Ridge*, 237–239.

255 *". . . don't feel safe":* Self, *Two Wars*, 231–232; Grau and Billingsley, *Operation Anaconda*, 269–270; MacPherson, *Roberts Ridge*, 247–248, 256–257; Naylor, *Not a Good Day to Die*, 364–366.

255 *several others weeping:* Naylor, *Not a Good Day to Die*, 367; MacPherson, *Roberts Ridge*, 262; Self, *Two Wars*, 239.

255 *cost any more men their lives:* Briscoe et al., *Weapon of Choice*, 318; MacPherson, *Roberts Ridge*, 266–267; Naylor, *Not a Good Day to Die*, 367; Self, *Two Wars*, 245.

255 *dead or gone:* Grau and Billingsley, *Operation Anaconda*, 293–330.

255 *death toll at 800:* Wright et al., *A Different Kind of War*, 173.

255 *during the fracas:* Naylor, *Not a Good Day to Die*, 375–376.

256 *any war in US history:* Tim Dyhouse, "'Black Ops' Shine in Iraq War: The Scope of U.S. Special Operations in the Iraq War Was the Largest in American Military History," *VFW Magazine*, February 1, 2004.

257 *exclusively for the Rangers:* Donald Rumsfeld, *Known and Unknown: A Memoir* (New York: Sentinel, 2011), 653.

257 *don the black one:* Bradley Graham, *By His Own Rules: The Ambitions, Successes, and Ultimate Failures of Donald Rumsfeld* (New York: PublicAffairs, 2009), 255.

257 *conventional forces would support them:* Linda Robinson, *Masters of Chaos: The Secret History of the Special Forces* (New York: PublicAffairs, 2004), 193–292; Gregory Fontenot, E. J. Degen, and David Tohn, *On Point: The United States Army in Operation Iraqi Freedom* (Fort Leavenworth, KS: Combat Studies Institute Press 2004), 402–405; Thomas K. Adams, *The Army After Next: The First Post-Industrial Army* (Westport, CT: Praeger, 2006), 155–156.

258 *keep Saddam from sabotaging them:* Charles H. Briscoe, Kenneth Finlayson, Robert W. Jones Jr., Cherilyn A. Walley, A. Dwayne Aaron, Michael R. Mullins, and James A. Schroder, *All Roads Lead to Baghdad: Army Special Operations Forces in Iraq* (Fort Bragg, NC: USASOC History Office, 2006), 112, 211–219; Smith, *Killer Elite*, 250–251.

258 *not a single Scud was found:* Michael R. Gordon and Bernard E. Trainor, *Cobra II: The Inside Story of the Invasion and Occupation of Iraq* (New York: Pantheon, 2006), 335–336.

258 *ended up supporting conventional units:* Briscoe et al., *All Roads Lead to Baghdad*, 142–148, 154–163; Robinson, *Masters of Chaos*, 253–259.

258 *without a single American casualty:* Richard B. Andres, "The Afghan Model in Northern Iraq," in Thomas G. Mahnken and Thomas A. Keaney, eds., *War in Iraq: Planning and Execution* (London: Routledge, 2007), 60–64; Briscoe et al., *All Roads Lead to Baghdad*, 194; Frank Antenori and Hans Halberstadt, *Roughneck Nine-One: The Extraordinary Story of a Special Forces A-Team at War* (New York: St. Martin's Press, 2006).

259 *sixth-floor office:* Gordon and Trainor, *Cobra II*, 332–334; Briscoe et al., *All Roads Lead to Baghdad*, 292–304.

260 *come to know in Afghanistan:* Gordon and Trainor, *Cobra II*, 329–330.

260 *final defense of the Iraqi capital:* Kevin M. Woods, Michael R. Pease, Mark E. Stout, Williamson Murray, and James G. Lacey, *Iraqi Perspectives Project: A View of Operation Iraqi Freedom from Saddam's Senior Leadership* (Norfolk, VA: Joint Center for Operational Analysis, 2006), 131–132, 142–145.

261 *cross the airwaves:* Blaber, *The Mission, the Men, and Me*, 8–12.

CHAPTER 9: COUNTERINSURGENCY AND COUNTERTERRORISM

267 *formerly omnipotent man:* Steve Russell, *We Got Him! A Memoir of the Hunt and Capture of Saddam Hussein* (New York: Threshold, 2011), 307–323; Eric Maddox and Davin Seay, *Mission: Black List #1* (New York: Harper, 2008), 221–255; Phil Zabriskie, "Inside Saddam's Hideout," *Time*, December 15, 2003; "Candy Bars, Hot Dogs and Dirty Dishes in Saddam's Hideaway," Associated Press, December 15, 2003; Michael R. Gordon and Bernard E. Trainor, *The Endgame: The Inside Story of the Struggle for Iraq, from George W. Bush to Barack Obama* (New York: Pantheon, 2012), 38.

268 *pulled it down:* Peter Maass, "The Toppling: How the Media Inflated a Minor Moment in a Long War," *New Yorker*, January 10, 2011.

268 *". . . way to freedom":* "Liberated Iraqis Cheer Troops," *Washington Times*, April 10, 2003.

268 *". . . face of Saddam Hussein":* William Safire, "Jubilant V-I Day," *New York Times*, April 10, 2003.

268 *six months' time:* Michael R. Gordon and Bernard E. Trainor, *Cobra II: The Inside Story of the Invasion and Occupation of Iraq* (New York: Pantheon, 2006), 458–460.

269 *erupted in the summer of 2003:* Mark Moyar, *A Question of Command: Counterinsurgency from the Civil War to Iraq* (New Haven, CT: Yale University Press, 2009), 214–219.

270 *troops to attack:* Rob Schultheis, *Waging Peace: A Special Operations Team's Battle to Rebuild Iraq* (New York: Gotham, 2005); R. Alan King, *Twice Armed: An American Soldier's Battle for Hearts and Minds in Iraq* (St. Paul, MN: Zenith Press, 2006); David Tucker and Christopher J. Lamb, *United States Special Operations Forces* (New York: Columbia University Press, 2007), 28–36.

270 *CT for short:* Charles H. Briscoe, Kenneth Finlayson, Robert W. Jones Jr., Cherilyn A. Walley, A. Dwayne Aaron, Michael R. Mullins, and James A. Schroder, *All Roads Lead to Baghdad: Army Special Operations Forces in Iraq* (Fort Bragg, NC: USASOC History Office, 2006), 423.

271 *gunning down terrorists:* Interviews with SOF veterans, 2014–2016.

271　*elite Emergency Response Brigade:* Kevin Wells, "Eight Years of Combat FID: A Retrospective on Special Forces in Iraq," *Special Warfare*, January-March 2012; Dick Couch, *The Sheriff of Ramadi: Navy SEALs and the Winning of Al-Anbar* (Annapolis, MD: Naval Institute Press, 2008), 72–73, 96–97; Office of the Special Inspector General for Iraq Reconstruction, "Iraqi Security Forces: Special Operations Force Program Is Achieving Goals, But Iraqi Support Remains Critical to Success," March 25, 2010, 1–4; Michael O'Brien, "Foreign Internal Defense in Iraq: ARSOF Core Tasks Enable Iraqi Combating-Terrorism Capability," *Special Warfare*, January-March 2012.

271　". . . *doomed to failure*": Sean Naylor, "More Than Door Kickers," *Armed Forces Journal*, March 2006.

271　". . . *can do manhunts*": Sean Naylor, *Relentless Strike: The Secret History of the Joint Special Operations Command* (New York: St. Martin's Press, 2015), 165.

271　*available to the regional combatant commanders:* Jennifer Kibbe, "The Rise of the Shadow Warriors," *Foreign Affairs* 83, no. 2 (March/April 2004), 102–115; Rowan Scarborough, *Rumsfeld's War: The Untold Story of America's Anti-Terrorist Commander* (Washington, DC: Regnery, 2004), 22–23; Thomas K. Adams, *The Army After Next: The First Post-Industrial Army* (Westport, CT: Praeger, 2006), 199–201.

272　*support SOCOM's operations:* Glenn W. Goodman Jr., "Expanded Role for Elite Commandos," *Armed Forces Journal*, February 2003.

272　*large bedrooms:* Naylor, *Relentless Strike*, 226–228.

273　*prima-donna character of special operations forces:* Interviews with US Army and Marine Corps officers, 2004–2010.

273　*keeping watch over the battlefield:* Mark Urban, *Task Force Black: The Explosive True Story of the Secret Special Forces War in Iraq* (London: Little, Brown, 2010), 78–79.

273　*suffocate the insurgency:* Donald P. Wright and Timothy R. Reese, *On Point II: Transition to the New Campaign* (Ft. Leavenworth, KS: Combat Studies Institute Press, 2008), 225–227.

274　". . . *threat to our forces*": Rumsfeld, Bremer Pentagon Briefing, July 24, 2003, IIP Digital, US Department of State, http://iipdigital.usembassy.govl.

274　". . . *terrorist acts in Iraq*": "Capture Should Speed Progress in Iraqi Politics," *Washington Times*, December 14, 2003.

275　*relieve his own team sergeant for laziness:* Stanley McChrystal, *My Share of the Task* (New York: Penguin, 2013), 33.

275　". . . *ever come across," Lamb remembered:* Dexter Filkins, "Stanley McChrystal's Long War," *New York Times Magazine*, October 14, 2009.

276　". . . *attitudes or arrogance*": McChrystal, *My Share of the Task*, 52.

276　". . . *seen up close*": Ibid., 65.

276　*low expectations:* Urban, *Task Force Black*, 35.

276　*pressed ahead:* Naylor, *Relentless Strike*, 272; McChrystal, *My Share of the Task*, 149, 161–162.

277　". . . *disrupting the enemy in foreign lands*": Walter Pincus and Dan Morgan, "Congress Supports Doubling Special Operations Funding," *Washington Post*, June 5, 2003.

277　*further targeting information:* Michael Flynn, Rich Juergens, and Thomas L. Cantrell, "Employing ISR: SOF Best Practices," *Joint Force Quarterly* 50, no. 3

(2008): 56–61; Spencer Ackerman, "How Special Ops Copied Al-Qaida to Kill It," *WIRED*, September 9, 2011.

278 *". . . ambassadors and advocates":* Naylor, *Relentless Strike*, 276; Christopher J. Lamb and Evan Munsing, *Secret Weapon: High-Value Target Teams as an Organizational Innovation* (Washington, DC: National Defense University Press, 2011), 16–18.

278 *". . . eliminate somebody":* Yochi Dreazen, "Joint Special Forces, CIA Hit Teams Are McChrystal's Legacy," *National Journal*, September 1, 2011; Naylor, *Relentless Strike*, 255–256; Urban, *Task Force Black*, 82–83.

278 *". . . Do it":* McChrystal, *My Share of the Task*, 155.

278 *three hundred per month in 2006:* Stanley McChrystal, with Tantum Collins, David Silverman, and Chris Fussell, *Team of Teams: New Rules of Engagement for a Complex World* (New York: Penguin, 2015), 218.

279 *". . . this is their life":* Naylor, *Relentless Strike*, 275.

279 *". . . perform at that level":* Ibid., 275.

279 *body parts of the targets:* Dana Priest and William M. Arkin, *Top Secret America: The Rise of the New American Security State* (New York: Little, Brown, 2011), 228; Urban, *Task Force Black*, 156.

280 *forces on patrol:* Couch, *The Sheriff of Ramadi*, 40–41, 68–69, 167–180.

280 *target the insurgent leaders:* Daniel P. Bolger, *Why We Lost: A General's Inside Account of the Iraq and Afghanistan Wars* (New York: Houghton Mifflin Harcourt, 2014), 197–198; Lamb and Munsing, *Secret Weapon*, 30.

280 *rather than launching raids themselves:* Gregory Wilson, "Anatomy of a Successful COIN Operation: OEF-Philippines and the Indirect Approach," *Military Review* 86, no. 6 (November-December 2006): 38–48.

281 *ramp up operations beyond Iraq and Afghanistan:* Harold Kennedy, "SOCOM Creates New Hub for Fighting War on Terror," *Defense Media Network*, February 2004.

281 *". . . past few years?" he demanded:* Bradley Graham, "Shortfalls of Special Operations Command Are Cited," *Washington Post*, November 17, 2005.

281 *". . . micro standpoint":* Andrew deGrandpre, "Task Force Violent: The Unforgiven," *Military Times*, March 12, 2015.

282 *"special operations capable":* John P. Piedmont, *Det One: U.S. Marine Corps U.S. Special Operations Command Detachment* (Washington, DC: US Marine Corps History Division, 2010), 8–20.

282 *pro-American Iraqi leader:* Bing West, *No True Glory: A Frontline Account of the Battle for Fallujah* (New York: Bantam, 2005), 208–251; Piedmont, *Det One*, 48–71; Moyar, *A Question of Command*, 229–230.

283 *Hagee concurred:* Piedmont, *Det One*, 91–93.

283 *smaller reconnaissance units:* Peter Nealen, "A Brief, Recent History of Force Recon and MARSOC," *SOFREP*, March 8, 2013; Piedmont, *Det One*, 93–96; Andrew Feickert, "U.S. Special Operations Forces (SOF): Background and Issues for Congress," Congressional Research Service, November 19, 2015.

283 *stint in the new units:* Andrew deGrandpre, "Task Force Violent: The Unforgiven," *Military Times*, March 12, 2015.

283 *segregated from the rest of the Army:* Linda Robinson, "The Future of Special Operations Forces," Council on Foreign Relations, April 2013, 9.

283 *"elite" any longer:* Tucker and Lamb, *United States Special Operations Forces*, 47; Dalton Fury, *Kill Bin Laden: A Delta Force Commander's Account of the Hunt for the World's Most Wanted Man* (New York: St. Martin's Press, 2008), 48.

284 *58 percent of Marine respondents said the same:* Moyar, *A Question of Command*, 299.

284 *Sunni and Shiite alike:* Peter R. Mansoor, *Surge: My Journey with General David Petraeus and the Remaking of the Iraq War* (New Haven, CT: Yale University Press, 2013); Bing West, *The Strongest Tribe: War, Politics, and the Endgame in Iraq* (New York: Random House, 2008); Kimberly Kagan, *The Surge: A Military History* (New York: Encounter, 2009).

284 *forestall the arrests:* Gordon and Trainor, *The Endgame*, 542–545.

285 *alleviating pressure on the Sunni insurgents:* Dave Butler, "Lights Out: ARSOF Reflect on Eight Years in Iraq," *Special Warfare*, January-March 2012, 32; Gordon and Trainor, *The Endgame*, 607, 759–760; Wells, "Eight Years of Combat FID."

285 *transiting from Pakistan into Afghanistan:* Donald P. Wright, with the Contemporary Operations Study Team, *A Different Kind of War: The United States Army in Operation Enduring Freedom, October 2001–September 2005* (Fort Leavenworth, KS: Combat Studies Institute, 2005), 213–218.

286 *". . . situation is worse":* Linda Robinson, *One Hundred Victories: Special Ops and the Future of American Warfare* (New York: PublicAffairs, 2013), 12–13.

286 *aversion to the use of force:* Jonathan Alter, *The Promise: President Obama, Year One* (New York: Simon and Schuster), 225; Vali Nasr, *The Indispensable Nation: American Foreign Policy in Retreat* (New York: Doubleday), 13–14.

287 *removed the terrorists:* Fred Kaplan, *The Insurgents: David Petraeus and the Plot to Change the American Way of War* (New York: Simon and Schuster, 2013), 297; Bob Woodward, *Obama's Wars* (New York: Simon and Schuster, 2010), 101–102, 166–167, 235–236; Alter, *The Promise*, 368; Robert M. Gates, *Duty: Memoirs of a Secretary at War* (New York: Knopf, 2014), 364.

287 *control of much of the country:* Woodward, *Obama's Wars*, 104, 190, 273–275; Gates, *Duty*, 364, 373–374.

288 *responsible for controlling:* Mark Moyar, "The Third Way of COIN: Defeating the Taliban in Sangin," Orbis Operations, 2011, 45.

288 *number of villages:* Mark Moyar, *Village Stability Operations and the Afghan Local Police* (Tampa, FL: Joint Special Operations University Press, 2014), 9–10.

288 *bolstering economic activity:* Brian Petit, "The Fight for the Village," *Military Review* 91, no. 3 (May-June 2011): 25–32.

288 *known as Village Stability Operations:* Todd C. Helmus, *Advising the Command: Best Practices from the Special Operations Advisory Experience in Afghanistan* (Santa Monica, CA: Rand, 2015). McChrystal assigned other white SOF and international SOF to the development of elite Afghan units such as the Commandos and the Provincial Response Companies.

289 *villages and their environs day and night:* Moyar, *Village Stability Operations and the Afghan Local Police*, 12–15.

290 *tête-à-tête:* Gates, *Duty*, 488–491; Karen DeYoung and Rajiv Chandrasekaran, "Gen. McChrystal Allies, Rolling Stone Disagree over Article's Ground Rules," *Washington Post*, June 26, 2010.

291 *authorize Local Police for the village:* Moyar, *Village Stability Operations and the Afghan Local Police*, 17–26.

292 *first 10,000 Local Policemen:* Joseph A. L'Étoile, "Transforming the Conflict in Afghanistan," *Prism* 4, no. 2 (September 2011): 3–16.

292 *varying levels of effectiveness:* Damon Robins, "Special Operations Forces and Conventional Forces Integration: Lessons Learned in Village Stability Operations," May 22, 2012.

292 *Afghan government could offer:* Moyar, *Village Stability Operations and the Afghan Local Police,* 77–86.

293 *". . . go out without fear":* Carmen Gentile, "Afghan Self-Defense Groups Give Communities Freedom," *USA Today,* August 16, 2012.

293 *". . . work with you":* Luke Mogelson, "Bad Guys vs. Worse Guys in Afghanistan," *New York Times,* October 19, 2011.

294 *taken root:* Human Rights Unit of the United Nations Assistance Mission in Afghanistan, "Afghanistan Mid-Year Report 2012: Protection of Civilians in Armed Conflict," July 2012; United Nations Assistance Mission in Afghanistan, "Treatment of Conflict-Related Detainees in Afghan Custody: One Year On," January 2013.

294 *ten raids per night:* US Department of Defense, Office of the Assistant Secretary of Defense (Public Affairs), "DoD Media Roundtable with Gen. McChrystal NATO Headquarters in Brussels," June 10, 2010; Rajiv Chandrasekaran, *Little America: The War Within the War for Afghanistan* (New York: Knopf, 2012), 277; Carlotta Gall, "Night Raids Curbing Taliban, But Afghans Cite Civilian Toll," *New York Times,* July 8, 2011.

295 *corruption and other flaws:* Naylor, *Relentless Strike,* 361–362; Emma Graham-Harrison, "NATO's Afghan Night Raids Come with High Civilian Cost," Reuters, February 24, 2011; Gall, "Night Raids Curbing Taliban"; Nick Paton Walsh, "U.S., Afghanistan May Be Close to 'Night Raids' Deal," CNN, April 4, 2012.

295 *rather than just individuals:* Yochi Dreazen, "Joint Special Forces, CIA Hit Teams Are McChrystal's Legacy," *National Journal,* September 1, 2011.

295 *mines around the exterior:* Marty Skovlund Jr., with Charles Faint and Leo Jenkins, *Violence of Action: The Untold Stories of the 75th Ranger Regiment in the War on Terror* (Colorado Springs, CO: Blackside Concepts, 2014), 320–378.

295 *". . . take casualties":* Naylor, *Relentless Strike,* 366.

295 *incriminating evidence:* Richard A. Oppel Jr. and Rod Nordland, "U.S. Is Reining in Special Operations Forces in Afghanistan," *New York Times,* March 15, 2010; Naylor, *Relentless Strike,* 369–370.

296 *unilateral operations by one or the other:* William B. Ostlund, "Irregular Warfare: Counterterrorism Forces in Support of Counterinsurgency Operations," Institute of Land Warfare, Land Warfare Papers no. 91, September 2012, www.ausa .org/publications/ilw/ilw_pubs/landwarfarepapers/Documents/LWP_91_web .pdf. See also "Generation Kill: A Conversation with Stanley McChrystal," *Foreign Affairs,* March/April 2013; Lamb and Munsing, *Secret Weapon,* 50.

CHAPTER 10: OVERREACH

299 *heat and noise:* Nicholas Schmidle, "Getting Bin Laden," *New Yorker,* August 8, 2011.

301 *whiff of him:* Declan Walsh, "In Hiding, Bin Laden Had Four Children and Five Houses," *New York Times*, March 29, 2012.

301 *"enhanced interrogation techniques" of the Bush administration:* Mark Bowden, *The Finish: The Killing of Osama bin Laden* (New York: Atlantic Monthly Press, 2012), 112–116, 248–249.

301 *small number of senior Pakistani officials:* Carlotta Gall, *The Wrong Enemy: America in Afghanistan, 2001–2014* (New York: Houghton Mifflin Harcourt, 2014), 247–251.

301 *identities of the inhabitants:* M. Ilyas Khan, "Bin Laden Neighbours Describe Abbottabad Compound," BBC News, May 2, 2011; Sam Greenhill, David Williams, and Imtiaz Hussain, "How a 40-Minute Raid Ended Ten Years of Defiance," *Daily Mail*, May 3, 2011; "What Was Life Like in the Bin Laden Compound?" BBC News, May 9, 2011.

302 *he did not possess:* Bowden, *The Finish*, 161.

302 *"a perfect grand strategy":* William H. McRaven, "Special Operations: The Perfect Grand Strategy?" in Bernd Horn, J. Paul de B. Taillon, and David Last, eds., *Force of Choice: Perspectives on Special Operations* (Kingston, Ontario: McGill-Queens University Press, 2004), 61–78.

302 *Bin Laden's presence:* Bowden, *The Finish*, 155–156.

302 *". . . complicating factor":* Peter L. Bergen, *Manhunt: The Ten-Year Search for Bin Laden from 9/11 to Abbottabad* (New York: Crown, 2012), 166–167.

303 *struck from the air:* Daniel Klaidman, *Kill or Capture: The War on Terror and the Soul of the Obama Presidency* (New York: Houghton Mifflin Harcourt, 2012), 235; Bergen, *Manhunt*, 199.

303 *wounded banshee:* Richard Lardner, "After Bin Laden's Death, a Hunt for Information," Associated Press, March 16, 2012; Barbara Starr, "Pentagon Double Checked Actions of Seals During Bin Laden Raid," CNN, September 7, 2012.

304 *arrival of Pakistani authorities:* Schmidle, "Getting Bin Laden."

304 *". . . compound in Abbottabad, Pakistan":* "Remarks by the President on Osama bin Laden," May 2, 2011, www.whitehouse.gov/blog/2011/05/02/osama-bin-laden-dead.

304 *commander-in-chief who had authorized it:* John Hudson, "More Revisions to the Official Bin Laden Raid Story," Atlantic Wire, April 12, 2012.

305 *safety of their families:* Sara Sorcher, "Top Officials Warn Against Leaks in Wake of Bin Laden Raid," *Government Executive*, May 19, 2011.

305 *"Shut the fuck up":* David E. Sanger, *Confront and Conceal: Obama's Secret Wars and Surprising Use of American Power* (New York: Crown, 2012), 107.

305 *". . . celebrity profit from their service":* Barbara Starr, "Scathing Message Sent to Navy SEALS On Discussing Secret Work," CNN, September 5, 2012.

305 *impede former SEALs:* The problem persisted to such a degree that Pybus's successor, Rear Admiral Brian L. Losey, felt compelled to issue the same warning across Naval Special Warfare Command two years later. Kelsey Harkness, "Top Navy SEAL Officials Aren't Happy with Teammates Spilling Bin Laden Secrets," *Daily Signal*, November 6, 2014. For a detailed analysis of the issue, see Forrest S. Crowell, *Navy SEALs Gone Wild: Publicity, Fame, and the Loss of the Quiet Professional*, Master's Thesis, Naval Postgraduate School, December 2015.

305 *deemed high threats to the United States:* Government Accountability Office, "Foreign Police Assistance: Defined Roles and Improved Information Sharing Could Enhance Interagency Collaboration," May 2012, 14.

306 *resurgence of those groups in Pakistani cities:* Bruce Riedel, *Avoiding Armageddon: America, India, and Pakistan to the Brink and Back* (Washington, DC: Brookings Institution Press, 2013), 169; Jeffrey Goldberg and Marc Ambinder, "The Ally from Hell," *Atlantic,* December 2011; Zia Ur Rehman, "The Pakistani Taliban's Karachi Network," *CTC Sentinel* 6, no. 5 (May 2013): 1–5; Kathy Gannon, "In Pakistan's Punjab Area, Militants Plan for Next Afghanistan War After Foreign Troops Leave," Associated Press, September 7, 2013; Tom Hussain, "U.S. Pullback in Lahore Another Sign of Growing Al Qaida Violence in Pakistan," McClatchy, August 9, 2013.

306 *ground forces by 100,000 troops:* US Department of Defense, "Defense Budget Priorities and Choices," January 2012; White House Office of the Press Secretary, "Remarks by the President on the Defense Strategic Review," January 5, 2012.

307 *substitute for a broad counterinsurgency campaign:* Rajiv Chandrasekaran, *Little America: The War Within the War for Afghanistan* (New York: Knopf, 2012), 278–279.

307 *offset their losses:* Robert M. Gates, *Duty: Memoirs of a Secretary at War* (New York: Knopf, 2014), 364; Bob Woodward, *Obama's Wars* (New York: Simon and Schuster, 2010), 190; "Generation Kill: A Conversation with Stanley McChrystal," *Foreign Affairs,* March/April 2013.

307 " . . . *change anything":* Sean Naylor, *Relentless Strike: The Secret History of the Joint Special Operations Command* (New York: St. Martin's Press, 2015), 424.

307 *thirty-eight people aboard the helicopter survived:* Jeffrey N. Colt, "Executive Summary (Crash of CH-47D Aircraft in Wardak Province, Afghanistan on 6 August 2011)," September 9, 2011, http://nsarchive.gwu.edu/NSAEBB /NSAEBB370/docs/Document%2012.pdf.

308 *thirty were injured:* "Details Emerge of Afghanistan Raid in Which Four GIs Were Killed," *Stars and Stripes,* October 10, 2013.

308 *from 2,886 to 12,560:* Jim Thomas and Chris Dougherty, "Beyond the Ramparts: The Future of U.S. Special Operations Forces," Center for Strategic and Budgetary Assessments, May 10, 2013, x; Michele L. Malvesti, "To Serve the Nation: U.S. Special Operations Forces in an Era of Persistent Conflict," Center for a New American Security, June 2010, 32.

308 *between 9/11 and the middle of 2014:* John D. Gresham, "Interview with 75th Ranger Regiment Commander Col. Christopher Vanek, USA," *Defense Media Network,* June 30, 2014.

309 *"signed by an automatic pen":* Marty Skovlund Jr., with Charles Faint and Leo Jenkins, *Violence of Action: The Untold Stories of the 75th Ranger Regiment in the War on Terror* (Colorado Springs, CO: Blackside Concepts, 2014), 432.

309 *deeply troubled the senior SOF leadership:* Thom Shanker and Richard A. Oppel Jr., "War's Elite Tough Guys, Hesitant to Seek Healing," *New York Times,* June 5, 2014; Thomas and Dougherty, "Beyond the Ramparts," 39–41.

310 *bureaucratic brawl with the regional military commanders:* "Leaders Shift from Rumsfeld Strategy," Associated Press, May 11, 2008.

310 *beck and call:* USSOCOM, "Global SOF Network Operational Planning Team: A History," March 2014.

310 *assistant secretary of defense for special operations and low intensity conflict:* Linda Robinson, "The Future of Special Operations Forces," Council on Foreign Relations, April 2013, 18.

312 *capabilities of the Washington office:* House Report 113–113, Committee on Appropriations, 2014 Department of Defense Appropriations Bill, June 17, 2013.

313 " . . . *directives and regulations":* House Report 113–473, Committee on Appropriations, 2015 Department of Defense Appropriations Bill, June 13, 2014.

313 *integral to the Global SOF Network Campaign Plan:* Howard Altman, "McRaven Legacy: More Globally Agile Command, Better Care for Troops," *Tampa Tribune,* August 27, 2014.

314 *evidence to support the accusations:* Kimberly Dozier, "Inside the Takedown of the Top Navy SEAL," *Daily Beast,* May 13, 2016.

314 *career to an abrupt end:* Craig Whitlock, "Powerful Admiral Punishes Suspected Whistleblowers, Still Gets Promotion," *Washington Post,* October 21, 2015; Meghann Myers, "Navy SEAL Admiral's Promotion Denied After Review," *Navy Times,* March 21, 2016.

314 " . . . *decades of service":* William H. McRaven, "A Warrior's Career Sacrificed for Politics," *Tampa Tribune,* April 24, 2016.

315 " . . . *manipulate them":* Sydney J. Freedberg Jr., "Killing Is Not Enough: Special Operators," *Breaking Defense,* December 16, 2014.

315 *intervention became necessary:* Charles T. Cleveland and Stuart L. Farris, "Special Operations—An Army Core Competency," *Army,* June 2014, 25–28.

315 " . . . *indirect action is decisive":* Department of the Navy, Naval Special Warfare NWP 3-05, May 2013, 4–10.

315 *large percentage of them special operators:* Joel D. Rayburn, "Rise of the Maliki Regime," *Journal of International Security Affairs,* no. 22 (Spring/Summer 2012): 45–54; Richard R. Brennan Jr., Charles P. Ries, Larry Hanauer, Benn Connable, Terrence K. Kelly, Michael J. McNerney, Stephanie Young, Jason Campbell, and K. Scott McMahon, *Ending the U.S. War in Iraq: The Final Transition, Operational Maneuver, and Disestablishment of United States Forces– Iraq* (Santa Monica, CA: Rand, 2013), 310–311; Patricia Dias, Tobias Feakin, Ken Gleiman, Peter Jennings, Daniel Nichola, Simone Roworth, Benjamin Schreer, and Mark Thomson, "Strike from the Air: The First 100 Days of the Campaign Against ISIL," Australian Strategic Policy Institute, December 2014.

316 *ISIS facility near Kirkuk:* Matthew Cox, "Delta Force KIA Led Assault Team on ISIS Prison in Iraq, Source Says," Military.com, October 27, 2015, www .military.com/daily-news/2015/10/27/delta-force-kia-led-assault-team-isis -prison-iraq-source-says.html.

316 *no combat role:* Gayle Tzemach Lemmon, "When Combat Isn't Combat," *Atlantic,* October 24, 2015; Charles Hoskinson, "Iraq Raid Signifies Stepped-Up Effort Against ISIS," *Washington Examiner,* October 24, 2015.

316 *"this is combat":* Kristina Wong, "Officials Parsing Words over 'Combat' in Iraq," *The Hill,* October 25, 2015.

317 *required much larger forces:* "U.S. Sees Syria Rebels in Political, Not Military Solution: Asharq Al-Awsat Newspaper," Reuters, October 27, 2014.

317 *"four or five":* Luis Martinez, "General Austin: Only '4 or 5' US-Trained Syrian Rebels Fighting ISIS," ABC News, September 16, 2015.

317 *terminated the program in October 2015:* Phil Stewart and Kate Holton, "U.S. Pulls Plug on Syria Rebel Training Effort; Will Focus on Weapons Supply," Reuters, October 9, 2015; Martin Matishak, "Obama Abandons $500 Million Program to Train Syrian Rebels," *Fiscal Times*, October 9, 2015.

318 *high-priority targets:* Michael M. Phillips, "Treading Line Between War and Peace, U.S. Special Forces Groom Afghan Troops," *Wall Street Journal*, August 28, 2015; Heath Druzin, "Fresh Taliban Assaults Test Boundaries of US 'Noncombat' Mission," *Stars and Stripes*, December 15, 2015.

318 *entirely under Taliban sway:* US Department of Defense, "Enhancing Security and Stability in Afghanistan," December 2015, www.defense.gov/Portals/1/Documents/pubs/1225_Report_Dec_2015_-_Final_20151210.pdf; Bill Roggio, "Taliban Overruns District in Southern Afghanistan," *Long War Journal*, December 9, 2015.

318 *". . . remnants of al-Qaida":* White House, Office of the Press Secretary, "Statement by the President on the End of the Combat Mission in Afghanistan," December 28, 2014; White House, Office of the Press Secretary, "Statement by the President on Afghanistan," October 15, 2015.

319 *small counterterrorism force:* John Vandiver, "Security Concerns Delay NATO Assistance to Libya," *Stars and Stripes*, May 19, 2014; Christopher S. Chivvis and Jeffrey Martini, *Libya After Qaddafi: Lessons and Implications for the Future* (Santa Monica, CA: Rand, 2014), 82–83.

320 *permission was denied by the State Department:* Mark Moyar, *Countering Violent Extremism in Mali* (Tampa, FL: Joint Special Operations University Press, 2015), 21–34.

320 *". . . government last March":* Vicki Huddleston, "Why We Must Help Save Mali," *New York Times*, January 14, 2013.

321 *improvements in skills and organizational culture:* Moyar, *Countering Violent Extremism in Mali*, 55.

321 *frequent reshuffling:* Simon J. Powelson, *Enduring Engagement Yes, Episodic Engagement No: Lessons for SOF from Mali*, Master's Thesis, Naval Postgraduate School, December 2013.

321 *". . . weed whacker":* Brian Dodwell and Marielle Ness, "A View from the CT Foxhole: An Interview with Captain Robert A. Newson," *CTC Sentinel* 8, no. 2 (February 2015): 1–4.

321 *did not have plans to attack American interests:* David S. Cloud and Kathleen Hennessey, "Obama's Pakistan Gamble Fails to Pay Off," *Los Angeles Times*, May 22, 2012.

321 *300 to more than 1,000:* Gregory D. Johnsen, *The Last Refuge: Yemen, Al-Qaeda, and America's War in Arabia* (New York: W. W. Norton, 2013), 264; Robert F. Worth, "Yemen, Hailed as Model, Struggles for Stability," *New York Times*, February 18, 2013; "Yemeni Parliament in Non-Binding Vote Against Drone Attacks," Reuters, December 15, 2013.

322 *directed the surgical strikes:* Greg Botelho and Hakim Almasmari, "State Department: U.S. Pulls Remaining Forces out of Yemen," CNN, March 23, 2015; Brian Bennett and Zaid Al-Alayaa, "Iran-Backed Rebels in Yemen Loot Secret Files About US Spy Operations," Tribune Content Agency, March 25, 2015; Greg Miller, "Al-Qaeda Franchise in Yemen Exploits Chaos to Rebuild, Officials Say," *Washington Post*, April 5, 2015.

322 *assault rifles in hand:* Ken Dilanian and David S. Cloud, "U.S. Raids on Al Qaeda Operatives Show Shift Away from Drone Strikes," *Los Angeles Times*, October 6, 2013; Ernesto Londoño and Scott Wilson, "U.S. Strikes Al-Shabab in Somalia and Captures Bombing Suspect in Libya," *Washington Post*, October 5, 2013; Karen DeYoung, "Heeding New Counterterror Guidelines, U.S. Forces Backed Off in Somalia Raid," *Washington Post*, October 7, 2013; Abdalle Ahmed, Spencer Ackerman, and David Smith, "How the US Raid on Al-Shabaab in Somalia Went Wrong," *Guardian*, October 9, 2013.

322 *video of the act online:* Michael D. Shear and Eric Schmitt, "In Raid to Save Foley and Other Hostages, U.S. Found None," *New York Times*, August 20, 2014.

323 *aboard the USS* Makin Island: Karen DeYoung and Adam Goldman, "Hagel: U.S. Hostage 'Murdered' in Yemen," *Washington Post*, December 6, 2014; Adam Entous, "Luke Somers Raid in Yemen: How It Went Wrong," *Wall Street Journal*, December 8, 2014.

323 *2,900 of 2001:* Government Accountability Office, "Special Operations Forces: Opportunities Exist to Improve Transparency of Funding and Assess Potential to Lessen Some Deployments," July 2015, 22–23.

323 *women into combat positions:* Gayle Tzemach Lemmon, "Special Ops Survey Showed 85% Opposed Serving with Women," *Defense News*, December 4, 2015.

323 *interpersonal conflicts:* Lolita C. Baldor, "Special Ops Troops Doubt Women Can Do the Job," Associated Press, April 4, 2015.

323 *emerged in the Cultural Support Team program:* Interviews with SOF personnel, 2013–2015.

324 *". . . him to cover":* Lolita C. Baldor, "U.S. Commandos Say No to Women in Special Operations Jobs," Associated Press, December 10, 2015.

CHAPTER 11: CONCLUSION

330 *promulgating definitions of special operations:* According to the Defense Department's current doctrine, special operations are "operations requiring unique modes of employment, tactical techniques, equipment and training often conducted in hostile, denied, or politically sensitive environments and characterized by one or more of the following: time sensitive, clandestine, low visibility, conducted with and/or through indigenous forces, requiring regional expertise, and/or a high degree of risk." Joint Publication 3-05, "Special Operations," July 16, 2014, GL-11.

330 *specifying a set of SOF missions:* The current list includes: "direct action, special reconnaissance, countering weapons of mass destruction, counterterrorism, unconventional warfare (UW), foreign internal defense, security force assistance, hostage rescue and recovery, counterinsurgency, foreign humanitarian

assistance, military information support operations, and civil affairs operations." Joint Publication 3-05, "Special Operations," July 16, 2014, II-3.

340 *facilities management and transportation:* For a discussion of this issue and the research behind it, see Mark Moyar, *A Question of Command: Counterinsurgency from the Civil War to Iraq* (New Haven, CT: Yale University Press, 2009), 261–265.

344 "*. . . primarily for personal glory*": Bob Schoultz, "Ethos or Mythos?" Bob Schoultz's Corner, November 5, 2010, https://bobscorner.wordpress.com/2010/11/05/ethos-or-mythos/.

344 *tight-knit organization:* Interviews with Navy SEAL officers, 2014–2016.

345 "*. . . should and should not be used*": Alexander Powell, "Advice from SOF on the Use of SOF for the Next Administration," Center for Naval Analyses, October 2016.

INDEX

©Denis Largeron

MARK MOYAR IS the director of the Center for Military and Diplomatic History in Washington, DC. He has served as a consultant for US Special Operations Command, Senior Fellow at Joint Special Operations University, and professor at Marine Corps University. He lives in Oak Hill, Virginia.